ORNAMENTAL TREES

*An Illustrated Guide
to Their Selection
and Care*

by EVELYN MAINO and FRANCES HOWARD
illustrated by Evelyn Maino

UNIVERSITY OF CALIFORNIA PRESS
Berkeley, Los Angeles, London

Preface

This book is an attempt to anticipate and answer the questions which would occur to a home owner when he is considering the planting and care of trees for his garden. In the book, more than 300 desirable ornamental trees are described and their cultural and climatic requirements defined, and 182 are illustrated. The list is naturally a selective one, made up of some of the best trees for various garden purposes in each type of western climate. Charts are also included which will facilitate the selection of individual trees for different climatic regions and landscaping uses and will show at a glance the particulars of flower, fruit, foliage, and habit. These charts are found at the ends of each of the four sections which list deciduous trees, broad-leaved evergreen trees, conifers, and palms.

The nomenclature is based on *Standardized Plant Names,* by Harlan P. Kelsey and William A. Dayton, published by the J. Horace McFarland Company of Harrisburg, Pennsylvania. This book seems to represent the clearest and most orderly approach to a very complicated subject. An attempt was made throughout the book to reduce botanical terminology to understandable language; but because this was not always possible, a glossary has been included which will help to clarify difficult words.

The text of the book was written by Frances Howard, and the illustrations were drawn from living specimens by Evelyn Maino. The information in the book is based on research by both collaborators, working together and separately. In this connection, thanks are due Professor Harry Shepherd of the University of California, who read the manuscript and made invaluable suggestions. Thanks are also due the editorial staff of the University of California Press, who were kind enough to take an interest at the book's inception and to suggest the manner of presentation.

University of California Press
Berkeley and Los Angeles, California
University of California Press, Ltd., London, England
Copyright, 1955, by the Regents of the University of California
Sixth printing, 1975
Manufactured in the United States of America
ISBN: 0-520-00795-6
Library of Congress Catalogue Card Number: 55-9882

Contents

Introduction	1
Deciduous Trees	11
Charts for the Ornamental Use and Climatic Tolerance of Deciduous Trees	95
Broad-leaved Evergreen Trees	101
Charts for the Ornamental Use and Climatic Tolerance of Broad-leaved Evergreen Trees	158
Conifers	163
Climatic Tolerance Charts for Conifers	197
Palms and Other Tropicals	199
Chart for the Ornamental Use and Climatic Tolerance of Palms, Tree Ferns, and Other Tropical-appearing Plants	210
Glossary	211
Bibliography	213
Index	214

Introduction

1. THE USE OF TREES

Trees are used in landscaping in several specific ways. These are: to provide shade; to decorate streets or avenues; to provide hedging, screens, and windbreaks; to serve as lawn specimens; to decorate patios; and as espaliers to provide design. In selecting a tree for any of these purposes, attention must be paid to the soil, climatic, and exposure preferences of the tree; its root system; its conformity with its surroundings; and its rate of growth. This information is recorded in the text of the book under the proper subject headings.

Shade trees

In planting for shade, the important factor to consider is the depth of shade required. A heavy, dense tree will produce deep shade, whereas an open tree will filter the light. All descriptions of this nature are given under "Conformation" in the text. With this section as a guide, it should be relatively easy to find the tree to meet the requirement. However, all selections should be made with full consideration of the seasonal aspects. For example, in climates where summers are extremely hot and winters are extremely cold and wet, deep shade should be provided during the summer months and little or none throughout the winter. Obviously, a dense deciduous tree is the answer; for in summer the foliage will provide adequate protection from the heat, and in winter the bare silhouette will allow the maximum of light to come through. It follows, also, that in foggy areas where heat is seldom a problem, open-headed trees are more happily used. Finding the tree which best meets the need is highly important.

Street trees

In the selection of trees for the street, there are four important points to remember: the tree must be of medium size; its root system must be deep; it must be provided with enough open ground from which to obtain the necessary food elements; and it must be a clean tree.

The presence of telephone and power lines and the size of the buildings in the particular area should be taken into consideration, and only trees that will not grow too tall should be planted. Overhead wires are a necessity of modern living; trees planted in complete disregard of their presence are subject to mutilation by maintenance crews who necessarily must trim them away from the wires. For street trees it is wise to select those trees which can be kept to a reasonable height for a rather long time. From an artistic point of view, this limitation of size is also desirable. Street trees are meant to grace an area and to enhance its beauty; there is nothing beautiful in long rows of enormous trees completely dwarfing and overpowering the buildings behind them. They are at variance with the unity of the picture, making everything around them seem like queer Liliputian distortions.

FILTERED SHADE TREE ..... PISTACIA

DECIDUOUS SHADE TREE ..... CATALPA

COMPACT DENSE SHADE TREE ..... MAPLE

SHADE TREES

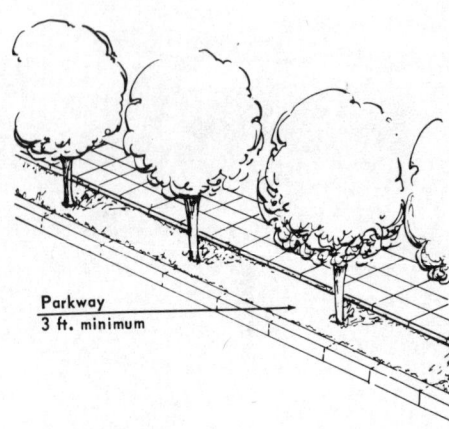

STREET TREES
Parkway 3 ft. minimum

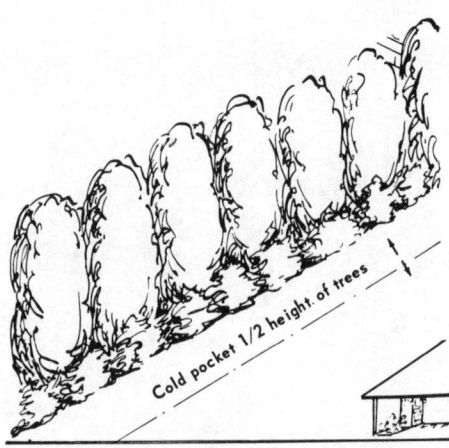

Cold pocket 1/2 height of trees

←—Minimum of 60 ft.; 100 ft. best—→
Protection 10 to 20 times height of trees

WINDBREAKS

TRIMMED HEDGE OF TREES

For obvious reasons, street trees should not have voracious or shallow roots that are likely to wind round and crack sewer pipes or heave up pavements. To avoid this, only trees that have roots which reach downward for sustenance and spread out at a safe level below the ground should be planted. In this connection, it is also important to consider the size of parkways assigned to the tree. It must be emphasized again and again that trees are enormous subjects and need plenty of room in which to develop. Six-foot parkways are adequate for the proper development of most street trees, but unfortunately that amount of space is not always available. If the parkway is only three or four feet wide, smaller trees requiring less space for development should be used. The larger the space, however, the better the tree will develop, for this small space around the tree is the cup through which life-giving elements are admitted. Too frequently it is packed down and hardened by trampling feet and by neglect until it is so packed that no food or water could possibly penetrate the surface. Under these conditions, a naturally deep-rooted tree, starved and reaching toward the surface for food, will upheave and break up pavements.

Street trees should not be of the type that continually drops residue of one kind or another. In particular, those which exude and drop great blobs of sticky gum, or those which produce large or prickly fruit should be avoided. Trees which shed their bark in huge strips and those which drop innumerable twigs are also undesirable.

Windbreaks

In areas where high winds are prevalent and likely to become a menace to plant life or a nuisance to comfortable living, some sort of barrier must be erected to offset their effect. Trees used for this purpose must have root systems and wood growth which are strong enough to prevent their toppling or breaking under pressure. Windbreaks should be planted in single rows or in double or triple alternating rows, depending upon the velocity of wind in the area. One should first determine the direction of the wind and then plant the trees very close together; this crowding allows young trees to help each other withstand the wind and also affords almost immediate wind protection to the area they are meant to serve. A windbreak is effective approximately six times the height of the trees comprising it.

Screens

In every garden there is almost always some view that is not pleasant, and the proximity of neighbors today often threatens privacy. It is to relieve these conditions that screens are planted. If a screen is needed, it is usually needed immediately; therefore it stands to reason that material for screens should be selected from among those trees that have a rapid or a moderate rate of growth. Whether light or heavy screens are used depends upon the requirements of the situation. By reference to the charts and text of this book, the reader can select the tree suitable for any particular garden and any specific purpose.

Hedges

Hedges are used to mark property lines or to create areas of design. To assist them in serving their purpose, pruning is frequently necessary. Therefore, trees selected for hedges should be able to tolerate shearing and to prosper under it. They should also exhibit some tendency to a natural uniformity of growth and should be able to survive and thrive under crowded conditions.

Espaliers

Ordinarily espaliers are used in small gardens where space will not permit the natural development of the tree. This is probably the most unnatural form in which a tree can be used, and almost constant attention is necessary to achieve and maintain it. The trees are planted against walls or fences and are pruned to keep them in a flat design against these structures. Trees with supple branches and those which do not become very large or grow very fast provide the best material. Designs are then determined, and the tree is pruned in a manner to spur growth which will carry out the design. Branches which threaten the design should be eliminated, and the tree's natural tendencies should be channeled by pinching back the branches. It need hardly be pointed out that much of the natural beauty of the tree is destroyed in this process. But espaliering has found favor as a practical means of providing design, and, more especially, it is a good method of growing a variety of fruit trees in gardens that are too small for trees grown in the usual way.

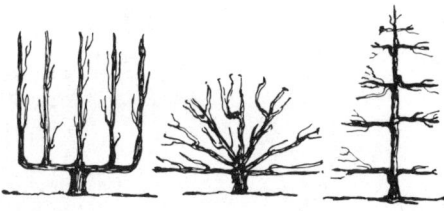
FORMAL

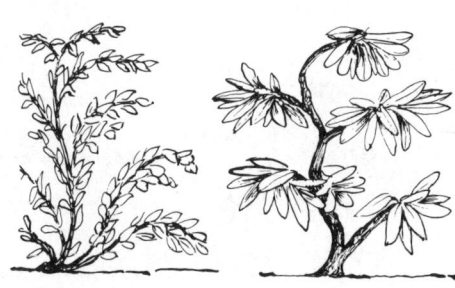
INFORMAL

Patio and tub trees

The trees designated in the charts and text of this book as useful in patios and for tub culture all have restrained root and growth habits and commendable form. Most of them have some additional feature which would make them desirable as specimen plants, such as bloom, or fruit, or type and color of leaf, or winter design. It is especially important to choose such plants carefully, for they are a particular center of interest, and an incorrect choice can utterly destroy the charm of the limited area in which they are grown. The color and type of architecture they are asked to complement should be taken into consideration, and a type of leaf and color of bloom should be chosen that will blend well with their surroundings. For instance, gray-foliaged plants are beautiful with redwood surroundings and are almost completely nondescript with white ones.

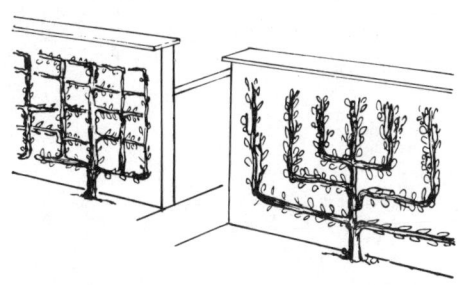
AS WALL DECORATION

2. THE CARE OF TREES

Purchasing and planting trees

The first step in buying a tree is to choose a reliable nursery. Your local nurseryman — if he knows his business — can give you more information than anyone else on what to plant in your area, for he has the advantage of being in the field and, with a practiced eye, watching the performance of every type of tree. He knows the shades of climatic variations in your neighborhood, which may mean the difference between success and failure. This is particularly necessary in the selection of fruit-tree varieties.

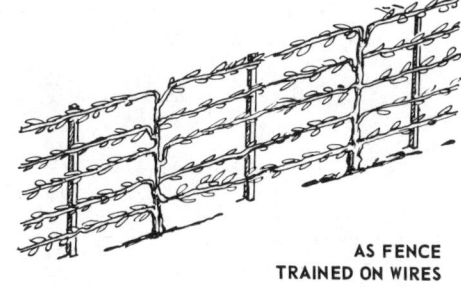
AS FENCE
TRAINED ON WIRES

ESPALIER

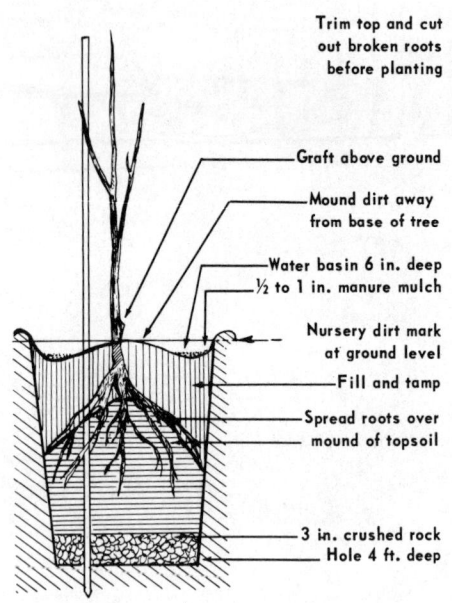

BARE-ROOT TREE

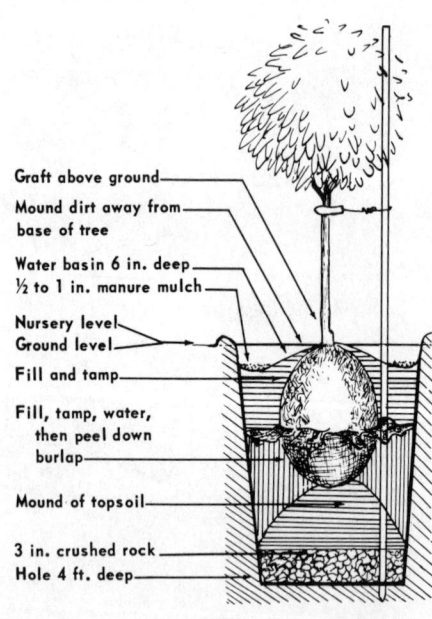

TREE BALLED IN BURLAP

HOW TO PLANT A TREE

When purchasing bare-rooted trees from a nursery, select a specimen with a strong, straight trunk. The thickness of the trunk at this stage is not so important as the general health of the tree, which is indicated by an extensive and strong root system. One of the most important points to remember is not to let the roots dry out from the time the tree has left the nursery until it is planted.

When the site has been selected for the tree, prepare a hole at least 4 feet deep, removing the soil and mixing it with good topsoil to which leaf mold or peat moss has been added. Do not use manure in the bottom of the hole or in the soil mixture. Place 2 to 3 inches of crushed rock in the bottom of the hole, to allow for drainage, and fill with the topsoil to a point where the roots can be comfortably spread. Tamp down the soil to keep it from shifting. Mound the earth in the hole at this point in an inverted V-shape, spreading the roots around it, filling in the soil mixture, and tamping it down lightly. Then, water the area and, after the soil has settled, fill in the rest of the soil mixture, allowing for a basin round the tree in which to receive water. Top mulch the area with ½ to 1 inch of well-rotted manure. For the first few months after planting, careful attention must be paid to watering, for it is at this stage that the tree is taking hold, and any undue dryness may retard it seriously.

Trees planted from containers require the same treatment as bare-rooted ones. The exceptions to this rule — citrus trees, for instance, require mounding of the earth *away* from the base of the tree — are noted in the text. When handling trees in burlap wrappings or in containers, care must be taken not to break the ball of earth which is protecting the roots. Tin containers should be cut in two or four places, folded back, and carefully removed; the plant should then be set at the proper level in the hole. Balled and burlapped plants should be placed in the hole at the proper level with the wrappings still round them; the strings should then be cut and the sack folded back from the ball. In time, the sack will rot away.

It is very important to plant the tree at the same depth as it was in the container or in the nursery field. To be planted too deeply is detrimental to the health of any tree and — for conifers and some others — it is often fatal.

Recognizing good specimens is one of the first considerations. Look for trees with straight trunks and well-formed heads and never accept a plant which appears starved or unhappy. Three good rules to follow are these:

1. Do not buy a plant which is obviously suffering from an attack by insects. No matter how desirable the plant or how light the infestation, you should not take it home until your nurseryman has cleared up the trouble. You may be able to get rid of the insects yourself; but if you are not successful in this, you may start an infestation in your garden.

2. Do not buy a plant which is one-sided or badly misshapen. It will take some time to train it to a presentable shape, and it

is foolish for you to do the work for which you are paying the nurseryman.

3. Do not think you are getting a bargain because you are able to buy an oversized plant in an undersized container. In all likelihood the plant is suffering from a too-small root system, and it will develop with relative slowness in your garden while trying to restore its balance.

The spacing of trees is important. They should be planted far enough away from any structure — and from each other — to permit their proper development. Individual trees differ in their space requirements; these are noted for each tree under "Spread" in the text.

Pruning

Young broad-leaved evergreen trees and conifers require only occasional pruning. Usually this is in the form of pinching back or nipping out the ends of branches which have a tendency to grow out of proportion to the rest of the tree. If special pruning is necessary for an individual tree, it is so noted in the text. It is always better to underprune than to overprune, for it sometimes takes years for the plant to replace injudiciously cut branches.

Young deciduous trees, however, must be pruned for the first three or four years of their life. The easiest and best method for training young trees is the central-leader method. The procedure is as follows: A central leader and two primary branches on opposite sides of the trunk are selected to establish the framework; all other branches are removed from the tree. The two primary branches are then cut back to one-half the length of the central leader, which is allowed to grow without being topped. In the second year, the two primary branches are shortened by one-third of their previous year's growth; all laterals are removed from the two shortened branches, with the exception of two or three near the tips; on the central leader, three or four laterals are allowed to develop near the tip, and all the rest are removed. The third and fourth-year pruning consists of the removal of all crossing or interfering branches which have developed on the framework. When selecting the framework, remember that branches will always remain at their original height from the ground; the tree must therefore be pruned early at the height desired.

The pruning formula given above is flexible and can be modified to produce differences in habit. For example, a specimen is encouraged in its wide-spreading habit by permitting laterals to take their full outward development, whereas a tree is made compact by nipping the laterals at the ends. A further example is the process of espaliering, in which fixed patterns are established and all branches are removed or pinched back which do not conform to the specific design. The pruning of fruit trees is treated in the text under the names of the individual trees.

Although the practice of leaving the side branches on a young tree for the first few years results in a vigorous and strong tree, it does not always result in a well-shaped one. The point

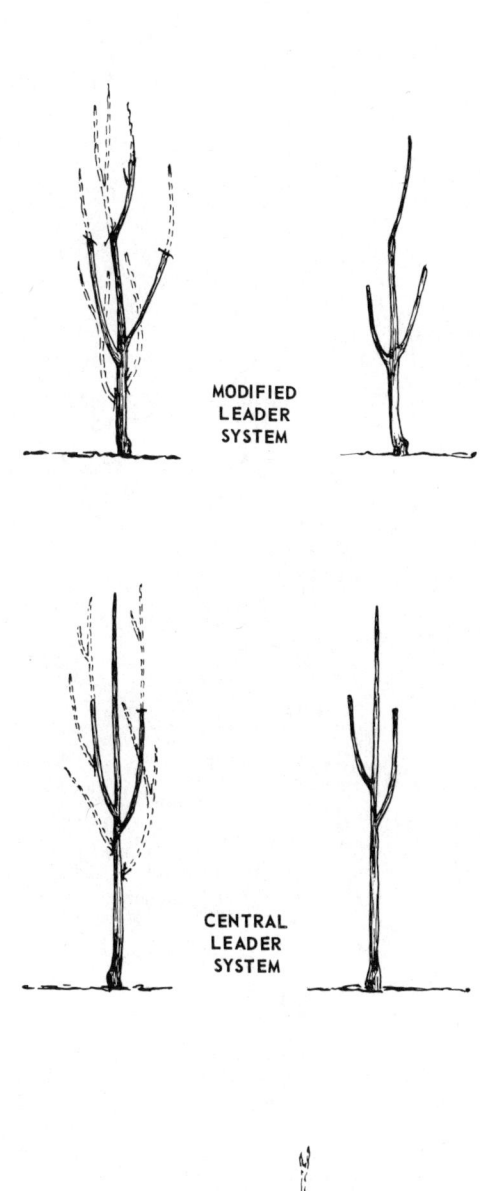

MODIFIED LEADER SYSTEM

CENTRAL LEADER SYSTEM

HEDGE

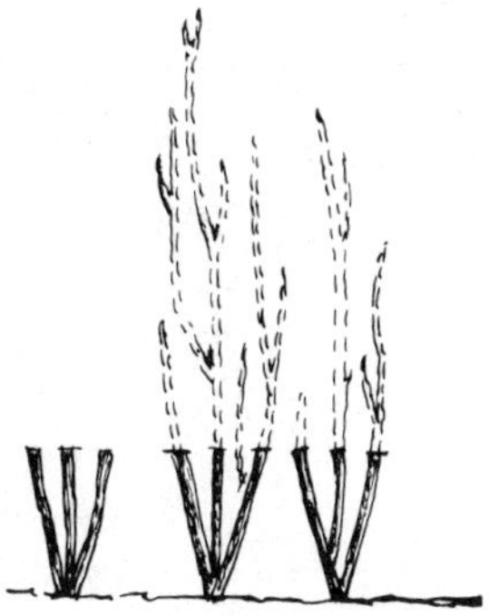

PRUNING AT TIME OF PLANTING

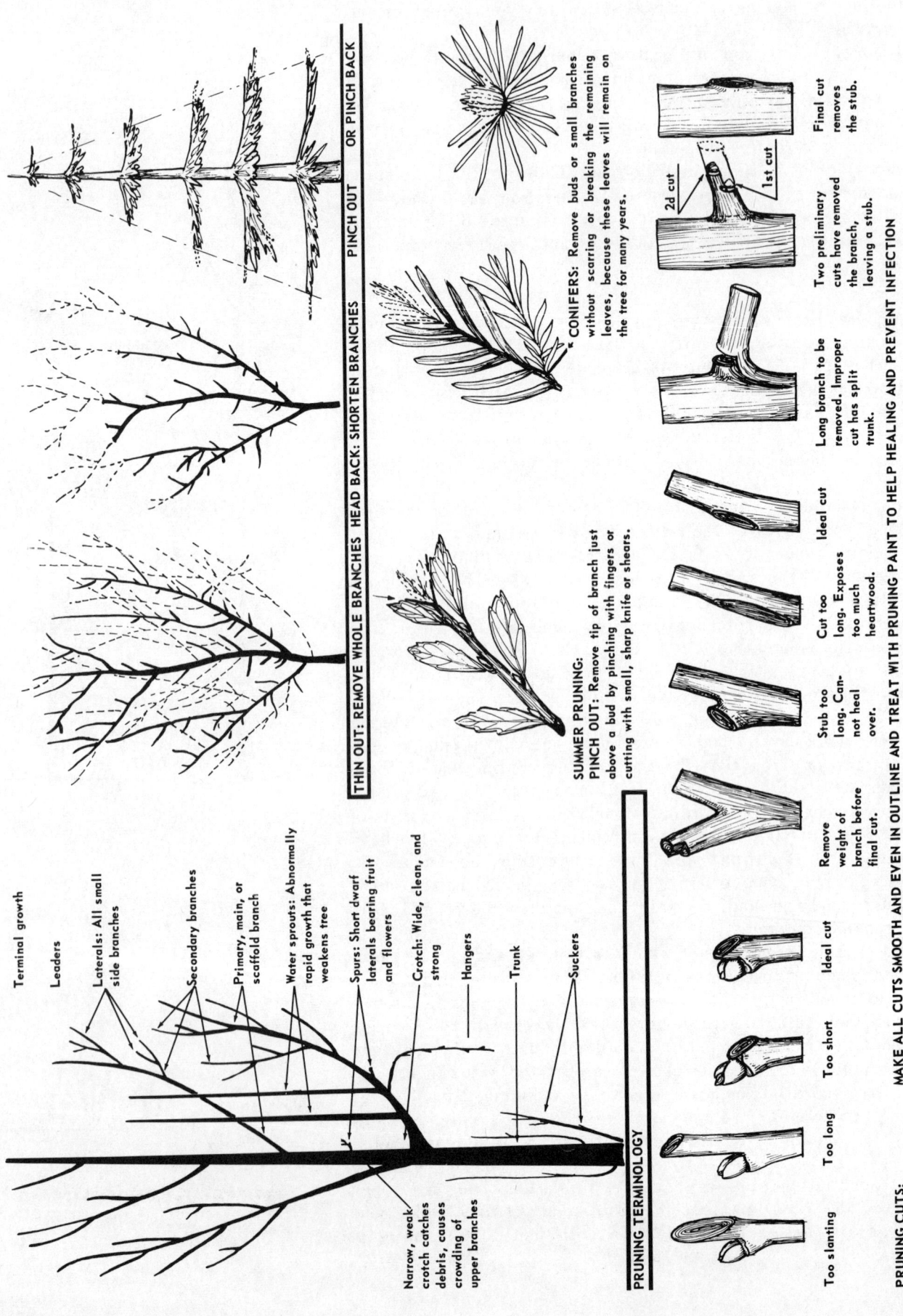

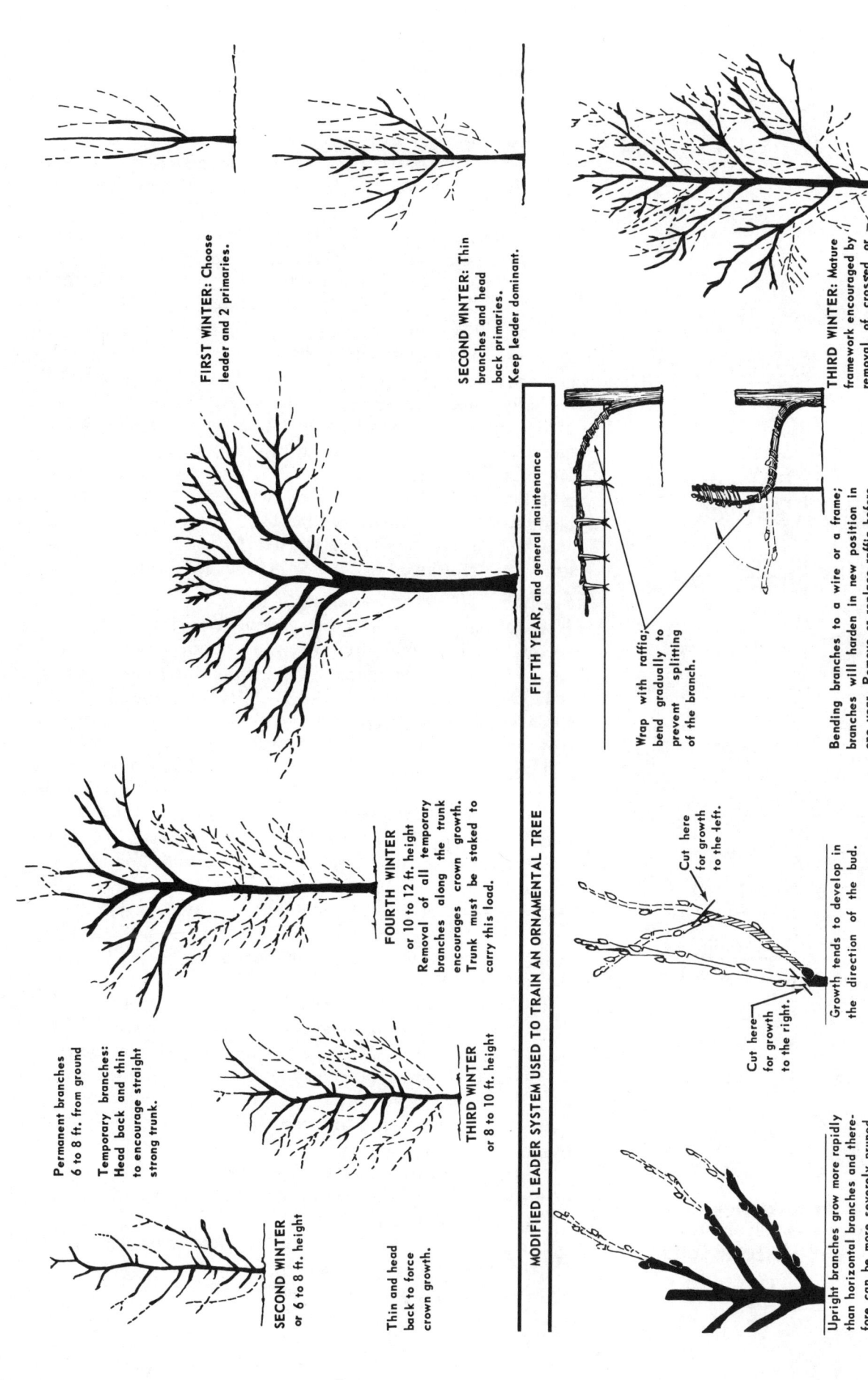

RELATIVE RATE OF WATER ABSORPTION BY TWO DIFFERENT SOILS

(Sandy Loam: 15 min., 40 min., 1 hour, 24 hours. Clay Loam: 4 hours, 24 hours, 36 hours, 48 hours. Width of Basin; 6 in. Depth of Basin; Mound water away from base of tree.)

at which the superfluous branches should be removed is always a difficult one for the home gardener to decide; often the branches are never removed and a misshapen tree is the consequence.

Large trees sometimes require pruning to improve their appearance and to preserve their health. Branches that take on disproportionate growth should be removed or shortened; and suckers on the branches, trunk, and at the base of the tree should be cut out at their point of origin. Most pruning for appearance, however, is based on individual preference for certain forms.

Pruning to improve the health of a tree consists in cutting back to a healthy crotch all dead, diseased, broken, or crossing branches. Crossing branches must be removed to admit light to the crown and permit air to circulate through it. Dead and broken branches not only are a menace to life and property but may also harbor insects and fungi which may attack the healthy parts of the tree and spread to other areas in the garden. Cutting out diseased branches is, of course, a way of fighting the disease; the branches should be cut to a point well below the point of infection. All cuts should be clean ones, for jagged tears are unsightly and do not heal rapidly or correctly. The larger cuts should be treated with pruning paint immediately after the operation, to help them heal and to prevent infection.

Feeding

Although any well-balanced commercial fertilizer is entirely adequate for feeding trees, the most successful results have been obtained from those which contain nitrogen, phosphorus, and potash in a ratio of 10-8-6. Nitrogen helps to produce the green color in the leaves and stimulates abundant twig and leaf growth; it should be used carefully, for it has a tendency to burn if overapplied. Phosphorus stimulates root and tissue growth and the production of flowers and seeds. Potash hastens the maturity of the plant, helps to overcome brittleness in the wood, and intensifies the colors of the flowers. Nitrogen seems to be the element that benefits trees the most, but it should not be used to the exclusion of the other two. Various other elements — such as calcium, magnesium, zinc, and iron — play a part in the growth of the plant. These are usually present in the soil; their absence is evidenced by a yellowing of the leaves.

Most trees need fertilizing about once every two or three years. Specific exceptions are noted in the text under the names of the individual trees. Of course, an obviously starved tree which is growing poorly and is not affected by disease may need fertilizer more often. However, in fertilizing, it is better to underdo than to overdo. Two points to remember are these:

1. Never fertilize a diseased plant. Water it carefully and combat the disease before putting an added strain on the plant by stimulating growth.

2. Never fertilize a dry plant. Soak the area thoroughly before fertilizer is applied, to make it easier for the plant to take up the fertilizer and to prevent burning.

Fertilizer is applied to trees at the rate of 2 pounds for each inch of the diameter of the trunk. For example, a tree with a trunk thickness of 12 inches requires an application of 24 pounds of fertilizer. Applications should be only by the punch-bar method, in order that the material will be distributed evenly and at a safe depth. Slanting holes should be drilled, 18 inches deep and 24 inches apart, in a circular pattern and extending outward beyond the farthermost branches. These holes should start 12 inches from the base of small trees, and at a distance of three times the diameter of the trunk of larger ones. Usually ten holes are needed for each inch of trunk diameter; they are easily made with a sharp stick or crowbar. After the holes are drilled, the fertilizer should be apportioned equally among them. Usually, it is good to plug each hole with manure after the fertilizer has been inserted. However, some trees take unkindly to manure applications; the holes around such a tree, as noted in the text, should be plugged with peat moss or topsoil. The tree should then be watered by letting a slow stream of water run into the earth at its base until it is thoroughly soaked.

When yellowing of the leaves is apparent, it is advisable to apply leaf feed; trees have been found to benefit from applications of this material, which can be found at most nurseries. It should be diluted according to directions and sprayed on the tree. Each leaf should be covered by the spray material, to ensure good results.

Watering

Water is the main source of food for plant life, and its importance cannot be exaggerated. Trees described in this book as drought tolerant generally will not need so much water as others in their adult life; but in youth they will need just as much attention as the others, and they will benefit from sensible attention at all times. The amount of water to apply and the frequency of the applications will depend on the type of soil and the climate in the vicinity. Very young trees which have just been planted require weekly watering for the first few months. Under ordinary conditions, monthly waterings are about right for the majority of established trees. It must be pointed out that surface sprinkling is one of the most dangerous ways of watering a tree. This causes the roots to spread upward instead of growing firmly downward, and produces a shallow system which eventually may heave up the ground around the tree. Basins should be made to receive the water, and a slow stream should be allowed to run into them for a rather long time.

Pests and Diseases

Trees, like other plants, are subject to disease and to insect infestations. In the text of this book, the insects and diseases most likely to attack individual trees are named. Most diseases on plants can be avoided if the plant is kept healthy by proper planting, feeding, and watering. The same principle applies to trees as to human beings—proper living is the best insurance against disease. At the first sign of disease, the plant should be treated by spraying it with materials particularly suited to combat the specific diseases. These spray applications should

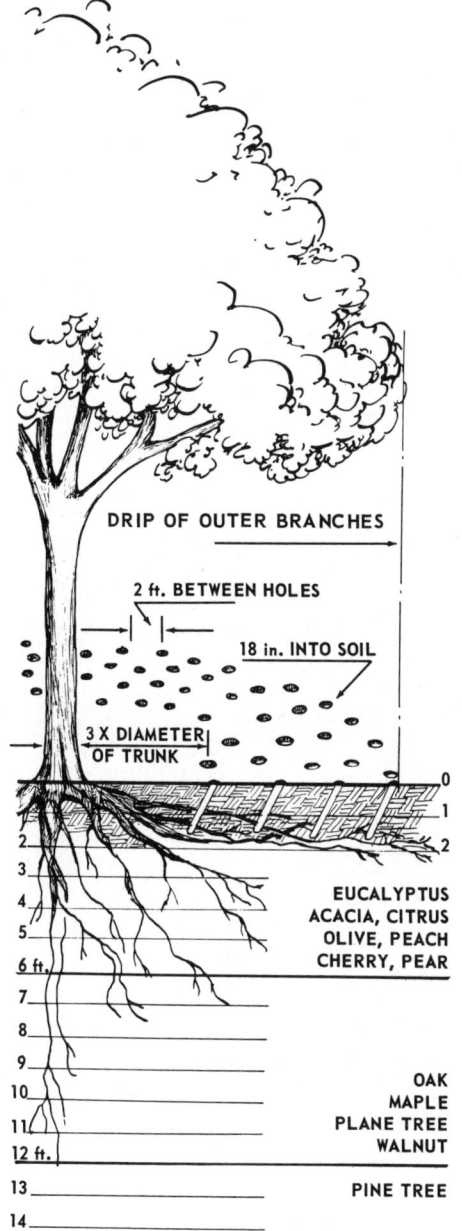

COMPARATIVE ROOT DEPTHS

PUNCH-HOLE METHOD OF APPLYING FERTILIZER

be made at twice-monthly or monthly intervals until all traces of the disease have disappeared. Sometimes it is necessary to eliminate infected branches in order to rid the tree of a disease; but this should not be done unless other methods have proved ineffective. The appearance of an infection on your plant is no reason for despair, for intelligent treatment has proved effective in a high percentage of cases. It is only rarely —in trees afflicted with chestnut blight or with Dutch elm disease, for instance—that infections are absolutely incurable and cause decimation of the types.

Insect infestations occur when hosts are present; the insects are just as likely to attack healthy plants as they are sickly ones. In fact, the vigorous growth of healthy specimens is doubly attractive to hungry insects. The frequent hosing off of the leaves with a stiff spray of water is a good combat method; a regular spray program in spring and fall is also a good preventive. In these preventive treatments, all-purpose insecticides are used. Of course, for a tree subject to attack by specific insects, the chemical that has been found most effective to combat that insect is used. If insects should appear in spite of the hosing and the usual spraying, the tree should be sprayed immediately with the proper insecticide, and the treatment should be repeated at two-week or monthly intervals until three applications have been made. This usually is effective; but if the infestation persists, spraying should be continued until all the insects have disappeared. When the infestations are persistent, it is best to vary the spray material, spraying with one element and then changing to another type in the next operation. Remember to avoid the use of oil sprays during the growing season, and of poisonous sprays on fruit trees at fruit-ripening time.

With the introduction of new insecticides, many kinds of insects are being eliminated easily today which heretofore were difficult to combat. However, this situation is by no means permanent, for insects develop immunity to spray materials over a period of time, and other methods must be employed. Local nurserymen should be able to supply the latest information on these matters. And, of course, complete details can be obtained from universities by addressing inquiries to them.

DECIDUOUS TREES

Deciduous trees shed their leaves every year and usually remain bare throughout the winter. Some of them—the Buckeye, for example—drop their leaves late in the summer and have two full seasons of nakedness. Others, such as the Cherimoya and the Jacaranda, drop their leaves unseasonally for a very short time. As a group, they have the most to offer in ornamental qualities, providing interest at every season of the year, with flowers, edible or ornamental fruit, striking fall color, or winter design. Their use in landscaping is unlimited, and they are found in enough variety and number to suit every individual taste.

Acer circinatum

A´cer circina´tum
Vine Maple; Mountain Maple

Pacific Coast of the United States and Canada

Features: Habit, foliage, fall color (red and orange), winter design.

Use: Patio, tub, specimen, accent, espalier

Growing in mountainous areas, in its natural state, Vine Maple has twisted, ropelike branches which sometimes sprawl along the ground and spread laterally, almost like heavy vines. Under cultivation, it is usually a multiple-trunked tree with delicate, arching branches which assume many artistic shapes. The leaves are large and many-lobed and turn brilliant red and orange before dropping in the fall; and in winter the twisted, leafless branches intertwine to picturesque designs. The tree makes an excellent specimen for use in restricted areas and in tubs, and its pliable branches lend themselves easily to espalier. It grows best in partial shade with protection from wind.

Conformation

Height: 25 to 35 ft. Spread: 25 to 35 ft.

A wide-spreading, arching tree usually branching severally from the base. The branches are twisted, and the young stems are a bright red. The bark is red-brown, thin, and seamed. The leaves are simple, opposite, and very thin; 5- to 11-lobed and sharp-toothed; 2 to 7 in. long and about as wide. Reddish when they first open, they turn a dull, dark green above, paler beneath, and become brilliant red and orange before dropping in the fall.

Flowers

Minute flowers with reddish or purple sepals and greenish-white petals, in small drooping clusters. April.

Fruit

Red, winged seed pods, 1½ in. long, in pairs. Summer. Persist until the following spring.

Root System: Deep

Rate of Growth: Moderate

Natural Requirements

Climate: Tolerates heat and cold, even at high altitudes.
Soil: Tolerates a wide variety of soils. Prefers a fairly fertile, moist soil which is rich in humus.
Exposure: Prefers partial shade. Tolerates some wind but assumes a better shape when afforded some protection.

Care

Pruning: Allow the tree to assume its natural shape when it is young. Prune and train to desired espalier form. Never prune after growth starts in spring, for the tree bleeds profusely. Time: Winter or early spring before growth starts; in mild areas, prune in the fall.
Feeding: Apply manure once every two years, in the fall.
Watering: Provide plenty of moisture.
Pests and Diseases: Aphids. Spray with nicotine, lindane, or malathion when needed.

ZONES 3-9

Acer negundo

A´cer negun´do

(Negundo aceroides;
 N. fraxinifolium; Rulac negundo)

Box-Elder; Ashleaf Maple

Eastern and central North America

Feature: Foliage

Use: Screen, erosion control, quick effects

Box-Elder is a short-lived tree, important in landscaping for its rapid rate of growth and its remarkable tolerance of hot, dry, arid regions. It is also useful in new gardens to provide quick effects while slower-growing, more desirable trees are maturing to take its place. Varieties of Box-Elder with silver or gold variegated leaves are much more handsome than the species and are more frequently planted. *Acer negundo californicum* (California Box-Elder), a native plant, is recommended as superior to the species for western garden culture.

Conformation

Height: 50 to 70 ft. Spread: 70 to 100 ft.

A rounded tree of dense habit, with branches starting close to the ground. The bark is grayish brown and thin, and cracks in interlacing fissures. The leaves are opposite and compound, and usually are composed of three to five sharp-pointed, irregularly toothed and lobed leaflets, 2 to 4 in. long and 1½ to 2½ in. wide. They are a dull green and turn an indifferent pale yellow before dropping in the fall. Desirable varieties with leaves marked with silver or gold are available. The native variety *Acer negundo californicum,* California Box-Elder, grows to a height of about 60 ft. It has compound leaves composed of 3-lobed and irregularly toothed yellow-green leaflets 1½ to 5 in. long.

Flowers

Small greenish flowers; not effective ornamentally.

Fruit

V-shaped, winged seeds, 1½ to 2 in. long, in drooping racemes 6 to 8 in. long. Summer. Persist throughout the winter.

Root System: Deep

Rate of Growth: Rapid

Natural Requirements

Climate: Tolerates heat and cold, even at high altitudes. Becomes brittle and misshapen in mild, humid areas. Tolerates desert atmosphere.

Soil: Grows best in fairly rich, moist, well-drained loam. Tolerates poor soil and drought.

Exposure: Sun. Protect from strong winds.

Care

Pruning: Remove lower branches and head high, when plant is young, if treelike specimen is desired. Never prune after growth starts in spring, for the tree bleeds excessively. Time: Winter or early spring before growth starts.

Feeding: No special feeding necessary.

Watering: Water deeply once a month. Withstands neglect.

Pests and Diseases: Box-elder bug; spray with a contact insecticide containing pyrethrum, when needed. Aphids: Spray with nicotine, lindane, or malathion when needed. Wilt fungus causes wilting of whole branches and the eventual death of the tree; there is no cure: remove and burn the tree and treat the soil with Bordeaux.

Faults

Short life. Branches are brittle. Reseeds. Stump sprouts.

ZONES: 2-

Acer palmatum

A´cer palma´tum
A. polymorphum palmatum

Japanese Maple

Japan; Korea

Features: Habit, foliage, fall color (red), winter design
Use: Lawn, water edge, patio, tub, specimen, accent

Japanese Maple is a tree of artistic branching habit with small, delicate, deeply lobed, light-green leaves, which turn red before dropping in the fall. The highly individual grace and charm of each picturesque specimen is accentuated in the winter months when the slender, leafless branches stand out in stark design. There are many varieties of Japanese Maple, some with deeply cut, threadlike leaves, and others varying in leaf color from yellow to bronze, red, and purple. The tree and its varieties make excellent specimens for small lawns and are particularly adaptable for use in patios and tubs. They need protection from wind and from the direct rays of the sun. *A. palmatum* should not be confused with *A. japonicum,* which has leaves of about the same size but not so acutely or deeply lobed.

Conformation

Height: 10 to 25 ft. Spread: 8 to 30 ft.

A picturesque, graceful tree with slender, irregular branches and light grayish-brown bark. The leaves are simple, opposite, double-toothed, and deeply lobed; they are 2 to 4 in. long and as wide. Very thin, with an almost transparent quality, they are reddish when they first open, change to a clear light green, and in the fall become a brilliant red. Seedlings offered at nurseries are not always dependable.

Flowers

Small purple flowers, in flat clusters, which appear before the leaves. Spring.

Fruit

V-shaped, winged seeds, 3/4 in. long. Summer. Persist on the tree throughout the winter.

Root System: Shallow, but roots are not voracious.

Natural Requirements

Climate: Tolerates heat and cold, even at high altitudes.
Soil: Prefers a moist, well-drained loam to which plenty of humus has been added.
Exposure: Partial shade. Protect from the direct rays of the sun and also from wind.

Care

Pruning: May be pruned to meet any particular artistic demand, or may be permitted to assume its natural shape. Never prune after growth starts in spring, for the tree bleeds profusely. Time: Winter or early spring before growth starts.
Feeding: Apply manure annually in the fall.
Watering: Provide plenty of moisture. Do not allow the plant to dry out. Avoid overhead watering or splashing of the leaves.
Pests and Diseases: Aphids: spray with nicotine, lindane, or malathion when needed. Wilt fungus causes wilting of whole branches and eventual death of the tree; there is no cure: remove and burn the tree and treat the soil with Bordeaux.

ZONES: 6-10

Acer platanoides

A´cer platanoi´des
Norway Maple

Features: Foliage, fall color (bright yellow)
Use: Shade, lawn, specimen

Norway Maple grows to a wide-spreading, dense, rounded tree with large, bright green foliage which casts heavy shade. In the fall, the handsome leaves make a brilliant display, turning bright yellow before dropping from the tree. Norway Maple is easy of culture and grows readily under adverse soil and climatic conditions. However, it must be pruned annually to lessen the strain on its branches and thus prevent hazardous breakage.

Europe and western Asia

Conformation
Height: 25 to 60 ft. Spread: 20 to 50 ft.

A roundheaded, compact tree with large, wide-spreading branches. The bark is very dark brown—almost black—and is closely ridged. The leaves are simple and opposite, deeply and acutely lobed, and sharp-toothed; they are 3 to 6 in. long and as wide. They are a clear, bright green and turn bright yellow before dropping in the fall.

Flowers
Greenish-yellow flowers, in clusters, which appear before the leaves unfold. Spring.

Fruit
V-shaped, winged seeds, 1½ to 2 in. long. Summer. Persist on the tree throughout the winter.

Root System: Deep
Rate of Growth: Rapid

Natural Requirements
Climate: Tolerates heat and cold, even at high altitudes.
Soil: Tolerates a wide variety of soils. Grows best in light, well-drained, fertile loam. Tolerates alkali. Endures drought but prefers moisture.
Exposure: Sun. Tolerates seacoast conditions and smog.

Care
Pruning: Remove lower branches and head high when tree is young. Thin annually to reduce heavy crown. Never prune after growth starts in spring, for the tree bleeds badly. Thinning is particularly important in lawn specimens. Time: Winter or early spring before growth starts.
Feeding: No special feeding necessary.
Watering: Water deeply once a month.
Pests and Diseases: Aphids are particularly plentiful on Norway Maple. Spray each spring and fall with nicotine, lindane, or malathion as a preventive measure and repeat when needed.

Faults
Branches may become brittle and break if crown is not thinned annually.

ZONES: 4-8

A´cer platanoi´des schwed´leri is a smaller tree than the species. Its leaves are red when they open in spring and gradually become green in summer; before dropping in the fall they turn a brilliant gold. A variety of *Acer platanoides schwedleri*, Crimson King, retains its red foliage throughout the spring and summer and becomes a riot of orange, red, and yellow before the leaves drop in the fall. Both trees are resistant to cold but not to dry heat. They should be given some protection from the direct rays of the sun.

Acer rubrum

A´cer ru´brum

Red Maple; Swamp Maple; Scarlet Maple

Eastern North America

Features: Foliage, flowers, fruit, fall color (scarlet, orange)
Use: Shade, street, lawn, water edge, accent

The bright red flowers of Red Maple appear in profusion in early spring and are followed by red foliage which gradually turns bright green, though the leaf stems and veins retain the red throughout the summer. Young twigs are also red, and in summer the tree is dotted with bright red, winged seeds. Red Maple is one of the first trees to drop its leaves in the fall, and early in the season the tree is a blaze of vivid orange and scarlet. Excellent as a street or lawn specimen, it grows to its best advantage in places where plenty of water is available.

Conformation

Height: 50 to 100 ft. Spread: 40 to 80 ft.

A dense, oval-topped tree with erect, upright-spreading branches. The bark is dark gray and flaked. The leaves are simple and opposite, slightly lobed and unequally toothed, and 2 to 4 in. long and as wide. Red when they first open, they gradually turn a soft, bright green on top and grayish underneath. Early in the fall they turn scarlet and orange before dropping from the tree.

Flowers

Bright red flowers, small but conspicuous. They bloom in profusion all over the tree before the leaves have opened. Spring.

Fruit

Bright red, V-shaped, winged seeds, which occur in profusion and make a brilliant display against the bright green summer foliage. Summer. They turn color and persist on the tree throughout the winter.

Root System: Average depth

Rate of Growth: Rapid

Natural Requirements

Climate: Tolerates cold and humid heat but not dry heat.
Soil: Prefers a fertile, moist loam. Tolerates alkali. Stands inundations.
Exposure: Sun. Tolerates seacoast conditions. Protect from strong winds.

Care

Pruning: Remove lower branches and head high, when tree is young. Never prune after growth starts, for the tree bleeds profusely. Time: Winter or early spring before growth starts.
Feeding: Apply manure once every two years, in the fall.
Watering: Provide plenty of moisture.
Pests and Diseases: Aphids; spray with nicotine, lindane, or malathion when needed. Wilt fungus causes wilting of whole branches and eventual death of the tree; there is no cure: remove and burn the tree and treat the soil with Bordeaux.

ZONES: 3-10

Acer saccharinum

A´cer sacchari´num

(*A. dasycarpum; A. eriocarpum*)

Silver Maple; Soft Maple; White Maple; River Maple

Eastern North America

Features: Foliage, fall color (pale yellow to brilliant yellow)
Use: Shade, lawn, screen, water edge, accent

Silver Maple is an upright-spreading tree with a somewhat open habit of growth and large, thin, deeply lobed leaves which cast medium heavy shade. The leaves are light green above, silvery beneath, and have a delicate, sparkling quality. In the fall, they turn a brilliant yellow before dropping from the tree. Silver Maple must be pruned annually to lessen the strain on its brittle branches and to prevent hazardous breakage under pressure from the wind. The tree grows best in extremely cold areas.

Conformation

Height: 60 to 100 ft. Spread: 50 to 100 ft.

A wide, oval-topped, upright-spreading tree with numerous, slender branches. The bark is gray and smooth when young and turns reddish brown and flakes with age. The leaves are simple and opposite, irregularly double-toothed, and deeply lobed; they are 6 to 7 in. long and nearly as wide, and very thin. Light green above, silvery beneath, they turn a pale to brilliant yellow before dropping in the fall.

Flowers

Greenish-yellow flowers, in clusters; not effective ornamentally. Spring.

Fruit

V-shaped, winged seeds, 2½ in. long; not effective ornamentally. Summer. Persist on the tree throughout the winter.

Root System: Shallow, spreading, with a small taproot
Rate of Growth: Rapid

Natural Requirements

Climate: Tolerates heat and cold, even at high altitudes.
Soil: Tolerates a wide variety of soils. Prefers a rich, moist, well-drained loam.
Exposure: Sun or partial shade. Protect from strong winds.

Care

Pruning: Remove lower branches and head high, when tree is young. Thin annually to prevent wind damage. Never prune after growth starts in spring, for the tree bleeds excessively.
Time: Winter or early spring before growth starts.
Feeding: No special feeding necessary.
Watering: Water deeply once a month.
Pests and Diseases: Aphids; spray with nicotine, lindane, or malathion when needed. Wilt fungus causes wilting of whole branches and eventual death of the tree; there is no cure: remove and burn the tree and treat the soil with Bordeaux.

Faults

Branches are brittle.

A´cer sac´charum, Sugar Maple, grows to the same height and spread as Silver Maple and has the same cultural and natural requirements. Its rate of growth is slower and its root system deeper; it is also more tolerant of alkali and less tolerant of boggy soils. Sugar maple has a beautiful symmetry and grows to a dense, oval-topped specimen which casts deep and heavy shade. The remarkable fall coloring of its large leaves varies in intensity according to the severity of the climate. Maple syrup and sugar are made from the sap of this tree.

ZONES 4-8
ZONES: 4-8

Aesculus californica

Aes´culus califor´nica
California Buckeye

California

Features: Flowers, habit, fall and winter design
Use: Hillsides, erosion control, accent

California Buckeye assumes many picturesque shapes depending upon the conditions under which it grows. Rounded and domelike in sheltered areas, it sprawls and leans with the wind when fully exposed—seeming to roll with the slopes of hills in perfect conformity with the landscape. In spring, tiny pink flowers, grouped tightly in long, compact spikes, appear all over the outer edges of the crown, standing out stiffly from the branches like huge candles. Too uncertain and wide-spreading for use in small gardens, California Buckeye makes a striking accent tree in large, open areas or on hillsides, and its roots are excellent for fixing sliding soils. It grows to its best advantage in cool, coastal areas.

Conformation
Height: 15 to 40 ft. Spread: 30 to 80 ft.

A broad, dense, open-crowned tree, generally domelike but assuming many picturesque shapes according to its situation and the pressure of the wind on its branches. Seldom erect, it is often multiple-trunked and low-branching, with twisted, crooked stems. The bark is smooth and pale gray. The leaves are dark green. They are opposite, palmately compound, composed of (usually) five fine-toothed leaflets 3 to 6 in. long and 1½ to 2 in. wide. They drop from the tree in late summer, leaving it completely bare and displaying interesting design patterns of the branches for two full seasons of the year.

Flowers
Pinkish-white flowers, ½ in. long, in stiff, erect, compact spikes 6 to 10 in. long, studded all over the tree. They make a handsome display. May—June.

Fruit
Large, pear-shaped brown pods, 1½ to 2 in. long, which persist on the branches even when the tree is leafless. The seeds are poisonous. Fall.

Root System: Shallow, spreading

Rate of Growth: Moderate

Natural Requirements
Climate: Grows best in cool, coastal areas.
Soil: Grows best in moist, well-drained loam. Tolerates drought.
Exposure: Sun or shade. Tolerates wind and seacoast conditions.

Care
Pruning: None required or advised. The tree is best when it is allowed to develop naturally.
Feeding: No special feeding necessary.
Watering: No special attention necessary.
Pests and Diseases: The tree is a host plant for thrips; spray with DDT, lindane, or malathion in spring and fall as a preventive measure and repeat when needed. Leaf-blotch fungus causes blotches in the leaves; spray with Bordeaux just as the leaf buds are opening in the spring.

Faults
The tree makes much litter, dropping twigs, flowers, fruits, and leaves. Seeds are poisonous to foraging animals.

Aesculus carnea

Aes´culus car´nea

Red Horse-Chestnut

Hybrid between *A. hippocastanum* and *A. pavia*

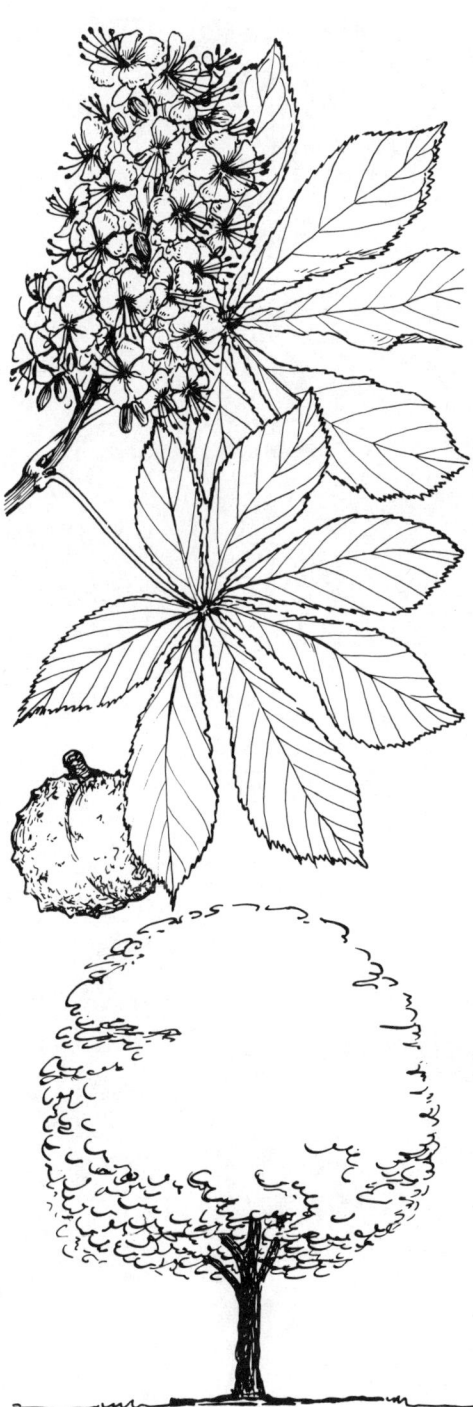

Features: Flowers, habit
Use: Shade, street, lawn

The Red Horse-Chestnut is an erect, roundheaded tree with an excellent habit of growth and a spectacular late spring display of light- to dark-red flowers. The color of the flowers varies in individual plants. If a particular shade is desired, it is necessary to purchase the tree when it is in bloom, except Var. *brioti*, which is consistent in having scarlet flowers. Red Horse-Chestnut casts medium shade and makes an excellent specimen for lawns. As a street tree, it maintains uniformity of shape and size but is likely to become a nuisance by its constant dropping of leaves, twigs, and fruit. The tree tolerates heat but will not thrive in dry atmospheres.

Conformation

Height: 30 to 40 ft. Spread: 25 to 30 ft.

A roundheaded, dense tree with an erect, straight trunk. The leaves are opposite and palmately compound, composed of (usually) five leaflets, 6 to 8 in. long and 1½ to 2½ in. wide and fine-toothed. They are a shiny medium to light green and drop from the tree early in the fall.

Flowers

Spectacular light- to dark-red flowers ¾ to 1 in. across, in loose, triangular spikes, 5 to 8 in. long. They bloom in profusion all over the tree. Var. *brioti* has bright scarlet flowers. May–June.

Fruit

Brown, globelike, prickly pods, 1 to 1½ in. long. They are interesting and rather attractive. They persist on the tree after the leaves have fallen. Fall.

Root System: Deep
Rate of Growth: Moderate to rapid

Natural Requirements

Climate: Tolerates heat. Does not grow well in dry atmospheres.
Soil: Grows best in moist, cool, well-drained soil. Tolerates drought to some extent.
Exposure: Sun. Protect from wind.

Care

Pruning: Prune occasionally to shape. Time: Winter or early spring.
Feeding: No special feeding necessary.
Watering: Water deeply once a month. Grows best with plenty of moisture.
Pests and Diseases: Relatively free from both.

Faults

Drops leaves, twigs and fruit, making much litter. Branches are brittle.

ZONES: 4-9

Aes´culus hippocasta´num bau´manni, Baumann's Common Horse-Chestnut, grows to a height of 30 to 60 ft. and a spread of 20 to 50 ft.; it is a low-branching tree with large, dense, dark-green foliage which casts heavy shade. It bears long, compact spikes of creamy-white double flowers in the late spring. It does not produce the messy seed pods of the species. It has the same natural and cultural requirements as *A. carnea* and is used for the same landscaping purposes.

Ailanthus altissima

Ailan´thus altis´sima
(*A. glandulosa*)

Tree-of-Heaven; Heaven-Wood;
Chinese Sumac; Paradise Tree

North China

Features: Foliage, fruit
Use: Shade, screen, water edge, erosion control, quick effects

Tree-of-Heaven is a rapid-growing, dense tree with large, luxuriant, tropical-appearing foliage. It is excellent for providing quick, light shade or screens in new gardens while more desirable trees are maturing to take its place. The landscaping value of this tree lies in its amazing indestructibility: it grows in places where no other vegetation will survive, tolerating heat, cold, wind, smog, and wet, dry, or salty soils, and displaying a remarkable resistance to insects and disease. The attractive, winged fruit appears only on female trees and is infertile unless pollinized; male trees should never be planted, for fertilized seeds reproduce the plant to such an extent that it is difficult to eradicate. Varieties of Tree-of-Heaven are available with handsome, red young leaves, or purplish stems, or bright red fruit.

Conformation
Height: 30 to 70 ft. Spread: 40 to 70 ft.

A tall, dense, flat-topped tree with smooth, striped, light-brown bark. The leaves are alternate and compound, 12 to 36 in. long, and composed of eleven to thirty-one leaflets 3 to 5 in. long and 1 to 2 in. wide. They are entire except for a few blunt teeth near the base, and are red when young, light green when mature.

Flowers
Yellowish flowers in large, pyramidal, terminal clusters. Male and female flowers are on different trees. The male flowers have an offensive odor. Spring.

Fruit
Yellowish to coppery red, winged seeds, $1\frac{1}{2}$ in. long; the wings twisted somewhat in the manner of an airplane propeller. They grow in large, compact clusters and are useful for flower arrangements and other indoor decoration. They occur on female trees only and are infertile unless pollinized. Varieties are available with bright red fruit. Fall.

Root System: Shallow
Rate of Growth: Rapid
Natural Requirements
Climate: Tolerates heat and cold. Adaptable.
Soil: Thrives in any soil but prefers a moist, light loam. Tolerates acid, alkali, salt, and drought, and also swamps and boggy areas.
Exposure: Sun or shade. Tolerates smog and wind.

Care
Pruning: Prune to a single trunk and remove suckers. Staking in youth is essential. Time: Any time of year.
Feeding: No special feeding necessary.
Watering: No special attention necessary. For best growth, provide plenty of moisture.
Pests and Diseases: Resistant to both.

Faults
Suckers excessively. Reseeds excessively and is difficult to eradicate if male trees are planted. Male flowers have an obnoxious odor.

Albizzia julibrissin

Albiz´zia julibris´sin

(Acacia julibrissin; Acacia nemu)

Silk Tree; Mimosa; Constantinople-Acacia

Persia; China

Features: Foliage, flowers

Use: Shade, tub, quick effects, accent

In its natural state, the Silk Tree is wide-spreading and often has a multiple trunk with branches arranged in tiers. It derives its name from the quality of its graceful dark-green foliage, which is exceptionally fine and feathery. The flowers appear as pink, fluffy balls which somewhat resemble a pincushion; they open consecutively and thus prolong the flowering season. Young trees do well in tubs, but they suffer and die back if confined for too long a time. However, the tree is remarkably tolerant of adverse conditions and stands climatic extremes.

Conformation

Height: 20 to 35 ft. Spread: 15 to 80 ft.

A dense, wide-spreading, low-branching, flat-topped tree with heavy branches arranged in tiers and spaced far apart. The bark is smooth and dark gray. Although the trunk often assumes a multiple form, the tree may be pruned when young to a single trunk, and can be headed high and trained into an umbrella shape. The leaves are alternate and compound, 5 to 8 in. long and 4 to 5 in. wide, and are composed of thirty to forty very tiny leaflets 1/4 to 3/8 in. long. They are a handsome dark green.

Flowers

Dainty, fluffy masses of pink stamens in ball-like clusters 1 to 1¼ in. wide. They open consecutively in the summer months. Var. *rosea* has deeper-pink flowers. Late spring to August and intermittently throughout the fall.

Fruit

Large, strap-shaped, flat pods, 5 to 6 in. long. Fall.

Root System: Shallow

Rate of Growth: Rapid

Natural Requirements

Climate: Tolerates heat, and stands cold to 0° F. Needs protection from frost when young.

Soil: Grows best in well-drained, sandy soil. Tolerates a poor or gravelly soil and also alkali and drought. Stands a good deal of moisture but grows best in dryer soils.

Exposure: Sun. Tolerates wind and seacoast conditions.

Care

Pruning: If umbrella shape is desired, prune to head high, removing lower branches. Time: Winter or early spring.

Feeding: No special feeding necessary.

Watering: No special attention necessary. Provide good drainage for best results.

Pests and Diseases: Pest resistant and relatively free from disease. Occasionally subject to an incurable wilt in hot, humid regions.

Faults

Relatively short-lived. Makes much litter.

Alnus rubra

Al´nus ru´bra
(*A. oregana*)
Red Alder

Pacific Coast of North America

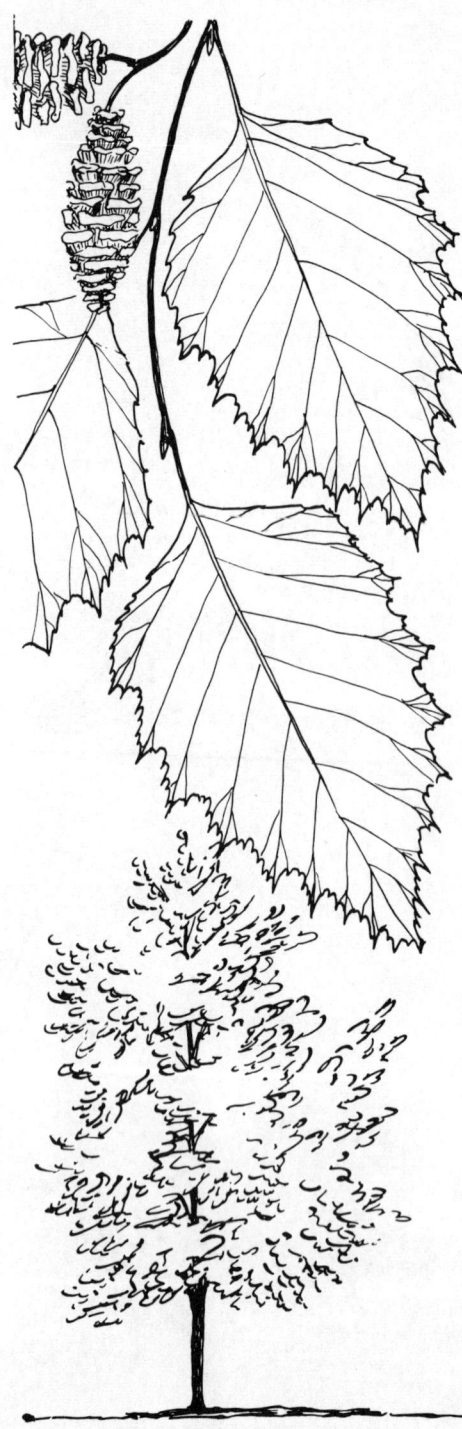

Features: Habit, bark
Use: Lawn, screen, copse, water edge, erosion control, quick effects

Red Alder is a light, supple tree with delicate, slightly pendulous branches and glistening gray-white bark which becomes blotched brown with age. The tree often grows in clumps, with several straight trunks rising from a single base and creating an excellent natural screen. Red Alder is also useful as a lawn specimen and for this purpose can be pruned to a single trunk. It has a remarkable ability to withstand wet or boggy soils and is highly tolerant of extremes of heat and cold.

Conformation

Height: 40 to 80 ft. Spread: 20 to 40 ft.

A narrow, pyramidal tree with intertwining, slightly pendulous branches. It often grows in clumps, with multiple trunks. The bark is gray-white, but it develops brown blotches with age and as it peels. The leaves are simple, alternate, and sharp-toothed, 2½ to 6 in. long and 1½ to 3 in. wide. They are dark, shiny green above, grayish and hairy beneath.

Flowers

Greenish catkins; not effective ornamentally.

Fruit

Dark orange-brown cones, 3/4 to 1 1/8 in. long, in short, branched clusters. Aug.–Sept. They persist on the tree throughout the winter.

Root System: Shallow
Rate of Growth: Rapid

Natural Requirements

Climate: Tolerates heat and cold.
Soil: Prefers a fertile, moist or wet soil. Tolerates swamps and boggy areas.
Exposure: Sun or shade.

Care

Pruning: Prune to a single trunk, if a specimen tree is desired. Little pruning is necessary. Time: Winter.
Feeding: No special feeding necessary.
Watering: Provide plenty of moisture.
Pests and Diseases: Caterpillars; spray with lindane, DDT, or malathion when needed.

Faults

The tree is relatively short-lived.

Al´nus rhombifo´lia, White Alder, has the same cultural and climatic requirements as Red Alder and is used for the same landscaping purposes. It grows to about the same height and has the same general habit but varies in having much smaller leaves, which are much more densely arranged on the branches.

Feature: Fruit
Use: Patio, tub, novelty

The Cherimoya is a subtropical tree which can be grown in only a few areas of the United States; specifically, it is suited only to the mild, protected regions of southern California and Florida, needing summer warmth to develop the fruit but being entirely intolerant of extreme heat, dry air, and cold. It is a spreading tree with large, tropical-appearing leaves, which drop from the tree for a short period in spring and are replaced almost immediately by lush, new growth. The fruit is elongated and heart-shaped and has a white, custard-like pulp with a sweetly acid, pineapple flavor. The tree is a temperamental bearer, setting few and generally inferior fruits unless it is pollinated by hand. It is best used in the garden as a novelty.

Conformation
Height: 15 to 25 ft. Spread: 15 to 25 ft.

A dense tree with horizontal-spreading branches. The leaves are oval, simple, alternate, and entire; 4 to 8 in. long and 2 to 4½ in. wide. They are smooth, light yellowish green above and velvety beneath. They drop from the tree in spring and are replaced almost immediately by lush new growth.

Flowers
Fragrant yellow flowers, 1 in. in length. Late spring–summer.

Fruit
Edible, light-green, elongated, heart-shaped fruit, 3 to 5 in. long; the outer surface either smooth or covered with tubercles which somewhat resemble overlapping leaves. The fruit is sliced and eaten like a melon. The flesh is white and has a texture like custard or ice cream, and a sweetly acid, pineapple-like flavor. Winter. The tree bears when four to five years old. Local nurserymen should be consulted for desirable varieties.

Root System: Average depth
Rate of Growth: Moderate to rapid

Natural Requirements
Climate: Tolerates heat that is not extreme or dry. Will not endure cold. Survives only in mild or semitropical areas.
Soil: Prefers a light, well-drained loam.
Exposure: Sun. Will not tolerate seacoast conditions.

Care
Pruning: Prune lightly each year to stimulate new growth. Time: Spring.
Feeding: Apply manure annually in the fall.
Watering: Provide plenty of moisture. Good drainage is essential.
Pests and Diseases: The tree may be susceptible to thrips; spray with lindane, DDT, or malathion when needed. Mealy bug; spray with a malathion solution or an oil emulsion when needed.

Annona cherimola

Anno´na cherimo´la

Custard-Apple; Ice-Cream Tree; Cherimoya

Peru

Betula pendula

Bet´ula pen´dula
(*B. alba*; *B. verrucosa*)
White Birch; European Birch

Europe, Asia Minor

Features: Habit, bark, winter design
Use: Lawn, screen, copse, water edge, accent

White Birch is a narrowly pyramidal tree with slender, gently pendulous branches and a clean white bark, irregularly marked and ringed with black. Light passes freely through its framework; the fine foliage seems to catch highlights from the rays of the sun and to twinkle with the least motion of the branches. In winter, the straight white trunk and slender, gracefully drooping branches of the bare tree form an exquisitely delicate and dainty design. White Birches make excellent screens or lawn specimens, whether planted singly or in clumps. They have a wide climatic adaptability and thrive almost anywhere except in the desert.

Conformation

Height: 20 to 60 ft. Spread: 8 to 15 ft.

A slender, pyramidal tree with an open habit and gently pendulous branches. The trunk is straight and tapering; the bark is smooth and white, marked irregularly with black patches or rings. The leaves are simple, alternate, and unevenly toothed, 1 to 2½ in. long and ¾ to 1½ in. wide. They are a shiny bright green and turn yellow before dropping in the fall. Among the varieties are: Var. *dalecarlica*, Cutleaf Weeping Birch, which grows to a height of about 30 ft. and a spread of 15 ft.; it is remarkably uniform in shape, with a decidedly pendulous habit and deep-cut leaves. Var. *youngi*, which can be trained to a wicket shape for use by pools or in oriental gardens.

Flowers

Not effective ornamentally.

Fruit

Narrow, woody, brown catkins, 1 in. long, bearing many small, winged seeds. Aug.–Sept. Persist throughout the winter.

Root System: Deep
Rate of Growth: Rapid

Natural Requirements

Climate: Tolerates heat and cold. Adaptable, but will not tolerate desert areas and is short-lived in warmer regions.
Soil: Tolerates a wide variety of soils. Prefers a moist loam but will survive in dry, sandy soils.
Exposure: Sun or shade. Tolerates seacoast conditions.

Care

Pruning: Little pruning is required. Trees bleed badly if pruned in the growing season. Time: Winter or early spring before growth starts.
Feeding: No special feeding necessary.
Watering: Provide plenty of moisture, especially in summer.
Pests and Diseases: Borer; spray with DDT in April, May, or June and repeat three weeks after the first spraying.

ZONES: 3-8

Bet´ula papyrif´era, Canoe or Paper Birch, has the same cultural and climatic requirements as White Birch and is used for the same landscaping purposes; but it is a taller tree, sometimes growing to 100 ft., and has a broader crown, which is definitely round. The bark is whitish. The leaves are almost twice as large as those of the White Birch.

ZONES: 2-8

Carpinus betulus

Carpinus betulus
European Hornbeam

Europe; Persia

Features: Habit, foliage
Use: Hedge, accent

European Hornbeam is a dense, shrubby tree with smooth gray bark and shiny bright green leaves. It can be trained to a very effective and handsome hedge. Many varieties are available, which differ in habit and foliage characteristics. Foliage types include cut-leaf, oak-leaf and purple-leaf; habit variations include a pyramidal and a narrowly columnar type. These varieties are valuable for supplying accents in many different garden plans. European Hornbeam and its varieties tolerate extremes of heat and cold and withstand a variety of adverse soil conditions.

Conformation
Height: 30 to 50 ft. Spread: 30 to 50 ft.

A dense, shrubby tree, pyramidal in youth, with a compact habit of growth. The bark is smooth and gray. The leaves are simple, alternate, and sharp-toothed, 2 to 4 in. long and 1 to 1¾ in. wide. They are shiny bright green, but turn yellow in the fall and persist on the tree throughout most of the winter.

Flowers
Catkins; not effective ornamentally.

Fruit
Winged seeds in light-green catkins 3 to 5½ in. long. They attract birds. Summer.

Root System: Average depth
Rate of Growth: Slow
Natural Requirements
Climate: Tolerates heat and cold.
Soil: Tolerates a wide variety of soils, including dry and rocky ones.
Exposure: Sun.

Care
Pruning: Stands a good deal of shearing. Time: Any time of year.
Feeding: No special feeding necessary.
Watering: No special attention necessary.
Pests and Diseases: Relatively free from both.

Faults
Does not transplant well.

ZONES: 6—

BUT AMERICAN HORNBEAM ZONES: 2—

Carya illinoiensis

Ca′rya illinoen′sis
(C. pecan; Hicoria pecan)

Pecan

South central United States

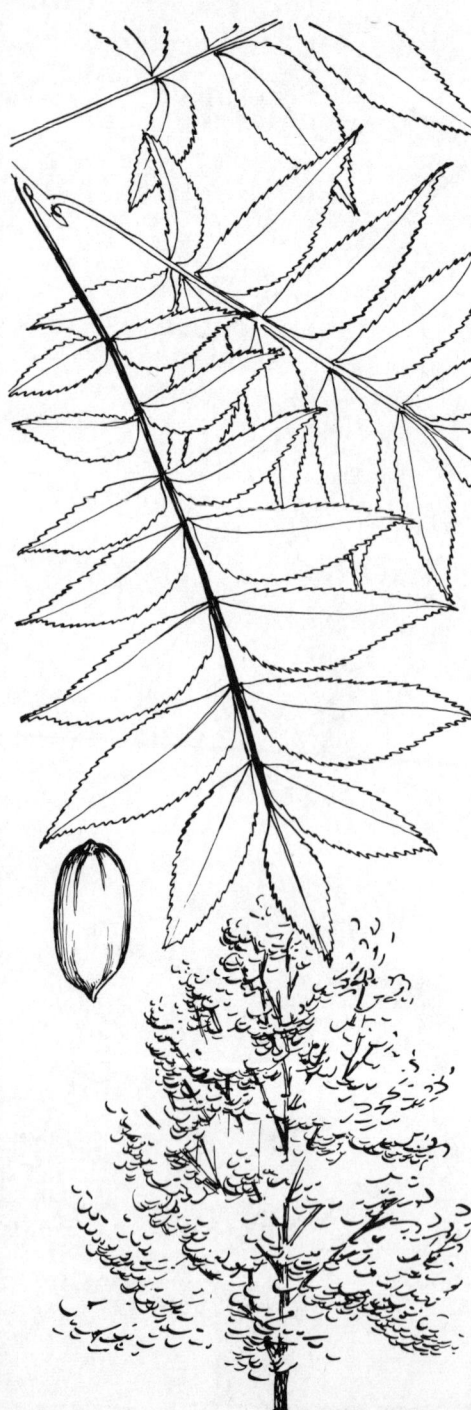

Features: Fruit, habit, fall color (gold)
Use: Shade, lawn, orchard

Pecan is a tall, upright, wiry tree with massive, gnarled branches and yellow-green foliage which casts light, filtered shade. Varieties are available for different climates; care should be taken to obtain the most suitable ones for the specific locality. The fruit, which is the pecan of commerce, requires plenty of summer heat for a good crop yield.

Conformation
Height: 60 to 150 ft. Spread: 45 to 70 ft.

An upright tree with massive branches and stout twigs. The bark is warm light brown and is irregularly and deeply furrowed. The leaves are alternate and compound, 12 to 18 in. long, and composed of eleven to fifteen fine-toothed leaflets 4 to 7 in. long and 1 to 3 in. wide. They are yellow green and turn clear gold before dropping from the tree in fall.

Flowers
Not effective ornamentally.

Fruit
Edible, reddish-brown or light-brown, long, slender, smooth fruit, 1 to 2½ in. long, with a very thin shell. Consult local nurserymen to determine the varieties best suited to the locality. Among the varieties are: Mahan (hot, dry areas), Nellis (coastal), Select (hot areas), and Success (cold areas). Fall. The tree bears when five years old; crops increase in yield each year.

Root System
Deep taproot with many long, shallow laterals. Deep cultivation can be injurious.

Rate of Growth: Slow. Increases after the first few years.

Natural Requirements
Climate: Prefers heat. Needs summer heat for fruiting but stands cool areas. Tolerates desert atmosphere.
Soil: Prefers a deep, rich, moist loam.
Exposure: Sun. Tolerates seacoast conditions but needs protection from strong winds.

Care
Pruning: Prune when tree is young if a specimen is desired. Later, prune only to train, shape, and thin. Time: Winter.
Feeding: Apply a small quantity of balanced commercial fertilizer annually in spring; apply manure in fall.
Watering: Provide plenty of moisture.
Pests and Diseases: Aphids (nicotine, lindane, or malathion), caterpillars (DDT, lindane, or malathion); spray when needed. Scale; spray with malathion or an oil emulsion in summer and repeat when needed. Bark bettle; spray with DDT in April, May, or June and repeat three weeks after the first spraying. Use dormant spray in winter. Pecan scab causes black spots on the undersurfaces of the leaves and on the twigs and fruit; at its inception, spray with Bordeaux at least three times at biweekly or monthly intervals.

Faults
Does not transplant well. Branches split and break in heavy storms. Woodpeckers release a liquid secretion which attracts insects.

Castanea dentata

Castánea dentáta
(*C. americana*)
American Chestnut

Northeastern United States

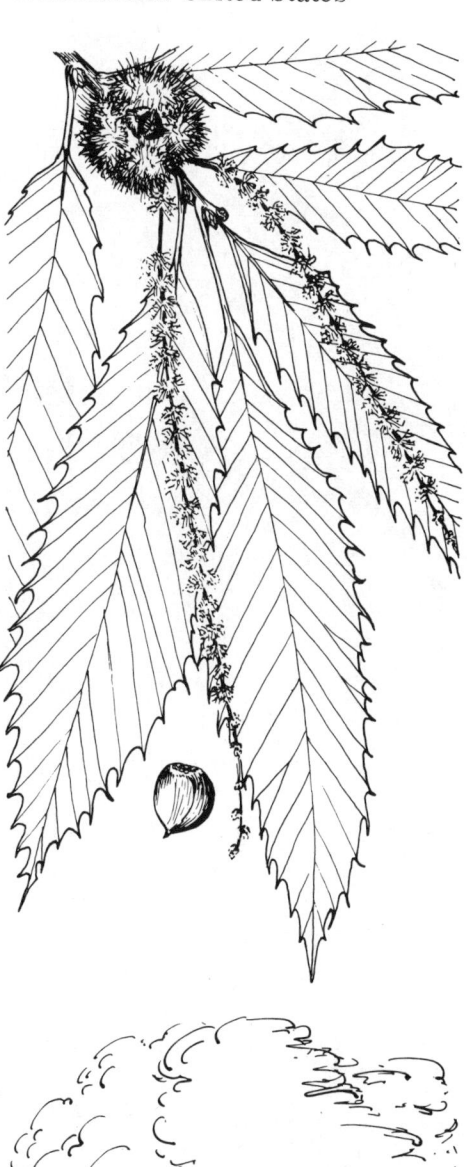

Features: Habit, fruit

Use: Shade, orchard, hillside

The wide-spreading, gracefully arching branches of the American Chestnut are clothed with pendulous, light-green leaves and cast ample but not oppressive shade. The fruit is a prickly bur containing edible nuts. This beautiful and productive tree has been decimated in a large part of the United States by a killing blight for which no cure has been found; the disease has not yet spread to California, nor to some areas in the Midwest. Research is being conducted by the Department of Agriculture to develop a blight-free strain. The tree needs winter chill to set fruit.

Conformation
Height: 50 to 100 ft. Spread: 70 to 110 ft.

A broad tree with a smooth, round crown and wide-spreading, arching branches. The bark is grayish brown and lightly ridged. The leaves are simple, alternate, and sharp-toothed, 5 to 11 in. long and 1½ to 4 in. wide. They are light green, thin, and pendulous on the tree.

Flowers
Fragrant white flowers in erect catkins, the male flowers being particularly conspicuous. June–July.

Fruit
Prickly brown bur, 2 to 2½ in. in diameter, enclosing (usually) two shiny, brown, edible nuts. Fall.

Root System: Deep

Rate of Growth: Moderate

Natural Requirements
Climate: Tolerates heat and cold. Needs winter chill to set good fruit.
Soil: Grows best in well-drained, warm, sandy loam. Tolerates rocky ground, acid soil, and drought. Will not stand boggy soils.
Exposure: Sun.

Care
Pruning: Prune to encourage growth of lateral branches, because fruit is produced on new wood. Time: Winter or early spring before growth starts.
Feeding: No special feeding necessary.
Watering: Water deeply once a month. Good drainage is essential.
Pests and Diseases: Weevil; spray with arsenate of lead in late summer to destroy adults and to prevent deposition of eggs. Destruction of larvae-infested nuts helps to control the pest. Blight causes shriveling of the leaves and eventually destroys the tree; there is no cure: remove infected tree immediately and burn it. This disease does not extend below the surface of the ground.

Faults: The tree suckers excessively.

Castánea mollis´sima, Chinese Chestnut, is apparently the only good ornamental chestnut which is resistant to the chestnut blight. For this reason, most of the research work is being done with this species, and with apparently good results.

Catalpa bignonioides

Catal´pa bignonioi´des
(Macrocatalpa; *C. syringaefolia*)

Cigar Tree; Common Catalpa;
Indian-Bean; Southern Catalpa

Southeastern United States

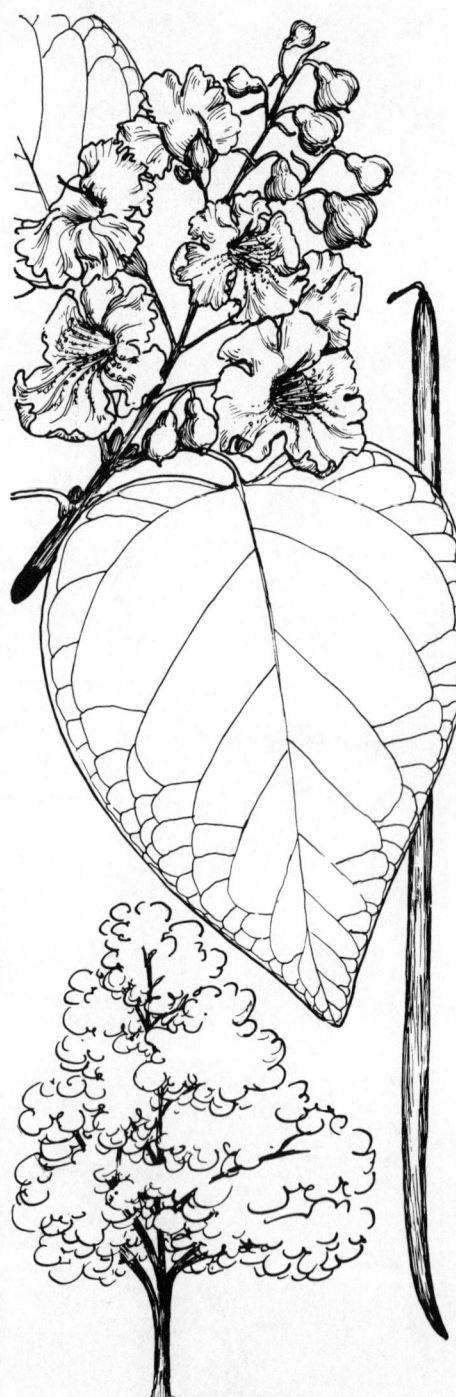

Features: Foliage, flowers, winter design

Use: Shade, lawn, specimen

Catalpa is an irregular, picturesque tree with a broad, round crown and large, dense, yellow-green foliage which casts heavy shade. In summer, showy white flowers make a handsome display against the tropical-appearing foliage; in autumn, these are followed by long, cylindrical seed pods, which persist throughout the winter. The long, narrow pods hanging from the crooked branches make an unusual and interesting winter display. Catalpa is too distinctive a specimen to be used indiscriminately; it should be considered only for large gardens where its bold features can be displayed to the best advantage. It is a vigorous tree with a wide climatic adaptability.

Conformation

Height: 40 to 60 ft. Spread: 40 to 65 ft.

A dense, irregular, picturesque tree with a broad, wide head and an upright central trunk. The branches are crooked and very wide-spreading. The bark is light brown and scaly. The leaves are a light yellow-green. They are simple, opposite, and entire, 6 to 12 in. long and 4 to 7 in. wide, and heart-shaped.

Flowers

White flowers, 1 to 1¾ in. long, spotted with purple-brown and striped with yellow, in large, erect, showy clusters, about 7 to 8 in. long, at the ends of the twigs. June–July.

Fruit

Slender, cylindrical brown seed pods, 6 to 12 in. long. The pods persist on the tree throughout most of the winter. The plant derives its popular name from these pods, which can be smoked like cigars. Fall.

Root System: Deep

Rate of Growth: Rapid

Natural Requirements

Climate: Grows best in dry atmosphere. Tolerates heat and cold.
Soil: Tolerates a wide variety of soils; grows best in moist, fertile, well-drained loam. Tolerates alkali and drought.
Exposure: Sun or shade.

Care

Pruning: Little is required. Time: Winter or early spring.
Feeding: Apply manure annually in fall.
Watering: Water deeply once a month.
Pests and Diseases: Pest resistant and relatively free from disease.

Faults

Leaves, twigs, and fruit make much litter.

Catal´pa specio´sa, Western Catalpa, has the same climatic and cultural requirements as the Common Catalpa but is a larger tree with huge, sharp-pointed, heart-shaped leaves and a loosely pyramidal habit. It should be used only where plenty of space is available for its development and the enhancement of its bold effect.

Celtis australis

Celtis australis

European Hackberry; Nettle Tree

Feature: Habit
Use: Street, shade, screen

European Hackberry is a rounded tree with a grayish bark and dense, gray-green foliage which casts heavy shade. Related to the elm and frequently used as a substitute for it, this tree lends itself well to street planting and is effective for use as a screen. It is a valuable ornamental because of its easy maintenance in difficult areas where drought, wind, dust, and dry heat are prevalent. However, it is not entirely hardy and will not tolerate bitterly cold areas.

Conformation

Height: 40 to 80 ft. Spread: 40 to 50 ft.

A round- to oval-topped tree with a straight trunk and many small, lateral branches. The bark is smooth and grayish brown. The leaves are simple, alternate, and sharp-toothed, 2 to 6 in. long and 1 to 2 in. wide. They are dark gray-green above, paler and slightly hairy beneath, and are densely arranged on the branches.

Flowers

Not effective ornamentally.

Fruit

Small, dark-purple berries, ½ in. in diameter. They are very attractive to birds. Summer and fall.

Root System: Average depth
Rate of Growth: Moderate

Natural Requirements

Climate: Tolerates heat and some degree of cold but will not endure extreme cold or prolonged freezing. Stands dry atmospheres.
Soil: Tolerates a wide variety of soils and also drought.
Exposure: Sun. Tolerates wind, smoke, and dust.

Care

Pruning: Little is required. Time: Winter or early spring.
Feeding: No special feeding necessary.
Watering: No special attention necessary. Stands neglect.
Pests and Diseases: Pest resistant and relatively free from disease.

ZONES: 6 −

BUT EASTERN HACKBERRY IS ZONE 4-9

Southern Europe

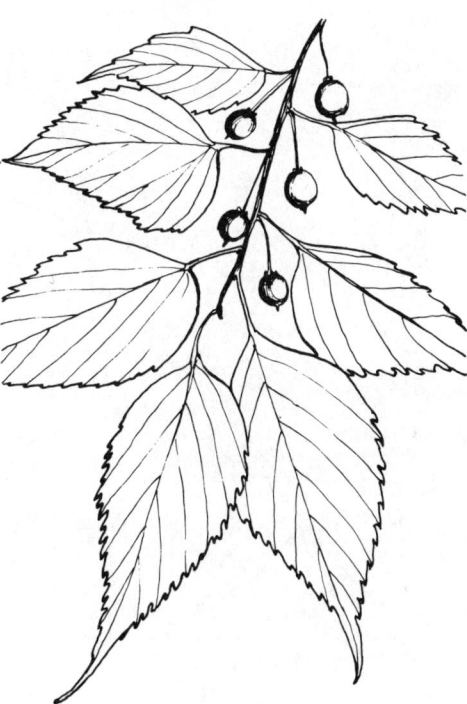

Cladrastis lutea

Cladras'tis lute'a
American Yellow-Wood

North Carolina; Kentucky; Tennessee

Features: Foliage, flowers, fall color (orange or yellow), winter design, bark

Use: Street, specimen

American Yellow-Wood is a dense, roundheaded tree with zigzagging branches and handsome, velvety, silver-green foliage. The fragrant white flowers hang in long, wistaria-like clusters; unfortunately they bloom only every second or third year. In the fall, the leaves turn orange and yellow before dropping from the tree; in winter, the interesting branches and light-gray bark make a striking design display. The tree is excellent for use in streets or for specimen planting in gardens. It has a wide climatic adaptability, withstanding extremes of heat and cold.

Conformation

Height: 30 to 45 ft. Spread: 15 to 25 ft.

A dense, roundheaded tree with zigzagging branches and a tall, straight trunk. The leaves are alternate and pinnately compound, 8 to 12 in. long, composed of seven to nine leaflets 2 to 4 in. long and 1½ to 2 in. wide and entire. They are shiny silver-green and turn orange and yellow before dropping in the fall.

Flowers

Fragrant, pea-shaped white flowers, 1 in. long, in wistaria-like clusters 10 to 15 in. long, at the ends of the twigs. The tree blooms once every two or three years. June.

Fruit

Narrow, flat brown pods, 2 to 4 in. long.

Root System: Deep

Rate of Growth: Moderate

Natural Requirements

Climate: Tolerates heat and cold and also desert conditions.

Soil: Prefers a deep, fertile, friable soil. Tolerates alkali and drought.

Exposure: Sun.

Care

Pruning: Thin branches in crown, when tree is young.
    Time: Summer only.

Feeding: No special feeding necessary.

Watering: No special attention necessary.

Pests and Diseases: Relatively free from both.

Faults

Branches are brittle if crown is not properly thinned.

ZONES: 3 -

Features: Flowers, fruit, foliage, fall color (brilliant red), winter design, bark

Use: Street, lawn, water edge, patio, tub, specimen

The branches of Flowering Dogwood spread out in horizontal tiers to form a wide, flat-topped tree. In early spring, flowers, consisting of small greenish clusters surrounded by four large white bracts, completely cover the tree. From amid this cloud of white, rosy-tinged leaves appear and gradually change to a clear, bright green as the season progresses. In autumn, the tree is a brilliant display of scarlet berries and fiery red leaves, which finally drop to leave the tiered branches and checkered brown bark in handsome, stark design throughout the winter months.

Conformation

Height: 10 to 30 ft. Spread: 15 to 25 ft.

A low-branching, flat-topped tree with branches arranged in horizontal tiers. The bark is a medium brown and is checkered somewhat like an alligator's hide. The leaves are simple, opposite, and entire; 3 to 6 in. long and 2½ to 4 in. wide; and sharply pointed at the tips. They are a rosy color when they open and change to a clear bright green; in the fall, they turn brilliant red before dropping from the tree.

Flowers

Tiny greenish flowers which are surrounded by four pure-white, deeply notched bracts cover the tree. The whole flower measures 4 to 5 in. across. A variety, *rubra*, which has pink bracts, is available. March-May.

Fruit

Tiny scarlet berries in large, round, showy clusters. They are highly ornamental and also serve as food for wildlife. Sept.-Oct.

Root System: Deep

Rate of Growth: Moderate

Natural Requirements

Climate: Grows best in cold areas. Tolerates heat and cold. Protect from early frost, which may damage the flowers.

Soil: Tolerates a wide variety of soils, including acid ones, if they are moist and well-drained.

Exposure: Sun or shade. Grows best in partial shade. Protect from wind.

Care

Pruning: Prune as little as necessary to maintain shape. Flowers are produced on new growth. Time: Winter.

Feeding: No special feeding necessary.

Watering: Provide plenty of moisture.

Pests and Diseases: Thrips (host); spray with DDT, lindane, or malathion in spring and late fall and repeat when needed. Disease resistant.

ZONES: 5-9

Cornus nuttálli, Pacific Dogwood, is a rather temperamental tree which varies in habit depending upon exposure conditions. At its best, it is pyramidal, with slender branches and a narrow crown. The flowers are surrounded by six bracts, which are white, faintly tinged with pink. It has the same cultural and climatic requirements as Flowering Dogwood.

Cornus florida

Cornus florida
(Cynoxylon floridum)
Flowering Dogwood

Eastern United States

Corylus maxima

Cor′ylus max′ima
Giant Filbert

Western Asia; southeastern Europe

Feature: Fruit

Use: Orchard, novelty

Giant Filbert is ordinarily pruned to an open-growing, vase shape for garden use. It is cultivated for its edible fruit, which consists of nuts that have a sweet, rich flavor. The tree grows to a good size and yields well only in climates which approximate that of the Pacific Northwest, where coolness and moisture are prevalent. Named varieties are obtainable and cross-pollination is necessary to set fruit.

Conformation

Height: 15 to 30 ft. Spread: 10 to 25 ft.

A sturdy, strong-growing tree of open, vase shape, which is determined by early and continued pruning. The leaves are simple and alternate, slightly lobed and fine-toothed, 3 to 4½ in. long and 2 to 3½ in. wide. They are bright green and are somewhat hairy. The twigs also are hairy.

Flowers

Greenish-white flowers in sparse clusters. They appear before the leaves on one-year-old lateral spurs. Not effective ornamentally. March–April.

Fruit

Large, oblong, edible, hard-shelled nuts enclosed in a leafy tube, one to three in a cluster, usually in pairs, on one-year-old spurs. Since cross-pollination is necessary to set fruit, two or more varieties should be planted. Among the varieties are Barcelona, DuChilly, and White Aveline. Fall. The tree bears when four years old.

Root System: Average depth

Rate of Growth: Moderate

Natural Requirements

Climate: Thrives only in cool, moist areas. Yields well only in climates which approximate that of the Pacific Northwest. Not practical for use in mild or tropical regions.

Soil: Grows best in fairly rich, well-drained, moist soil.

Exposure: Sun.

Care

Pruning: Prune whips to a height of 2 ft., allowing six branches to develop around the tree in vase form. Head back strong branches to promote spurs. Prune annually to remove all old wood which has borne fruit. Remove suckers. Time: March or April, after the flowering season, to avoid removal of bearing spurs.

Feeding: Apply a small quantity of balanced commercial fertilizer annually in early spring; apply manure annually in the fall.

Watering: Water deeply once a month. Good drainage is essential. Do not allow water to stand at the base of the tree.

Pests and Diseases: Aphids and mites; spray with malathion in spring and repeat when needed.

Faults

Sends out many suckers.

Cotinus coggygria

Coti´nus coggyg´ria
(Rhus cotinus)
Smoke Tree

Southern Europe to central China

Features: Fruiting panicles, fall color (orange to scarlet)
Use: Accent, novelty, difficult areas, erosion control

Smoke Tree, when mature, has a bushy, bowl-like shape and a broad, rounded crown. In late summer, pinkish fruiting clusters in plumy branched panicles cover the tree and, when seen from a distance, create the impression of billowing smoke. In early fall, the leaves, before dropping, turn blazing orange and scarlet. A variety, *purpurea*, has purplish fruiting clusters and young leaves which are a deep red when they first open. The trees are excellent in small gardens for novelty effects or for accent purposes. They tolerate dry, infertile soils and desert atmosphere and withstand rather severe cold.

Conformation

Height: 12 to 15 ft. Spread: 10 to 15 ft.

A dense, broadly rounded, shrublike tree with many slender, upright-spreading branches. When mature it has a bowl-like shape. The leaves are simple, alternate, and entire, 2 to 3 in. long and 1¼ to 2 in. wide. They are bright green and turn blazing orange and scarlet before dropping in the fall.

Flowers

Small yellowish flowers in branched terminal clusters. May–June.

Fruit

Pinkish fruiting clusters in feathery branched panicles 7 to 10 in. long, consisting of a few seeds and the lengthened stalks of the numerous, sterile flowers. They cover the tree and give it a "smoky" appearance. June–July. They persist for many weeks.

Root System: Average depth
Rate of Growth: Moderate

Natural Requirements

Temperature: Tolerates heat and cold and also desert conditions.
Soil: Prefers a well-drained, infertile soil. Tolerates rocky, gravelly soil and drought.
Exposure: Sun

Care

Pruning: Little is required.
Feeding: No special feeding necessary.
Watering: No special attention necessary.
Pests and Diseases: Relatively free from both.

Crataegus lavallei

Crataeˈgus lavalˈlei
(*C. carrierei*)
Carriere Thorn; Lavalle Thorn

Hybrid between *C. crusgalli* and *C. pubescens*

Features: Flowers, fruit, fall color (red)
Use: Street, lawn, screen, patio, tubs, specimen

The branches of Carriere Thorn start low on the trunk and spread out in every direction, frequently crossing and impeding one another in their development; annual pruning is therefore necessary if a specimen plant is to be obtained. The tree offers much seasonal interest, from the masses of white flowers in late spring to the handsome orange-red berries which form in the fall and persist throughout the winter. In autumn, the leaves turn red and remain on the tree for some time before dropping. Although Carriere Thorn tolerates mild climates, it does not produce its best fruit or most brilliant fall coloring in these regions. The tree prefers winter cold and will not stand extreme, dry heat.

Conformation
Height: 15 to 30 ft.   Spread: 8 to 10 ft.

A slender tree with dense, stout-thorned branches which cross frequently. The bark is smooth and brown and breaks into scaly plates, with age. The leaves are simple, alternate, and toothed, 2 to 4 in. long and 1 to 1½ in. wide. They are wedge-shaped and are pointed at the tips. A gray-green, they turn coppery red in the fall and persist on the tree well into the winter months.

Flowers
White flowers, ¾ in. in diameter, with red center discs, massed on the tree in large, showy clusters 4 to 5 in. across. May.

Fruit
Orange-red berries, 3/4 to 7/8 in. long. They are very profuse. The berries are often cut to prune the tree in winter and for use in indoor decoration. Sept.-Oct. Persist throughout the winter.

Root System: Deep

Rate of Growth: Moderate

Natural Requirements
Climate: Tolerates cold; will not stand extreme, dry heat. Will grow in coastal areas but will not produce fruit well or give good fall color in these regions.
Soil: Prefers an open, rich, well-drained, sandy loam with a limestone base. Tolerates alkali and also drought.
Exposure: Sun. Tolerates wind and seacoast conditions.

Care
Pruning: Thin head and remove cross branches frequently. Remove suckers. The tree will stand heavy pruning. Time: Winter.
Feeding: Apply manure and bone meal annually in the fall.
Watering: No special attention is necessary. Good drainage is essential.
Pests and Diseases: Aphids; spray with nicotine, lindane, or malathion when needed. Scale; spray with malathion or an oil emulsion in summer and repeat when needed; spray with oil in winter. Disease resistant.

Faults
Sends out many suckers.

Features: Flowers, habit

Use: Street, lawn, hedge, patio, tub, specimen, accent

English Hawthorn is a roundheaded tree of symmetrical shape with a straight trunk and a steeply ascending habit of growth. The white flowers bloom in late spring; their compact clusters, strung all along the branches, completely cover the tree. Varieties are available with double white, single pink, or double red flowers. English Hawthorn and its varieties make neat and handsome street, lawn, patio, and tubbed specimens and because of their symmetrical habit are well adapted for use as hedges. The trees stand severe cold and thrive in coastal regions; they will not tolerate hot, dry atmosphere.

Conformation
Height: 10 to 25 ft. Spread: 12 to 20 ft.

A dense, roundheaded, symmetrical tree with very erect, upright-spreading, thorny branches. The trunk is straight; the bark is very smooth and brownish. The leaves are simple, alternate, and toothed, ¾ to 2 in. long and ½ to 1¼ in. wide. They are distinctly three- to five-lobed and are a handsome bright green.

Flowers
Single white flowers, ½ in. in diameter, in tight clusters, 2 to 2½ in. wide, strung all along the branches. The varieties of the species differ in having single pink, double red, or double white flowers. Pauls Scarlet Thorn, a double red variety, is probably the most widely planted of the group. May–June.

Fruit
Small scarlet berries, ½ in. long, in clusters; very sporadic in the varieties. Fall.

Root System: Deep

Rate of Growth: Moderate

Natural Requirements
Climate: Tolerates heat and cold. Tolerates coastal conditions; will not thrive in hot, dry regions.
Soil: Prefers an open, rich, well-drained, sandy loam with a limestone base. Tolerates alkali and drought.
Exposure: Sun. Tolerates wind and seacoast conditions.

Care
Pruning: Prune to eliminate occasional crossing branches. Remove suckers. Time: Winter.
Feeding: Apply manure and small quantities of bone meal annually in the fall.
Watering: No special attention necessary. Good drainage is essential.
Pests and Diseases: Aphids; spray with nicotine, lindane, or malathion when needed. Scale; spray with malathion or an oil emulsion in summer and repeat when needed; spray with oil in winter. Fire blight causes twigs and branches to become blackened as though having been burned by fire; cut out infected areas to 12 in. below the point of infection and spray the tree with Bordeaux.

Faults
Has a tendency to sucker.

ZONES: 5-9

Crataegus oxyacantha

Cratae´gus oxyacan´tha
(C. oxyacanthoides)
English Hawthorn

Europe; North Africa

Crataegus phaenopyrum

Cratae´gus phaenopy´rum
(*C. cordata; C. acerifolia;
C. populifolia*)
Washington Thorn

Eastern United States

Features: Fruit, flowers, foliage, habit, fall color (red), winter design

Use: Street, lawn, hedge, patio, tub, specimen, accent

Washington Thorn is a highly ornamental specimen tree which is delightful at every season of the year. It grows to a dense, rounded shape with graceful, zigzagging branches springing horizontally from a handsome, straight trunk. The flowers bloom in large white clusters in late spring and early summer and are followed in the fall by red berries. The tree is excellent for use in streets, lawns, hedges, patios, and tubs. It needs winter cold to produce its best development and will not thrive where hot, dry atmosphere is prevalent. It tolerates coastal conditions but will not perform at its best in these regions.

Conformation

Height: 20 to 30 ft. Spread: 20 to 25 ft.

A dense, roundheaded, high-branching tree with slender, intertwining, zigzagging, thorny branches which spread horizontally from a straight trunk. The bark is smooth and brownish and breaks into scaly plates when the tree is old. The leaves are simple, alternate, and toothed, 1 to 2½ in. long and as wide, and are 3- to 5-lobed. They are densely arranged on the branches. Shiny light green, they turn red or sometimes orange in the fall.

Flowers

Small white flowers, ½ in. in diameter, in huge clusters, 4 to 6 in. wide. They bloom in profusion all over the tree after the leaves are fully open. May–June.

Fruit

Bright red berries, ¼ in. in diameter, in large, flat-headed, compact clusters which are pendulous and are suspended from the branches on long stems. They make a brilliant display. Sept.–Oct. Persist well into the winter months.

Root System: Deep

Rate of Growth: Moderate

Natural Requirements

Climate: Tolerates cold; will not thrive in hot, dry atmospheres. Tolerates seacoast conditions but does not reach its best development in coastal areas.

Soil: Prefers an open, rich, well-drained, sandy loam with a limestone base. Tolerates alkali and drought.

Exposure: Sun. Tolerates wind and seacoast conditions.

Care

Pruning: Prune occasionally to thin head. Remove suckers. The tree will stand heavy pruning. Time: Winter.

Feeding: Apply manure and small quantities of raw bone meal annually in the fall.

Watering: No special attention necessary. Good drainage is essential.

Pests and Diseases: Aphids; spray with nicotine, lindane, or malathion when needed. Scale; spray with malathion or an oil emulsion in summer and repeat when needed; spray with oil in winter. Disease resistant.

Feature: Flowers
Use: Novelty, specimen

Dove Tree is unpredictable in shape, but it is usually a loose pyramid with graceful, arching branches. The flowers are highly unusual, consisting of a group of red anthers surrounded by two long white bracts, which are pendulous and resemble the wings of a dove. Any disturbance in the atmosphere causes the bracts to flutter like a bird in flight, creating a remarkable effect. The The tree is an interesting and effective novelty specimen. It grows best in northern areas where the winters are cold.

Conformation
Height: 30 to 60 ft. Spread: 15 to 40 ft.

A tree of unpredictable shape. It is usually a pyramid, with slender, arching branches and a dense habit of growth. The leaves are simple, alternate, and toothed, 2 to 4½ in. long, and oval. They are light green above, lighter green beneath.

Flowers
A group of red anthers within two creamy white, pendulous bracts. The bracts are of different lengths, one being about 6 in. long, the other about 3 in. long. They resemble the wings of a dove. May.

Fruit
Fleshy, green, pear-shaped fruit, about 1½ in. long. June.

Root System: Average depth
Rate of Growth: Moderate. Growth is more rapid in northern areas.

Natural Requirements
Climate: Grows best in northern areas where winters are cold. Tolerates both heat and cold.
Soil: Prefers a light, sandy loam to which plenty of humus has been added.
Exposure: Sun or partial shade.

Care
Pruning: Prune only to shape, when tree is young.
  Time: Winter.
Feeding: Apply leaf mold annually at any season of the year.
Watering: Water deeply once a month.
Pests and Diseases: Relatively free from both.

Davidia involucrata

David´ia involucra´ta
Dove Tree

Western China

Diospyros kaki

Diospy̆ros kaki

Kaki Persimmon

China, Korea

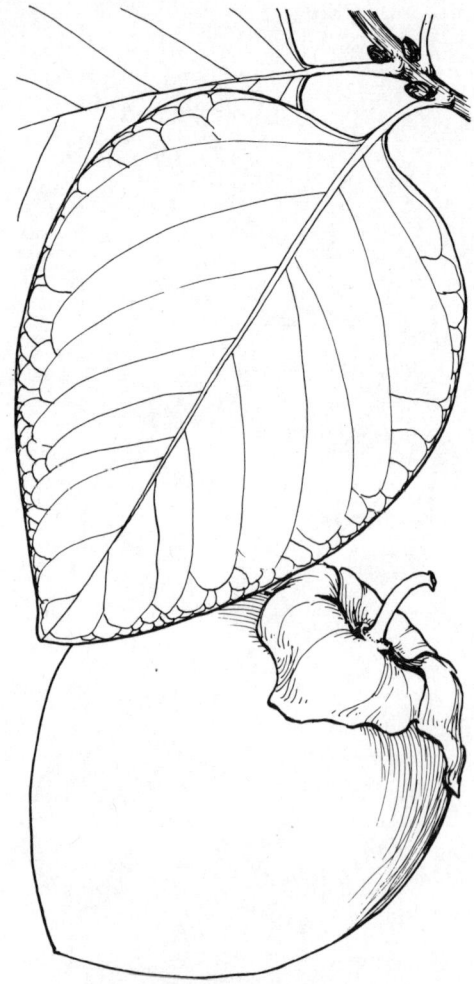

Features: Fruit, fall color (orange-red)

Use: Orchard, patio, tub, novelty, specimen, accent, espalier

Kaki Persimmon has wide-spreading, pliable branches which are easily trained to any desired shape. The orange-red fruit decorates the tree in the fall and early winter, persisting after the leaves have turned fiery red and orange and have dropped from the branches. The brilliant fall coloring of the leaves is consistent even in mild climates. Kaki Persimmon stands some cold and will produce well even in temperate regions.

Conformation

Height: 20 to 40 ft. Spread: 20 to 40 ft.

A compact, roundheaded tree with a straight, erect trunk and widespreading branches. The bark is gray. The leaves are simple, alternate, and entire, and are 3 to 7 in. long and 2 to 3½ in. wide. They are a shiny dark green and turn a brilliant orange-red in fall.

Flowers

Not effective ornamentally.

Fruit

Edible, brilliant orange-red fruit, 3 to 4 in. long and almost round. The fruit ripens on the tree after the leaves have fallen; but when used for food, it is picked while firm and allowed to ripen. Neither winter chill nor pollination is necessary to set fruit. Varieties available are Hachiya (fruit astringent until soft) and Fuyu (fruit nonastringent, ripening to firm, sweet flesh). Sept.–Dec. The tree will bear when four years old.

Root System: Deep

Rate of Growth: Moderate

Natural Requirements

Climate: Tolerates heat and cold but needs protection from prolonged freezing. Grows well in temperate areas.

Soil: Tolerates a wide variety of soils. Prefers a moist, well-drained soil.

Exposure: Sun. Protect from strong winds.

Care

Pruning: Train to a modified leader and thin branches to produce fruiting wood in center of tree. Cut to laterals and never leave stubs. Thin fruit to lessen strain on branches. Persimmons bear on current season's growth. To keep trees to dwarf size, thin and cut back branches severely to within four to eight buds each year. Espaliers also demand annual pruning and constant pinching. Time: Winter.

Feeding: Apply manure annually in the fall. If tree is growing poorly, apply a nitrogen fertilizer in early spring.

Watering: Water deeply once a month. Good drainage is essential.

Pests and Diseases: Relatively free from both.

Faults: Branches are brittle.

Diospy̆ros virginiána, Common Persimmon, is a wide-spreading, low-branching, pendulous tree with a thick, ridged bark and leaves which turn a brilliant orange-red in the fall. The fruit is decorative but is small and of indifferent quality. The tree is a good ornamental for extremely cold areas where Kaki Persimmon will not thrive.

Features: Habit, foliage, bark, fall color (bronze), winter design
Use: Shade, lawn, windbreak, hedge, specimen

Fagus sylvatica

Fágus sylvática
European Beech

Central and southern Europe

European Beech is a graceful, upright-spreading tree with beautiful light-gray bark and dense dark-green foliage. The leaves turn bronze in late fall and tend to persist on the tree, combining with the gray bark and slender branches to make a handsome winter display. There are many varieties of European Beech, including columnar, weeping, cut-leaved, and round-leaved types. The best known and most widely planted is var. *atropunicea,* or Purple Beech. Numerous gradations of leaf color are found under the name Purple Beech, varying from coppery red to crimson-purple; it is well to see the tree in foliage before purchasing it.

Conformation
Height: 50 to 60 ft. (100 ft.). Spread: 35 to 50 ft.

A compact, dense, roundheaded tree with slender, spreading branches forming a pyramid. The smooth, light-gray bark is occasionally speckled and blotched with darker gray. The leaves are simple, alternate, and remotely toothed, 2 to 4 in. long and 1 to 2 in. wide. They are a lustrous dark green and in mild climates tend to persist well into winter. Before dropping, they turn bronze. Var. *atropunicea* has young leaves of cherry red that darken to purple-black at maturity.

Flowers
Not effective ornamentally.

Fruit
A prickly bur, ¾ in. long; not effective ornamentally. Persists on the tree throughout the winter.

Root System: Spreading, with a long taproot. The fibrous roots are near the surface and are voracious.

Rate of Growth: Moderate

Natural Requirements
Climate: Tolerates heat but does not like dry heat. Tolerates cold.
Soil: Prefers a deep, rich, well-drained, sandy loam with a limestone base. Var. *atropunicea* tolerates alkali.
Exposure: Sun. Tolerates wind and seacoast conditions. Protect bark from blistering in hot, exposed situations.

Care
Pruning: Stands a good deal of pruning. Prune, when tree is young, to establish framework. Later, it needs little pruning, for it grows naturally to a good shape. Time: Winter.
Feeding: Apply manure and raw bone meal once every two years, in the fall.
Watering: Provide plenty of moisture. Good drainage is essential.
Pests and Diseases: Relatively free from both.

Faults
Roots are voracious. Tree does not transplant well.

ZONES: 5 —

Fágus grandifolia (*F. americana*), American Beech, stands even more severe cold than European Beech but is not cultivated to any great extent in western gardens. The bark is a lighter gray; the leaves are larger and turn a clear, bright yellow in the fall.

ZONES: 3 —

Ficus carica

Fi´cus cari´ca

Domestic Fig; Common Fig

Western Asia

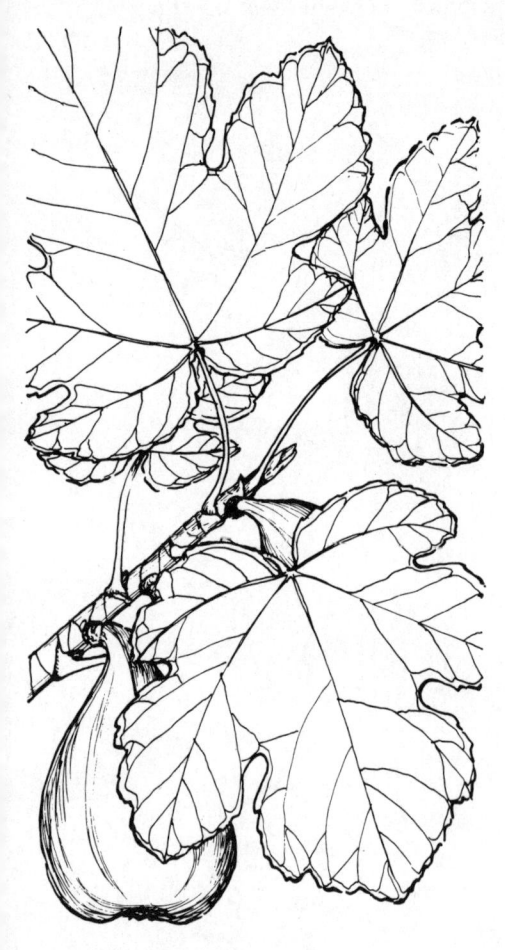

Features: Fruit, foliage, bark

Use: Shade, lawn, orchard, patio, tub, espalier

Fig is a roundheaded tree with handsome gray bark and wide-spreading branches which grow in many picturesque shapes. The foliage is dark green and has a lush, tropical appearance. The fruit is a fleshy receptacle containing many small fruits which resemble seeds. However, even without the fruit, the tree is a valuable ornamental. It will survive in northern areas if given proper winter protection.

Conformation

Height: 20 to 40 ft. Spread: 30 to 60 ft.

A picturesque tree with wide-spreading branches forming a broad, rounded crown. The trunk is often multiple and is covered with smooth, dark-gray bark. The leaves are simple, alternate, three- to five-lobed, with slightly toothed or wavy margins, and 4 to 12 in. long and about as wide. They are rich dark green and rough above and hairy beneath.

Flowers

Not effective ornamentally.

Fruit

A fleshy edible receptacle containing many minute fruits which resemble seeds. It is purple or white, 1 to 3 in. long, and variable in shape. Local nurserymen should be consulted about the varieties that have proved best for their regions. Among those available are: Adriatic, Brown Turkey, Brunswick (Magnolia), Kadota, Mission, Trojano, and White Genoa. Brunswick has proved very successful for home gardens, having a wide climatic tolerance and setting fruit easily. The first crop matures in early summer; the second, from midsummer to fall. The tree bears when three years old.

Root System: Deep

Rate of Growth: Slow

Natural Requirements

Climate: Thrives in desert atmosphere and tropical climates; sets best crops in hot, dry areas. Protect from winter cold.

Soil: Tolerates a wide variety of soils, even sterile ones. Prefers a deep loam. Tolerates drought but grows best with moisture.

Exposure: Sun. Tolerates wind and seacoast conditions.

Care

Pruning: Prune young trees to 24 to 30 in. above ground, allowing three or four main branches to develop to establish the framework for fruiting branches. Thereafter, pruning should be slight and only to shape the tree. Fruit bears on young branches. Time: Winter or early spring.

Feeding: Apply manure once every two years, in the fall. Avoid too rich a soil, which is unconducive to fruiting. Climate is a greater determining factor than soil in fruit production.

Watering: Water deeply once a month. Good drainage is essential.

Pests and Diseases: Scale; spray with malathion or an oil emulsion in summer and repeat when needed; spray with oil in winter. Red spider; spray with malathion when needed. Avoid the use of poisonous materials near fruit-ripening time.

Firmiana simplex

Firmiāna sim´plex
(Sterculia platanifolia)

Chinese Parasol Tree; Japanese Varnish Tree; Phoenix Tree

China; Korea

Features: Foliage, unusual fruit, winter design
Use: Shade, street, lawn, patio, accent

The branches of the Chinese Parasol Tree are covered with shiny, light gray-green bark and extend steeply upward to form a rounded crown of large, bright green leaves. The fruit is highly unusual, splitting into four leafy sections, like the petals of a flower, each section bearing pealike seeds along the margins. Late in the year, when the leaves have fallen, the precise, upright branches and shiny bark make a bright and charming winter picture. Chinese Parasol Tree is an excellent street, lawn, or patio tree and is useful for creating lush, tropical effects. It tolerates some degree of cold but will not stand prolonged freezing, and needs protection from strong winds.

Conformation

Height: 20 to 40 ft. Spread: 15 to 40 ft.

A dense, high-branching and upright-spreading tree with a rounded crown. The bark of both trunk and branches is gray-green, smooth, and shiny. The leaves are simple and alternate, 6 to 12 in. long and as broad, and are three- to five-lobed, each lobe being sharply pointed. They are a shiny green.

Flowers

Small greenish-white flowers, in branched terminal clusters.

Fruit

Pods, 2 to 4 in. long, which separate into four expanded, leafy sections, like the petal of a flower, with pealike seeds along the margins. A brown fluid is released when the pods open.

Root System: Average depth
Rate of Growth: Moderate

Natural Requirements

Climate: Tolerates heat and some degree of cold but will not endure prolonged freezing.
Soil: Tolerates any good, moist, well-drained garden soil.
Exposure: Sun. Protect from strong winds.

Care

Pruning: Little pruning is required.
Feeding: No special feeding necessary.
Watering: Provide plenty of moisture. Good drainage is essential.
Pests and Diseases: Relatively free from both.

Fraxinus velutina

Frax´inus veluti´na
(F. standleyi)

Arizona Ash; Velvet Ash

Arizona; New Mexico; Mexico

Features: Foliage, fall color (deep yellow)

Use: Shade, street

Narrow and pyramidal when young, Arizona Ash develops to a wide-spreading shade tree with cool, yellowish-green foliage which turns deep yellow in the fall. The remarkable durability of this tree under desert as well as seacoast conditions and its tolerance of a variety of soils place it high on the list of rugged plants for difficult areas. The variety *glabra*, Modesto Ash, has smooth leaves and is more widely planted than the species.

Conformation

Height: 30 to 40 ft. Spread: 15 to 30 ft.

An open-growing, roundheaded tree, rather heavy at maturity though definitely light and pyramidal when young. The bark is gray tinged with red and is deeply furrowed. The leaves are opposite and compound, 4 to 8 in. long, and composed of (usually) five somewhat variable, sometimes hairy, toothed or untoothed leaflets 1 to 1½ in. long and ¾ to 1 in. wide. The foliage is light yellowish green and turns deep yellow in the fall.

Flowers

Male and female flowers on separate trees: the female flowers greenish, male ones yellowish. Not effective ornamentally. March-April, before the leaves.

Fruit

Light-brown, winged seeds, 1 in. long, which resemble coarse paddles and grow in long, drooping clusters, on female trees only. Interesting but not effective ornamentally. Spring. Persist until fall.

Root System: Deep

Rate of Growth: Moderate to rapid

Natural Requirements

Climate: Tolerates heat and desert atmosphere. Will not endure extreme cold or prolonged freezing.

Soil: Prefers a rich, moist, well-drained soil. Tolerates drought and alkali.

Exposure: Sun. Tolerates wind and seacoast conditions.

Care

Pruning: Head high, when tree is young. Maintains a good shape without pruning. Time: Fall.

Feeding: Apply manure annually in the fall.

Watering: No special attention necessary.

Pests and Diseases: Relatively free from both. Red spider is sometimes present; spray with malathion at first sign of infestation and repeat when needed.

Fraxinus velutina coriacea, Leatherleaf Ash, is a variety with larger, deeper green, leathery foliage. It is more resistant to attack from red spider than the species and is an excellent plant for growing in clumps.

Gleditsia triacanthos inermis

Gledit´sia triacan´thos iner´mis

Thornless Honey Locust; Thornless Sweet Locust

Central United States

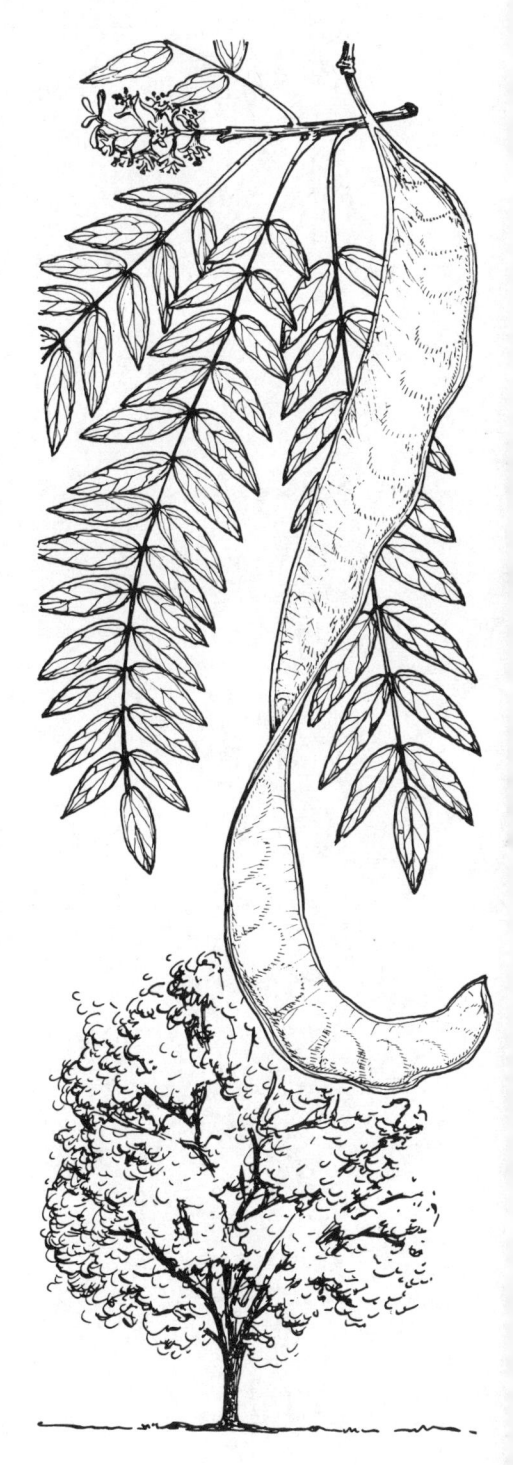

Features: Habit, foliage, fall color (yellow)

Use: Shade, street, lawn, windbreak, hedge

Thornless Honey Locust is a wide-spreading, symmetrical tree with bright green, finely divided, fernlike leaves which turn a clear yellow in the fall. Strong-growing and rugged, it is well equipped to take care of itself under adverse conditions, tolerating wind, drought, and poor soils and presenting no maintenance problem. Although it adapts itself well to shade, street, lawn, windbreak, and hedge plantings, its use should be limited to large gardens where it has plenty of room to develop. When buying this tree, it is important to make certain it is the thornless variety, for the species is equipped with cruel thorns which are a real menace under city or garden conditions. A podless, thornless variety, Moraine Locust, has been widely preferred because of its neat habit and the vaselike shape it has when young. The trees are very hardy, tolerating extremes of heat and cold.

Conformation

Height: 50 to 75 ft. Spread: 50 to 70 ft.

A flat-topped, open-growing, horizontal tree with branches starting close to the ground and often drooping. The twigs are slim and polished. The bark is smooth and nearly black and breaks into long, scaly ridges, with age. The leaves are alternate and compound, 6 to 10 in. long, and composed of many smooth-margined leaflets, ¾ to 1½ in. long and ¼ to ½ in. wide. They create an airy, graceful, fernlike effect; they are bright green until they turn yellow in the fall.

Flowers

Small, fragrant, greenish flowers in narrow racemes, 2 to 3 in. long. They are very attractive to bees. May–July.

Fruit

Dark-brown seed pods, 10 to 16 in. long, contorted in all manner of twisted shapes. They are rose-colored when young. The gummy pulp round the seeds is sweet when the pods are young and becomes bitter when they mature. Fall. Persist on the tree after the leaves have fallen.

Root System: Deep, wide-spreading

Rate of Growth: Rapid

Natural Requirements

Climate: Tolerates heat and cold and desert atmosphere.
Soil: Tolerates a wide variety of soils, including alkali. Tolerates drought.
Exposure: Sun. Tolerates wind, smoke, and dust.

Care

Pruning: Prune annually to lighten crown and thus prevent breakage. Time: Fall.
Feeding: No special feeding necessary.
Watering: No special attention necessary.
Pests and Diseases: Resistant to and relatively free from both.

Faults

Pods drop and make much litter.

ZONES: 5–

Halesia carolina

Hale´sia caroli´na
(H. tetraptera)

Silverbell; Snowdrop Tree

West Virginia to Florida and Texas

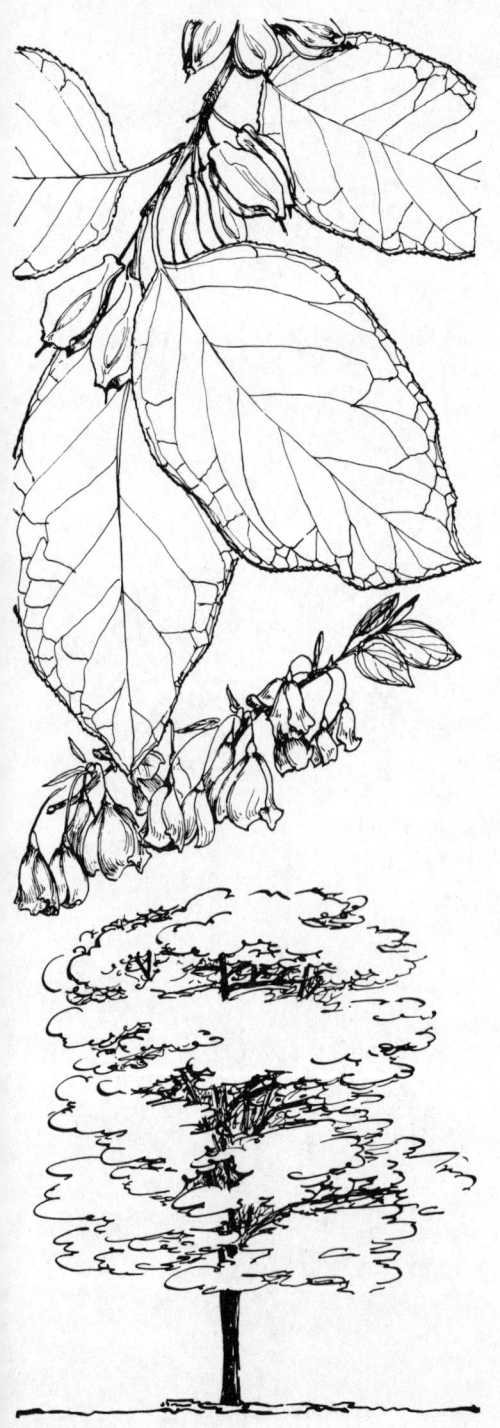

Features: Flowers, fall color (yellow)

Use: Lawn, patio, tubs, specimen

Silverbell is a graceful, roundheaded tree with slender branches and an open habit of growth. In spring, myriads of bell-shaped white flowers literally cover the tree, hanging all along the branches in delicate, pendulous clusters. In the fall, the neat, bright green foliage turns clear yellow before dropping. Silverbell is well suited for use in small gardens, patios, or tubs, and it makes an excellent lawn specimen. It tolerates heat and some degree of cold but will not stand prolonged freezing.

Conformation

Height: 20 to 40 ft. Spread: 15 to 30 ft.

A roundheaded, open-growing tree, pyramidal in youth, with slender horizontal-spreading branches. The bark is rough and separates into small, close scales. The leaves are simple, alternate, and fine-toothed, 2 to 4 in. long, and oblong. They are bright green and turn clear yellow before dropping in the fall.

Flowers

Bell-shaped white flowers, ½ to ¾ in. long, in short, drooping axillary clusters of two to four flowers in a cluster. The buds are light pink. May.

Fruit

Dry, winged pods, 1 to 1½ in. long, in clusters. Fall.

Root System: Average depth

Rate of Growth: Moderate

Natural Requirements

Climate: Tolerates heat. Stands some cold but will not endure prolonged freezing.

Soil: Prefers a rich, moist, well-drained loam. Tolerates acid soils.

Exposure: Partial shade. Protect from wind.

Care

Pruning: Prune only when tree is young, to establish framework. Time: Winter.

Feeding: Apply manure annually in fall.

Watering: Provide plenty of moisture. Good drainage is essential.

Pests and Diseases: Relatively free from both.

Features: Flowers, foliage

Use: Street, patio, tub, specimen, accent

Jacaranda has a tendency to straggle; to keep it in shape, some attention to pruning is necessary. The large, light-green foliage has a delicate, fernlike appearance. In late spring and summer, long, showy clusters of large, lavender-blue flowers bloom in profusion and make a handsome display. When trained properly, Jacaranda is an excellent specimen for street, patio, or tub use. It is not tolerant of wet soils or wind and will do well only in frost-free climates.

Conformation

Height: 25 to 60 ft. Spread: 20 to 45 ft.

An irregular, rather scraggly tree with smooth, light grayish-brown bark. The leaves are opposite and twice compound, 16 to 20 in. long, and composed of twenty to forty pinnae. There are eighteen to forty-eight oblong leaflets on each pinna; these are 1/4 to 1/3 in. long, except the terminal one, which is 1/2 in. They are light green and have the appearance of a fern frond. The leaves drop for a short period in April and May.

Flowers

Lavender-blue, tubular flowers, 2 in. long and 1½ in. wide, in handsome showy panicles 8 in. long, on the tips of the current year's growth. Summer and fall. The petals drop from the flowers and spread like a lavender carpet on the ground; they last for an appreciable time after falling.

Fruit

Hard, dark-brown, woody pods, 1 to 2 in. long. They are used for indoor decoration, or are strung for use as beads; they last for years. Fall.

Root System: Deep

Rate of Growth: Rapid

Natural Requirements

Climate: Tolerates heat; will not tolerate frost. Protect young trees in winter, even in mild areas.
Soil: Prefers a light, fertile, well-drained soil. Tolerates drought.
Exposure: Sun or shade. Protect from wind.

Care

Pruning: Prune to establish framework, when tree is young. Later, prune to shape and cut out any inner branches affected by dieback. Time: Early spring.
Feeding: No special feeding necessary.
Watering: Water deeply once a month. Good drainage is essential.
Pests and Diseases: Relatively pest-free.

Jacaranda acutifolia

Jacaran'da acutifo'lia
(J. ovalifolia; J. mimosaefolia)
Green-Ebony; Sharpleaf Jacaranda

Brazil

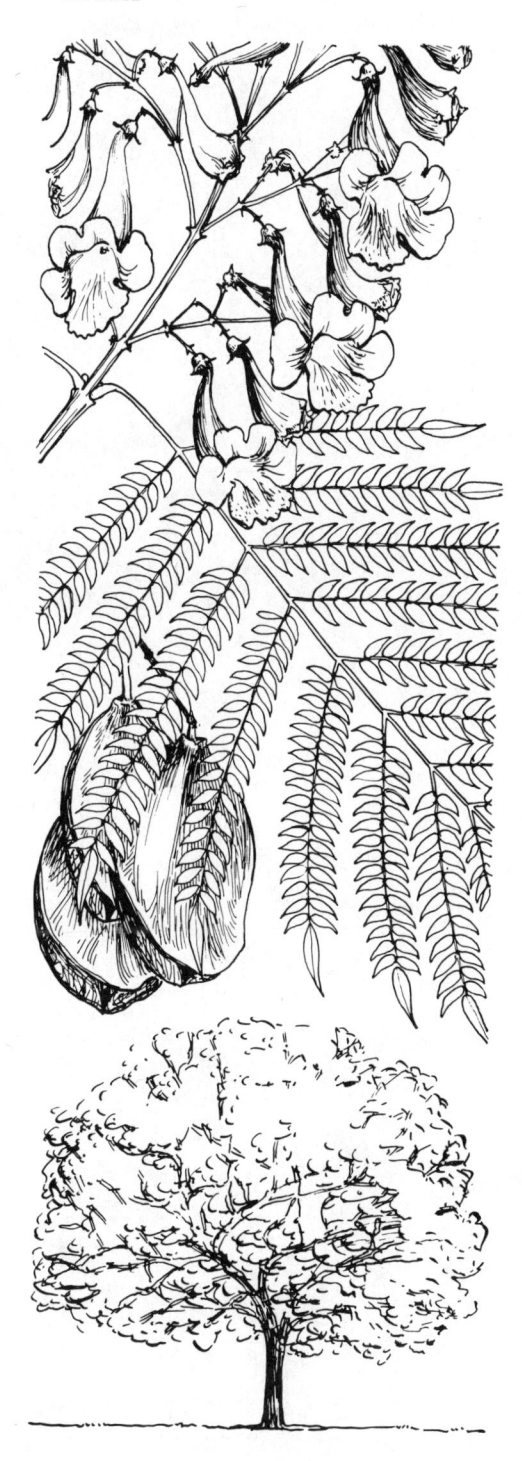

Juglans regia

Ju´glans re´gia

English Walnut; Persian Walnut

Southeastern Europe; China

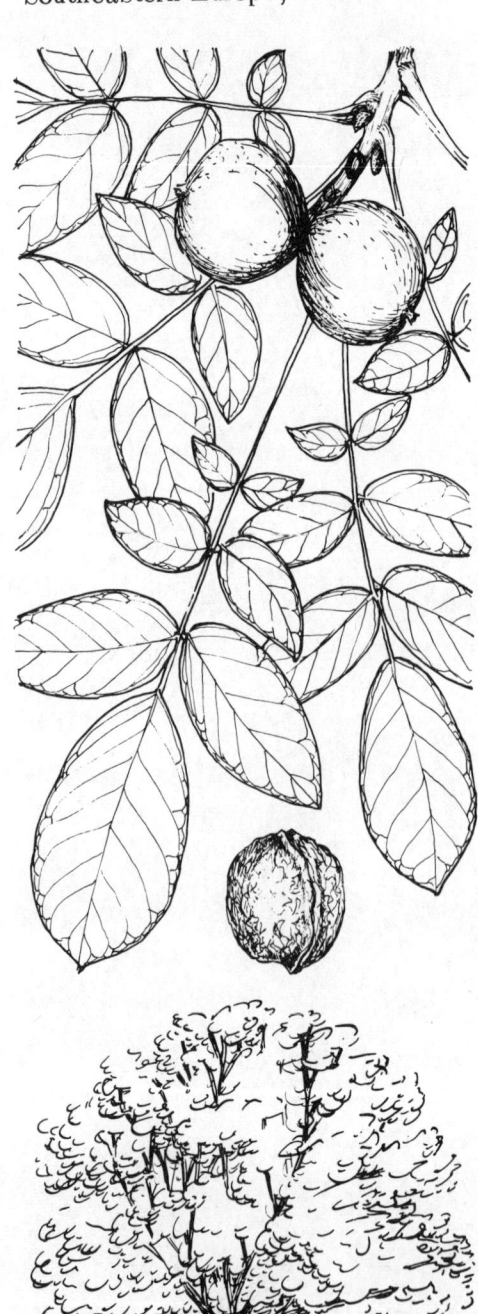

Features: Fruit, habit, foliage

Use: Shade, lawn, orchard

English Walnut is a good ornamental, casting heavy shade from its wide canopy of graceful, bright green leaves. It has a wide climatic tolerance, standing extremes of heat and cold and thriving in mild and coastal areas.

Conformation

Height: 40 to 50 ft. (75 ft.). Spread: 40 to 70 ft.

A broad, open-headed tree with wide-spreading branches. The bark is smooth and silvery gray. The bright green leaves are alternate and compound, 8 to 16 in. long, and composed of seven to nine oblong, entire leaflets 2 to 5 in. long and 1 to 1½ in. wide.

Flowers

Not effective ornamentally.

Fruit

Edible, dark-brown nuts, 1½ to 2 in. in diameter. Cross-pollination is not necessary to set fruit. Among the varieties are Concord (coastal valley), Franquetta (inland valley), Payne (mild regions), Placenta (mild regions), and Wasson (coastal). Fall.

Root System: Deep

Rate of Growth: Slow; moderate when young.

Natural Requirements

Climate: Tolerates heat and cold. Frost sometimes kills fruiting wood in the north.

Soil: Tolerates a variety of soils but will produce good fruit only in a deep, fertile, well-drained, light loam. Will not tolerate alkali or boggy soils.

Exposure: Sun. In hot areas, protect trunk from sunburn by whitewashing the bark. Tolerates wind.

Care

Pruning: Cut back young trees to two or three buds, or to about 12 to 18 in. from the ground; in summer, select the most vigorous young shoot as the leader and remove all others. The next spring, from the laterals beginning to form, select a framework of branches starting 5 to 6 ft. from the ground and allow at least 2 ft. between the branches. Thereafter, remove all branches which develop below it. Little pruning is needed after the framework is established. Time: Winter.

Feeding: Apply nitrogen in early spring if yield is poor.

Watering: Provide plenty of moisture, especially in summer. Good drainage is essential.

Pests and Diseases: Aphids; spray with lindane, nicotine, or malathion when needed. Codling moth; spray with DDT or malathion when needed. Blight causes irregular black spots on the leaves and fruit and prevents setting of fruit; spray with Bordeaux just before buds open in spring and repeat immediately after they have opened. A yellowing of the leaves is sometimes caused by zinc deficiency in the soil; spray with leaf feed.

Jug´lans ni´gra, Black Walnut, has the same climatic and cultural requirements as English Walnut, but it is not so ornamental and becomes ragged with age. The nuts have a pungent taste and are used mostly for cooking. *Juglans hindsi*, Hinds Black Walnut, is distinguished for its high-branching habit.

Koelreuteria paniculata

Koelreutéria paniculáta

Goldenrain Tree; Varnish Tree; China Tree; Pride-of-India

China; Korea; Japan

Features: Flowers, fall and winter design

Use: Shade, street, lawn, patio, specimen, accent

Goldenrain Tree is a compact, roundheaded tree with an interesting framework of twisted branches. In summer, bright yellow flowers in long, branched clusters literally cover the tree. The leaves are red when they open in the spring and become a shiny bluish-green when mature; they drop early in the fall and leave the design of branches as a decorative autumn and winter feature. Goldenrain is particularly noteworthy for its remarkable tolerance of various climates and soils; and it presents no maintenance problem, being pest-free and drought tolerant and growing naturally to a good shape.

Conformation

Height: 10 to 30 ft. Spread: 10 to 20 ft.

A compact, roundheaded tree with wide-spreading branches and interesting twisted stems. The leaves, which are alternate and compound, are 8 to 14 in. long and composed of seven to fifteen lobed leaflets 1¼ to 3 in. long and ¾ to 1¾ in. wide. They are red when they open in the spring and turn a shiny bluish green; by midsummer the whole tree has a bluish cast. The leaves drop early, and the tree is deciduous for two full seasons.

Flowers

Bright yellow flowers, ½ in. in diameter, orange-marked at the base, in branched panicles 15 in. long. They literally cover the tree. May–June.

Fruit

Inflated, papery-walled, bladder-like capsules, 1 to 2 in. long, containing three black seeds. They are light yellow-brown at first and change gradually to light red-brown. October. Persist into winter.

Root System: Deep

Rate of Growth: Moderate to slow

Natural Requirements

Climate: Tolerates heat and cold. Should be protected from prolonged freezing. Tolerates mild, temperate, and coastal areas.

Soil: Tolerates any well-drained soil. Tolerates alkali and drought.

Exposure: Sun. Grows scraggly in shade. Tolerates wind, smoke, and dust.

Care

Pruning: Little is required. Time: Winter.

Feeding: No special feeding necessary.

Watering: No special attention necessary. Good drainage is essential.

Pests and Diseases: Relatively free from both.

ZONES: 6-8

Koelreutéria formosána, Chinese Flame Tree, resembles Goldenrain Tree in foliage and flowers but is a larger tree, growing 40 to 60 ft. high. It has flame-colored fruit in the form of lantern-like, papery-walled capsules, which are a highly decorative feature. This tree suffers damage in bitterly cold areas.

47

Laburnum watereri

Labur´num waterer´i
(*L. vossi; L. parksi*)
Goldenchain Tree
Hybrid bet. *L. anagyroides* and *L. alpinum*

Feature: Flowers

Use: Lawn, accent, espalier

Goldenchain Tree is shrublike and rather scraggly; the tree needs annual pruning to keep it in any semblance of good shape. It is grown exclusively for its magnificent spring display of light-yellow flowers which hang in long, drooping clusters all over the tree. Pruning is usually done in the flowering period, so that the showy, fragrant sprays may be used for indoor decoration. Goldenchain Tree is easily adapted to espalier form and is probably most effective when used in this manner. It blooms at its best in areas where the winters are cold.

Conformation

Height: 15 to 30 ft. Spread: 10 to 20 ft.

An upright-growing, low-branching tree with an uneven, shrubby habit of growth. The bark is olive green and the twigs have a grayish-green cast. The leaves are alternate, and pinnately trifoliate; the leaflets are entire and are 1 to 2 in. long. They are gray-green and are silky on the undersurfaces, when young.

Flowers

Light-yellow flowers, 1 in. in diameter, in graceful, drooping sprays 6 to 12 in. long, which suggest loose chainwork. May.

Fruit

Brown pods, 2 in. long. They persist on the tree and are unsightly. Fall.

Root System: Shallow

Rate of Growth: Moderate

Natural Requirements

Climate: Tolerates both heat and cold. Will not thrive in mild regions.

Soil: Tolerates a wide variety of soils. Prefers a cool, moist soil with a limestone base.

Exposure: Sun or shade. Prefers partial shade, especially in hot areas where leaves are likely to burn in full exposure. Tolerates seacoast conditions.

Care

Pruning: Prune annually to shape. Time: During or after flowering.

Feeding: Apply a nitrogen fertilizer in early spring if the tree is not growing well.

Watering: Provide plenty of moisture. Good drainage is essential.

Pests and Diseases: Relatively free from both.

Faults

Ragged habit. Unsightly pods.

Lagerstroemia indica

Lagerstroe´mia in´dica
Crape-Myrtle

China

Features: Flowers, fall color (red and gold)

Use: Street, patio, tub, accent

The Crape-Myrtle must be pruned to a single trunk and headed high, when young, if a tree shape is desired; thereafter the new lateral growth must be pruned annually if the best flowering potential of the tree is to be realized. The lovely crinkled and fringed blossoms are pink to red in the species and are obtainable, in variety, in white, pink, rose, red, purple, lavender, and blue. They open from July to September and bloom in such amazing profusion that the whole tree appears to be one gigantic flower. Another feature of Crape-Myrtle which adds to its desirability as an ornamental is the display of warm reds and golds in the fall before the leaves drop. This tree is one of the best accent plants available for use in small gardens, tubs, or patios in regions where the summers are dry and hot. It should not be considered for coastal areas, for the flowers will not open and the tree mildews badly in moist atmospheres.

Conformation

Height: 10 to 25 ft. Spread: 10 to 20 ft.

A dense, vase-shaped tree with smooth brown bark which flakes with age to reveal a reddish inner bark. The leaves are simple, opposite, and entire, 1 to 2 in. long and ¾ to 1¼ in. wide. They are dark green and turn red and gold in the fall.

Flowers

Crinkled and fringed flowers, 1½ in. in diameter, in panicles 4 to 8 in. long. They bloom in profusion all over the tree. In the species they are pink to red. Varieties are available with white, pink, rose, red, purple, lavender, and blue flowers. July—Sept. Bloom later in drier regions.

Fruit

Brown woody capsules in clusters. Persist and are unsightly.

Root System: Shallow

Rate of Growth: Moderate to slow

Natural Requirements

Climate: Tolerates heat and also cold but will not stand prolonged freezing. In cold areas protect roots by mulching. Grows best in hot, dry atmosphere.

Soil: Tolerates a variety of soils. Prefers a deep, moist, fertile, well-drained loam. Tolerates alkali to some extent.

Exposure: Sun. Will not tolerate coastal conditions.

Care

Pruning: Head high and prune to a single trunk, when plant is young. Flowers develop on current year's growth. Cut back lightly two or three times during the growing season to encourage new, lateral growth. In winter, head back 8 to 12 in. all around the tree. Remove fruit clusters and suckers.

Feeding: No special feeding necessary.

Watering: Water deeply once a month.

Pests and Diseases: Relatively pest-free. Likely to mildew if planted in foggy areas.

Faults

Difficult to transplant. Sends out suckers.

ZONES: 7—

Liquidambar styraciflua

Liquidam'bar styracif'lua

Sweet Gum; Red Gum; Alligator Wood

Eastern United States

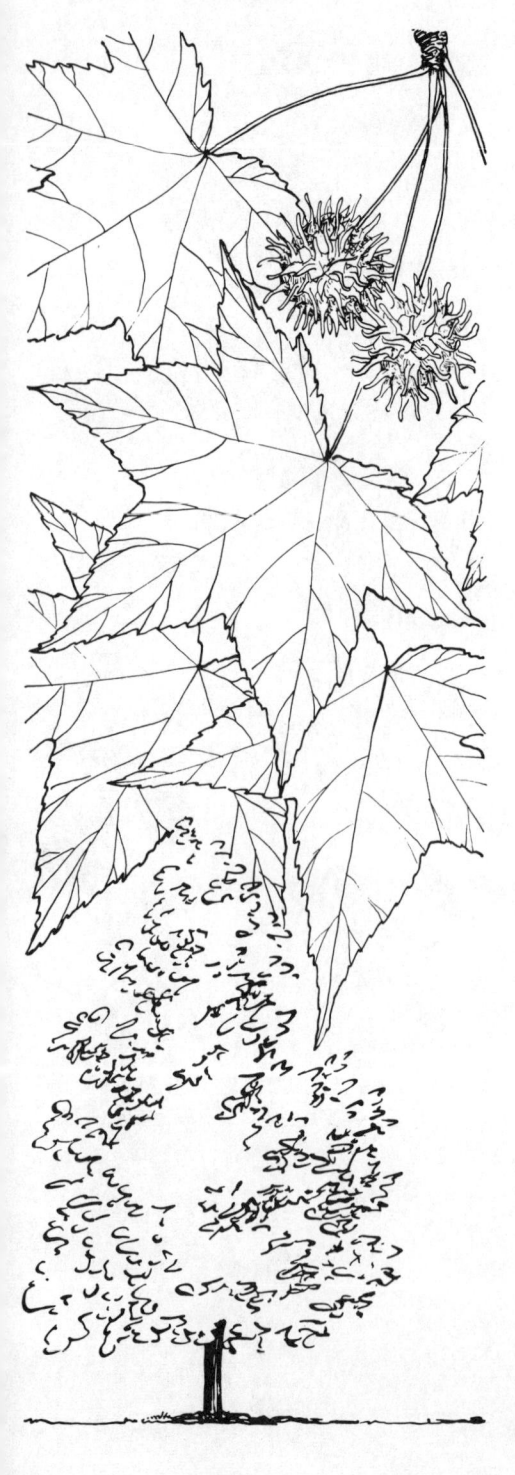

Features: Habit, foliage, fall color (crimson, yellow, and orange), winter design

Use: Street, lawn, water edge, specimen, accent

Liquidambar is a symmetrical tree growing in a pyramidal shape, with gray-brown, corky branches and a tall, straight trunk. The leaves are star-shaped and bright green and make a riotous display of crimson, orange, and yellow before dropping in the fall. Although the autumn coloring is consistent in mild areas, it increases in intensity in proportion to the coldness of the winters; northern plantings stimulate the greatest brilliance. Liquidambar makes an outstanding specimen for use in small or large gardens, and very few trees are comparable to it in habit and performance.

Conformation

Height: 10 to 40 ft.   Spread: 8 to 25 ft.

A symmetrical, pyramidal tree with a tall, straight trunk and gray-brown, deeply furrowed bark, which exudes a resinous, gummy substance. The branches are gray-brown and corky. The leaves are simple, alternate, and five- to seven-lobed; they are 4 to 6 in. long and as broad. The lobes are sharply pointed and very fine-toothed. A bright, shimmering green in spring and summer, the leaves turn crimson, yellow, and orange before dropping in the fall.

Flowers

Yellowish flowers, 1 in. in diameter, in dense, globe-shaped clusters; not effective ornamentally. Early spring.

Fruit

Thorny, brown, burlike balls, 1 in. in diameter. Fall. They persist on the tree after the leaves have fallen.

Root System: Deep

Rate of Growth: Slow

Natural Requirements

Climate: Tolerates both heat and cold. Adaptable.
Soil: Prefers a deep, fertile, moist loam.
Exposure: Sun or partial shade. Tolerates seacoast conditions.

Care

Pruning: Prune, when tree is young, to a single trunk. For the next few years, thin at properly spaced intervals to establish framework of branches. Time: Winter.

Feeding: Apply manure annually in fall. Apply a nitrogen fertilizer in early spring if growth is too slow.

Watering: Provide plenty of moisture.

Pests and Diseases: Resistant to and relatively free from both.

Faults

Prickly burs sometimes become a nuisance.

ZONES: 7-9

Liriodendron tulipfera

Lirioden´dron tulipif´era

Tulip Tree; Saddle Tree; Canoe Wood; Whitewood; Yellow-Poplar; Blue-Foplar

Eastern United States

Features: Flowers, foliage, fall color (yellow)
Use: Water edge, specimen

Tulip Tree is a narrow, compact, pyramidal tree with a tall, straight trunk and grayish-brown, furrowed bark. Growing to a towering height, it needs plenty of room in which to display its unique beauty; it should never be planted in small gardens. The light-green leaves are saddle-shaped and are notched at the ends; they turn a clear yellow before dropping in the fall. Large, greenish-yellow, tulip-shaped flowers bloom among the leaves in summer; they are interesting and unusual but not particularly showy. The tree tolerates extremes of heat and cold and grows at its best in areas where plenty of moisture is available.

Conformation

Height: 50 to 70 ft. (150 ft.). Spread: 25 to 35 ft. (60 ft.).

A narrowly pyramidal tree with a straight, tall trunk, without branches for a good part of its length. The bark is grayish brown and is covered with diamond-shaped furrows. The leaves are simple, alternate, and entire, 3 to 8 in. long and about as broad and two- to four-lobed. They are truncated or broadly notched at the apex. They are a shiny light green and turn to clear yellow in the fall.

Flowers

Greenish-yellow, tulip-shaped flowers, 2 in. wide, marked with a wide orange band at the base. They bloom singly, among the leaves, but not until the tree is ten years old. Summer.

Fruit

Dark-brown, conelike fruit, 2 to 3 in. long, bearing winged seeds. Fall.

Root System: Deep and spreading

Rate of Growth: Moderate to slow

Natural Requirements

Climate: Tolerates heat and cold.
Soil: Prefers a deep, rich, moist soil.
Exposure: Sun. Tolerates seacoast conditions.

Care

Pruning: Prune, when tree is young, to establish framework. Little pruning is required thereafter. Time: Winter.
Feeding: No special feeding necessary.
Watering: Provide plenty of moisture.
Pests and Diseases: Scale; spray with malathion or an oil emulsion in summer and repeat when needed; spray with oil in winter. Aphids; spray with nicotine, lindane, or malathion when needed. Leaf drop and spot gall; spray with Bordeaux when needed.

ZONES: 5-9

Maclura pomifera

Maclur′a pomif′era
(M. aurantiaca; Toxylon pomiferum)
Osage-Orange

South central United States

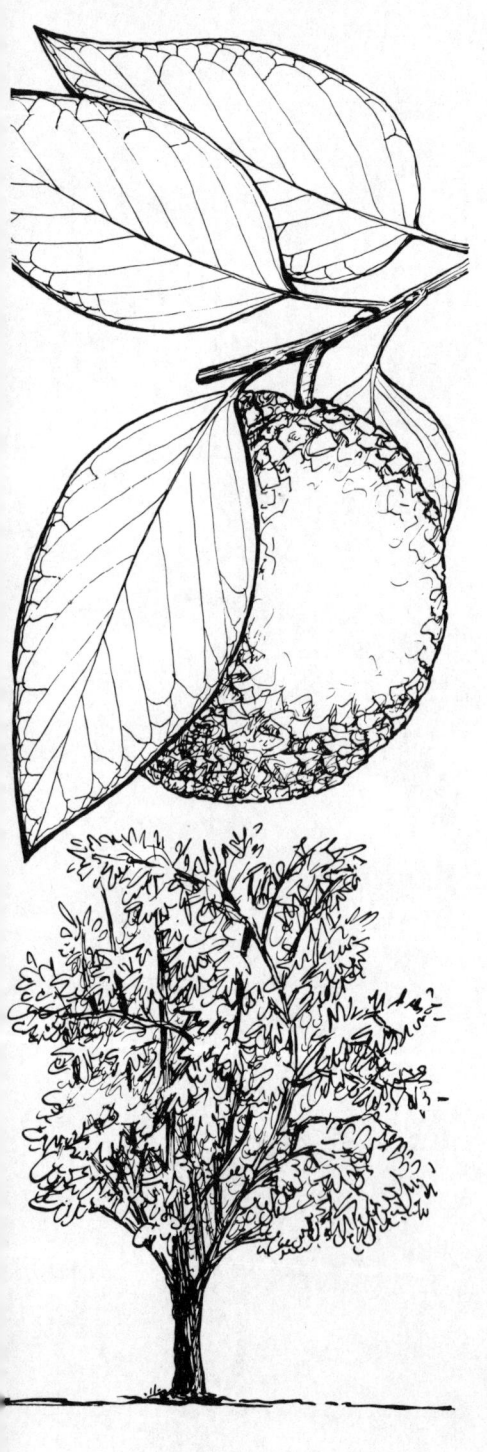

Feature: Fruit

Use: Shade, windbreak, hedge, erosion control, difficult areas

The landscaping value of Osage-Orange lies in its remarkable ability to stand poor soils, extreme climates, and full exposure to strong winds. Although it has no distinctive feature which would recommend it as an ornamental, it is a useful tree for reclamation purposes and erosion control and provides welcome shade in hot, dry regions where many other plants find survival difficult. The Osage-Orange should be limited to the outlying areas of the garden where its invasive, voracious roots cannot penetrate sewers, drains, or other installations.

Conformation

Height: 25 to 60 ft. Spread: 20 to 40 ft.

A low-branching, roundheaded, compact tree with zigzagging, upright, thorny branches and a rather unkempt habit. The bark is light brown and rough. The leaves are simple, alternate, and entire, 2 to 5 in. long and 1½ to 2 in. wide. They are a lustrous bright green and turn yellow before dropping in the fall.

Flowers

Not effective ornamentally.

Fruit

Round, hard fruit, 5 to 6 in. in diameter, green at first and a clear, bright orange when mature. The fruit is inedible, but it closely resembles that of the orange tree except that it is coarsely stippled with rounded bumps. September.

Root System: Roots long, spreading, and voracious

Rate of Growth: Rapid

Natural Requirements

Climate: Tolerates heat and cold. Will grow in desert areas.
Soil: Will grow in poor soil. Tolerates alkali and drought.
Exposure: Sun. Tolerates wind.

Care

Pruning: Tolerates heavy pruning. Time: Any season, but preferably winter.
Feeding: No special feeding necessary.
Watering: No special moisture requirements.
Pests and Diseases: Relatively free from both.

Faults

Fruit drops and makes much litter. Voracious roots are a menace to sewers, drains, and other installations. Branches are thorny.

Magnolia soulangeana

Magnolia soulangeana

Saucer Magnolia; Japanese Magnolia

Hybrid bet. *M. denudata* and *M. liliflora*

Features: Flowers, habit

Use: Lawn, patio, tub, specimen, accent, espalier

Saucer Magnolia is a wide-spreading, picturesque tree which becomes compact and oval-topped when mature. The branches are exceedingly pliable, especially when young, and are easily trained to assume many artistic shapes. The flowers open like gaily colored, giant tulips and unfold to become wide white saucers of dazzling brightness. The outer side of the petals is purplish pink, the inner side white, and the flowers are sometimes, though not often, fragrant. Varieties are available which differ in the outside color of the petals; this ranges from pure white, through rose, to purple-black. The trees are excellent lawn, patio, tub, or espalier specimens and are especially adaptable for use in small gardens. They prefer mild, humid areas but will tolerate cold if grown in protected areas.

Conformation

Height: 10 to 20 ft. (25 ft.). Spread: 10 to 30 ft. (40 ft.).

A wide-spreading tree of irregular habit which becomes compact and oval-topped when it is mature. The bark is light brown. The leaves are simple, alternate, and entire, 4 to 7 in. long and 2½ to 4½ in. wide. They are very thin and are a soft, bright green.

Flowers

Gaily colored, sometimes fragrant, tulip-shaped flowers, 5 to 6 in. long, which unfold to a wide saucer shape. The flowers appear all along the branches before the leaves have opened. They are purplish pink on the outside of the petals, creamy white on the inside. Varieties of *M. soulangeana* differ in the outside color of their petals, which ranges from pure white, through rose, to purple-black. March–April. Flowers will bloom on very young plants.

Fruit

Not effective ornamentally.

Root System: Deep. Roots are fibrous.

Rate of Growth: Slow

Natural Requirements

Climate: Prefers mild, humid areas. Tolerates high altitudes and is hardy in the north in protected areas.

Soil: Prefers a rich, moist, well-drained loam.

Exposure: Shade or partial shade. Protect from wind.

Care

Pruning: Prune lightly and only to preserve shape. Even small cuts should be treated with pruning paint. Time: June, or after flowering.

Feeding: Apply manure once every two years.

Watering: Provide plenty of moisture. Plants should never be allowed to dry out. Good drainage is absolutely essential.

Pests and Diseases: Resistant to and relatively free from both.

Faults

Leaves burn in sun. Does not transplant well.

Malus pumila

Ma′lus pu′mila
Apple

Europe; Asia

Features: Fruit, flowers, habit

Use: Shade, lawn, orchard, patio, novelty, accent, espalier

The Apple is a roundheaded tree with spreading, arching branches which assume many picturesque shapes. It is an excellent ornamental for use in lawns or for shade. Although some apples are self-pollinating, or partially so, the greatest number need cross-pollination to develop good fruit; and since different varieties bloom at different times in spring, selection should be made from among those which bloom at about the same period so that cross-pollination may be effected. Apples have the widest climatic adaptability of any fruit tree, and there are varieties suited for each locale. Probably the desert is the only region where apples will not perform satisfactorily. To the tens of hundreds of varieties now available, new ones are being added each year. Only a few are listed here, for it is impossible to list them all. Local nurserymen should be consulted on regional and blossoming differences.

Conformation

Height: 20 to 40 ft. Spread: 30 to 45 ft.

A wide-spreading tree with a rounded, somewhat arching top, a short, muscular trunk, and downy branches. The bark is steel gray and is deeply indented with spiral ridges. The leaves are simple, alternate, and blunt-toothed, 1¾ to 4 in. long. They are shiny bright green above and downy beneath. Dwarf varieties are available which, with proper pruning, may be contained to a height of 10 to 15 ft.

Flowers

Pink-and-white flowers, 1 to 1¼ in. in diameter, which entirely cover the branches and make a spectacular display. Early and late spring.

Fruit

Edible, red, yellow, or red-and-yellow fruit, 2 to 4 in. in diameter, and nearly round. In most varieties, cross-pollination is necessary to set fruit; selection should be made from those which bloom about the same time. Some varieties are infertile and are useless as pollinizers. Among the many hundreds of excellent varieties are: Delicious (midseason bloom; fruits in late fall or early winter), Golden Delicious (midseason bloom; fruits in late summer or early fall), Gravenstein (infertile, early bloom; fruits in summer), Grimes (self-pollinating, midseason bloom; fruits in late fall and early winter), Jonathan (midseason bloom; fruits in early fall), McIntosh (early bloom; fruits in fall), Red Astrachan (early bloom; fruits in summer), Rome Beauty (self-pollinating, late bloom; fruits in late fall), Stayman Winesap (infertile, midseason bloom; fruits in late summer), Winter Banana (midseason bloom; fruits in late fall), Yellow Newtown (self-pollinating, midseason bloom; fruits in late fall or early winter) and Yellow Transparent (self-pollinating, early bloom; fruits in summer).

For small gardens or for areas where space is limited, multiple apple trees are available and recommended; on these, three to five different, compatible varieties are grafted on one rootstock, to insure pollination and extend the fruiting period. Summer, fall, or winter. The tree bears when four to eight years old.

Malus pumila

Ma´lus pu´mila
Apple

Europe; Asia

Root System: Shallow
Rate of Growth: Moderate

Natural Requirements
Climate: Tolerates heat and cold. Grows best in humid areas with moderate summer heat and winter cold. Tolerates coastal areas. Will not thrive in desert atmosphere.
Soil: Tolerates a wide variety of soils. Grows best in deep, moist, well-drained loam.
Exposure: Sun.

Care
Pruning: Pruning may be either of two types: (1) Prune young tree to 36 in. from ground, allowing three main branches to develop in the upper 18 in. of the tree at well-spaced intervals around the trunk to establish framework; in summer, remove all but two well-spaced outside shoots from each of the three branches. In second year, cut framework branches to half their previous season's growth. Head back branches to side shoots for the next two years. After four years, little pruning is necessary except for occasional cutting back to strong laterals and eliminating crossing, dead, or diseased branches. If tree grows poorly, prune back to revitalize. The fruit develops on spurs two or more years old. Thin fruit for health of tree and for better-quality fruit. Remove suckers. (2) Head high to a central leader and allow branches to develop, except for occasional thinning. Use this type of pruning for specimen or lawn trees. Dwarf trees should be cut back severely to four to eight buds each year. Espaliers also require annual pruning and constant pinching. Time: Winter.
Feeding: Apply nitrogen fertilizer in early spring if growth in previous year was poor. Apply manure annually or every other year, in the fall.
Watering: Provide plenty of moisture. Good drainage is essential.
Pests and Diseases: Codling moth; spray with DDT when needed. Worms; spray with lindane when needed. Aphids; spray with nicotine, lindane, or malathion when needed. Scale; spray with malathion or an oil emulsion in summer and repeat when needed; spray with oil in winter. Mites; spray with malathion when needed. Do not use poisonous materials at fruit-ripening time. Scab causes black splotches on leaves and fruit and eventual defoliation; spray with Bordeaux in early spring as buds are about to open. Mildew causes a white, powdery residue on buds, twigs, and foliage; spray with sulphur when needed.

The edible Crabapple *(M. bacca´ta or M. ioen´sis)* has the same cultural requirements as the Apple and should be treated in the same manner. The difference between the Apple and the Crabapple is in the size of the fruit, that of the Crabapple being 2 in. or less in diameter; and the Crabapple will develop good fruit with less winter chilling. Among the varieties available are Florence, Hyslop, Transcendent, Montreal Beauty, and Whitney.

Malus species

Malus

Flowering Crabapple

Asia

Features: Flowers, foliage, habit

Use: Street, lawn, hedge, patio, specimen, accent

Seedling discoveries and hybrid developments from Flowering Crabapple have contributed some of the most valuable ornamental trees in use today. They vary from erect, horizontal-spreading specimens to columnar and weeping types. The flowers, which cover the trees in spring, range from a very delicate pink to deep pink and red. In the different named types the leaves are of various colors, from bright or dark green to red or purple. In some varieties the fruit provides red or yellow autumn color; the fruit often persists into the winter months.

Conformation

Height: 15 to 35 ft. Spread: 25 to 35 ft.

Usually a stiff, oval-topped tree, low-branching and often multiple-trunked, with crooked, twisted branches. There are also columnar and weeping types. The leaves are simple, alternate, and fine-toothed, 2 to 4 in. long, and oval or oblong. The color of the foliage varies from bright or dark green to red or purple, in the varieties. Bright green to dark-green foliage: Arnold, Bechtel, Eleyi, Hall, Hopa, Pink Weeper, Sargent, and Scheideckeri. Red to purple foliage: Carmine, Lemoine, Niedzwetzkyana, and Red Silver.

Flowers

Often fragrant, pale- to deep-pink or red flowers, $1\frac{1}{4}$ to 2 in. wide, all over the tree. Varieties with pale-pink flowers: Arnold, Bechtel, Pink Weeper, and Sargent. Deeper-pink flowers: Hall, Hopa, and Scheideckeri. Red flowers: Carmine, Eleyi, Lemoine, Niedzwetzkyana, and Red Silver. April–May.

Fruit

Small, fleshy, acid pomes; yellow, orange, or red. Inedible, but the fruit of Hopa may be used for jellies or preserves. Varieties are: Arnold (yellow and red), Carmine (yellow to red, persists in winter), Eleyi (red), Hall (red, persists in winter), Hopa (orange and red), Lemoine (purplish red), Niedzwetzkyana (red), Red Silver (red), Sargent (red, persists in winter), Scheideckeri (yellow and orange). The fruits of Bechtel and Pink Weeper are not effective ornamentally. Fall.

Root System: Average depth

Rate of Growth: Moderate

Natural Requirements

Climate: Tolerates heat and cold. Adaptable.

Soil: Tolerates a variety of soils; prefers a rich, moist, well-drained, sandy loam.

Exposure: Sun. Tolerates seacoast conditions.

Care

Pruning: Prune to shape, when necessary. Cutting for flowers will thin tree sufficiently. Time: May or early June.

Feeding: Apply manure annually in the fall.

Watering: Water deeply once a month.

Pests and Diseases: Relatively free from both. Borer; spray with DDT in April, May, or June and repeat three weeks after first spraying. Scale; spray with malathion or an oil emulsion in summer and repeat when needed; spray with oil in winter.

ZONES: 3-10

Melia azedarach umbraculiformis

Me´lia azed´arach umbraculifor´mis

Texas Umbrella Tree

Himalaya

Features: Habit, flowers, fruit

Use: Shade, quick effects

The Texas Umbrella Tree grows in a uniform shape, with branches rising stiffly upward to form a flattened crown. The large, feathery leaves are densely crowded on the branches and hang downward to give the tree the appearance of a giant umbrella. In spring, fragrant lilac-colored flowers appear in long, loose clusters. These are followed by yellow fruits, which are dried and used to make strings of beads or rosaries. Texas Umbrella Tree is useful in hot areas, where it grows quickly and casts deep and heavy shade. It is highly tolerant of poor soils and desert conditions and withstands winter temperatures of 0° F.

Conformation

Height: 25 to 40 ft. Spread: 30 to 60 ft.

A dense, compact tree with sharply ascending, spreading branches forming a flat-topped crown. The bark is dark brown, rough, and furrowed. The shiny, bright green leaves are alternate and twice compound, 12 to 36 in. long, and composed of many sharp-toothed leaflets, 1 to 2½ in. long and ½ to 1 in. wide. They are crowded on the branches and hang downward.

Flowers

Fragrant lilac-colored flowers, ¾ in. in diameter, in loose clusters, 4 to 8 in. long, at the tips of the shoots. April–May.

Fruit

Smooth, shiny, yellow fruit, ½ to ¾ in. in diameter. It is used as food for cattle and birds and sometimes for making stimulants. When dried, it is used to make strings of beads and rosaries. Fall. Persists on the tree into winter.

Root System: Average depth to deep

Rate of Growth: Very rapid

Natural Requirements

Climate: Tolerates heat and desert atmosphere. Tolerates cold as low as 0° F.

Soil: Prefers a deep, well-drained or dry, sandy loam. Tolerates alkali and drought.

Exposure: Sun. Will not tolerate seacoast conditions. Protect from strong winds.

Care

Pruning: Little is required. The tree grows naturally to a good shape. Time: Fall.

Feeding: Apply a nitrogen fertilizer in spring, but only if the tree appears starved and is growing poorly.

Watering: No special attention necessary. Good drainage is essential.

Pests and Diseases: Relatively free from both.

Faults

Branches are brittle. Tree is short-lived. Reseeds. Makes much litter.

Morus nigra

Mo´rus ni´gra
Black Mulberry; Persian Mulberry

Persia

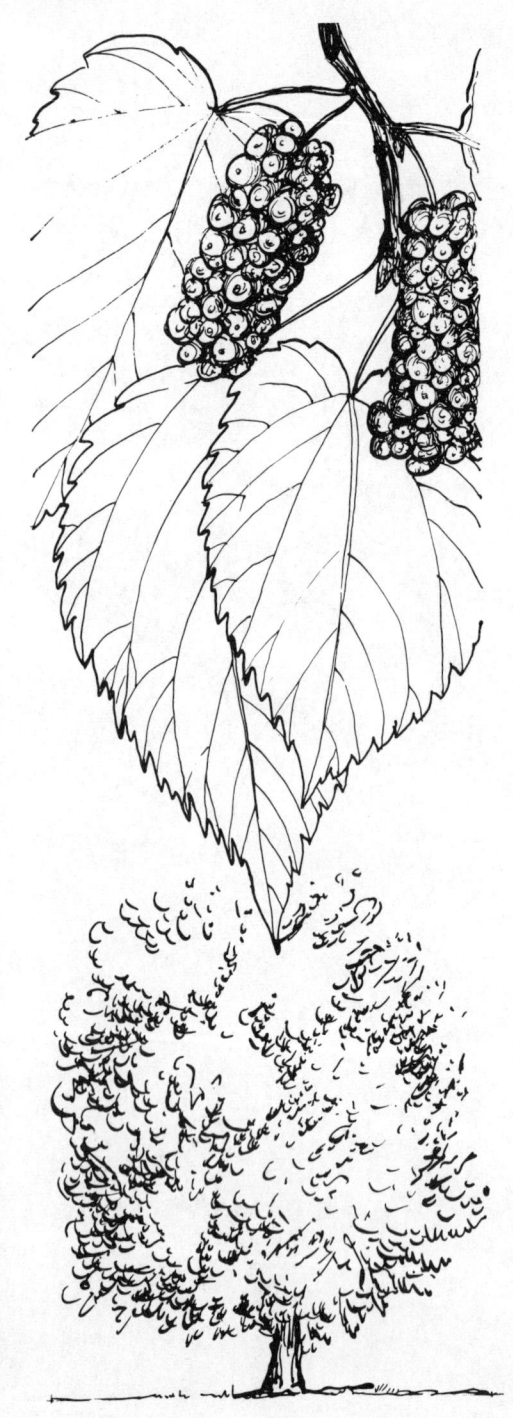

Feature: Fruit

Use: Street (Kingan Mulberry only), shade, erosion control

Mulberry trees have fallen into disfavor as ornamentals because of their untidy fruits, which not only litter the ground but also stain sidewalks and clothing. For this reason, the fruiting varieties should never be used near sidewalks, paved paths, or patios However, in outlying areas of the garden, Mulberry makes an excellent open-headed shade tree; it is also used successfully for erosion control and reclamation purposes. The fruit is tasty when eaten fresh or made into jams and preserves. White Mulberry *(M. Alba)* and Red Mulberry *(M. rubra)* produce good fruit, but it is considered inferior in quality to that of Black Mulberry. A variety of *M. alba,* Kingan Mulberry, is a fruitless type which is frequently planted as a street tree in hot, dry climates. It grows to a height of approximately 30 feet and has a 25-foot spread.

Conformation

Height: 30 to 40 ft. Spread: 35 to 50 ft.

A roundheaded, open-growing tree with wide-spreading branches, which start close to the ground, and a very rough bark. The leaves are simple, alternate, toothed, and variously lobed, 2½ to 5 in. long and 2 to 3½ in. wide. They are a dull green.

Flowers

Not effective ornamentally.

Fruit

Edible, purple to black, oblong fruit, ¾ to 1 in. long. The berries are juicy and have a very sweet flavor. They are eaten fresh or are used to make jam and preserves. Birds are attracted by the fruit of this tree, and it is often planted to deter them from ravaging more valuable trees. Early summer.

Root System: Shallow

Rate of Growth: Rapid

Natural Requirements

Climate: Heat and cold tolerant. Adaptable.

Soil: Tolerates a wide variety of soils; grows best in rich, moist, well-drained soil. Stands gravelly soils. Tolerates alkali and drought.

Exposure: Sun. Protect from strong winds.

Care

Pruning: Prune, when tree is young, to head high. Little Pruning is necessary for older trees. Time: Winter.

Feeding: Apply manure annually in the fall.

Watering: No special attention necessary.

Pests and Diseases: Relatively free from both.

Faults

Fruit makes litter and stains. Branches are brittle.

ZONES: 5-10

Nyssa sylvatica

Nys´sa sylvat´ica

Black Tupelo; Sour-Gum; Black-Gum; Pepperidge

Eastern United States

Features
Habit, foliage, fall color (flaming scarlet to orange), winter design

Use: Screen, water edge, swamps, accent

Black Tupelo is a dense tree of narrowly pyramidal habit with a tall, straight trunk which extends well into the crown. The numerous, slender branches spring from the trunk on a sharply horizontal plane and in some trees are gently pendulous at the tips. In the fall, the glossy dark-green leaves turn vivid orange and scarlet and rival the most spectacular trees in their brilliant display. Black Tupelo is useful as a screen and is particularly valuable in areas where boggy soils are prevalent. It has a wide climatic adaptability, growing well in mild regions and tolerating extremes of heat and cold.

Conformation
Height: 30 to 60 ft. (100 ft.) Spread: 15 to 25 ft.

A dense, compact, pyramidal tree with a conical crown which flattens with age. The branches spread on a horizontal plane and on some trees are pendulous at the tips. The trunk is straight and tall, frequently extending into the top of the crown. The reddish-brown bark is deeply and irregularly ridged. The leaves are simple, alternate, and entire or (rarely) coarse-toothed, 2 to 5 in. long and ¾ to 2½ in. wide. They are leathery and glossy, a deep dark green above, paler beneath, and turn brilliant scarlet and orange in the fall.

Flowers
Small, greenish-white flowers; not effective ornamentally. April–June.

Fruit
Bluish-black, plumlike fruit, 1/2 to 5/8 in. long, usually hidden by the foliage. It is very attractive to birds. Sept.–Oct.

Root System: Deep

Rate of Growth: Moderate

Natural Requirements
Climate: Tolerates heat and cold. Performs well in mild, temperate areas.
Soil: Prefers a moist or wet soil.
Exposure: Sun. Tolerates seacoast conditions. Should be protected from strong winds.

Care
Pruning: Little is required. Time: Fall.
Feeding: No special feeding necessary.
Watering: Provide plenty of moisture.
Pests and Diseases: Relatively free from both.

Faults
Difficult to transplant. Tree topples and branches break in heavy winds.

Zones: 5-

Oxydendrum arboreum

Oxyden´drum arbo´reum
(*Andromeda arborea*)
Sourwood; Sorrel Tree

Eastern and Southeastern United States

Features: Flowers, habit, foliage, fruit, fall color (scarlet), winter design

Use: Patio, tub, specimen

Sourwood is a well-formed tree of pyramidal shape with slender, spreading branches and a narrow crown. Tiny white flowers in delicate, branched clusters bloom in summer and are followed by greenish capsules which are a silvery gray when mature and persist on the tree into winter. In the fall, the bright green leaves turn flaming scarlet before dropping from the tree. Sourwood grows slowly and remains small for a good many years; consequently it is well adapted for use in small gardens, confined areas, or tubs. It tolerates heat and cold but does not grow well in mild or coastal regions.

Conformation

Height: 15 to 30 ft. Spread: 10 to 20 ft.

An open-growing, pyramidal tree with slender, spreading branches and a dense foliage habit. The bark is reddish gray and smooth, becoming scaly with age. The leaves are simple, alternate, and fine-toothed, 4 to 7 in. long, and narrowly oblong. They are leathery in texture. Reddish when they open in spring, they change to bright green and finally turn brilliant scarlet in the fall.

Flowers

Tiny, bell-shaped white flowers, 1/3 in. long, which hang from the tree in branched terminal panicles, 6 to 10 in. long. June-Aug.

Fruit

Hairy, greenish capsules, which turn silvery gray when mature, in branched clusters. The capsules are 1/3 to 1/2 in. long; each contains many seeds. Fall, persist into winter.

Root System: Average depth. Roots have spreading fibrous laterals.

Rate of Growth: Slow

Natural Requirements

Climate: Tolerates heat and cold. Does not grow well in mild or coastal areas.
Soil: Prefers a deep, moist, well-drained soil. Tolerates acid soils.
Exposure: Sun or shade. Prefers sunny areas.

Care

Pruning: Little is required. The tree grows slowly and has a good natural shape. Time: Fall.
Feeding: No special feeding necessary.
Watering: Water deeply once a month.
Pests and Diseases: Relatively free from both.

ZONES: 5-9

Paulownia tomentosa

Paulow′nia tomento′sa
(P. imperialis)
Empress Tree; Royal Paulownia

China

Features: Flowers, foliage

Use: Shade, lawn, patio, tub

Royal Paulownia is a low-branching, wide-spreading tree with large, bright green, tropical-appearing leaves. In early spring, before the leaves unfold, large, fragrant, violet-blue flowers, striped yellow and flecked with dark spots, bloom in terminal clusters 6 to 10 in. long. The flowers are attractive individually, and, combined in the huge clusters, they make a spectacular show. The habit of the Royal Paulownia is unpredictable; the tree must be pruned annually to keep it in shape. It is entirely intolerant of frost, and it should be used only in warm, temperate areas.

Conformation

Height: 25 to 40 ft. Spread: 35 to 45 ft.

A compact, roundheaded, low-branching tree with a short, thick, often multiple trunk and wide-spreading branches. The leaves are simple, opposite, and entire or three-lobed, 5 to 12 (or more) in. long and 4 to 8 (or more) in. wide. They are bright green and heart-shaped and have a decidedly tropical appearance.

Flowers

Very fragrant, violet-blue flowers, 1½ to 2 in. long, striped yellow on the inside and flecked with dark spots; in terminal clusters 6 to 10 in. long. They bloom before the leaves unfold; their fragrance is vanilla-like. The flower buds are exposed in winter; the tree must be protected from frost. March–April.

Fruit

Light-brown, leathery, oval, woody capsules, 1 to 1½ in. long, in grapelike clusters. Each capsule contains some 2,000 winged seeds. Fall. Persist on the tree after the leaves have fallen.

Root System: Deep

Rate of Growth: Rapid

Natural Requirements

Climate: Grows best in mild, temperate areas. Tolerates heat; will not stand any frost.

Soil: Prefers a deep, rich, moist, well-drained, light loam.

Exposure: Partial shade, or sun if summers are not too extreme. Tolerates seacoast conditions, but should be protected from wind. Tolerates smoke and dust.

Care

Pruning: Prune annually to shape. Flowers develop on mature wood. Time: Winter.

Feeding: Apply a nitrogen fertilizer annually in early spring.

Watering: Provide plenty of moisture.

Pests and Diseases: Relatively free from both.

Faults

Leaves burn in very hot sun. Branches are brittle.

Pistacia chinensis

Pistac´ia chinen´sis
(*P. sinensis*)
Chinese Pistache

China

Features: Fruit (decorative only), fall color (orange and red)

Use: Shade, street, patio, tub, specimen, accent

Chinese Pistache is a roundheaded tree with heavy, arching branches which spread widely from a short, stout trunk. The foliage is large, feathery, and exceptionally graceful. Red when it opens in the spring, it is bright green when mature, and turns vivid orange and red before dropping in the fall. Male and female flowers occur on separate trees; the female trees produce clusters of small, red, decorative fruits, which are not edible but from which a valuable oil is obtained. As an ornamental for small gardens or for street plantings, Chinese Pistache is a charming and graceful tree, providing good shade and plenty of seasonal interest. It tolerates dry air and extreme heat but will not stand severe cold or prolonged freezing.

Conformation

Height: 30 to 60 ft. Spread: 30 to 60 ft.

A broad, roundheaded tree with heavy, spreading and arching branches springing from a short, stout trunk. The leaves are alternate and compound, composed of five to six pairs of small, lance-shaped leaflets arranged in feather fashion. They are bright green and turn brilliant red and orange in the fall. The new growth is red. The foliage is more dense on male trees.

Flowers

Not effective ornamentally. Male and female flowers are on separate trees.

Fruit

Small, decorative, red fruit, ¼ in. long, which grows in clusters and develops into a nut from which an oil is extracted and used in cooking. Fruit is produced by female trees only. Fall.

Root System: Deep

Rate of Growth: Slow

Natural Requirements

Climate: Tolerates extreme heat and also desert atmosphere. Tolerates cold (safely) to 20° F.

Soil: Tolerates a variety of soils. Prefers a deep, well-drained soil. Tolerates drought.

Exposure: Sun. Tolerates seacoast conditions.

Care

Pruning: Little is required. Time: Winter.
Feeding: No special feeding necessary.
Watering: No special attention necessary.
Pests and Diseases: Relatively free from both.

Pistacia vera, Common Pistache, is a smaller tree than Chinese Pistache, attaining a maximum height of 30 ft. The edible pistachio nut is derived from the fruit of this tree. Only female trees bear fruit; male trees must be planted as pollinizers—one male tree will pollinate five female trees. Common Pistache stands cold as low as 0° F. and needs winter chill to set the fruit. Its cultural requirements are the same as those of the Chinese Pistache.

Platanus racemosa

Plat´anus racemo´sa

(P. californica)

California Sycamore; California Plane Tree; Buttonwood

Southern California

Features: Habit, foliage, bark, winter design
Use: Shade, water edge, erosion control, specimen

In its natural state, California Sycamore assumes a variety of picturesque shapes, with heavy, twisted branches spreading widely from a massive, gnarled, often multiple trunk. The bark on the trunk flakes to color patterns of gray, white, green, and brown; the foliage is large, prominently lobed, and a soft light green. When planted in the garden, California Sycamore should be allowed plenty of room in which to develop, for though it can be pruned to many shapes, it is far more beautiful when left to develop naturally. The tree stands heat and cold and has a wide climatic adaptability.

Conformation

Height: 40 to 50 ft. (90 ft.). Spread: 50 to 70 ft.

A sprawling, round-topped, open-headed tree with heavy, contorted branches springing from a massive, gnarled, often twisted and sometimes multiple trunk. At times, the trunk leans horizontally or is prostrate. The twigs arise from the branches in zigzagging patterns. The flaking bark is marbled green, brown, gray, and white. The leaves are simple, alternate, sharp-toothed, and three- to five-lobed, 4 to 9 (or 12) in. long, and 5 to 10 (or 18) in. wide. They are a soft light green above, paler and covered with yellowish hairs beneath.

Flowers: Not effective ornamentally.

Fruit

Dark-brown ball-like fruits containing many seeds. Summer. Persist on the tree.

Root System: Shallow, spreading
Rate of Growth: Rapid

Natural Requirements

Climate: Tolerates heat and cold. Adaptable.
Soil: Tolerates a variety of soils; prefers a deep, rich, moist loam. Tolerates alkali.
Exposure: Sun or shade. Tolerates wind to some degree; but branches are brittle and tend to snap in too exposed a location.

Care

Pruning: Stands heavy pruning but is best when allowed to develop naturally. Time: Winter.
Feeding: No special feeding necessary.
Watering: No special attention necessary.
Pests and Diseases: Red spider; spray with malathion when needed. Blight; spray with Bordeaux in early spring as a preventive measure and repeat when needed.

Faults: Branches are brittle. Hairs on undersurfaces of the leaves shed in summer and cause nasal irritation.

ZONES: 6-

Plat´anus acerifo´lia, London Plane Tree, is a roundheaded tree with wide-spreading branches which grows to a height of 30 to 70 ft. with an equal spread. Because of its remarkable climatic adaptability and easy culture, this tree has enjoyed an unmerited popularity and has been vastly overplanted. Its use is best restricted to large areas for erosion control and reclamation purposes. It is often sold as *P. orientalis*.

ZONES: 6-

Populus alba

Pop´ulus al´ba
White Poplar

Europe; Western Siberia

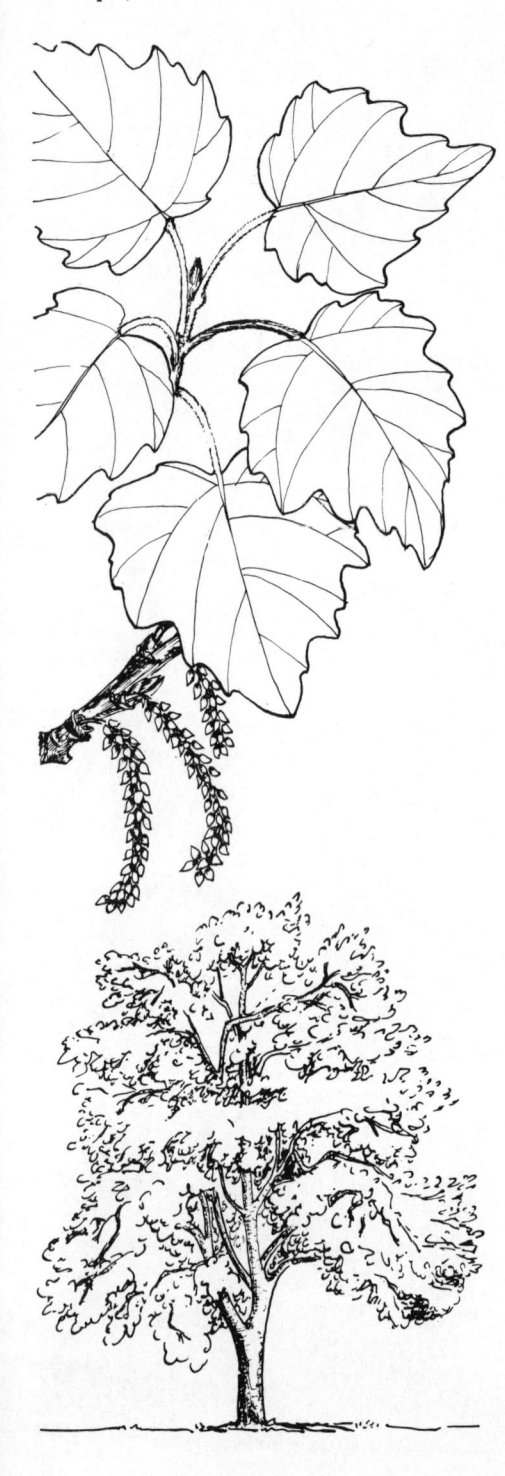

Features: Foliage, bark
Use: Shade, quick effects, hillsides, erosion control

The White Poplar is an open-growing, irregular tree with wide-spreading branches and grayish-white bark. It does not assume a good natural shape; early pruning is necessary if a specimen plant is desired. The leaves — dark green above and chalk white beneath — provide an effective contrast accent in the landscape. However, because the White Poplar has brittle branches and voracious roots, it should be planted only in the outlying parts of the garden, for shade purposes, reclamation, or erosion control. A variety of White Poplar, *pyramidalis,* or Bolleana Poplar, is a dense, narrow, columnar tree with leaves more disk-shaped than the species but similarly colored. The trees have a wide climatic adaptability and thrive in wet or dry soils under almost every adverse condition.

Conformation

Height: 40 to 60 ft. (90 ft.). Spread: 40 to 60 ft.

An irregular, wide-spreading, open-growing tree with steeply ascending and arching branches. The bark is grayish white; the branches are greenish white; and the twigs and buds are covered with white woolly hairs. The leaves are simple and alternate, 2 to 5 in. long and 1½ to 3½ in. wide, toothed, and lobed. The upper surface is a dark shiny green, the undersurface a dead white and covered with woolly hairs.

Flowers

Catkins; not effective ornamentally.

Fruit

Not effective ornamentally.

Root System: Shallow, spreading. Roots are voracious.

Rate of Growth: Rapid

Natural Requirements

Climate: Heat and cold tolerant. Adaptable.
Soil: Thrives in any soil. Tolerates wet soils and drought.
Exposure: Sun or shade. Tolerates seacoast conditions, including moderate winds; but branches break and the tree topples in very strong winds.

Care

Pruning: Stands heavy pruning. Shape well and head high, when young. Time: Fall.
Feeding: No special feeding necessary.
Watering: No special moisture requirements.
Pests and Diseases: Leaf hoppers, thrips (host); spray with DDT or malathion in spring and fall as a preventive measure and repeat when needed. Poplar canker is not so likely to occur on White Poplar as on other species.

Faults: Roots are voracious and invasive and heave up the ground around them. Plant at least 30 ft. from drains, sewers, and other installations. Tree topples and branches break in strong winds. Suckers.

ZONES: 3-

Popúlus canadénsis eugénei, Carolina Poplar, is a large, wide-spreading tree of no particular ornamental value. Although it has the faults of the other poplars and none of their redeeming features, it has enjoyed a long period of popularity. The tree is not recommended here for garden use.

Populus nigra italica

Pop´ulus ni´gra ital´ica
Lombardy Poplar
Clon of *P. nigra*

Europe; Western Asia

Features: Habit, foliage, fall color (rich yellow), winter design
Use: Screen, windbreak, water edge, quick effects, accent

Narrowly columnar, Lombardy Poplar rises like an exclamation point in the landscape, its wealth of bright green leaves shimmering in the sunlight and turning in the fall into a rich, bright butter yellow. In spite of its beauty, the tree should be used only in outlying areas of large gardens where its voracious roots cannot become a danger to sewers, drains, and other installations. It is excellent to mark outer property lines on ranches, farms, or estates. When used as a windbreak, the trees should be planted fairly close together so that the roots will intertwine and sustain each other to prevent toppling. Lombardy Poplar stands wet and dry soils and has a wide climatic tolerance.

Conformation
Height: 40 to 90 ft. Spread: 10 to 25 ft.

A dense, narrow, oval-topped tree with a tapering trunk, which is covered nearly its whole length with many slender, upright-spreading branches. The leaves are simple, alternate, toothed, and 2 to 3½ in. long and 1¾ to 3 in. wide. They are a shiny bright green and turn a rich bright yellow before dropping in the fall.

Flowers: Not effective ornamentally.

Fruit: Not effective ornamentally.

Root System: Shallow, spreading, voracious roots. They should be pruned annually in the fall by inserting a sharp spade well down into the ground at an outer circumference 12 ft. or more from the base of the tree.

Rate of Growth: Rapid

Natural Requirements
Climate: Tolerates heat and cold. Adaptable.
Soil: Thrives in any soil but needs fair depth. Tolerates wet soils and drought.
Exposure: Sun or shade. Tolerates some wind and seacoast conditions. Protect from strong winds.

Care
Pruning: Prune occasionally to head in branches. Time: Fall.
Feeding: Apply manure annually in the fall. Regular feeding helps to prevent the voracious roots from spreading out in search of food.
Watering: No special moisture requirements. Regular watering, however, helps to prevent voracious roots from spreading out in search of water.
Pests and Diseases: Thrips (host); spray with DDT, lindane, or malathion in spring and fall and repeat when needed. Poplar canker attacks twigs and trunk; cut out infected parts and adjacent areas and paint cuts with Bordeaux.

Faults
Voracious and invasive roots cause damage; plant at least 30 ft. away from drains, sewers, and other installations. Tree topples and branches break in strong winds. Suckers. Does not live long.

Populus tremuloïdes, Quaking Aspen, has the same cultural and natural requirements as Lombardy Poplar and is used for the same landscaping purposes. It is a narrow, delicate tree, growing to a height of 60 ft. and a spread of 30 ft.

Prunus amygdalus

Prunus amygdalus

Almond

Asia

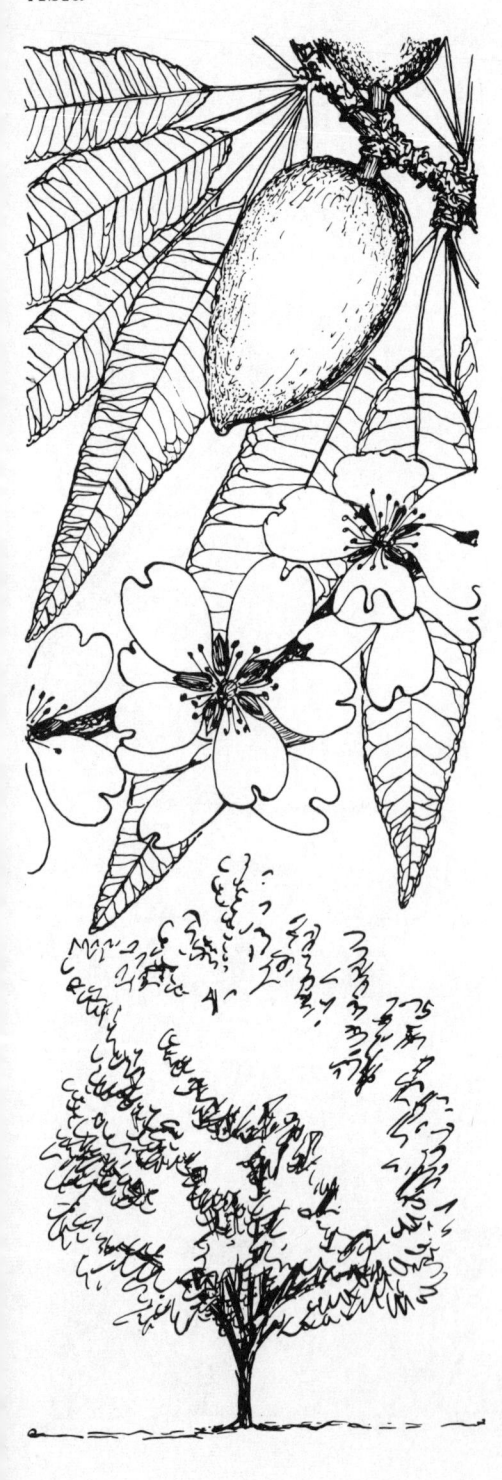

Features: Fruit, flowers
Use: Orchard, patio, novelty, accent

Almond needs hot summer temperatures and dry air to set good fruit but does not require much winter chilling. Since the tree blooms early in the spring and the partially formed fruits are likely to be severly damaged by late spring frost, the tree should not be planted in extremely cold areas.

Conformation
Height: 25 to 40 ft. Spread: 20 to 35 ft.

A tall, upright-growing tree with picturesque, wide-spreading branches and a rough gray bark. The leaves are simple, alternate, and fine-toothed, 4 to 5½ in. long and 1 1/8 to 1¾ in. wide. They are a cool, bright green.

Flowers
Pink flowers, 1½ in. in diameter, which completely cover the tree and make a spectacular display. Early spring.

Fruit
Brown, oblong, edible nut, 1½ in. long, enclosed in a leathery hull which splits open when mature. Hot summer temperatures and cross-pollination of compatible varieties are necessary for fruit production. Among the better varieties are: Drake (midseason), Jordanalo (midseason), Ne Plus Ultra (midseason), Nonpareil (early), and Texas or Mission (late). July–September. The tree bears when three years old.

Root System: Deep, with wide-spreading laterals
Rate of Growth: Moderate

Natural Requirements
Climate: Prefers hot, dry summer climate. Tolerates cold but needs protection from late spring frost.
Soil: Prefers a deep, fertile, well-drained sandy loam. Tolerates a wide variety of soils from sand to adobe, but good drainage is essential. Will not tolerate alkali or salt soils.
Exposure: Sun.

Care
Pruning: Prune young trees to a distance of 24 to 30 in. above ground, allowing three main branches in top 18 in. of tree at well-spaced intervals around trunk, to establish framework; in summer, remove all but two well-spaced outside shoots from each of the three framework branches. In second year, cut back all branches to half their previous season's growth. Thereafter, little pruning is necessary. Almonds bear on one-year-old spurs. The spurs are productive for about five years. Time: Winter.
Feeding: Apply manure every year in the fall. Apply nitrogen in early spring only if the tree is growing poorly.
Watering: Water deeply once a month. Provide good drainage.
Pests and Diseases: Mites; spray with malathion when needed. Peach twig borer; spray with DDT in April, May, or June and repeat three weeks after first spraying. Brown rot causes blossoms and twigs to wither and die; remove diseased twigs and spray with Bordeaux just before the leaves open in spring and repeat immediately after they have opened. Shot-hole fungus; spray with Bordeaux after the leaves fall in winter. Oak-root fungus is caused by wet soils; there is no cure.

Prunus armeniaca

Prúnus armeniáca

Apricot

Western Asia

Features: Fruit, flowers

Use: Shade, orchard, patio, novelty, accent

Apricots are usually pruned to a vase shape for best fruit production; but when allowed to develop naturally, they become handsome, wide-spreading shade specimens. Being among the earliest of flowering plants, they are subject to blossom damage by frost. It is therefore necessary to limit their planting to regions where there is some winter chill but no extreme cold or killing frosts. Also, though the Apricot needs summer warmth for good fruit development, it suffers severe crop damage in extremely hot areas; and it performs indifferently and is subject to disease in cool, humid, foggy coastal climates. Best results are obtained in coastal valleys and foothills. Since most varieties of apricots are self-pollinating, it is not necessary to plant two trees of different varieties in order to set the fruit.

Conformation

Height: 15 to 30 ft. Spread: 20 to 30 ft.

Vigorous, wide-spreading trees which are best pruned to a vase shape for good fruit production. The bark is brown and ridged. The leaves are simple, alternate, and fine-toothed, 3 to 4 in. long, and 2¼ to 3½ in. wide. They are a shiny bright green. Dwarf trees are available which, with proper pruning, may be kept to a height of 10 to 12 ft.

Flowers

Pink or white flowers, 1 in. in diameter, which appear in great profusion before the leaves unfold. They are solitary flowers and are quite showy. Feb.-March.

Fruit

Edible, round, orange-colored (sometimes red-flecked) fruit, 1¾ to 2¾ in. in diameter. Some of the varieties available: Moorpark, Reeves (needs cross-pollination), Royal, and Tilton. June-July. The tree bears when three to four years old.

Root System: Average depth

Rate of Growth: Moderate

Natural Requirements

Climate: Tolerates moderate heat and some degree of cold but needs protection from frost. Will not tolerate extremely hot, cold, or foggy areas.

Soil: Prefers a deep, fertile, well-drained, light loam. Will not tolerate alkali or boggy soils.

Exposure: Sun.

(Continued on next page)

ZONES: 6-

Prunus armeniaca

Pru′nus armeni′aca
Apricot

Western Asia

Care

Pruning: Prune young tree to 24 in. above ground, allowing three main branches in top 18 in. of the tree at well-spaced intervals around the trunk, to establish framework; in summer, remove all but two well-spaced outside shoots from each of the three branches. In the second year, cut back branches to half their previous season's growth. Thereafter, prune to thin top for open growth; to develop new fruiting spurs; and to remove excess wood and dead, diseased, or pendulous branches. In April or May, thin, leaving fruit 1½ to 3 in. apart on the branches. Fruit is borne on two-year-old or older, short-lived spurs. Time: Winter.

Feeding: Apply nitrogen fertilizer annually in early spring. Apply manure every year or every other year, in the fall.

Watering: Provide plenty of moisture. Good drainage is essential.

Pests and Diseases: Twig borer; spray with DDT in April, May, or June and repeat three weeks after first spraying. Aphids (nicotine, Lindane, or malathion), thrips (DDT, lindane, or malathion), codling moth (DDT); spray when needed. Scale; spray with malathion or an oil emulsion in summer and repeat when needed; spray with oil in winter. Do not use poisonous materials at fruit-ripening time. Brown rot causes blossoms and twigs to wither and die; remove diseased parts and spray tree with Bordeaux once just before, and again just after, the leaves open. This disease is difficult to control when it attacks the fruit. Shot-hole fungus causes reddish spots and holes in the leaves and fruit; spray with Bordeaux after the leaves fall in winter and before rains start. Gummosis causes the bark to crack and a gummy substance to ooze out; cut away the infected parts and adjacent areas and treat cuts with Bordeaux. Other diseases attack the apricot but if the tree is planted in the proper climate and given the proper care, no disease is likely to develop.

Flowering Apricot *(Pru′nus mu′me)* is an early flowering tree which does well in any area where frost is not present to damage its blossoms. It is roundheaded and open-growing, with slender, arching branches. Cutting sprays of blossoms for indoor decoration in February is the usual method of pruning. Named varieties are available in fragrant, double and single, pink, red, and white blooms. Perhaps the most beautiful of these is Dawn, with a soft, pink, double blossom. Flowering Apricot is used for patios and novelty planting and for accent.

Prunus avium

Pru´nus a´vium
Sweet Cherry

Eurasia

Features: Fruit, flowers
Use: Orchard, patio, novelty, accent

Sweet Cherries are temperamental trees both in climatic and soil requirements. They will not perform well in areas where the summers are extremely hot or adequate moisture is not available. They do not grow well in boggy soils, and though they stand some degree of cold and need some winter chill to set the fruit, they will not endure prolonged freezing. Nor do they prosper in mild, foggy, humid coastal areas. They do well in areas where the atmosphere is fairly dry, the summers are warm but not hot, and the winters cold but not bitterly so. Cross-pollination is necessary for fruit production, and compatible varieties should be selected with the aid of local nurserymen.

Conformation
Height: 25 to 40 ft. Spread: 15 to 30 ft.

A tall tree of upright-branching habit, which must be pruned, when young, to force lateral growth. The bark is mottled light brown, smooth, and shiny. The leaves are simple, alternate, and sharp-toothed, 2½ to 6 in. long, and oblong. They are a shiny bright green. Dwarf trees available at nurseries are smaller than the regular trees but are not true dwarfs.

Flowers
White flowers, ¾ in. wide, in clusters, 3 to 4 in. in diameter. They are profuse and very showy. Spring.

Fruit
Small, edible, black, red, or cream-colored with a red blush, globe-shaped or oblong fruit, in clusters on long stems. Cross-pollination is necessary to set fruit; two or more varieties should be planted together. For this purpose, the multiple trees are available in different combinations of varieties; these plants are especially suitable for small home grounds. Among the varieties are: Black Tartarian (early), Bing (midseason), Republican (late), Lambert (late), and Royal Ann or Napoleon (midseason). Of these, the Lambert is the best variety, especially for eating fresh. May–June. The tree bears when four to six years old.

Root System: Shallow

Rate of Growth: Moderate

Natural Requirements
Climate: Tolerates some degree of cold but will not stand prolonged freezing; some winter chill is needed to set fruit. Will not tolerate extremely hot or foggy, humid areas.
Soil: Prefers a deep, moist, well-drained loam. Will not tolerate excessively boggy or sandy soils.
Exposure: Sun.

(Continued on next page)

Prunus avium

Care

Pruning: Prune young trees to 24 in. above ground, allowing three main branches in top 18 in. of the tree at well-spaced intervals around the trunk, to establish the framework; in summer, remove all but two well-spaced, outside shoots from each of the three branches. In the second year, cut back branches to half their previous season's growth. For the next two years, head back branches to side shoots. After four years little pruning is necessary except for occasional cutting back to strong laterals and eliminating crossing branches and dead or diseased wood. The fruit is borne on long-lived spurs.

Time: Winter.

Feeding: Apply nitrogen fertilizer in early spring only if growth is poor or weak. Apply manure every year or every other year, in the fall.

Watering: Provide plenty of moisture. Good drainage is essential; water should never be allowed to stand at the base of the plants.

Pests and Diseases: Aphids (nicotine, lindane, or malathion), cherry fruit fly and cherry slug (arsenates); spray when needed. Scale; spray with malathion or an oil emulsion in summer and repeat when needed; spray with oil in winter. Do not use poisonous materials at fruit-ripening time. Gummosis causes cracks in the bark and a gummy substance to ooze from them; cut out affected parts and adjacent areas and treat cuts with Bordeaux. Brown rot causes decay of blossoms and fruit, and yellow leaf causes spotting of leaves and defoliation; spray with Bordeaux before and after blossoms open, spray again just before fruit is mature, and repeat once more just after it is harvested. Diseases on cherries are most prevalent in humid areas or in places where water has been allowed to accumulate at the base of the plant.

Prúnus cerásus (Sour or Pie Cherry) grows to a height of 20 ft. with a 30-ft. spread. It has a more wide-spreading habit of growth and is not so temperamental as Sweet Cherry. It endures extremes of heat and cold, tolerates coastal areas, tolerates drought to some extent, and is far less subject to insects and diseases than Sweet Cherry. The fruit has firm, tart flesh. Varieties are English Morello, Montmorency, and Early Richmond.

The Duke Cherry (a hybrid between *P. avium* and *P. cerasus*) more closely resembles Sweet Cherry in its climatic and soil requirements and cultural demands, and also in habit and size. Its fruit is like that of Sour Cherry in tartness and flavor.

Features: Flowers, bark, winter design
Use: Street, lawn, screen, patio, specimen, accent

Flowering Cherry never achieves great height but is wide-spreading, with an open, graceful habit of growth and gray bark which has a satiny sheen. In spring, large clusters of showy white, light-pink, or deep-pink flowers completely cover the branches. These flowers are single, double, or semidouble in the different varieties, and some of them are distinctly fragrant. Deviations from the type are found in weeping or columnar varieties, which make excellent specimen or accent plants. Whether used for street, lawn, screen, or patio, Flowering Cherry is a charming and dependable tree at every season of the year.

Conformation
Height: 15 to 25 ft. Spread: 15 to 25 ft.

An open-headed tree of graceful, wide-spreading, upright habit. Its smooth, gray, spotted bark has a satiny sheen. The leaves are simple, alternate, and sharp-toothed, $3\frac{1}{2}$ to 5 in. long, and 2 to $2\frac{1}{2}$ in. wide. They are a clear bright green. Amanogawa, a narrow, columnar type, and Weeping Park, a pendulous type, are deviations from the standard form.

Flowers
Sometimes fragrant, white, light-pink, or deep-pink flowers, 1 to $1\frac{1}{2}$ in. in diameter, double, semidouble, or single, which appear in clusters or singly all along the branches. Among the varieties are: Amanogawa (semidouble, light pink), Akebono (single, light pink), Kwanzan (double, deep pink), Mount Fuji (double, white, Naden (semidouble, light pink) Shirofugen (double, light pink, opening from a deep-pink bud), and Weeping Park (single or double, light pink). April.

Fruit: Either nonexistent or not effective ornamentally.
Root System: Average depth
Rate of Growth: Moderate
Natural Requirements
Climate: Tolerates heat and cold. Grows well in mild areas. Adaptable.
Soil: Prefers a fairly rich, moist, well-drained soil.
Exposure: Sun (except in extremely hot areas, where partial shade is best). Tolerates seacoast conditions. Protect from wind.

Care
Pruning: Prune carefully and only when necessary, for branches are slow to replace themselves. When pruning for flowers, cut to lateral growth. Time: Midsummer, when new growth is slowing down.
Feeding: Apply manure annually in the fall.
Watering: Water deeply once a month. Good drainage is essential.
Pests and Diseases: Aphids (nicotine, lindane, or malathion) and worms (DDT, or lindane); spray when needed. Scale; spray with malathion or an oil emulsion in summer and repeat when needed; spray with oil in winter. If borers appear, spray with DDT in April, May, or June and repeat three weeks after first spraying. A regular preventive spray program in spring and fall is advisable.

Faults: The tree is short-lived. Branches split easily.

ZONES: 5-9

Prunus species

Pru´nus

Flowering Cherry

Japan

Prunus persica

Pru'nus per'sica

Peach

China

Features: Fruit, flowers

Use: Orchard, novelty

Peaches will develop fruit only in areas where summer heat is available. Also, most varieties require deep winter chilling, though some are adaptable for milder winter climates. Any degree of excess moisture in the soil or air is detrimental to the health of the tree, and boggy, alkali, or salty soils are fatal. With the exception of a very few varieties, Peaches are self-pollinating; it is therefore not necessary to plant two trees of different varieties to set the fruit. However, varieties must be selected for their climatic adaptability; local nurserymen should be consulted about the ones which do best in their areas.

Conformation

Height: 15 to 25 ft. Spread: 15 to 25 ft.

A rather loose-growing tree, usually pruned to a vase shape, which is the most practical type for its fruiting habit. The bark is warm brown and rough. The leaves are simple, alternate, and fine-toothed, about 5 in. long and ¾ to 1 in. wide, tapering at the tips. They are light green. Dwarf trees are available which, with proper pruning, may be contained to a height of 10 to 12 ft.

Flowers

Attractive, showy pink flowers, which appear in profusion before the leaves. Altair, a double-flowered fruiting variety, has the most handsome flowers of this group. They are deep pink and very profuse. Spring.

Fruit

Edible, round, yellowish-pink fruit, 2½ to 4 in. in diameter, covered with a soft, downy fuzz. Among the many hundreds of excellent varieties available are: Altair (white freestone, maturing late), Babcock (white freestone, maturing in midseason), Early Crawford (yellow freestone, maturing in midseason), Early Elberta (yellow freestone, maturing early), Elberta (yellow freestone, maturing in midseason), Four Star (white, maturing early), J. H. Hale (yellow freestone, maturing in midseason; needs cross-pollination), Late Crawford (yellow freestone, maturing late), Mayflower (white cling, maturing early), Miller's Late (yellow freestone, maturing very late), Nectar (white freestone, maturing early), Rio Oso Gem (yellow freestone, maturing late), Sims (yellow canning cling, maturing late), Three Star (white, maturing midseason), and Two Star (white, maturing late midseason). Of these varieties, Altair, Babcock, Four Star, Sims, Three Star, and Two Star do fairly well without much winter chilling. June to mid-October. The tree bears when three years old.

Root System: Shallow, spreading

Rate of Growth: Moderate

Climate: Most varieties grow best where summers are hot and winters cold; some need deep winter chill to set fruit, and some are adaptable to milder climates. None thrive in coastal areas.

Prunus persica

Soil: Grows best in deep, well-drained, warm, light loam. Will not tolerate alkali or salt. Will not tolerate boggy soils.

Exposure: Sun.

Care

Pruning: Prune young tree to 24 in. above ground, allowing three main branches in top 18 in. of tree, spaced at proper intervals around the trunk, to establish the framework; in summer, remove all but two well-spaced outside shoots from each of the three branches. In second year, cut back branches to half their previous season's growth. Thereafter, each year, head back all one-year-old twigs, cutting off one-third of their length; prune out all dead and diseased wood and branches which have put on disproportionate growth; keep center of tree open for free circulation of air. If natural dropping of fruit in June has not resulted in proper spacing, thin until peaches are 10 in. apart. Fruit is borne on previous season's growth. Time: Winter.

Feeding: Apply a balanced commercial fertilizer annually in early spring. Apply manure every year or every other year in the fall.

Watering: Provide plenty of moisture while fruit is maturing. Good drainage is essential.

Pests and Diseases: Trunk borer and peach twig borer; spray with DDT in April, May, or June and repeat three weeks after first spraying. Aphids (nicotine, lindane, or malathion), moth (DDT); spray when needed. Do not use poisonous materials at fruit-ripening time. Peach leaf curl: spray with Bordeaux just before and immediately after buds open in spring. No further treatment is effective. Mildew, brown rot, and blight are controlled by sulphur sprays. Rust should be treated by spraying with "fermate." Mosaic and stony pit are virus diseases for which there is no known cure.

Faults

Branches are brittle. Tree is short-lived (to 20 years). Does not transplant well.

Nectarine *(P. pérsica nectariña)* is a bud mutation, or sport, of the Peach; the two are identical in every way except that the fruit of the Nectarine is smaller and sweeter, and it has a smooth skin. The climatic, natural, and cultural requirements are the same as for the Peach. Among the recommended varieties are: Freedom (yellow freestone, maturing in midseason), Pioneer (yellow freestone, maturing in midseason), Quetta (white cling, maturing in midseason), Silver Lode (white freestone, maturing early), Stanwick (white freestone, maturing late) and Victoria (white freestone, maturing late). The climatic adaptability of the varieties can be ascertained by consulting local nurserymen.

Prunus persica

Pru'nus per'sica
Flowering Peach

China

Features: Flowers
Use: Novelty

Although the blossoms of Flowering Peach are exceptionally large and beautiful, they occur only on new wood; the tree must be cut back severely each year to ensure blooms. For this reason, the habit of the tree does not conform to the best ornamental standards. In addition, the tree is subject to attack by peach borer and peach leaf curl, which are very stubborn and injurious. It should be used in gardens solely as a novelty in places where it can be given special care. Weeping and pyramidal types of Flowering Peach are available, but they do not compare satisfactorily with similar types in the flowering crabapples and cherries. Flowering Peach tolerates heat and cold but is very subject to peach leaf curl in coastal areas.

Conformation
Height: 25 ft. Spread: 20 ft.

A shrubby tree of rather uncertain habit because of the severe pruning which it needs to produce flowers. Weeping, pyramidal, and dwarf types are available. The leaves are simple, alternate, and fine-toothed, 3 to 4 in. long and 1 to 1¼ in wide, and tapering at the tips. They are bright green.

Flowers
Double pink, red, white, and variegated (combinations of pink, red, and white) flowers, sometimes 1½ to 2 in. in diameter. They usually appear singly, but occasionally in clusters, before the leaves. Early and late-blooming types are available. Among the varieties are: Altair (double, pink), Burbank (double, pink), Helen Borchers (double, pink), Peppermint Stick (red, white, and pink), and the Star series (double, pink). Early and late spring.

Fruit
In most varieties, fruit is nonexistent or not effective ornamentally. Altair and the Star series have handsome flowers and good fruits; they should not be pruned too heavily after flowering. Summer to fall.

Root System: Average depth
Rate of Growth: Moderate

Natural Requirements
Climate: Tolerates heat and cold.
Soil: Prefers a light, well-drained, warm, sandy or gravelly soil. Will not tolerate boggy, heavy, or alkali soils. Tolerates drought.
Exposure: Sun.

Care
Pruning: Cut back all flowering branches severely to spur new growth; flowers develop on new wood. Time: Immediately after flowering, except for fruiting varieties, which are pruned in winter.
Feeding: Apply manure annually in the fall.
Watering: Water deeply once a month. Good drainage is essential.
Pests and Diseases: Borer; spray with DDT in April, May, or June and repeat three weeks after first spraying. Peach leaf curl; spray with Bordeaux immediately before leaf buds open in spring. No further treatment is effective.

Faults: Has an unshapely habit. Does not live long.

Prunus species

Pru´nus
Plum

Europe; Asia

Features: Fruit, flowers
Use: Orchard, patio, novelty, accent, espalier

There are three important types of edible Plums under cultivation: the European and Damson, which do well in rigorous climates and need extreme heat and cold to perform satisfactorily; and the Japanese, which requires heat in summer and some winter chill but is likely to be injured by frost because of its early blooming habit. The great majority of fresh-fruit varieties are derived from the Japanese and European types. Japanese types will sometimes produce in coastal areas, but their fruiting is uncertain and sporadic in these regions. With a few exceptions, Plums need cross-pollination to produce fruit. Since not all varieties will pollinate each other, local nurserymen should be asked for advice regarding those best planted together.

Conformation

Height: 15 to 30 ft. Spread: 12 to 25 ft.

A roundheaded tree with upright-spreading branches and dark-brown bark. The leaves are simple, alternate, and blunt-toothed, 3¼ to 5 in. long, and oblong, elliptic, oval, or shaped like those of a willow. They are a clear bright green. Dwarf varieties are available which, with proper pruning, may be contained to 10 or 12 ft. in height.

Flowers

Fragrant white flowers, ¾ to 1 in. in diameter, in clusters. The number in the cluster varies with the different species. Japanese varieties bloom in early spring; European and Damson in late spring.

Fruit

Edible, round, red, yellow, blue, or purple fruit, varying in size from 1 to about 3 in., depending upon the variety. The skin is smooth and shiny. With a few exceptions, plums need cross-pollination to produce fruit. The Japanese types are large and juicy and generally are eaten fresh; among the varieties are: Beauty (medium-sized, red with crimson flesh, early), Climax (large-sized, red and yellow with yellow flesh, early), Inca (medium-sized, yellow skin and flesh, late), Late Satsuma (medium-sized, red skin and flesh, late), Mariposa (large-sized, purplish with red flesh, midseason), Santa Rosa (large-sized, purplish with red flesh, early), Satsuma (medium-sized, red skin and flesh, midseason). The European types vary from sweet to tart, some are eaten from the tree and all are used in cooking; among the varieties are: Earliana (medium-sized, purplish with reddish flesh, early), Emilie (large-sized, purplish with reddish flesh, midseason), and Green Gage (medium-sized, yellow skin and flesh, late). Damson produces tart fruit, which is used for jellies and preserves; it is usually sold under the name Damson, though Shropshire is a variety sometimes offered. June–Sept. The tree bears when three to five years old.

Root System: Shallow, with many spreading laterals
Rate of Growth: Moderate
Natural Requirements
Climate: European and Damson: Tolerate heat, cold, and high altitudes. Japanese: Tolerates heat and also cold but needs

(Continued on next page)

Prunus species
Prúnus
Plum

Europe; Asia

protection from spring frost. Will grow in coastal areas, but fruiting is uncertain in these regions. Some varieties are adaptable to mild winter climates.

Soil: Tolerates a variety of soils. Prefers a deep, well-drained, fertile, moist loam; will not tolerate boggy or alkali soils.

Exposure: Sun.

Care

Pruning: Prune young tree to 24 to 30 in. above ground, allowing three main branches in top 18 in. of the tree, spaced at proper intervals around the trunk, to establish framework; in summer, remove all but two well-spaced outside shoots from each of the three branches. In second year, cut back branches to half their previous season's growth. Thereafter for ten years, head back all branches, cutting off a quarter of their length, or more, if a branch has taken on disproportionate growth; prune out dead, diseased, or crossing branches and those which do not benefit the shape of the tree; remove suckers. Since plums bear on long-lived spurs, these should be preserved. Thin fruit to 6 in. apart on branches when the fruit is partially formed. Dwarf trees should be thinned out and cut back severely to within four to eight buds each year. Espaliers also require annual pruning and constant pinching. Time: Winter.

Feeding: Apply nitrogen fertilizer annually in early spring. Apply manure annually or every other year in the fall. If leaves become small and yellowish, zinc deficiency is indicated; spray the tree with leaf feed.

Watering: Provide plenty of moisture. Good drainage is essential.

Pests and Diseases: Mites (malathion) and thrips (DDT, lindane, or malathion); spray when needed. Peach twig borer; spray with DDT in April, May, or June and repeat three weeks after first spraying. Do not use poisonous material at fruit-ripening time. Brown rot causes blossoms and twigs to wither and die; remove diseased twigs and spray with Bordeaux just before the leaves open in the spring and again after they have unfolded. This disease is difficult to control when it attacks the fruit. Leaf spot causes mottling of the leaves; spray with Bordeaux when needed. Gummosis causes cracks in the bark and exudation of a gummy substance; cut out infected parts and adjacent areas and treat the cuts with Bordeaux. This disease is likely to occur only on trees growing in boggy soils.

Prunes are plums with a very high sugar content; they dry easily without fermenting at the pit. They are varieties of the European Plum and can be eaten fresh, though they are very sweet. Among the varieties are French, Italian, and Sugar. All have a wide climatic tolerance.

ZONES: 5-10

Prunus species

Pru′nus

Flowering Plum

Eurasia

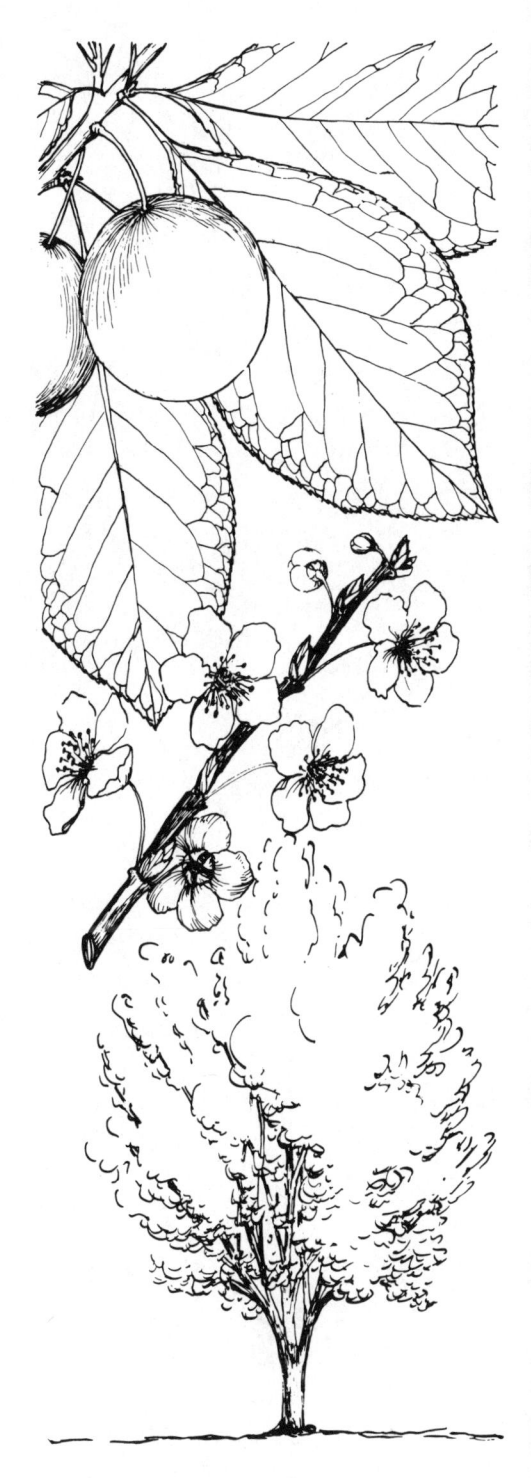

Features: Flowers, foliage

Use: Street, lawn, screen, patio, tub, specimen, accent

Flowering Plum is a vase-shaped tree with an open habit of growth and steeply ascending branches. It is one of the first trees to bloom in the spring, and the plentiful pink or white flowers cover the branches densely. They are followed by purple foliage, which varies in depth of color depending upon the variety. The tree is a valuable ornamental, excellent for use in streets, lawns, patios, or tubs, and particularly suitable for handsome, light screens. In addition, it is easy to cultivate and tolerates a wide range of climatic conditions.

Conformation

Height: 20 to 25 ft. Spread: 10 to 15 ft.

A vase-shaped, open-growing tree with slender, steeply ascending branches. The leaves are simple, alternate, and finely toothed, 2 to 3½ in. long and 1½ to 2 in. wide. They are reddish purple, deepening to black-purple in the several varieties. Vesuvius has the darkest foliage of the group.

Flowers

Pink or white, double or single flowers, ¾ to 1 in. in diameter, blooming singly or (rarely) in clusters. They densely cover the tree. Among the varieties are Blireiana (double, pink), Pissardi (single, pink or white), Thundercloud (single, white).
Feb.–March.

Fruit

Not effective ornamentally. Small, purplish-red fruits.

Root System: Average depth

Rate of Growth: Moderate

Natural Requirements

Climate: Tolerates heat and cold. Grows well in mild or coastal areas.

Soil: Tolerates a variety of soils and also drought to some extent.

Exposure: Sun. Tolerates shade but produces foliage of inferior color in shady areas. Tolerates both dry air and seacoast conditions.

Care

Pruning: Prune to a single trunk and establish good framework, when tree is young. Prune annually to eliminate cross branches and keep the tree open. Time: Immediately after flowering.

Feeding: Apply manure annually in the fall.

Watering: Water deeply once a month.

Pests and Diseases: Aphids (nicotine, lindane, or malathion) and worms (DDT or lindane); spray when needed.

Pterocarya stenoptera

Pteroca´rya stenop´tera

Chinese Wingnut

Caucasus to Northern Persia

Features: Foliage, fruit

Use: Shade, street

Chinese Wingnut is usually a multiple-trunked tree with branches starting close to the ground. It has shiny light-green foliage and decorative light-green, winged fruit, which hangs from the branches in long, drooping clusters. A strong-growing tree with a remarkable tolerance of poor soils, drought, and heat, Chinese Wingnut makes an excellent shade or street tree for difficult areas. It will stand some degree of cold but will not endure extreme cold or prolonged freezing.

Conformation

Height: 30 to 60 ft. Spread: 30 to 50 ft.

An open-headed, low-branching tree with an upright-spreading habit and a multiple trunk. The leaves are compound and alternate, 6 to 12 in. long, and composed of eleven to twenty-three very fine-toothed leaflets 2 to 4 in. long and ¾ to 1¾ in. wide. They are shiny bright green above and lighter beneath.

Flowers

Not effective ornamentally.

Fruit

Numerous light-green, winged nuts in long, drooping racemes 9 to 12 in. long. They are very fragile appearing and decorative and turn brown before dropping from the tree. Summer.

Root System: Average depth

Rate of Growth: Moderate

Natural Requirements

Climate: Tolerates heat; will not stand extreme cold. Tolerates desert atmosphere.

Soil: Grows best in rich, moist, well-drained loam, but tolerates poor soils.

Exposure: Sun. Tolerates wind.

Care

Pruning: Prune to train and shape. Time: Fall.

Feeding: No special feeding necessary

Watering: Water deeply once a month.

Pests and Diseases: Relatively free from both.

Faults

Fruit makes much litter.

Pyrus communis

Pyrus commu´nis
Pear

Eurasia

Features: Fruit, flowers
Use: Shade, lawn, orchard, patio, novelty, ascent, espalier

Pears prefer dry atmosphere and need moderately warm summer temperatures and some winter chill to set good fruit. In cold areas, it is necessary to provide protection from unseasonal spring frosts, which damage the blossoms. Wide-spreading, and growing to broadly rounded shapes, they make fine shade trees and lawn specimens. Cross-pollination almost always results in better fruit production, and it is a necessity for some varieties and under some climatic conditions.

Conformation

Height: 15 to 45 ft. Spread: 12 to 30 ft.

A broad-topped, upright-growing tree with rough brown bark. The leaves are simple, alternate, and fine-toothed, 2½ to 4 in. long and 1¾ to 2¼ in. wide. They are bright green. Dwarf varieties of Pear are available which, with proper pruning, may be contained to a height of 10 ft.

Flowers: Fragrant white flowers, ¾ to 1 in. in diameter, in clusters. They appear at the same time as the leaves. Early spring.

Fruit

Edible large fruit, 3 to 4 in. long; yellow, flushed with pink or red. Pears should be picked from the tree while still hard and brought indoors to ripen. Cross-pollination is always beneficial and sometimes necessary. For this purpose, multiple trees are available with two or more compatible varieties grafted on the same root stock. Among the varieties are: Anjou (August), Bartlett (August), Comice (August), Seckel (August-October), Winter Bartlett (November), and Winter Nellis (September).

Aug.–Dec. The tree bears when five to eight years old.

Root System: Average to deep
Rate of Growth: Moderate

Natural Requirements

Climate: Tolerates heat but prefers moderately warm, dry areas. Tolerates cold but needs protection from spring frost. Subject to disease in highly humid areas.

Soil: Prefers a moist, deep, fertile loam. In sandy soil, the growth is usually rapid and the foliage is apt to be wispy and the tree short-lived.

Exposure: Sun.

Care

Pruning: Pears require the same pruning as almonds. The fruit is borne on long-lived spurs; these should be preserved. Prune in winter.

Feeding: Apply nitrogen fertilizer annually in early spring; manure every year, or every other year, in the fall. Applications should be very light.

Watering: Provide plenty of moisture; the tree requires a constant moisture content.

Pests and Diseases: Aphids (nicotine, lindane, or malathion), mites (malathion), codling moths (DDT), pear slug (arsenates); spray when needed. Do not use poisonous materials at fruit-ripening time. Fire blight causes leaves and twigs to turn black; cut out infected areas to 12 in. below point of infection and use Bordeaux in spring and fall as a preventive spray. Scab causes leaves and fruit to become distorted and deposits a black, moldlike growth; spray with Bordeaux when needed.

ZONES: 5-9

Quercus coccinea

Quer´cus coccin´ea
Scarlet Oak

Eastern and central United States

Features: Habit, foliage, fall color (scarlet), winter design
Use: Shade, street, specimen

Scarlet Oak is a graceful, open-growing tree with slender, wide-spreading branches which ascend gradually and dip gently at the tips to arch downward. The delicate branches and willow-like twigs are covered with thin, silky-smooth, clear green leaves which are bright red when they open in the spring and turn blazing scarlet before dropping in the fall. In winter, when the tree is bare of leaves, the dark bark and graceful design of branches make a delicate and charming display. The uniformity of shape and the controlled habit of Scarlet Oak make it an excellent tree for use on streets. It has a wide climatic tolerance, enduring extremes of heat and cold.

Conformation
Height: 60 to 80 ft. Spread: 50 to 65 ft.

An open-headed tree with a rather narrow crown and slender, gradually ascending branches which are somewhat pendulous at the ends. The trunk tapers rapidly; the bark is gray to black and is rough, scaly, and ridged. The silky-smooth leaves are simple and alternate, 3 to 6 in. long and 2 to 4 in. wide, with seven (or rarely nine) bristle-tipped lobes. The young leaves are bright red when they open in the spring. They become bright green and shiny above, paler beneath, and turn blazing scarlet before dropping in the fall.

Flowers: Not effective ornamentally.

Fruit
Reddish-brown acorn with the cup enclosing one-third to one-half of the nut. The nut is ovoid to hemispheric, ½ to 1 in. long. Sept.–Oct. Matures the second season.

Root System: Deep, with many spreading laterals
Rate of Growth: Rapid

Natural Requirements
Climate: Tolerates heat and cold. Adaptable.
Soil: Tolerates dry, rocky, or sandy soil and also drought.
Exposure: Sun.

Care
Pruning: Prune only when tree is young, to establish framework.
  Time: Fall.
Feeding: No special feeding necessary.
Watering: No special moisture requirements.
Pests and Diseases: Scale; spray with malathion or an oil emulsion in summer and repeat when needed; spray with oil in winter. Caterpillars; spray with DDT, arsenate, lindane, or malathion as a preventive in spring and fall and repeat when needed.

Faults: Difficult to transplant.

ZONES: 4-9

Quer´cus borea´lis, Red Oak, assumes a pyramidal shape when young and matures to a roundheaded specimen with stout, wide-spreading branches. It grows rapidly to a height of 40 to 60 ft. and spread of 60 to 85 ft. The leaves are large and deeply lobed, a dull green above with grayish undersurfaces; they turn dark red before dropping in the fall. Red Oak has the same natural and cultural requirements as Scarlet Oak and is used in landscaping as a deep shade tree for large gardens.

ZONES: 4-8

Quercus douglasi

Quer´cus doug´lasi
California Blue Oak

California

Features: Habit, foliage, winter design
Use: Shade, erosion control

Blue Oak is a sturdy tree which thrives in difficult areas, welcoming dry, arid soils and seeming to resent the slightest amount of moisture. It flourishes in regions where intense heat is prevalent, providing pleasant shade where it is most needed. The tree grows to unusual, picturesque shapes, with many short, spreading branches. The bark is light gray, and the leaves are bluish green with yellowish undersurfaces. Because it does not thrive when given much care and attention, Blue Oak is best used in outlying sections of the garden or on rocky hillsides, or for purposes of fixing sliding soils.

Conformation

Height: 20 to 60 ft. Spread: 25 to 50 ft.

A picturesque tree with short, spreading branches forming a round-topped crown. The bark is light gray and is checkered into thin scales. The leaves are simple and alternate, 2 to 4 in. long and ¾ to 2¼ in. wide, and irregularly lobed to entire. They are bluish green above, yellow-green beneath, and are quite firm and rigid.

Flowers

Not effective ornamentally.

Fruit

An acorn with a shallow cup, one-fourth to one-third as long as the nut. The nut is usually ovoid, and ¾ to 1¼ in. long. Sept.–Oct. Matures the first year.

Root System: Shallow
Rate of Growth: Rapid

Natural Requirements

Climate: Tolerates extreme heat and stands desert atmosphere.
Soil: Tolerates a variety of poor soils. Prefers a dry, arid soil.
Exposure: Sun.

Care

Pruning: None required.
Feeding: None required.
Watering: Not required after plant is established.
Pests and Diseases: Subject to disease, especially dry rot, which destroys whole branches when the tree matures. Dry rot is caused to some extent by wounds in the bark and branches when the tree is young.

Faults

Makes litter. Branches are brittle.

Quer´cus kel´logi, California Black Oak, is another native California tree which attains its best form when left to develop naturally. It is a highly ornamental tree, growing 40 to 80 ft. high with stiffly ascending branches and a very dark brown, furrowed, and ridged bark. The leaves are light crimson when they open and are shiny yellow-green when mature, turning deep yellow before dropping in the fall. They are bristle-veined and sharp-lobed, 4 to 8 in. long and 2 to 4 in. wide. The tree tolerates dry heat and some cold but will not endure seacoast conditions.

Quercus palustris

Quer´cus palus´tris
Pin Oak

Central and mid-eastern United States

Features: Habit, fall color (scarlet), winter design

Use: Shade, lawn, specimen

Pin Oak is an exceptionally delicate and graceful tree. It grows to a pyramidal shape, with the topmost branches spreading stiffly upright, the middle branches leveling to a horizontal plane, and the lower branches pendulous and sweeping the ground. The leaves are dark green, glossy, and prickly, and turn scarlet in the fall. This tree is handsome in winter when it is without leaves and the perfect symmetry of form is clearly discernible. It tolerates extremes of heat and cold and needs plenty of moisture to attain its best development.

Conformation

Height: 50 to 80 ft. Spread: 25 to 40 ft.

A dense, symmetrical, broadly pyramidal tree with upright upper branches, horizontal-spreading middle branches, and pendulous lower branches. The branches are numerous but are smaller than on most oaks. The bark is light to dark grayish brown and has shallow, scaly ridges. The leaves are simple and alternate and are 4 to 6 in. long and 2 to 4 in. wide. They have five to seven bristle-tipped lobes and are deeply indented. Dark green and glossy above, paler beneath, they turn scarlet in the fall.

Flowers

Not effective ornamentally.

Fruit

An acorn with the saucer-shaped cup enclosing one-third of the nut. The nut is hemispheric, ½ in. long and as broad. Sept.–Oct. Matures the second year.

Root System: Shallow. Roots are fibrous.

Rate of Growth: Rapid

Natural Requirements

Climate: Tolerates heat and cold.

Soil: Grows best in rich, moist, well-drained clay loam. Will not tolerate dry or alkali soils.

Exposure: Sun.

Care

Pruning: None required.

Feeding: Apply manure annually in the fall.

Watering: Provide plenty of moisture.

Pests and Diseases: Caterpillars; spray with DDT, lindane, or arsenates as a preventive measure in spring and fall and repeat when needed. Scale; spray with malathion or an oil emulsion in summer and repeat when needed; spray with oil in winter.

ZONES: 5-9

Feature: Flowers

Use: Shade, street (difficult areas), quick effects, erosion control.

Common Locust tolerates extreme heat and cold and thrives in dry, sterile soils. Its most extensive landscape use is for erosion control, but it is often used in difficult areas as a shade or street tree. Many varieties of Common Locust are available, including thornless and pendulous types. Var. *decaisneana*, Pink Flowering Locust, has fragrant pink flowers and is more widely planted than the species.

Conformation

Height: 40 to 80 ft. (100 ft.). Spread: 30 to 60 ft. (80 ft.).

A tree of unpredictable habit, often multiple-trunked, with an irregularly rounded, open-headed crown and upward-spreading branches. The bark is dark gray, rough, and broken into ridges. The leaves are compound and alternate, 4 to 12 in. long, and composed of seven to nineteen entire, rounded leaflets 1 to 2 in. long. They are yellow-green when they open in spring and turn a deep blue-black.

Flowers

Very fragrant, pea-shaped flowers, ¾ in. long. They are white, spotted with yellow at the throat, and appear in drooping racemes 4 to 6 in. long. May–June.

Fruit

Reddish brown, beanlike pods, 1 to 4 in. long and ½ in. wide. Fall. Persist into winter.

Root System: Wide-spreading, fibrous roots, of average depth and with nitrogen-fixing nodules. They are quite voracious.

Rate of Growth: Rapid

Natural Requirements

Climate: Tolerates heat, cold, and desert conditions. Adaptable.

Soil: Prefers a deep, well-drained loam with a limestone base. Tolerates sandy, alkali, or sterile soils and drought.

Exposure: Sun; will stand full exposure in the hottest areas. Tolerates smoke and dust.

Care

Pruning: Tolerates severe pruning. Prune when tree is young, to establish framework; later, prune annually to shape.
Time: Fall.

Feeding: No special feeding necessary.

Watering: No special attention necessary.

Pests and Diseases: Borer; spray with DDT in April, May, or June and repeat three weeks after first spraying. Aphids (nicotine, lindane, or malathion) and leaf miner (lindane or malathion); spray when needed; destroy leaves infested with leaf miner.

Faults

Habit is unpredictable. Branches are brittle. Roots are voracious. Suckers.

Robin´ia neomexica´na, New Mexican Locust, is a small, spiny tree growing to a height of 25 ft. Its fragrant lavender, pink, or purplish flowers bloom from May to July. It has the same natural and cultural requirements as Common Locust and is used for the same landscaping purposes.

Robinia pseudoacacia

Robin´ia pseudoaca´cia

Common Locust; Black Locust; Yellow Locust; False-Acacia

Central and eastern United States

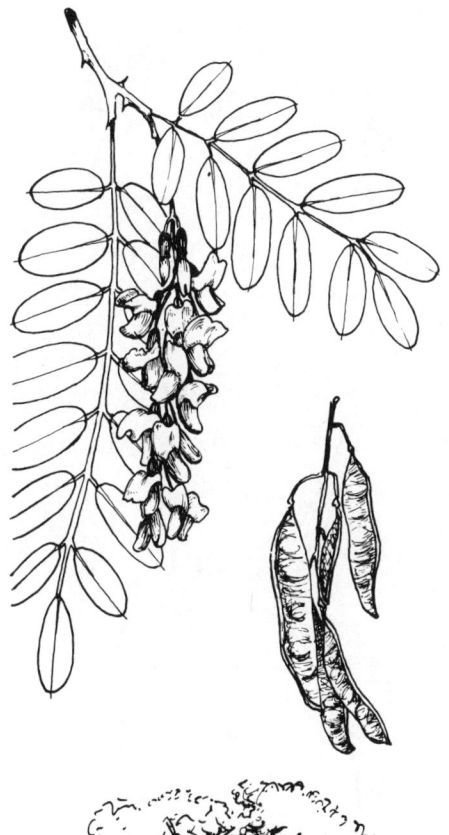

Salix babylonica

Sa´lix babylon´ica

Weeping Willow;
  Babylon Weeping Willow

China

Feature: Habit

Use: Shade, windbreak, screen, water edge, specimen, accent, erosion control

Weeping Willow is a heavy tree with long, limp, pendulous branchlets which droop to the ground. It is likely to become an oppressive tree unless it is pruned annually; sometimes it is necessary to remove whole branches to allow the light to filter through. This type of pruning also keeps the tree from having the unfortunate bobbed appearance which sometimes results from trimming the ends of the branches. Because of its peculiar habit, the Weeping Willow centers attention in the landscape and it should be used sparingly. A water-loving tree with strong, voracious roots, it should be planted in the outlying areas of the garden where its invasive tendencies will not become a problem.

Conformation

Height: 30 to 40 ft. Spread: 50 to 70 ft.

A roundheaded, compact, densely branched tree with heavily drooping branchlets. The bark is dark brown and rough, and the slender twigs are a highly polished olive-green or purple. When the leaves have fallen, the twigs make an attractive design in the winter landscape. The leaves are simple, alternate, and fine-toothed, 3 to 6 in. long and 1/2 to 7/8 in. wide. They are a light, shiny green above and glaucous beneath. They persist on the tree well into the winter months.

Flowers

Catkins, in spring with the leaves. Not effective ornamentally.

Fruit

Not effective ornamentally.

Root System: Shallow, spreading. Roots are voracious.

Rate of Growth: Rapid

Natural Requirements

Climate: Tolerates heat and cold. Adaptable.

Soil: Prefers a wet soil; will grow in boggy places.

Exposure: Sun or shade. Tolerates wind, but branches will break in very strong winds. Tolerates smoke and dust.

Care

Pruning: Prune when tree is young, to establish framework. Thin branches annually to shape tree. Do not lop off ends of branchlets. Time: Fall.

Feeding: No special feeding necessary.

Watering: Provide plenty of moisture.

Pests and Diseases: Thrips (host); spray with DDT, lindane, or malathion in spring and fall as a preventive measure and repeat when needed. Aphids; spray with nicotine, lindane, or malathion when needed.

Faults

Does not live long. Branches are brittle. Roots are voracious and tend to invade sewers, drains, and other installations, in search of water.

Sa´lix al´ba vitelli´na, Yellow-stemmed Weeping Willow, is not so dense a tree as *S. babylonica*, nor is its root system so voracious as that of the species. It is very graceful, with highly polished yellow twigs, and is well adapted for use as a windbreak or screen.

Features: Flowers, habit, winter design, foliage

Use: Shade, street, lawn, patio, tub, specimen

Japanese Pagoda Tree grows to a symmetrical, rounded shape, its wide-spreading branches assuming a precise, conventional form even when not pruned. In late summer, when most other trees have spent their brilliance, this one is covered with masses of cream-colored flowers which stand erect in rather loose clusters. Unfortunately, the tree must approach maturity before it will bloom, and sometimes it is twenty-five or thirty years before the first flowers appear. But while it is maturing it makes an excellent specimen, with its feathery, lustrous, dark-green foliage and handsome habit.

Conformation

Height: 20 to 40 ft. (80 ft.). Spread: 20 to 40 ft.

A compact, rounded tree with wide-spreading branches which start low on the trunk. The bark is dark brown and deeply fissured, and the young branches are a dark, shiny green. The feathery leaves are compound and alternate, 6 to 10 in. long, and composed of seven to seventeen entire leaflets, 1 to 2 in. long. They are dark green and lustrous above, hairy beneath.

Flowers

Numerous cream-colored, pea-shaped flowers, ½ in. in diameter, in loose, erect clusters, 12 in. long. A yellow dye is made from the buds and flowers. July-Aug.

Fruit

Yellowish pods, 2 to 3 in. long, which are soapy when crushed. Fall. Frequently persist throughout the winter.

Root System: Deep

Rate of Growth: Slow

Natural Requirements

Climate: Tolerates heat and cold and desert conditions.

Soil: Grows best in moist, well-drained, sandy loam. Tolerates poor, gravelly or rocky soils. Tolerates drought.

Exposure: Sun. Tolerates dust, smoke, and seacoast conditions.

Care

Pruning: Little is required. Time: Fall.
Feeding: No special feeding necessary.
Watering: Water deeply once a month.
Pests and Diseases: Relatively free from both.

Faults

Only mature plants bloom.

Zones 5-9

Sophora japonica

Sopho′ra japon′ica

(*Broussonetia*)

Japanese Pagoda Tree; Chinese Scholar Tree

China; Korea

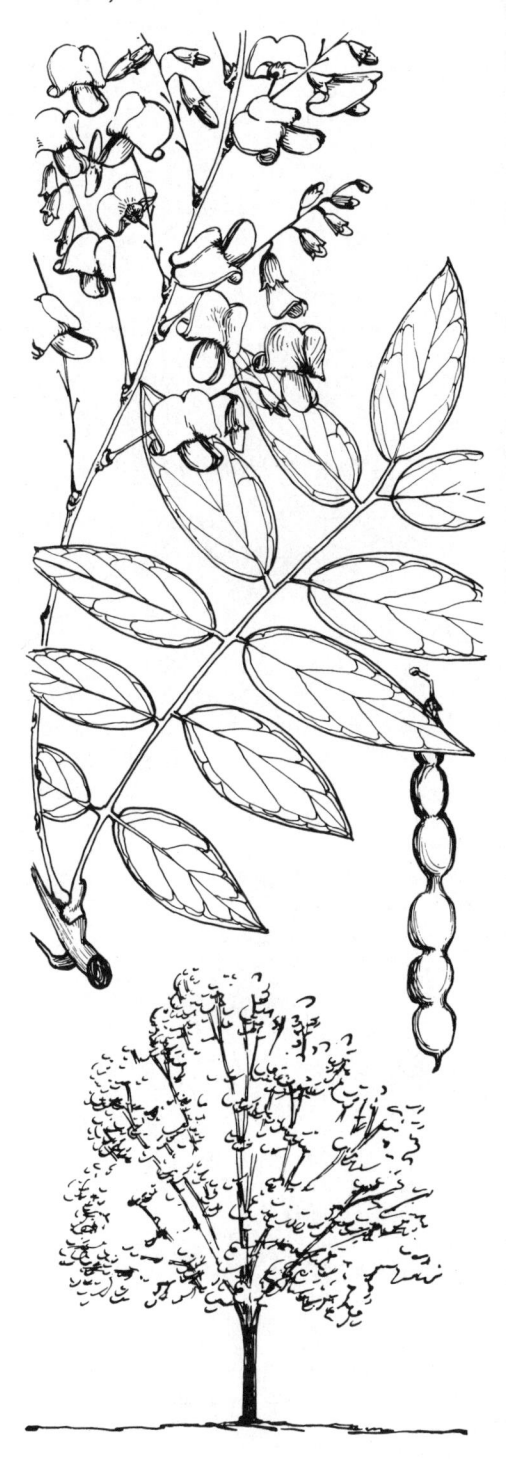

Sorbus aucuparia

Sor´bus aucupa´ria

(Pyrus aucuparia; Micromeles)

European Mountain Ash;
 Rowan Tree

Europe to western Asia

Features: Fruit, flowers, fall color (orange-red)

Use: Lawn, patio, tub, water edge, accent

Mountain Ash is a graceful, open-headed tree which attains its best development in cool, mountain areas. It grows in any soil and tolerates extreme cold. In late spring, large, flat-headed clusters of white flowers appear on the tree. In autumn, these are followed by masses of shiny, bright red berries. While the berries are at their height of brilliance, the rather quietly colored leaves begin to turn fiery orange and red and drop from the tree. There are many varieties of Mountain Ash under cultivation, including upright, pendulous, and cut-leaf types, as well as one with yellow fruits.

Conformation

Height: 15 to 30 ft. (45 ft.). Spread: 8 to 15 ft. (25 ft.).

A roundheaded, open-growing tree with graceful, spreading, somewhat pendulous branches. The bark is grayish brown. The handsome, fernlike leaves are compound and alternate, 5 to 7 in. long, and composed of nine to fifteen toothed leaflets ¾ to 2 in. long. They are dull green to gray-green above, paler beneath, and turn brilliant orange and red in the fall, before dropping from the tree.

Flowers

Tiny white flowers, 1/3 in. in diameter, in large, flat clusters, 4 to 6 in. in diameter. Late spring.

Fruit

Shiny, bright red berries, 3/8 in. in diameter, in large, flat clusters, 4 to 6 in. in diameter. The fruit is very attractive to birds. Fall.

Root System: Deep

Rate of Growth: Rapid

Natural Requirements

Climate: Prefers cool, mountain areas. Tolerates cold; will not perform well in mild climates.

Soil: Tolerates a wide variety of soils. Prefers a moist, rich loam with a limestone base.

Exposure: Sun or shade. Prefers partial shade.

Care

Pruning: Prune when tree is young, to establish framework. Time: Winter.

Feeding: No special feeding necessary.

Watering: Water deeply once a month.

Pests and Diseases: Borer; spray with DDT in April, May, or June and repeat three weeks after first spraying. Scale; spray with malathion or an oil emulsion in summer and repeat when needed; spray with oil in winter. Under good growing conditions, the tree is quite resistant to these insects.

Faults

Full exposure to sun in hot areas causes burning of leaves and branches.

Features: Flowers, bark
Use: Street, screen, patio, tub, specimen

Japanese Tree Lilac is an erect, neat, roundheaded tree with beautiful, smooth, shiny, gray-brown bark. The fragrant, cream-white flowers appear in upright, pyramidal clusters, resembling those of the common lilac but blooming later. This tree is more prolific in northern areas where winters are very cold, and it grows best in a rich, well-drained soil to which plenty of leaf mold has been added. It is very attractive in small gardens and performs especially well in tubs.

Conformation
Height: 15 to 30 ft. Spread: 10 to 25 ft.

A roundheaded, open-growing tree with upright-spreading branches. The bark is smooth, shiny, and gray-brown. The leaves are simple, opposite, and entire, 3 to 6 in. long and 1½ to 2½ in. wide, and rounded at the base. They are dark green and glossy above, paler beneath, and they drop early in the fall.

Flowers
Tiny, fragrant, cream-white flowers in compact, erect, pyramidal clusters, 8 to 12 in. long. June–July.

Fruit
Small, brown, leathery capsules; not effective ornamentally. Fall.

Root System: Average to deep
Rate of Growth: Moderate
Natural Requirements
Climate: Tolerates heat and cold. Grows best in northern areas where winters are very cold.
Soil: Prefers a moist, rich, well-drained soil to which plenty of humus has been added.
Exposure: Sun. Protect from strong wind. Will not tolerate fog.

Care
Pruning: Prune to shape. Time: After flowering in late summer. Do *not* prune in winter or early spring.
Feeding: Apply a balanced commercial fertilizer in early spring. Apply manure annually in the fall.
Watering: Provide plenty of moisture.
Pests and Diseases: Borer; spray with DDT in April, May, or June and repeat three weeks after first spraying. Scale; spray with malathion or an oil emulsion in summer and repeat when needed. Spray with oil in winter. Mildew attacks the tree in foggy areas.

Faults
Becomes woody and scraggly with age.

Syringa amurensis japonica

Syrin´ga amuren´sis japon´ica
(*S. japonica*)

Japanese Tree Lilac

Japan

Tamarix parviflora

Tam´arix parviflo´ra
(T. algerica)
Smallflower Tamarix

Southern Europe

Feature: Flowers

Use: Hedge, windbreak, patio, tub, erosion control

Tamarix is a shrubby little tree of irregular habit, with numerous, long, slender, spreading branches. In spring, the branches are covered from base to tip with tiny pink flowers in short, compact spikes. This tree tolerates extreme heat and drought and thrives in sandy, alkali, or salty soils. It is subject to cold and will not stand any degree of frost. It is used effectively as a windbreak or hedge in desert areas and on the seacoast and, if pruned properly, is effective in patios or tubs.

Conformation

Height: 10 to 20 ft. Spread: 12 to 20 ft.

A low-branching, wide-spreading, shrubby tree of loosely rounded habit, with many long, slender branches. The bark is rough and reddish brown. The leaves are scalelike, 1/8 in. long, and hug the twigs tightly, somewhat in the manner of the cypress. They are bright green.

Flowers

Numerous tiny pink flowers, in short clusters, 1 to 1½ in. long. Early spring.

Fruit

Not effective ornamentally.

Root System: Deep

Rate of Growth: Rapid

Natural Requirements

Climate: Tolerates extreme heat; will not stand cold. Tolerates salt air and desert atmosphere.

Soil: Thrives in any soil. Tolerates alkali, salt, and drought.

Exposure: Sun. Tolerates wind and seacoast conditions.

Care

Pruning: Prune as much as needed to maintain shape. Flowers develop on previous year's growth. Time: Immediately after flowering.

Feeding: None required.

Watering: Not required after plant is established.

Pests and Diseases: Relatively free from both.

Faults

Stump sprouts.

Feature: Foliage

Use: Shade, street, lawn, specimen

American Linden is a compact tree with a rounded crown and a steeply upward-branching habit. The handsome deep-green leaves, which are large and thin, cover the branches densely. An unusual feature of the tree is the manner in which the fruit and flowers form from the midrib of a ribbon-like leaf, produced especially for this purpose. Lindens make excellent shade and lawn specimens and are good for use on wide streets where provision can be made for their moisture requirements. They are heat and cold tolerant and grow best in moist, fertile soils.

Conformation

Height: 40 to 60 ft. Spread: 30 to 50 ft.

A compact, roundheaded, symmetrical tree with a steeply upward-spreading habit. The branches arch slightly downward at the extreme ends. The bark is light gray and is lightly ridged. The handsome leaves are simple, alternate, and coarse-toothed, 4 to 6 in. long and 3 to 4 in. wide. They are typically lopsided and heart-shaped, a soft dark green, and very thin.

Flowers

Tiny fragrant, creamy-white, star-shaped flowers, which dangle in branched clusters from the center of a special, bladelike, "ribbon-leaf." This is 4 to 5 in. long and very narrow. Each cluster contains five to twelve flowers. They attract bees and are a good source of honey. June–July.

Fruit

Round, gray-green, nutlike fruits; 3/8 to 1/2 in. long, which hang in pendulous clusters from the "ribbon-leaf." October. Persist into winter.

Root System: Deep

Rate of Growth: Rapid

Natural Requirements

Climate: Tolerates heat and cold.
Soil: Prefers a fertile, moist loam.
Exposure: Sun. Tolerates some shade.

Care

Pruning: Prune occasionally to shape. Time: Fall.
Feeding: No special feeding necessary.
Watering: Provide plenty of moisture.
Pests and Diseases: Aphids; spray with nicotine, lindane, or malathion when needed.

Til´ia corda´ta, Littleleaf Linden, varies from the American Linden in having a smaller leaf (2 to 3 in. long) and a slower rate of growth. Otherwise the trees are quite similar, having the same cultural and natural requirements and the same landscape uses.

ZONES: 4-8

Tilia americana

Til´ia america´na

(*T. glabra*; *T. nigra*)

American Linden;
American Basswood

Eastern United States;
southern Canada

Toona sinensis

Too´na sinen´sis
(Cedrela sinensis)
Chinese Cedrela; Chinese Toon

China

Features: Foliage, flowers, fruit
Use: Street, shade

Chinese Cedrela is an upright-branching tree with a very compact habit of growth and a rounded crown. The large, luxuriant, feathery foliage is at first a bright pink and later becomes a clear, bright green. Slightly fragrant and quite showy, the tiny white flowers hang in long, drooping clusters. The fruit is a large woody pod; when open it has the shape of a five-pointed star. Unfortunately, the tree does not produce fruit and flowers until it is well along in years; but its excellent habit and handsome foliage make it a valuable ornamental for use in streets or for shade. It stands heat but will not tolerate cold and is best in mild, temperate climates.

Conformation

Height: 15 to 40 ft. Spread: 15 to 40 ft.

A dense, roundheaded, symmetrical, compact tree of upright-branching habit. The bark is loose and shredding. The leaves are alternate and compound, 10 to 20 in. long, and composed of ten to twenty-two toothed leaflets 3½ to 7 in. long and 1¼ to 2 in. wide. They are bright pink at first and change to a beautiful, clear, bright green.

Flowers

Slightly fragrant, small white or greenish flowers in drooping panicles 8 to 12 in. long. June–July.

Fruit

Chocolate-brown, woody seed pods, 4 in. in diameter, which split open to form a five-pointed star. They last long and are used frequently in indoor decoration. Fall.

Root System: Average
Rate of Growth: Moderate

Natural Requirements

Climate: Tolerates heat. Should be protected from frost.
Soil: Tolerates a wide variety of soils; prefers a fertile loam.
Exposure: Sun.

Care

Pruning: Little is required. The tree assumes a good natural shape.
Feeding: No special feeding necessary.
Watering: Water deeply once a month.
Pests and Diseases: Resistant to and relatively free from both.

Ulmus americana

Ul′mus america′na

American Elm

Central and eastern North America

Features: Habit, fall color (gold), winter design
Use: Shade, lawn, specimen

American Elm is an upright-growing tree with stiffly ascending branches which arch firmly downward to form a perfect vase shape. In the fall, the cool bright green leaves change to dull gold and drop from the tree to reveal the marvelous symmetry of branch design in stark relief against the winter landscape. Although the Dutch elm disease, which has ravaged American elms in the eastern United States, has so far not appeared on the Pacific Coast, discretion should be used in selecting this tree for ornamental use, for the disease may yet come. However, since no other tree approximates the American Elm in its uniquely beautiful habit, the tree should be used in specimen plantings wherever this is feasible.

Conformation

Height: 60 to 100 ft. Spread: 40 to 70 ft.

A broad-headed, vase-shaped tree with strong, upright branches arching downward at the ends. The branches begin to form high up on the trunk, 15 to 30 ft. from the ground. The bark is dark ashy gray and deeply ridged. The leaves are simple, alternate, and toothed, 3 to 5 in. long and 1¼ to 2¼ in. wide. They are unequal at the base and are rough above. A cool, bright green, they turn gold in early fall.

Flowers: Not effective ornamentally.

Fruit

Honey-colored, winged seeds, 3/8 to 1/2 in. long, in clusters. May–June.

Root System: Shallow. Roots are fibrous.
Rate of Growth: Rapid

Natural Requirements

Climate: Tolerates heat and cold.
Soil: Prefers a rich, deep, moist soil.
Exposure: Sun.

Care

Pruning: Tolerates pruning, but little is needed to maintain the excellent natural shape. Remove all dead branches. Time: Fall.
Feeding: No special feeding necessary.
Watering: Water deeply once a month.
Pests and Diseases: Borer carries Dutch elm disease, for which no cure is known; spray with DDT in April, May, or June and again in the fall, whether or not borers are present. Should Dutch elm disease appear, with its attendant dying back of twigs and branches, remove and burn the tree immediately. Since dead branches harbor borers, they should be removed.

Faults: Suckers. Roots have a tendency to surface and heave up the ground around them.

Ul′mus pro′cera, English Elm, is a majestic tree with massive, wide-spreading branches forming a symmetrical, rounded crown. It grows to a height of 40 to 120 ft., with a 60- to 100-ft. spread; its use should be restricted to large gardens. The English Elm has the same cultural and natural requirements as the American Elm and is used for the same landscaping purposes. It is, however, less subject to disease.

Ulmus pumila

Ul′mus pu′mila

Siberian Elm; Asiatic Elm

Eastern Siberia;
northern China

Feature: Foliage
Use: Shade, screen, quick effects, erosion control

Siberian Elm is a rapid-growing tree which thrives in difficult areas. At its best, it grows to a neat, round-topped specimen with wide-spreading, somewhat pendulous branches. However, it is the least attractive of the elms and should be planted only in regions where more ornamental trees will not survive or where quick, temporary effects are desired.

Conformation
Height: 15 to 40 ft. Spread: 15 to 40 ft.

A round-topped, open-headed tree with rough, dark-brown bark. The leaves are simple, alternate, and toothed, ¾ to 3 in. long and ½ to 1 in. wide. They are glossy bright green above, paler and rough beneath.

Flowers
Not effective ornamentally.

Fruit
Not effective ornamentally.

Root System: Shallow roots are voracious.

Rate of Growth: Very rapid

Natural Requirements
Climate: Tolerates heat, cold, and also desert conditions.
Soil: Thrives in any soil except boggy ones. Tolerates drought.
Exposure: Sun or shade.

Care
Pruning: Tolerates heavy pruning. Time: Fall.
Feeding: No special feeding necessary.
Watering: No special moisture requirements.
Pests and Diseases: Relatively free from both.

Faults
Branches are brittle. Roots are voracious and invasive.

Zelkova serrata

Zelko´va serra´ta

(*Z. acuminata; Z. cuspidata; Z. keaki; Planera japonica*)

Japanese Zelkova; Sawleaf Zelkova

Japan

Features: Habit, fall color (red-yellow to dark red), winter design
Use: Shade, street, lawn, hedge, windbreak

Japanese Zelkova is a heavy, rounded tree with large, wide-spreading branches starting close to the ground. The handsome, dense foliage is elmlike and assumes a quiet beauty in the fall when it turns a rich dark red or dull red-yellow. The tree is easily adapted for use as a windbreak or hedge, and it makes a splendid shade, street, or lawn specimen. It is exceedingly easy of maintenance and has a wide climatic tolerance.

Conformation

Height: 50 to 90 ft. Spread: 50 to 90 ft.

A dense, broadly roundheaded tree with a short trunk dividing into several ascending stems. The branches are slender and wide-spreading. The bark is dark brown and scaly. The leaves are simple, alternate, and toothed, and of two kinds: those on the sterile branches are 4 to 6 in. long and 2 to 3½ in. wide; those on fruiting branches are 2 to 3 in. long and ¾ to 1¼ in. wide. They are dark green and rough above, nearly smooth beneath, and turn dull red-yellow to rich dark red in the fall.

Flowers

Not effective ornamentally.

Fruit

Not effective ornamentally.

Root System: Shallow

Rate of Growth: Rapid

Natural Requirements

Climate: Tolerates heat and cold. Will grow in altitudes as high as 4,000 ft.
Soil: Tolerates a variety of soils, including alkali ones, and also tolerates drought.
Exposure: Sun. Tolerates wind.

Care

Pruning: Prune occasionally to shape. Time: Fall.
Feeding: No special feeding necessary.
Watering: No special moisture requirements.
Pests and Diseases: Scale; spray with malathion or an oil emulsion in summer and repeat when needed; spray with oil in winter.

ZONES: 5-10

Zizyphus jujuba

Ziz-yphus juju´ba
(*Z. sativa; Z. vulgaris*)
Jujube; Chinese-Date

Southern Europe; Asia

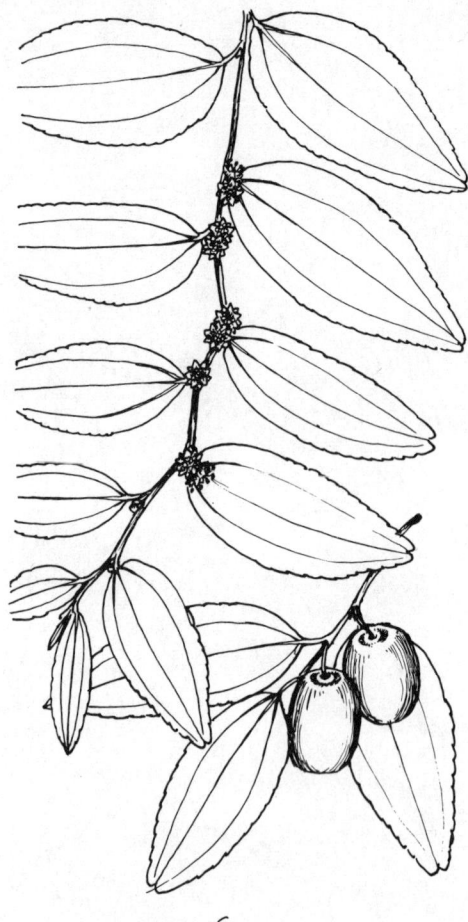

Features: Fruit, foliage, design of branches
Use: Lawn, patio, tub, specimen, espalier

Jujube will bear fruit only in areas where prolonged summer heat is available. But even in regions where the fruit will not set, Jujube is a good ornamental, with its wealth of clean, shiny, dark-green leaves and the interesting patterns of its zigzagging branches. The fruit is shiny reddish brown and medium-sized; the flesh is crisp and sweet. It is eaten fresh or candied and and makes excellent preserves.

Conformation
Height: 10 to 30 ft. Spread: 10 to 30 ft.

An open-growing tree with small, upright, prickly, zigzagging branches. The leaves are simple, alternate, and bluntly toothed, ¾ to 2½ in. long, and oblong. They are a clean, shiny dark green above, light green beneath.

Flowers
Small yellowish flowers, in clusters; not effective ornamentally. June-July.

Fruit
Shiny, edible, reddish-brown, roundish fruit, ½ to ¾ in. long, somewhat resembling a date in appearance. The flesh is sweet and crisp. The fruit is eaten fresh or candied, or is made into preserves. Among the varieties are Lang and Li. Sept.-Oct. The tree bears when two years old.

Root System: Deep
Rate of Growth: Moderate

Natural Requirements
Climate: Tolerates heat; needs prolonged summer heat to develop fruit. Tolerates cold; does not need winter chill to set fruit.
Soil: Prefers a moist, deep, well-drained loam. Tolerates alkali and also drought but prefers moisture.
Exposure: Sun.

Care
Pruning: Little pruning is necessary. Time: Winter.
Feeding: Apply manure annually in the fall.
Watering: Water deeply once a month.
Pests and Diseases: Relatively free from both.

CHART FOR THE ORNAMENTAL USE AND CLIMATIC TOLERANCE OF DECIDUOUS TREES

Rate of growth: R = rapid; M = medium; S = slow
Leaf-blade size: L = large, 6 or more in. long; M = medium, 2 to 6 in. long; S = small, less than 2 in. long
Leaf color: gr = green
Fruit: E = edible; O = ornamental

G: good fall color and (or) winter design
X: areas where the particular tree may be grown easily
(X): areas where the particular tree may be grown, but with some reservations

	Rate of Growth	Habit	Leaf-Blade Size	Leaf-Blade Color	Flowers	Fruit	Fall Color	Winter Design	Temperate Coastal	Desert	Cool Coastal	Temperate Inland	Cold Winters
ORNAMENTAL USE									\multicolumn{5}{l}{CLIMATIC TOLERANCE}				
STREET TREES													
Acer rubrum	R	Dense	L	Novelty	Red	O	G						X
Aesculus carnea	M	Dense	L	Light gr	Red				X		X	(X)	
Aesculus hippocastanum baumanni	M	Dense	L	Dark gr	White				X		X	X	
Celtis australis	M	Dense	M	Gray					X	X	X	X	
Cladrastis lutea	M	Dense	M	Gray	White	O	G	G	X	X	X	X	X
Cornus florida	M	Dense	M	Bright gr	White	O	G	G					X
Crataegus lavallei	M	Dense	M	Gray	White	O	G	G	(X)		X	(X)	X
Crataegus oxyacantha	M	Dense	S	Bright gr	White				X		X	(X)	X
Crataegus oxyacantha, Pauls Scarlet	M	Dense	S	Bright gr	Red				X		X	(X)	X
Crataegus phaenopyrum	M	Dense	S	Light gr	White	O	G	G	(X)		X	(X)	X
Firmiana simplex	M	Dense	L	Bright gr		O		G	X		X	X	
Fraxinus species	R	Dense	M	Bright gr		O	G	G	X	X	X	X	X
Gleditsia triacanthos inermis	R	Open	S	Bright gr					X	X	X	X	X
Jacaranda acutifolia	R	Open	S	Light gr	Blue				X		X		
Koelreuteria species	S	Dense	M	Dark gr	Yellow	O	G	G	X	X	X	X	
Lagerstroemia indica	S	Dense	S	Dark gr	Various		G	G	X	X	X	X	
Liquidambar styraciflua	S	Dense	M	Bright gr			G	G	X		X	X	X
Malus, Flowering Crabapple	M	Dense	M	Various	Various	(O)			(X)		X	X	X
Morus, Kingan	R	Dense	M	Bright gr					X	X	X	X	X
Pistacia chinensis	S	Open	S	Bright gr		O	G		X	X	X	X	X
Prunus, Flowering Cherry	M	Open	M	Bright gr	Various			G	(X)		X	X	(X)
Prunus, Flowering Plum	M	Open	S	Purple	Various				X	X	X	X	X
Pterocarya stenoptera	M	Open	L	Dark gr					X		X	X	X
Quercus borealis	R	Dense	M	Dark gr		O	G	G	X		X	X	X
Quercus coccinea	R	Dense	M	Bright gr		O	G	G	X		X	X	X
Robinia species	R	Open	S	Dark gr	Various	O		G	X	X	X	X	X
Sophora japonica	S	Dense	S	Dark gr	White			G	X		X	X	X
Syringa amurensis japonica	M	Open	M	Dark gr	White				X		X	X	X
Tilia species	R	Dense	M	Dark gr					X			X	X
Toona sinensis	M	Dense	M	Bright gr	White	O			X		X	X	(X)
Zelkova serrata	R	Dense	M	Dark gr			G	G	X	X	X	X	X
SHADE TREES													
Acer platanoides	R	Dense	L	Bright gr			G		X		X	X	X
Acer platanoides schwedleri	R	Dense	L	Red			G		X		X	X	X
Acer rubrum	R	Dense	L	Novelty	Red	O	G				X	(X)	X
Acer saccharinum	R	Dense	L	Light gr			G				X	(X)	X

ORNAMENTAL USE OF DECIDUOUS TREES

SHADE TREES (continued)

	Rate of Growth	Habit	Leaf-Blade Size	Leaf-Blade Color	Flowers	Fruit	Fall Color	Winter Design	Temperate Coastal	Desert	Cool Coastal	Temperate Inland	Cold Winters
Acer saccharum	M	Dense	M	Bright gr			G		X		X	X	X
Aesculus carnea	M	Dense	L	Light gr	Red				X		X	X	
Aesculus hippocastanum baumanni	M	Dense	L	Dark gr	White				X		X	X	X
Ailanthus altissima	R	Dense	M	Dark gr		O			X	X	X	X	
Albizzia julibrissin	R	Dense	S	Dark gr	Pink				X	X	X	X	
Carya illinoensis	S	Dense	M	Light gr		E, O			X	X	X	X	X
Castanea dentata	M	Dense	L	Light gr		E, O		G	X	X	X	X	X
Catalpa species	R	Dense	L	Light gr	White			G	X	X	X	X	
Celtis australis	M	Dense	M	Gray					X	X	X	(X)	X
Fagus sylvatica	M	Dense	M	Dark gr		E, O	G	G	X		X	(X)	X
Fagus sylvatica atropunicea	M	Dense	M	Purple		O		G	X		X	X	
Ficus carica	S	Dense	L	Dark gr					X	X	X	X	
Firmiana simplex	M	Dense	L	Bright gr			G	G	X		X	X	(X)
Fraxinus species	R	Dense	M	Bright gr					X	X	X	X	
Gleditsia triacanthos inermis	R	Open	S	Bright gr					X	X	X	X	X
Juglans species	S	Dense	M	Bright gr	Yellow	E, O			X	X	X	X	
Koelreuteria species	M	Dense	M	Dark gr		O	G	G	X	X	X	X	
Maclura pomifera	R	Open	M	Bright gr		O			X	X	X	X	
Malus, Apple	M	Open	S	Bright gr	Pink				X	X	X	X	X
Melia azedarach umbraculiformis	R	Dense	M	Bright gr	Purple	E, O			X	X	X	X	
Morus species	R	Dense	M	Bright gr	Violet	O			X	X	X	X	
Paulownia tomentosa	R	Dense	L	Bright gr					X	X	X	X	
Pistacia chinensis	S	Open	S	Bright gr			G	G	X	X	X	X	X
Platanus acerifolia	R	Dense	L	Bright gr			G	G	X	X	X	X	X
Platanus racemosa	R	Open	L	Light gr					X	X	X	X	(X)
Populus alba	R	Open	M	Novelty				G		X		(X)	(X)
Prunus, Apricot	M	Open	M	Bright gr	Various	E, O			X	X	X	X	(X)
Prunus, Flowering Apricot	M	Open	M	Bright gr	Various	O			X	X		X	X
Pterocarya stenoptera	M	Dense	S	Dark gr		O					X	X	X
Pyrus, Pear	M	Open	M	Bright gr	White	E, O		G	X		X	X	X
Quercus borealis	R	Dense	L	Dark gr		O	G	G	X	X	X	X	X
Quercus coccinea	R	Dense	M	Bright gr		O	G	G	X		X	X	X
Quercus douglasi	M	Dense	M	Blue gr		O		G	X	X	X	X	X
Quercus palustris	R	Dense	M	Dark gr		O		G	X		X	X	X
Robinia species	R	Open	S	Light gr	Various				X	X	X	X	X
Salix species	S	Dense	M	Dark gr	White			G	X		X	X	X
Sophora japonica	R	Dense	S	Dark gr					X	X	X	X	X
Tilia species	M	Dense	M	Bright gr	White				X		X	X	X
Toona sinensis	M	Dense	M	Bright gr		O			X	X	X	X	X
Ulmus americana	R	Dense	M	Dark gr			G	G	X	X	X	X	X
Ulmus procera	R	Dense	M	Dark gr				G	X	X	X	X	X
Ulmus pumila	R	Dense	S	Bright gr				G	X	X	X	X	X
Zelkova serrata	R	Dense	M	Dark gr			G	G	X	X	X	X	(X)

CLIMATIC TOLERANCE

ORNAMENTAL USE OF DECIDUOUS TREES

LAWN TREES	Rate of Growth	Habit	Leaf-Blade Size	Leaf-Blade Color	Flowers	Fruit	Fall Color	Winter Design	Temperate Coastal	Desert	Cool Coastal	Temperate Inland	Cold Winters
Acer palmatum	S	Open	M	Light gr		O	G	G	X		X	X	X
Acer palmatum vars.	S	Open	M	Various			G	G	X		X	X	X
Acer platanoides	R	Dense	L	Bright gr			G		X		X	X	X
Acer platanoides schwedleri	R	Dense	L	Red			G		X		X	X	X
Acer rubrum	R	Dense	L	Novelty	Red	O	G				X	(X)	X
Acer saccharinum	R	Dense	L	Light gr			G				X	(X)	X
Acer saccharum	M	Dense	M	Bright gr			G		X		X	X	X
Aesculus carnea	M	Dense	L	Light gr	Red				X		X	X	X
Aesculus hippocastanum baumanni	M	Dense	L	Dark gr	White				X		X	X	
Alnus species	R	Open	M	Dark gr								X	
Betula species	R	Open	M	Bright gr				G	X		X	X	X
Carya illinoensis	S	Dense	M	Light gr		E,O	G	G	X	X	X	X	X
Catalpa species	R	Dense	L	Light gr	White				X	X		X	X
Cornus florida	M	Dense	M	Bright gr	White	O	G	G	X		X	X	X
Cornus florida rubra	M	Dense	M	Bright gr	Red	O	G	G	X		X	X	X
Crataegus lavallei	M	Dense	M	Gray	White	O	G	G	(X)		X	(X)	X
Crataegus oxyacantha	M	Dense	S	Bright gr	White	O			X		X	(X)	X
Crataegus oxyacantha, Pauls Scarlet	M	Dense	S	Bright gr	Red	O			X		X	(X)	X
Crataegus phaenopyrum	M	Dense	S	Light gr	White	O			(X)		X	(X)	X
Fagus sylvatica	M	Dense	M	Dark gr			G	G	X		X	(X)	X
Fagus sylvatica atropunicea	M	Dense	M	Purple			G	G	X		X	(X)	X
Ficus carica	S	Dense	L	Dark gr		E,O		G	X	X	X	X	
Firmiana simplex	M	Dense	L	Bright gr		O			X	X	X	X	X
Gleditsia triacanthos inermis	R	Open	S	Bright gr				G	X	X	X	X	X
Halesia carolina	M	Open	M	Bright gr	White		G		X		X	X	
Juglans species	S	Dense	M	Bright gr		E,O			X	X	X	X	(X)
Koelreuteria species	M	Dense	M	Dark gr	Yellow	O	G	G	X	X	X	X	
Laburnum watereri	M	Open	M	Gray gr	Yellow				X		X	X	X
Liquidambar styraciflua	S	Dense	M	Bright gr				G	X		X	X	X
Magnolia soulangeana and vars.	S	Dense	M	Bright gr	Pink	E,O	G	G	(X)		X	X	X
Malus, Apple	M	Open	M	Various	Various	(O)			X		X	X	X
Malus, Flowering Crabapple	M	Dense	M	Bright gr	Violet				X			X	
Paulownia tomentosa	R	Dense	L	Bright gr	Various		G	G	X			X	
Prunus, Flowering Cherry	M	Open	M	Bright gr	Various				(X)		X	X	(X)
Prunus, Flowering Plum	M	Open	S	Purple	Various	E,O		G	X	X	X	X	(X)
Pyrus, Pear	M	Open	M	Bright gr	White	O	G	G				X	X
Quercus palustris	R	Dense	M	Dark gr				G	X		X	X	X
Sophora japonica	S	Dense	S	Dark gr	White			G	X	X	X	X	X
Sorbus aucuparia	R	Open	S	Bright gr	White	O	G					X	X
Tilia species	M	Dense	M	Dark gr					X	X	X	X	X
Ulmus americana	R	Dense	M	Bright gr			G	G	X	X	X	X	X
Ulmus procera	R	Dense	M	Dark gr			G	G	X			X	X

CLIMATIC TOLERANCE

ORNAMENTAL USE OF DECIDUOUS TREES

LAWN TREES (continued)	Rate of Growth	Habit	Leaf-Blade Size	Leaf-Blade Color	Flowers	Fruit	Fall Color	Winter Design	Temperate Coastal	Desert	Cool Coastal	Temperate Inland	Cold Winters
Zelkova serrata	R	Dense	M	Dark gr		E, O	G	G	X	X	X	X	(X)
Zizyphus jujuba	M	Open	S	Dark gr			G	G	X	X	X	X	
WINDBREAKS													
Fagus species	M	Dense	M	Dark gr			G		X		X	(X)	X
Gleditsia triacanthos inermis	R	Open	S	Bright gr				G	X	X	X	X	X
Maclura pomifera	R	Dense	M	Bright gr		O	G		X	X	X	X	X
Platanus acerifolia	R	Dense	L	Bright gr					X	X	X	X	X
Populus nigra italica	R	Dense	M	Bright gr			G	G	X	X	X	X	X
Populus tremuloides	R	Dense	M	Bright gr			G	G	X	X	X	X	X
Salix species	R	Dense	M	Light gr					X	X	X	X	X
Tamarix parviflora	R	Open	S	Bright gr	Pink				X	X	X	X	
Zelkova serrata	R	Dense	M	Dark gr			G	G	X	X	X	X	(X)
HEDGES													
Carpinus betulus	S	Dense	M	Bright gr					X		X	(X)	X
Crataegus oxyacantha	M	Dense	S	Bright gr	White	O			X		X	(X)	X
Crataegus oxyacantha, Pauls Scarlet	M	Dense	S	Bright gr	Red				X		X	(X)	X
Crataegus phaenopyrum	M	Dense	S	Light gr	White	O			(X)		X	(X)	X
Fagus species	M	Dense	M	Dark gr					X		X	(X)	X
Fagus sylvatica atropunicea	M	Dense	M	Purple					X		X	X	X
Gleditsia triacanthos inermis	R	Open	S	Bright gr			G	G	X	X	X	X	X
Maclura pomifera	R	Dense	M	Bright gr		O (O)		G	X	X	X	X	X
Malus, Flowering Crabapple	M	Dense	M	Various	Various		G		X	X	X	X	X
Tamarix parviflora	R	Open	S	Bright gr	Pink				X	X	X	X	
Zelkova serrata	R	Dense	M	Dark gr			G	G	X	X	X	X	(X)
SCREENS													
Acer negundo	R	Dense	M	Light gr			G		X	X	X	X	X
Acer negundo vars.	R	Dense	M	Novelty			G		X	X	X	X	X
Acer saccharinum	R	Dense	L	Light gr			G		X	X	X	X	X
Ailanthus altissima	R	Dense	M	Dark gr		O			X	X	X	X	X
Alnus species	R	Open	M	Dark gr					X		X	X	X
Betula species	R	Open	M	Bright gr				G	X	X	X	X	X
Celtis australis	M	Dense	M	Gray	White				X	X	X	X	
Crataegus lavallei	M	Dense	M	Gray		O	G		(X)	X	X	(X)	X
Nyssa sylvatica	M	Dense	M	Dark gr			G	G	X	X	X	X	X
Platanus acerifolia	R	Dense	L	Bright gr			G	G	X	X	X	X	X
Populus nigra italica	R	Dense	M	Bright gr			G	G	X	X	X	X	X
Populus tremuloides	R	Dense	M	Bright gr			G	G	X	X	X	X	X

CLIMATIC TOLERANCE

ORNAMENTAL USE OF DECIDUOUS TREES

CLIMATIC TOLERANCE

SCREENS (continued)	Rate of Growth	Habit	Leaf-Blade Size	Leaf-Blade Color	Flowers	Fruit	Fall Color	Winter Design	Temperate Coastal	Desert	Cool Coastal	Temperate Inland	Cold Winters
Prunus, Flowering Cherry	M	Open	M	Bright gr	Various			G	(X)		X	X	(X)
Prunus, Flowering Plum	M	Open	S	Purple	Various				X	X	X	X	X
Salix species	R	Dense	M	Light gr					X	X	X	X	X
Syringa amurensis japonica	M	Open	M	Dark gr	White							X	X
Ulmus pumila	R	Dense	M	Bright gr					X	X	X	X	X

ESPALIERS

Acer circinatum	M	Dense	M	Dark gr							X	X	
Diospyros kaki	M	Dense	M	Dark gr		O	G		X	X	X	X	X
Ficus carica	S	Dense	L	Dark gr		E,O	G		X	X	X	X	
Laburnum watereri	M	Open	M	Gray gr	Yellow						X	X	X
Magnolia soulangeana and vars.	S	Dense	M	Bright gr	Various				X		X	X	
Malus, Apple	M	Open	M	Bright gr	Pink	E,O			X		X	X	X
Prunus, Plum	M	Open	M	Bright gr	White	E,O			X	X	X	X	X
Pyrus, Pear	M	Open	M	Bright gr	White	E,O			X	X	X	X	X
Zizyphus jujuba	M	Open	S	Dark gr		E,O			X	X		X	(X)

PATIO AND TUB TREES

Acer circinatum	M	Dense	M	Dark gr							X	X	X
Acer palmatum	S	Open	M	Light gr			G	G	X		X	X	X
Acer palmatum vars.	S	Open	M	Various			G	G	X		X	X	
Albizzia julibrissin	R	Dense	S	Dark gr	Pink			G	X	X	X	X	
Annona cherimola	M	Open	L	Light gr		E,O			X				
Cornus florida	M	Dense	M	Bright gr	White	O	G	G	X		X	X	X
Cornus florida rubra	M	Dense	M	Bright gr	Red	O	G	G	X		X	X	X
Crataegus lavallei	M	Dense	M	Gray	White	O	G		(X)		X	(X)	X
Crataegus oxyacantha	M	Dense	S	Bright gr	White	O	G		(X)		X	(X)	X
Crataegus oxyacantha, Pauls Scarlet	M	Dense	S	Bright gr	Red	O	G		(X)		X	(X)	X
Crataegus phaenopyrum	M	Dense	S	Light gr	White	O	G	G	X		X	X	X
Diospyros kaki	M	Dense	M	Dark gr		E,O	G	G	X	X	X	X	X
Ficus carica	S	Dense	L	Dark gr		E,O			X	X	X	X	
Firmiana simplex	M	Dense	L	Bright gr	White	O		G	X	X	X	X	
Halesia carolina	M	Open	M	Bright gr	Blue		G		X		X		
Jacaranda acutifolia	R	Open	S	Light gr	Yellow				X	X			
Koelreuteria species	M	Dense	M	Dark gr		O		G	X		X	X	
Lagerstroemia indica	S	Dense	S	Dark gr	Various		G		X			X	

ORNAMENTAL USE OF DECIDUOUS TREES

PATIO AND TUB TREES (cont'd)

	Rate of Growth	Habit	Leaf-Blade Size	Leaf-Blade Color	Flowers	Fruit	Fall Color	Winter Design	Temperate Coastal	Desert	Cool Coastal	Temperate Inland	Cold Winters
Magnolia soulangeana and vars.	S	Dense	M	Bright gr	Various	E,O			X		X	X	
Malus, Apple	M	Open	M	Bright gr	Pink	(O)			X		X	X	X
Malus, Flowering Crabapple	M	Dense	M	Various	Various	O			X		X	X	X
Oxydendron arboreum	S	Dense	M	Bright gr	White		G	G			X	X	
Paulownia tomentosa	R	Dense	L	Bright gr	Violet		G		X			X	X
Pistacia chinensis	S	Open	S	Bright gr		O	G		X	X		X	
Pistacia vera	S	Open	S	Bright gr		E,O	G		X	X	X	X	
Prunus, Almond	M	Open	M	Bright gr	Pink	E,O			X			X	
Prunus, Apricot	M	Open	M	Bright gr	Various				X	X	X	(X)	(X)
Prunus, Flowering Apricot	M	Open	M	Bright gr	Various	E,O			X			X	(X)
Prunus, Cherry	M	Open	M	Bright gr	White			G	(X)		X	X	X
Prunus, Flowering Cherry	M	Open	M	Bright gr	Various	E,O			X	X	X	X	X
Prunus, Plum	M	Open	M	Bright gr	White				X	X	X	X	(X)
Prunus, Flowering Plum	M	Open	M	Purple	Various	E,O			X		X	X	X
Pyrus, Pear	M	Open	M	Bright gr	White			G	X	X	X	X	X
Sophora japonica	S	Dense	S	Dark gr	White	O	G			X		X	X
Sorbus aucuparia	R	Open	S	Bright gr	White							X	
Syringa amurensis japonica	M	Open	M	Dark gr	White				X	X		X	
Tamarix parviflora	R	Open	S	Bright gr	Pink				X	X	X	X	
Zizyphus jujuba	M	Open	S	Dark gr		E,O		G				X	

CLIMATIC TOLERANCE

BROAD-LEAVED EVERGREEN TREES

Broad-leaved evergreen trees are plants with relatively broad leaves which they retain throughout the year. They are distinct from evergreen conifers in that they do not bear cones. A few broad-leaved evergreens that are very sensitive to cold sometimes drop their leaves in regions that have severe winters; but since they do not do so in milder zones, they are classified as evergreens. In landscaping, broad-leaved evergreens provide a permanent garden picture, which is often brightened by highly ornamental flowers or fruit. Among the many edible fruits found in this group are the Citrus, Avocado, Olive, and Loquat. Depending upon the characteristics of the individual trees, broad-leaved evergreens serve useful purpose for shade, street, lawn, hedge, windbreak, screen, patio, or tubs. The majority of these trees are not hardy in extremely cold regions, and their climatic preferences should be closely studied before they are selected for garden use.

Acacia baileyana

Aca´cia baileya na

Cootamundra Wattle; Bailey Acacia

New South Wales

Features: Flowers, foliage

Use: Quick effects, patio, tub, erosion control, accent

Bailey Acacia does not assume a good natural shape, and pruning in its early years is essential to its ornamental use. When the tree is so controlled and trained, it may be effectively employed as an accent plant in patios or in tubs. The fine, feathery, blue-gray foliage provides a pleasing contrast at all seasons of the year; and in winter, tiny golden balls of fluffy flowers cover the tree. Unsightly pods, brittle wood, and a short life span count heavily against its extensive use in any permanent garden plan. This tree thrives in mild, temperate zones or in hot areas where frost cannot become a danger.

Conformation

Height: 15 to 30 ft. Spread: 15 to 35 ft.

A roundheaded tree with horizontal-spreading branches creating a loose, open appearance. The fine, feathery, blue-gray foliage is twice-compound, 1 to 3 in. long, and composed of forty to sixty leaflets about 1/4 in. long. It is very dense and is arranged spirally round the branches.

Flowers

Fluffy golden-yellow balls, 1/4 in. in diameter, in racemes 3 to 6 in. long. They are very profuse and brighten the tree for a long period in winter. Jan.-March.

Fruit

Unsightly seed pods, 2 to 4 in. long and 1/2 in. or less wide. They persist on the tree well into the winter months.

Root System: Shallow, spreading

Rate of Growth: Rapid; 11 to 12 ft. in one year, 25 ft. in six years

Natural Requirements

Climate: Grows best in temperate areas. Tolerates heat; will not tolerate cold.

Soil: Grows best in light, well-drained fertile soil. Tolerates alkali soils and drought; stands a moderate amount of salt.

Exposure; Sun or shade. Tolerates salt air and seacoast conditions. Protect from strong winds.

Care

Pruning: Head in and shape well in early years. Time: Summer.

Feeding: Apply fairly large quantities of manure annually in the fall.

Watering: Provide very little moisture.

Pests and Diseases: Relatively free from both; but since acacias are known to be host plants for thrips, spray with DDT, lindane, or malathion in spring and fall as a preventive measure and repeat when needed.

Faults

Makes much litter. Has brittle branches, unsightly pods. Does not live long (30 yrs.). Does not assume a good natural shape.

Aca´cia baileya´na purpu´rea is a variety with the same general characteristics as the species but with striking purplish-gray foliage. It is used for the same landscaping purposes as *A. baileyana* and has the same cultural and climatic requirements.

Acacia decurrens dealbata

Acácia decúrrens dealbáta
(A. dealbata)

Silver Wattle; Silver-Green Wattle

Australia

Features: Flowers, foliage

Use: Quick effects, erosion control, accent

Silver Wattle has an open habit of growth and feathery, silver-green foliage with a delicate, shimmering quality. In early spring, the tree is covered with clouds of clear yellow, fluffy, ball-like flowers which are fragrant and last for a rather long time. Unfortunately, Silver Wattle is too large and too unpredictable in shape for use in patios and tubs, and too light and brittle for most other landscaping purposes. It is best used for occasional surprise effects or contrast accents. It will stand more cold than most acacias but will not tolerate prolonged freezing.

Conformation

Height: 30 to 60 ft. Spread: 25 to 50 ft.

An open, roundheaded, and narrowly upright tree with wide-spreading or ascending branches. The leaves are alternate and compound, 4 to 6 in. long, and composed of numerous leaflets about 1/4 in. long. They are silver-green and feathery and are very densely arranged on the branches.

Flowers

Clear yellow, fragrant, fluffy, ball-shaped flowers, 1/4 in. in diameter, in branched racemes 12 to 14 in. long, and so profuse as to blanket the tree. Feb.-March.

Fruit

Unsightly red-brown pods, 2 to 4 in. long and 1/4 in. wide. They persist on the tree for a long time. Mar.-May.

Root System: Shallow, spreading

Rate of Growth: Rapid

Natural Requirements

Climate: Heat tolerant. Vulnerable to frost but will stand more than most acacias.

Soil: Grows best in light, well-drained, fertile soil. Tolerates alkali and drought. Stands a moderate amount of salt.

Exposure: Sun or shade. Tolerates salt air and seacoast conditions. Protect from strong winds.

Care

Pruning: Head in and shape well in early years. Time: Summer.

Feeding: Apply fairly large quantities of manure annually in the fall.

Watering: Provide very little moisture.

Pests and Diseases: Relatively free from both; but since acacias are known to be host plants for thrips, spray with DDT, lindane, or malathion in spring and fall as a preventive measure and repeat when needed.

Faults

Makes much litter. Has brittle branches, unsightly pods. Reseeds. It is short-lived, but is the longest-lived of the acacias.

Acacia longifolia

Acácia longifólia
Sydney Golden Wattle

Australia

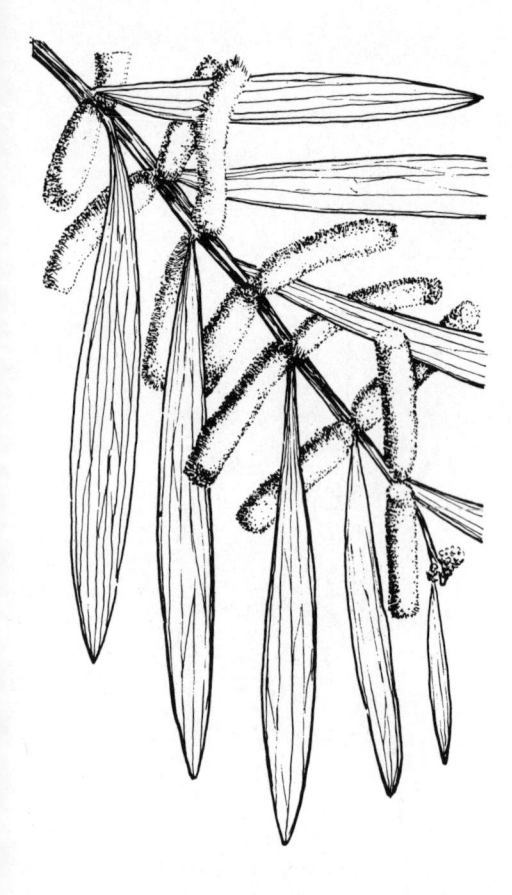

Features: Flowers, foliage

Use: Hedge, screen, tub, quick effects, erosion control

Hedge, screen tub, quick effects, erosion control

Sydney Golden Wattle is satisfactory for small gardens if planted in protected areas and pruned when young to establish a good framework. The flowers bloom in tiny, bright gold spikes and open all at once in a sudden brilliant display at the end of winter. Sydney Golden Wattle is often confused in the trade with *A. latifolia*, Broadleaf Acacia, and is sold under that name. A variety of *A. longifolia*, var. *floribunda*, Gossamer Wattle, has narrower leaves and quantities of pale-yellow flowers.

Conformation

Height: 15 to 30 ft. Spread: 10 to 20 ft.

A roundheaded, open-growing tree with arching, spreading branches which are pendulous at the tips. The foliage is comprised of bladelike "leaves," called phyllodes, which are modified leafstalks; they are simple, alternate, and entire, 2 to 6 in. long and ¼ to ½ in. wide.

Flowers

Bright gold, fluffy flowers in short, narrow spikes ¾ to 2¼ in. long. They completely cover the tree. Feb.–March.

Fruit

Unsightly, rounded brown pods, 3 to 4 in. long, which persist on the tree for a long time. May–June.

Root System: Shallow

Rate of Growth: Rapid

Natural Requirements

Climate: Prefers temperate regions. Tolerates heat. Will not stand cold.

Soil: Prefers a light, well-drained, fertile soil. Tolerates alkali and a moderate amount of salt and also drought.

Exposure: Sun or shade. Tolerates seacoast conditions. Protect from strong winds.

Care

Pruning: Head high and shape well in early years. Time: Summer.

Feeding: Apply fairly large quantities of manure annually in the fall.

Watering: Provide very little moisture.

Pests and Diseases; Relatively free from both; but since acacias are known to be host plants for thrips, spray with DDT, lindane, or malathion in spring and fall as a preventive measure and repeat when needed. Scale is sometimes a nuisance; spray with malathion or an oil emulsion in summer and repeat when needed. Spray with oil in winter.

Faults

Branches are brittle, pods unsightly. Makes much litter. Short-lived.

Two very satisfactory acacias used for the same landscaping purposes as Sydney Golden Wattle are *A. riceána*, Rice Acacia, and *A. verticillata*, Star Acacia. They grow to a height of about 20 ft. with an equal spread. Star Acacia has dark-green, needle-like foliage and pale-yellow, fluffy flowers from April to May. Rice Acacia has deeper-yellow flowers and blooms in March.

Acacia melanoxylon

Acácia melanóxylon
Blackwood Acacia

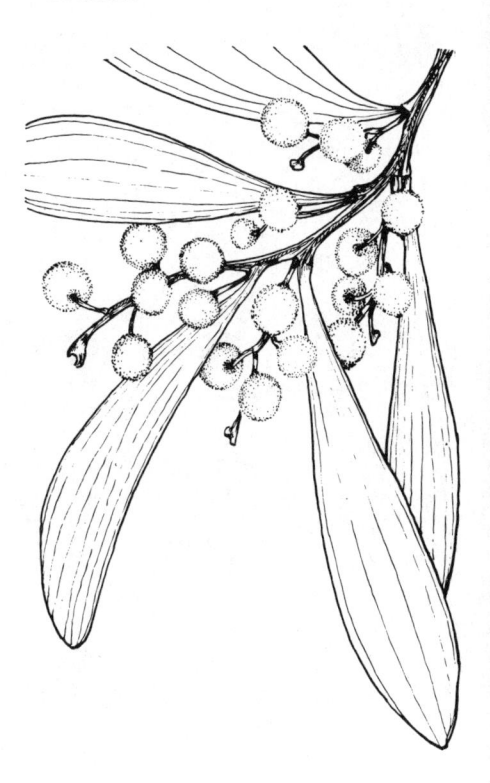

Australia

Features: Habit, foliage, bark
Use: Shade, street, hedge, windbreak, quick effects, erosion control.

Although frequently seen as a clipped, symmetrical street tree, Blackwood Acacia is a better ornamental when it is allowed to grow to its full shape and girth. For then its dense, dark-green foliage boils up in rounded patterns, casting deep shade and exemplifying a quiet, somber elegance accentuated by the dark-brown—almost black—bark. The tree is vulnerable to frost and will not survive in extremely cold areas.

Conformation
Height: 25 to 70 ft. Spread: 20 to 40 ft.

A dense, symmetrical tree with a broad, spreading crown, becoming pyramidal and roundheaded with age. The bark is deep, dark-brown. The dark-green foliage is composed of simple, alternate leafstalks, or phyllodes, 2½ to 5 in. long and ½ to 1 in. wide. When young it is compound and feathery. Both types of foliage may appear on the tree at the same time.

Flowers
Creamy-white, fluffy balls in short racemes. They are not effective if the tree has been sheared. The flowers do not make as spectacular a display as those of many other acacias. March–April.

Fruit
Unsightly purplish-brown seed pods, 3 to 5 in. long and 3/8 in. wide. They persist on the tree until the following season.

Root System: Shallow, spreading

Rate of Growth: Rapid

Natural Requirements
Climate: Heat tolerant. Vulnerable to frost but will stand some degree of cold.
Soil: Grows best in light, well-drained, fertile soil. Tolerates alkali and drought; stands a moderate amount of salt.
Exposure: Sun or shade. Tolerates salt air, seacoast conditions, and smog. Protect from strong winds.

Care
Pruning: Head high and shape well when tree is young; later, thin branches to reduce the mass. Time: Summer.
Feeding: Apply manure annually in the fall.
Watering: Provide very little moisture. Avoid surface watering, for this tends to make the roots come to the surface.
Pests and Diseases: Relatively free from both; but since acacias are known to be host plants for thrips, spray with DDT, lindane, or malathion in spring and fall as a preventive measure and repeat when needed.

Faults: Pods are unsightly on tree and make much litter when they drop. Branches are brittle, but not so brittle as those of other acacias. The tree is usually short-lived, though individual trees are known to have lived for eighty years.

Acácia pycnántha, Golden Wattle, grows to a height of 30 ft., with a 20-ft. spread. It has bladelike leaves and bright yellow, ball-like flowers in long, showy racemes. This acacia rivals all the others in profusion of blooms; but the habit of the tree is faulty and it becomes scraggly with age.

Agonis flexuosa

Ago′nis flexuo′sa
Peppermint Tree; Australian Willow-Myrtle

Australia

Features: Habit, bark, young twigs and foliage

Use: Shade, specimen

Australian Willow-Myrtle is a low-branching, wide-spreading, picturesque tree with pendulous twigs and foliage and a multiple trunk covered with warm reddish-brown, deeply furrowed bark. The fragrant, eucalyptus-like leaves are bright green, but the coppery red of the young leaves and twigs seems to suffuse the whole tree with a rosy flush. Compared with other weeping trees, Australian Willow-Myrtle is not fragile like the birch nor heavy and ponderous like the willow but grows with an individual grace which adds character to any garden position it occupies. It will tolerate heat and drought but will not stand extreme cold, and seems to prefer cool, mild, coastal areas.

Conformation

Height: 25 to 40 ft. Spread: 15 to 45 ft.

An irregular tree with heavy, low, horizontal-spreading branches and usually multiple trunk. The bark is rough and furrowed and is a warm reddish brown. The leaves are simple, alternate, and entire, 3 to 6 in. long and 3/8 to 1/2 in. wide. They somewhat resemble those of the eucalyptus and hang straight down from the branches. When crushed they exude a fresh, peppermint odor. When they first open, the leaves are a coppery red; later they change to a cool, bright green. The young twigs are also coppery red and pendulous.

Flowers

Small white flowers, 1/2 in. in diameter, quite profuse but not especially ornamental. They somewhat resemble those of *Leptospermum*. June–Aug.

Fruit

Small brown capsules, 1/4 in. across, which persist on the tree throughout the year. July–Sept.

Root System: Shallow, spreading

Rate of Growth: Slow

Natural Requirements

Climate: Grows best in mild areas and cool coastal climates. Tolerates heat but not extreme cold. Tolerates desert atmosphere.
Soil: Tolerates a variety of soils; grows best in light sandy loam. Tolerates drought.
Exposure: Sun. Tolerates wind and seacoast conditions.

Care

Pruning: Little is required. The tree is best when allowed to assume its natural shape.
Feeding: No special feeding necessary.
Watering: No special attention necessary.
Pests and Diseases: Relatively free from both.

Albizzia lophantha

Albiz´zia lophan´tha
(Acacia lophantha)

Plume Albizzia

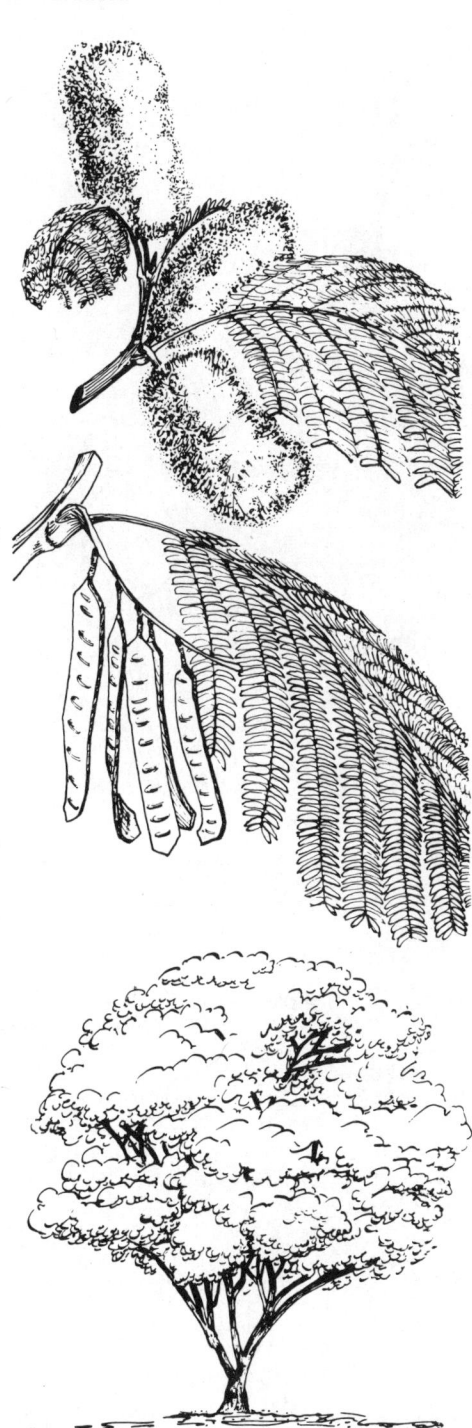

Australia

Feature: Foliage

Use: Quick effects, erosion control

Plume Albizzia is a rapid-growing, short-lived tree which becomes scraggly with age. It is ordinarily used in landscaping for quick effects or as a filler plant in difficult areas, for it flourishes in poor soil and under drought conditions, requiring little or no maintenance. The outstanding ornamental feature of the tree is its dark-green foliage, which is delicate and graceful and resembles a giant plume. Plume Albizzia is practical for use only in mild areas, for it will not stand cold.

Conformation
Height: 25 ft. Spread 35 to 40 ft.

A compact, roundheaded tree with many horizontal-spreading branches. As it matures, the tree loses its shape completely, spreads out unevenly, and becomes scraggly in appearance. The dark-green leaves are delicate and graceful. They are alternate and compound, 5 to 8 in. long and 4 to 6 in. wide, and are composed of fourteen to twenty-four pinnae. Each pinna is composed of forty to sixty leaflets 1/4 to 3/8 in. long.

Flowers
Tiny greenish-white flowers in spikes 1 to 2¼ in. long. Feb.–June

Fruit
Light-brown pods, 3 in. long and 1/2 in. wide, which detract from the pleasing appearance of the tree. June–Aug.

Root System: Shallow

Rate of Growth: Rapid

Natural Requirements
Climate: Thrives only in mild areas. Will not tolerate extreme dry heat or cold.
Soil: Tolerates sterile, alkali soils and also drought.
Exposure: Tolerates smoke, dust, and seacoast conditions.

Care
Pruning: Little is required.
Feeding: No special feeding necessary.
Watering: No special attention necessary.
Pests and Diseases: Relatively free from both.

Faults
Branches are brittle. Tree becomes scraggly with age. Does not live long.

Arbutus menziesi

Arbu´tus menzies´i
(*A. procera*)
Pacific Madrone

Northwestern United States

Features: Bark, fruit, branchlets
Use: Screen, copse, specimen, accent

Pacific Madrone varies in habit according to the conditions under which it grows; but whatever shape it takes, it is always charming and interesting. Its beautiful polished twigs and dramatic, peeling red bark make it a spectacular part of the landscape. In autumn, loose clusters of orange-red berries appear in profusion. Because of its striking qualities, the tree should be used to accent well-favored areas.

Conformation

Height: 20 to 80 ft. (100 ft.). Spread: 15 to 50 ft. (75 ft.).

A tree of unpredictable habit: it sometimes grows to an irregular picturesque shape with a twisted or multiple trunk, and sometimes it is completely roundheaded and symmetrical with a perfectly straight trunk. The bark is reddish brown or terra-cotta color and peels in long, vertical strips to reveal a smooth, tight, slippery underbark, which deepens gradually from light green to brownish red. The branchlets are polished, twisted, and angular, and are often variegated red and green, when young. The leaves are simple, alternate, and entire or fine-toothed, 3 to 6 in. long, and 1 to 3 in. wide. They are glossy and leathery, a dark green above and glaucous beneath. In the summer of the second year, they turn orange or scarlet and fall at irregular intervals; almost simultaneously their place on the tree is taken by new pale-green foliage.

Flowers

Waxy white, urn-shaped flowers 1/3 in. long, in terminal clusters 3 to 9 in. long and 6 in. wide. The flowers somewhat resemble those of a heather. They are slightly fragrant and are an important source of honey. March–May.

Fruit

Orange-red berries, 1/2 in. in diameter, in loose, grapelike clusters 8 to 14 in. long. Late summer and fall.

Root System: Average to deep

Rate of Growth: Moderate to slow

Natural Requirements

Climate: Tolerates heat and cold.
Soil: Grows best in well-drained, slightly acid loam. Tolerates poor soils and drought.
Exposure: Sun or shade. Tolerates seacoast conditions with some protection from wind, and altitudes as high as 4,000 ft.

Care

Pruning: Prune very little and only when absolutely necessary; then remove entire branch because stubs will not be covered by new growth. Time: Spring.
Feeding: No special feeding necessary.
Watering: Provide average to slight moisture.
Pests and Diseases: Scale, sucking insects, thrips (host plant), spray with an all-round insecticide each spring and fall and repeat when needed.

Faults

Difficult to transplant. Stump sprouts. Bark is untidy when shedding.

Brachychiton populneus

Brachychi'ton popul'neus
(Sterculia diversifolia)
Kurrajong Bottle Tree

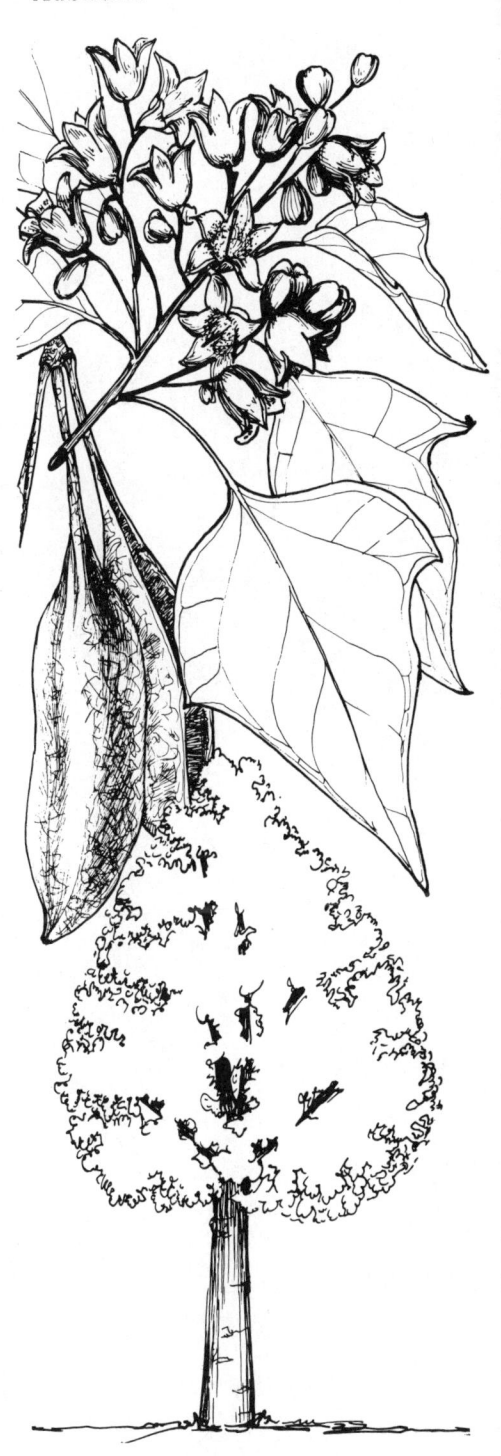

Australia

Features: Habit, foliage, pods

Use: Shade, street, lawn

Kurrajong Bottle Tree has an odd, bottle-shaped trunk which bulges at the base and rises to a dense, conical crown. The foliage occurs in many shapes and types on the same tree, making an interesting study in diversity. Although the bell-shaped white flowers add a charming note, the outstanding ornamental value of the tree lies in its excellent and predictable habit and its interesting foliage and trunk. It will not tolerate cold climates and thrives only in mild areas.

Conformation

Height: 25 to 60 ft. Spread: 20 to 40 ft.

A dense, erect, symmetrical tree with a distinctly conical crown. The trunk is straight, strong, and smooth, with a conspicuously swollen base. The bark is light gray. The leaves are simple and alternate and have various interesting shapes, many kinds on the same tree, lobed and unlobed. They are usually ½ to 3 in. long and 1 to 1½ in. wide and are a clear light green, glabrous, and glossy.

Flowers

Bell-shaped whitish flowers, ¾ in. across, often tinged with red inside, in terminal panicles 4 to 6 in. long. May–June.

Fruit

Woody brown pods, 1½ to 3 in. long. They split wide open to a canoe-like shape and tend to persist on the tree. Aug.–Sept.

Root System: Deep

Rate of Growth: Slow

Natural Requirements

Climate: Tolerates heat but not cold. Stands desert atmosphere.
Soil: Grows best in deep soil. Tolerates drought.
Exposure: Sun. Tolerates dust; should be protected from strong winds.

Care

Pruning: Little is required. Tree maintains a good shape to old age, even though neglected.
Feeding: No special feeding necessary.
Watering: No special attention necessary.
Pests and Diseases: Relatively free from both.

Casimiroa edulis

Casimiro´a ed´ulis
White Sapote; Mexican-Apple

Mexico; Central America

Features: Fruit, foliage

Use: Shade, patio, tub, orchard, novelty, specimen

The leaves of the White Sapote are very decorative; they are bright green, and the leaflets are arranged round the stalks in finger-fashion. The fruit resembles an apple in appearance and has a delicate flavor somewhat like that of a peach. White Sapote has practically the same climatic and cultural requirements as the Citrus family. It is indigenous to the subtropics and will not endure frost below 20° F. Probably the most important cultural requirement is adequate moisture combined with proper drainage; the tree will not survive in dry or boggy soils.

Conformation

Height: 30 to 50 ft. Spread: 30 to 40 ft.

A spreading tree with a broad, domed crown and a short, stout trunk. The bark is dark gray-black and somewhat rough. The leaves are alternate, palmately compound, and composed of three to seven (usually five) leaflets 3 to 5 in. long. They are bright green, leathery, and glossy; in spring, when they open, they are a coppery shade.

Flowers

Small, star-shaped yellowish flowers, not effective ornamentally. April-May.

Fruit

Yellowish-green fruit, 3 in. in diameter, resembling a small green apple in appearance. The skin is thin, and the edible pulp has a delicate texture and flavor somewhat like those of the peach. Among the varieties available are Suebelle and Wilson. Aug.-Nov. The tree will bear when four to six (or eight) years old.

Root System: Shallow. Do not cultivate soil around tree.

Rate of Growth: Moderate to rapid

Natural Requirements

Climate: Tolerates heat; will not stand cold below 20° F.
Soil: Grows best in well-drained sandy loam. Tolerates heavy clay if drainage is good. Tolerates acid, but will not survive in boggy soils.
Exposure: Sun. Tolerates humid atmosphere. Needs protection from wind.

Care

Pruning: Head low to start. Little pruning is required except to shape, thin, and remove dead or diseased branches. Time: Early spring.
Feeding: Apply manure annually in the fall. Apply nitrogen fertilizer in early fall if tree is growing poorly.
Watering: Maintain a uniform moisture content. Good drainage is essential.
Pests and Diseases: Scale; spray with malathion or an oil emulsion in summer and repeat when needed; spray with oil in winter.

Feature: Branchlets

Use: Hedge, windbreak, screen, quick effects, novelty, erosion control

Horsetail Beefwood is an open-growing, narrowly upright tree with numerous, slender, graceful branches. Assuming many picturesque shapes, this odd and quaintly beautiful tree is often mistaken for a pine because of its needle-like, apparently leafless branchlets, which are jointed with threadlike scales and represent the only foliage on the tree. The delicate appearance of Horsetail Beefwood seems to belie its rugged nature, for it is strong-growing, drought tolerant, and remarkably easy to cultivate. It stands hot, dry atmospheres and some degree of cold but not prolonged freezing.

Conformation

Height: 40 to 70 ft. (80 ft.). Spread: 20 to 35 ft.

A strikingly picturesque, feathery, thin-topped tree with a loose crown and upward-reaching, slender branches from which emerge spreading, drooping branchlets, needle-like in appearance. These branchlets are jointed with threadlike internodes, ¼ in. long. They are pale green or gray-green. *C. equisetifolia* is often confused in the trade with *C. stricta*, the She-Oak, which is a much smaller tree, growing 10 to 30 ft. high and 8 to 15 ft. across, with drooping branches and longer internodes on the branchlets. Old trunks on both trees are often gnarled and buttressed at the base.

Flowers

Not effective ornamentally.

Fruit

Reddish-brown, pinelike cones, ½ in. long. Spring. Persist throught the winter.

Root System: Shallow

Rate of Growth: Rapid

Natural Requirements

Climate: Tolerates heat and some degree of cold but not prolonged freezing. Tolerates desert atmosphere.

Soil: Grows best in light, sandy soil. Tolerates sandy or clayey soils and wet, brackish soils. Tolerates drought and also acid, alkali, and salt.

Exposure: Tolerates wind, semidesert, and seacoast conditions.

Care

Pruning: Little is necessary except to remove dead and broken branches annually. Time: Spring.

Feeding: No special feeding necessary.

Watering: No special moisture requirements.

Pests and Diseases: Relatively free from both.

Faults

Makes litter.

Casuarina equisetifolia

Casuari′na equisetifo′lia

Horsetail Beefwood; Beefwood

Australia

Ceratonia siliqua

Cerato´nia sili´qua

Carob; Caroub; St. John's Bread; Algaroba

Eastern Mediterranean region

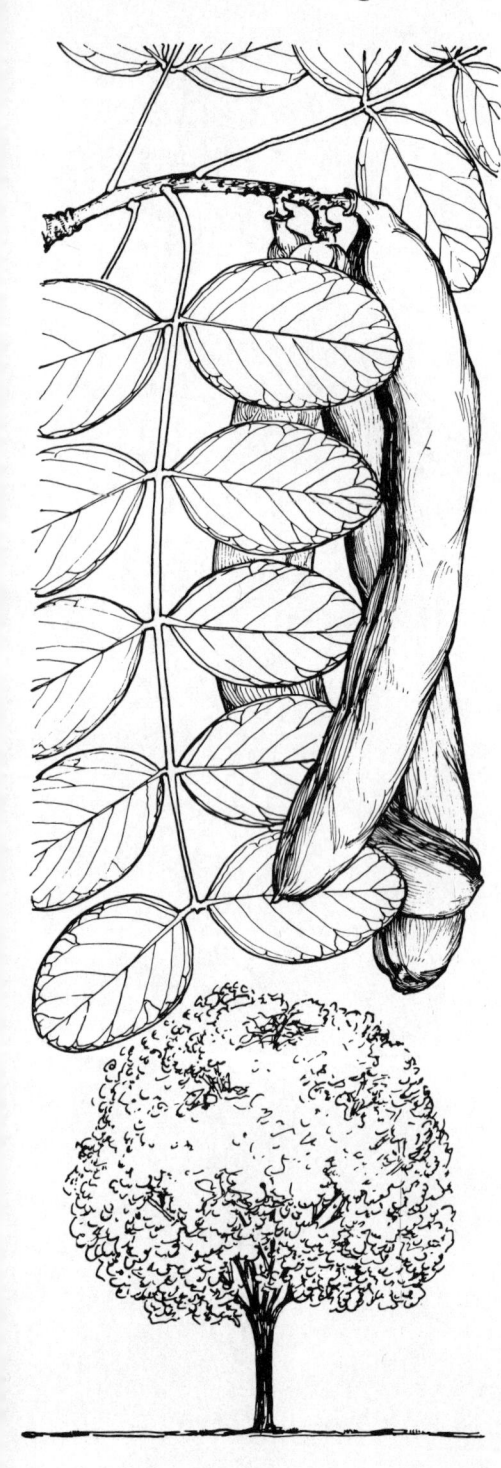

Features: Fruit, habit

Use: Shade, street, hedge, specimen

Carob is a handsome, fully rounded, compact tree with neat, clean foliage and narrow, flat, leathery fruit in the form of pods. These pods have a high nutritional value and a sweet, mealy flavor. Historically, they served as the principal food supply for Wellington's army in the fight against Napoleon, and they are supposed to have been the "locusts and wild honey" St. John ate in the wilderness. Today they are ground and used for bread and as an ingredient of cereal, candy, spirits, and syrup. The Carob is a highly effective ornamental, casting deep shade and adapting itself well to garden use. It tolerates adverse city conditions, drought, and alkali soils. Although it will not stand severe cold, it is extremely tolerant of heat and dry atmosphere.

Conformation

Height: 20 to 45 ft. (50 ft.). Spread: 20 to 55 ft.

A low-branching, dense, fully rounded, compact tree with artistically contorted branches; neat, clean foliage; and a rough, dark-brown bark. The leaves are compound and alternate, 6 to 9 in. long, and composed of 6 to 10 oval, entire leaflets 1 to 3 in. long. They are dark green above, paler beneath, glossy, and leathery.

Flowers

Small yellowish blossoms in lateral racemes. The male and female flowers are on separate trees. They open from red buds. Spring.

Fruit

Brown, glossy, flat, narrow, leathery pods, 4 to 12 in. long; on female trees only. Both male and female trees are necessary for crop production. The pods are edible. They are rich in protein, contain up to 40 per cent sugar, and are sweet and mealy. Fruit is produced in great abundance every second year. Aug.–Oct.

Root System: Deep

Rate of Growth: Slow. Tree lives to a great age.

Natural Requirements

Climate: Tolerates heat and some degree of cold but will not endure prolonged freezing. Tolerates dry air and desert atmosphere.

Soil: Grows best in light, well-drained soil. Tolerates gravelly, alkali soils and drought, though it grows better if it has some moisture. Will not stand heavy, wet, or stiff clay soils.

Exposure: Sun. Tolerates wind, dust, smoke, smog, and seacoast conditions.

Care

Pruning: Stands severe pruning. Thin out head annually. Time: Winter.

Feeding: No special feeding necessary.

Watering: Water deeply once a month. Good drainage is essential.

Pests and Diseases: Resistant to and relatively free from both.

Faults

Young trees are difficult to grow in uniform sizes.

Cinnamomum camphora

Cinnamo´mum campho´ra
*(Camphora officinarum;
Laurus camphora)*
Camphor Tree

China; Japan

Feature: Foliage (spring and winter color)

Use: Shade, street

Camphor grows to a wide-spreading, dense tree which casts deep and heavy shade. The foliage is neat, shiny, and attractive. The young leaves are pinkish bronze when they open, turn light green, and in winter take on a yellowish-bronze cast. In shallow soils or in places where only surface moisture is available, the extensive root system surfaces and heaves up the ground around it. For this reason, camphor trees when young should be provided with deep soil and plenty of water to force their roots downward. They should never be used in lawns or flower beds. Although the tree tolerates some degree of cold, it grows at its best in mild, humid regions.

Conformation

Height: 20 to 40 ft. Spread: 30 to 60 ft.

An open-headed, wide-spreading tree, becoming rounded and dense with age. The trunk is enlarged at the base, and the bark is a light red-brown. The leaves are simple, alternate, and entire, 2 to 4½ in. long and 1 to 2 in. wide. Light, shiny green above, paler beneath, they turn yellowish bronze in the cold months. The new growth is a pinkish bronze. The leaves are fragrant and exude a camphor odor when crushed. Commercial camphor is obtained from the leaves and the twigs of this tree.

Flowers

Tiny yellow flowers, in clusters which are shorter than the leaves. Not effective ornamentally. June.

Fruit

Beady black berries, 3/8 in. in diameter, set in a cuplike receptacle. Not effective ornamentally.

Root System: Roots stout and voracious.

Rate of Growth: Slow

Natural Requirements

Climate: Tolerates heat and some degree of cold but will not survive in extremely cold areas. Should be protected from frost when young. Grows best in mild, humid regions.

Soil: Tolerates a variety of soils, including heavy ones. Grows best in deep, sandy loam to which manure has been added. Tolerates alkali and when mature tolerates drought.

Exposure: Sun or partial shade. Tolerates wind, but young trees should be protected from it.

Care

Pruning: Head high and train, when plant is young, to shape as a tree. Thin out branches annually. Time: Fall.

Feeding: Apply manure annually in the fall.

Watering: Provide plenty of moisture, when tree is young, to force roots downward. Deep watering is essential.

Pests and Diseases: Relatively free from both.

Faults

Difficult to transplant. In shallow soils or in areas where only surface moisture is available, the extensive root system upheaves the ground around it.

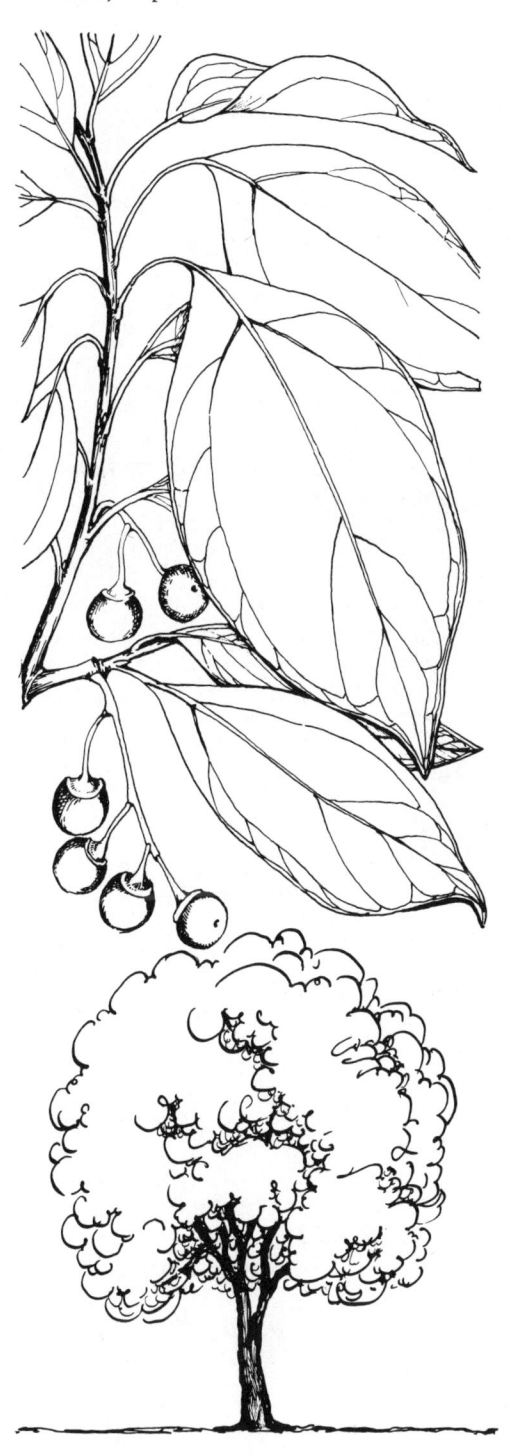

Citrus aurantifolia

Cit́rus aurantifo´lia
(*C. limetta*, in part)
Lime

Asia; subtropical areas

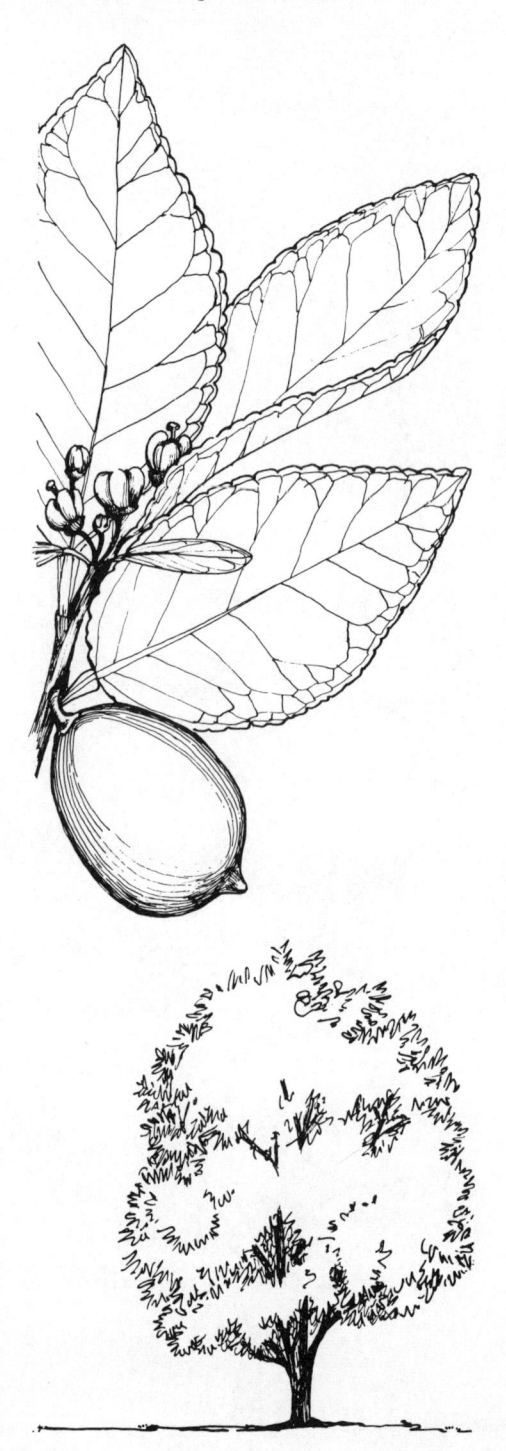

Features: Fruit, habit

Use: Hedge, orchard, patio, tub, specimen, espalier

Limes are very sensitive to cold and should never be planted in areas where winters are severe; temperatures of 28° to 30°F. are often fatal to them. They also need protection from extreme dry heat, drought, wind, and boggy soils. If proper attention is given to its climatic and cultural requirements, the Lime can be one of the most rewarding and beautiful of garden trees, compact in shape, clean-foliaged, and yielding a munificent harvest of fruit all year round. Although subject to a number of pests and diseases, the Lime will ward off most of its natural enemies if proper attention is paid to its climatic and cultural requirements.

Conformation

Height: 15 to 20 ft. Spread: 12 to 20 ft.

A compact, roundheaded tree with a short, stout trunk and many irregular, thorny branches. The leaves are a soft light green. They are compound but are composed of a single leaflet and have the appearance of a simple leaf. They are alternate and entire, 2 to 3½ in. long, and oblong or elliptic, with a narrowly winged leafstalk. Dwarf varieties of Lime are available, which grow to a height of 10 ft. or less.

Flowers

Clear white flowers, ½ in. long, in axillary clusters. They bloom intermittently throughout the year, most heavily in summer.

Fruit

Edible, oval or round-oval fruit, 1½ to 2½ in. long, greenish yellow when ripe and very acid in taste. The fruit is borne near the tips of the new growth. Pollination is not necessary for fruit production. The variety Bearss has proved satisfactory. The tree bears intermittently throughout the year, and most heavily in winter and spring. It begins to bear when three to five years old.

Root System: Shallow

Rate of Growth: Moderate

Natural Requirements

Climate: Sensitive to sudden and prolonged heat waves. Needs protection from extreme dry heat. Very sensitive to cold; temperatures of 28° to 30°F. are often fatal. Thrives in mild, temperate regions.

Soil: Grows best in rich, light, well-drained loam. Tolerates light and moderately heavy soils. Will not stand heavy, alkali, or boggy soils, and will not endure drought. In planting the tree, the ground should be prepared to a depth of 3 to 4 feet. Then the plant should be placed high, with the basin around it sloping downward from the trunk, to prevent the accumulation of moisture at the base of the tree (see Introduction).

Exposure: Sun. Protect from wind and cold drafts.

Care

Pruning: Limes should be pruned annually but never too violently at one time. Prune to the lowest upright-growing limbs to keep fruit within reach. Remove laterals and downward-growing branches, for the weight of the fruit and leaves on such branches will pull the tree downward and out of shape. Remove dead and broken branches and water sprouts in the head of the tree. These sprouts must be cut out at their base. Remove intertwining branches to keep head open. Time: Spring, before growth starts.

Feeding: Apply a small quantity of balanced fertilizer in spring, a light mulch of manure in the fall or early winter. If leaves become mottled or yellow and are of decreasing size toward the ends of the branches, a zinc deficiency is indicated; spray with leaf feed in late winter or early spring, making sure that each leaf is covered by the solution.

Watering: Irrigation is essential; the amount is determined by the nature of the soil, the size of the trees, and the weather conditions. Good drainage is essential. All applications of water should be thorough, but moisture should never be added to already wet soils.

Pests: Aphids (nicotine, lindane, or malathion), white fly (DDT, lindane, or malathion), red spider (malathion), thrips (DDT, lindane, or malathion); spray when needed. Scale and mealy bug; spray with malathion or an oil emulsion in summer and repeat when needed; spray with oil in winter.

Diseases: Anthracnose causes injury to the twigs and spotting or russeting of the fruit; prune out diseased parts and spray with Bordeaux. Foot rot attacks the bark of the crown roots and the base of the trunk, usually near the surface of the soil. Water standing round the plant is most often the cause. When the disease girdles the trunk, the tree dies; prune out infected and adjacent areas and paint the cuts with Bordeaux. If the trunk is more than half girdled by the disease, remove the tree. Gummosis causes the bark to crack and a pale-colored liquid gum to ooze out; cut away the infection and the surrounding areas and paint the cuts with Bordeaux.

Faults

Difficulty in transplanting can be avoided if the ball of earth round the roots is not broken, and if the tree is never transplanted when the ground is cold.

Limequat is a hybrid cross between the West Indian Lime and the Kumquat. It does not grow as strongly as either parent but is an exceedingly prolific tree. The flowers are porcelain white and are 3/8 to 1/2 in. in diameter; the leaves and flowers are both smaller than those of the Lime. The fruit is oval, 1½ in. long, light yellow, and has a sweet rind with a very acid pulp. Its culture is the same as that of the Lime, but its climatic tolerance is the greatest in the citrus group. Among the varieties are Eustis and Lakeland.

Citrus aurantifolia

Cit´rus aurantifo´lia

(*C. limetta,* in part)

Lime

Asia; subtropical areas

Citrus limon

Citrus limon'
(C. limonia)
Lemon

Asia

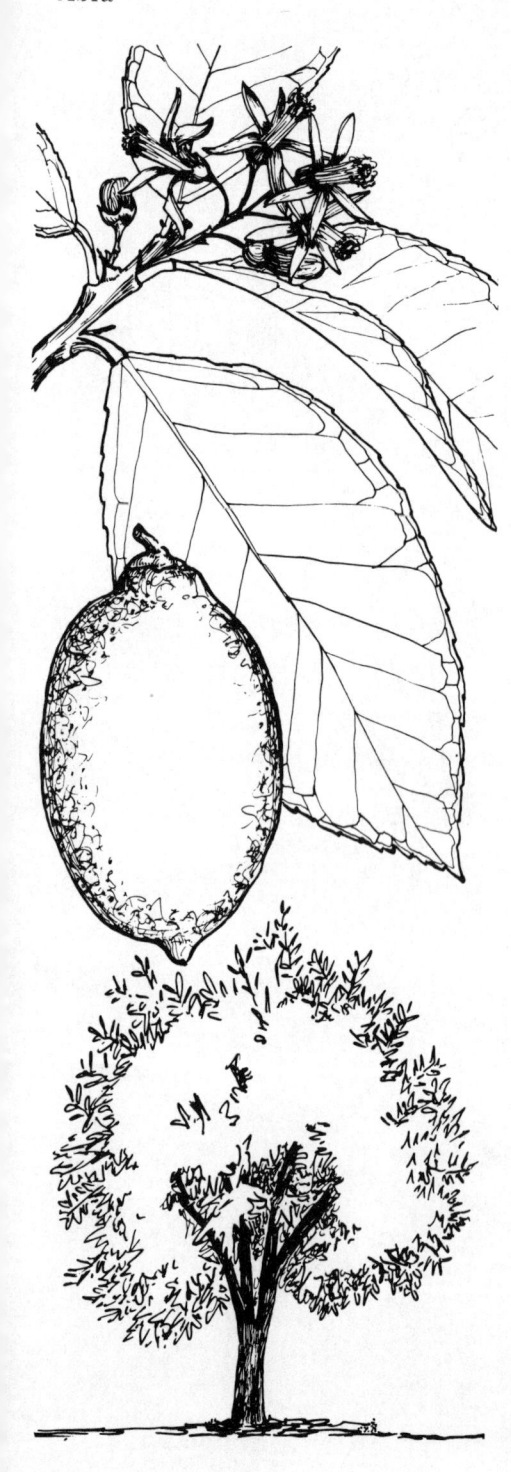

Features: Fruit, habit, flowers

Use: Hedge, orchard, patio, tub, specimen, espalier

Lemons are the most popular of all citrus trees for ornamental purposes. They have a neat habit, fragrant white flowers the year round, and excellent fruit, which has many culinary uses.

Lemons are very sensitive to frost but are not quite so tender as limes. They need protection from wind, drought, and boggy soils, and are very intolerant of sudden, prolonged hot spells. Although subject to attack by a number of insects and diseases, the Lemon will ward off most of its natural enemies if proper attention is paid to its climatic and cultural requirements.

Conformation

Height: 15 to 20 ft. Spread: 15 to 25 ft.

A round, somewhat open-growing tree with branches which are armed with many short, stiff spines. The light yellowish-green leaves are compound, but have the appearance of a simple leaf because they are composed of a single leaflet. They are alternate and oblong or elliptic, 2 to 4½ in. long, and finely but bluntly toothed. The leafstalk is narrowly winged or merely margined. Among the varieties of lemons, the Eureka and the Lisbon are very satisfactory. The Meyer Lemon is a lemon-orange hybrid and is classified as a shrub; it is deservedly popular for its hardiness and its prolific bearing. Dwarf trees of named varieties are also obtainable.

Flowers

Highly fragrant flowers, 1/3 to 2/3 in. in diameter, white with a purplish tinge on the outside of the petals. They are almost everblooming, but the main periods of bloom are in spring and fall.

Fruit

Edible, lemon-yellow, oval fruit, 2 to 4 in. long, which is very sour to the taste. Pollination is not necessary for fruit production. The fruit is produced throughout the year; more heavily in winter and summer. The tree will bear when four years old.

Root System: Shallow

Rate of Growth: Moderate, but more rapid than that of other citrus trees.

Natural Requirements

Climate: Heat tolerant but sensitive to sudden and prolonged heat waves. Sensitive to cold; temperatures which drop below 26° F. are impractical. Thrives in temperate regions.

Soil: Same as for Lime.

Exposure: Sun. Protect from wind and cold drafts.

Care

Pruning: Same as for Lime. In addition, the lateral branches of lemons should be pinched back in spring and again in summer to ensure the development of short, sturdy branches.

Feeding: Same as for Lime.

Watering: Same as for Lime.

Pests: Same as on Lime.

Diseases: Footrot and gummosis; see Lime.

Faults: Same as those of Lime.

Citrus paradisi

Cit´rus paradi´si

Grapefruit; Pomelo

Sport of *C. maxima*, originating in West Indies

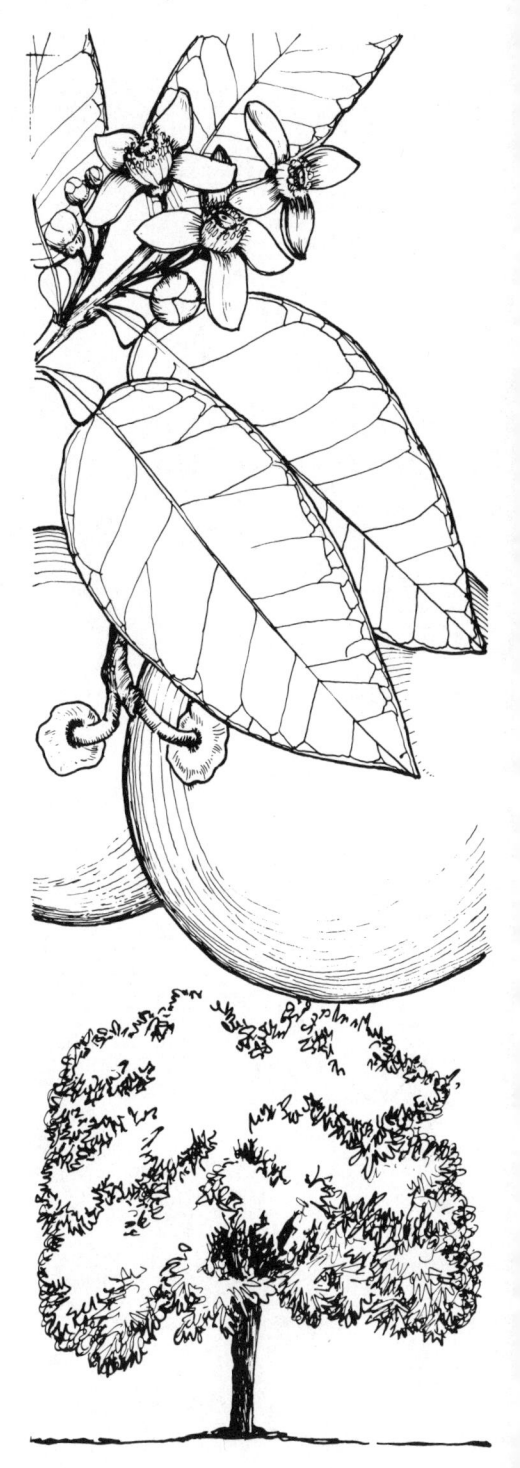

Features: Fruit, habit

Use: Hedge, orchard, patio, tub, specimen, espalier

A heat-loving plant, the Grapefruit flourishes in the tropics and in desert areas; although vulnerable to frost, it is considerably more hardy than the Lemon or the Lime. Like all citrus trees, it is an excellent ornamental, with its neat, controlled habit, clean foliage, and clusters of highly decorative fruit. Although subject to attack by a number of insects and diseases, it will ward off most of its natural enemies if proper attention is paid to its climatic and cultural requirements.

Conformation

Height: 20 to 30 ft. Spread: 20 to 30 ft.

A roundheaded tree with very regular, sometimes spiny branches. The glossy, dark-green leaves are compound but are composed of a single leaflet and thus have the appearance of a simple leaf. They are alternate and entire, ovate, and 4 to 8 in. long, with a broadly winged leafstalk. Dwarf varieties of Grapefruit are available which grow to a height of 8 to 10 ft.

Flowers

Large white flowers, borne singly or in clusters in the axils of the leaves. Spring.

Fruit

Edible, pale lemon-yellow, globose fruit, 4 to 6 in. in diameter, usually in clusters of three to twelve. It has a thick rind and a fine-grained, moderately acid pulp. Among the varieties available are Marsh (white flesh, seedless), Foster (pink flesh), and Thompson (pink flesh, seedless). Pollination is not necessary for fruit production. In favorable areas, where heat is prevalent, the fruit ripens nine to ten months after the flowering period. In zones where less heat is available, more than one growing season is required to ripen the fruit.

Root System: Shallow

Rate of Growth: Moderate

Natural Requirements

Climate: Thrives in hot climates. Vulnerable to frost but more tolerant of cold than the Lime or the Lemon; will not set good edible fruit in cold areas.

Soil: Same as for Lime.

Exposure: Sun. Tolerates some wind but needs protection from strong winds.

Care

Pruning: Requires less pruning than other citrus trees. Prune to the lowest upright-growing limbs. Remove laterals and all downward-growing branches; remove dead and broken branches and sucker growth in the crown. Keep head open. Time: Spring, before growth starts.

Feeding: Same as for Lime.

Watering: Same as for Lime.

Pests: Same as on Lime.

Diseases: Melanose causes small, rough, circular brown spots on the leaves, twigs, and fruit, and in severe cases the leaves become badly distorted; spray with Bordeaux. Foot rot and

Faults: Same as those of Lime.

Citrus sinensis

Cit´rus sinen´sis
Sweet Orange

China

Features: Fruit, habit, flowers

Use: Hedge, orchard, patio, tub, specimen, espalier

The fruit of the Orange will ripen only in areas having a high total amount of heat, though the heat requirements of individual varieties differ to some extent. Somewhat more tolerant of cold than the Lime or the Lemon, the Orange is nevertheless vulnerable to frost, and temperatures of 20° F. or lower are usually fatal. The tree needs protection from wind and from sudden, intense, and prolonged heat waves. The variety Valencia is highly ornamental, for blooms of the current year appear on the tree at the same time as the fruit ripening from the previous season's blossoms. The heavy, sweet fragrance of the flowers and their symbolic significance are well known. Although the Orange is subject to attack by a number of insects and diseases, it will ward off most of its natural enemies if its climatic and cultural requirements are satisfied.

Conformation

Height: 20 to 30 ft. Spread: 15 to 20 ft.

A dense, compact, rounded tree with a strong trunk and branches sometimes armed with a few blunt thorns. The bark is smooth and almost black. The shiny, deep-green leaves are compound but are composed of a single leaflet and have the appearance of a simple leaf. They are alternate and entire, oblong-oval, 3 to 5 in. long, and have a narrow-winged leafstalk. Dwarf trees are available which grow to a height of 8 to 10 ft.

Flowers

Highly fragrant flowers, ½ to ¾ in. in diameter, in tight clusters. Spring.

Fruit

Edible, round fruit, 3 to 4½ in. in diameter, with a very sweet pulp. Among the varieties are Valencia (a summer-ripening, seedless type) and Washington Navel (a fall- or winter-ripening, seedless type). Pollination is not necessary for fruit production. Valencia bears in summer from the previous season's bloom; Washington Navel bears in the fall or winter from the current season's bloom. The tree bears when three years old.

Root System: Shallow

Rate of Growth: Moderate

Natural Requirements

Climate: Grows best in subtropical or semitropical climates. Heat-loving, but sensitive to sudden, prolonged heat waves. Vulnerable to frost but more tolerant of cold than other citrus trees; temperature of 20° F. is usually fatal.

Soil: Same as for Lime.

Exposure: Sun. Protect from wind.

Care

Pruning: Same as for Lime.
Feeding: Same as for Lime.
Watering: Same as for Lime.
Pests: Same as on Lime.
Diseases: Melanose; see Grapefruit. Foot rot and gummosis; see Lime.

Faults: Same as those of Lime.

Feature: Foliage

Use: Hedge, screen, espalier

New Zealand Karaknut is shrubby in habit and must be pruned, when young, if a tree shape is desired. But since the tree is used principally for hedges or screens, it is usually allowed to assume its natural shape. The dark-green foliage is large and handsome and has a clean, fresh, shiny appearance; it is excellent for use in indoor arrangements. Unfortunately, New Zealand Karaknut has deceptively dangerous fruit which has an edible pulp and poisonous seeds; children are likely to be attracted by its large size and orange color. The tree prefers mild, temperate or cool, protected coastal areas and will not tolerate extremes of heat or cold.

Conformation
Height: 30 to 40 ft. Spread: 15 to 20 ft.

A slender, shrublike tree with numerous, upright-spreading branches. The dark-green leaves are simple, alternate, and entire, 6 to 8 in. long and 2½ to 3½ in. wide. They are glossy and glabrous and somewhat resemble the foliage of the southern magnolia.

Flowers
Tiny, greenish-white flowers in branched, terminal clusters, 3 to 4 in. long. May–June.

Fruit
Orange-colored, fleshy fruit, ½ to 1½ in. long. It is plumlike in appearance. The pulp is edible, but the seed is poisonous unless treated. Aug.–Sept.

Root System: Average depth

Rate of Growth: Moderate

Natural Requirements
Climate: Prefers mild, temperate or cool, protected, coastal areas. Will not tolerate extremes of heat or cold.
Soil: Prefers a light loam to which plenty of leaf mold has been added.
Exposure: Sun or shade. Prefers partial shade. Will burn in very hot sun.

Care
Pruning: Stands severe shearing for use as a hedge. To shape as a tree, prune when it is young.
Feeding: Apply leaf mold annually. Apply manure once every two years in the fall.
Watering: Water deeply once a month. Provide proper drainage.
Pests and Diseases: Relatively free from both.

Faults
Fruit makes much litter.

Corynocarpus laevigata

Corynocar´pus laeviga´ta
New Zealand Karakanut

New Zealand

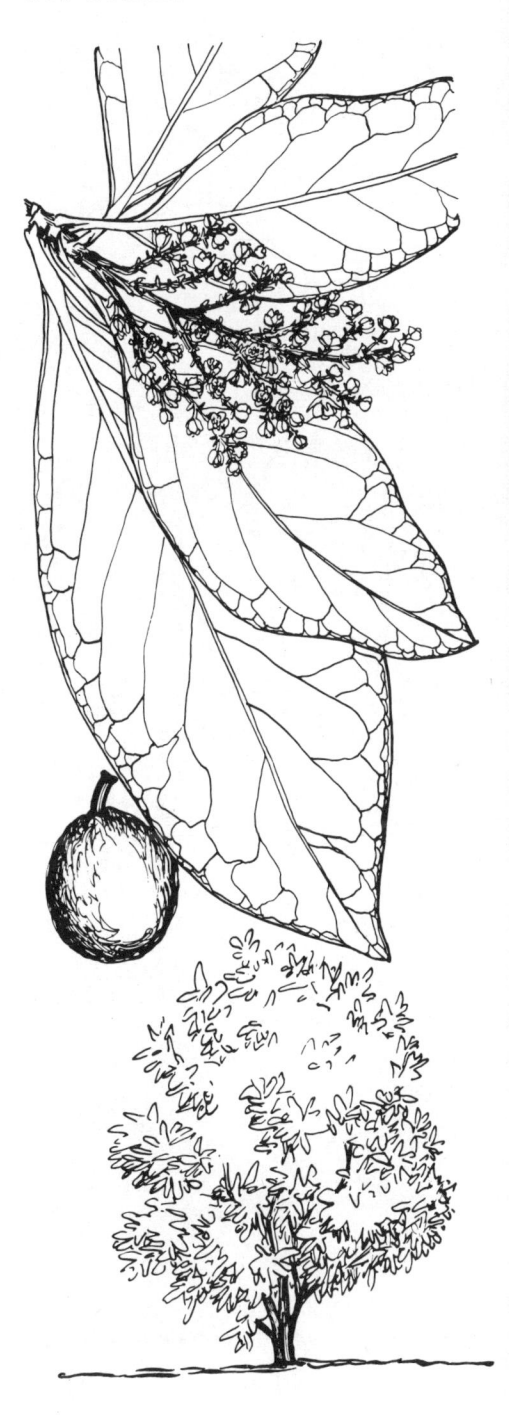

Crinodendron dependens

Crinoden´dron depen´dens
(Tricuspidaria dependens)
White Lily Tree;
  Lily-of-the-Valley Tree

Chile

Features: Flowers, fruit

Use: Street (when trained), lawn, specimen

The White Lily Tree has an unpredictable habit of growth and needs a good deal of pruning to shape as a tree; but once the framework is established, only perfunctory pruning is necessary to maintain a good shape. In summer, small bell-shaped flowers appear in profusion all over the tree; in the fall, these are replaced by cream-colored seed pods. The White Lily Tree makes a delightful lawn specimen. It tolerates heat and some degree of cold but will not stand prolonged freezing.

Conformation

Height: 30 ft.   Spread: 30 ft.

A tree of somewhat haphazard habit, with many branches spreading in all directions. Pruning is essential, if specimen trees are desired. The leaves are simple, (alternate or) opposite, toothed, 2 to 2½ in. long and 1 to 1½ in. wide. They are bright green.

Flowers

Small, bell-shaped white flowers, ¾ in. long, which bloom in profusion all over the tree. They somewhat resemble the Lily of the Valley. June–Aug.

Fruit

Cream-colored leathery capsules. Sept.–Nov. Persist through the winter.

Root System: Average depth

Rate of Growth: Moderate

Natural Requirements

Climate: Tolerates heat and desert atmosphere. Stands some degree of cold but will not endure prolonged freezing.
Soil: Tolerates a variety of soils. Prefers a moist, well-drained, light loam.
Exposure: Sun or partial shade. Prefers sun. Tolerates seacoast conditions.

Care

Pruning: Prune to establish framework, when tree is young. Thin and shape occasionally. Time: Fall.
Feeding: Apply manure annually in the fall.
Watering: Provide plenty of moisture. Good drainage is essential.
Pests and Diseases: Relatively free from both.

Faults

Haphazard habit of growth; must be corrected by pruning when tree is young.

Eriobotrya japonica

Eriobo´trya japon´ica
Loquat

Central China

Features: Foliage, habit, fruit

Use: Shade, street, lawn, windbreak, orchard, patio, tub, specimen, espalier

Loquat is a handsome tree which grows naturally to a good symmetrical shape. The large, dark-green, tropical-appearing leaves are used effectively in indoor decoration; and the orange-yellow fruit is both ornamental and edible. Loquat fits almost every garden need with ease and graciousness. It is excellent for small gardens. It is a durable tree and can be pruned to any desired shape.

Conformation

Height: 15 to 30 ft. Spread: 15 to 30 ft.

A densely roundheaded, compact tree with wide-spreading branches and light red-brown, fairly smooth bark. The leaves are simple, alternate, entire or remotely toothed, 5 to 12 in. long and 2 to 4 in. wide, and distinctly ribbed; they have the appearance of being bunched at the ends of the branches. They are a glossy dark green above, paler and rusty-hairy beneath. When they first open, they are a pale green, which contrasts interestingly with the deeper green of the older leaves.

Flowers

Slightly fragrant white flowers, ½ in. in diameter, in terminal clusters 5 to 6 in. long. Nov.–Jan.

Fruit

The fruits, borne in large clusters of three to ten to a cluster, have juicy, firm flesh of a sweet, slightly acid flavor and are orange-yellow, 1 to 3 in. long, and pear-shaped. They are eaten fresh and are used to make jelly and preserves. Named varieties include: Advance (early, yellow skin and white flesh), Champagne (early, yellow skin and white flesh), Gold Nugget (late, orange skin and flesh), and Thales (late, orange skin and flesh). March–June. The tree will bear when four to six years old.

Root System: Average depth

Rate of Growth: Moderate

Natural Requirements

Climate: Tolerates heat and some degree of cold but will not endure extreme cold. Requires heat for fruiting. Tolerates desert atmosphere.

Soil: Tolerates a wide variety of soils; prefers a heavy, deep, well-drained soil with a limestone base. Tolerates drought but needs irrigation for fruiting.

Exposure: Sun. Tolerates wind and seacoast conditions.

Care

Pruning: Tolerates any amount of pruning. Remove suckers below crown; thin, if desired. Time: Fall.

Feeding: Apply manure once every two years. If soil is sandy and infertile, apply commercial fertilizer in spring.

Watering: Provide plenty of moisture during dry season, if fruits are desired. Good drainage is essential.

Pests and Diseases: Scale; spray with malathion or an oil emulsion in summer and repeat when needed; spray with oil in winter. Pear blight causes blackening of twigs and leaves; cut out infected area and 12 in. below the lowest point of infection and spray with Bordeaux.

Eucalyptus citriodora

Eucalyp´tus citriodo´ra
(*E. maculata citriodora*)

Lemon Eucalyptus; Lemon-scented Gum

Australia

Features: Foliage, habit, bark
Use: Windbreak, screen, copse, specimen

Lemon Eucalyptus is a graceful tree with upright-growing branches and pendulous branchlets covered with bright green, lemon-scented leaves. The bark on the trunk and branches is a clear ivory white, affording a striking and dramatic contrast to the rest of the landscape. An oil obtained from the bark is used to perfume soap. Lemon Eucalyptus is excellent when used singly as a specimen or in small groups to simulate a grove. It will thrive only in warm, coastal areas and is intolerant of any degree of cold.

Conformation
Height: 30 to 130 ft. Spread: 10 to 70 ft.

An open-headed, slender, erect tree with upright-spreading branches, drooping branchlets, and a straight, tapering trunk. The outer bark is whitish or reddish gray and flakes off to disclose a smooth, ivory-white inner bark. The leaves are alternate, or opposite on young shoots, simple, and entire, 4 to 6 in. long and ½ to ¾ in. wide. They are equally bright green on both surfaces and exude a lemon odor when crushed.

Flowers
Creamy-white flowers, in stalked umbels, which bloom in profusion. They attract bees and are an important source of honey. Jan.-Feb. and July-Oct.

Fruit
Urn-shaped brown capsules, ½ in. long; not effective ornamentally.

Root System: Shallow. Roots spread laterally and are voracious.

Rate of Growth: Fairly rapid

Natural Requirements
Climate: Tolerates heat but will not stand cold. Prefers warm, coastal areas.
Soil: Prefers a rich, moist, well-drained soil. Will not tolerate alkali soils.
Exposure: Sun.

Care
Pruning: Head high and stake, when tree is young. Remove suckers and dead and broken branches. Time: Spring.
Feeding: Apply manure annually in the fall.
Watering: Water deeply once a month.
Pests and Diseases: Thrips; spray with DDT, lindane, or malathion in spring and fall as a preventive measure and repeat when needed.

Faults
Makes much litter. Branches are brittle.

Eucalyp´tus cae´sia, Gungurru Eucalyptus, grows to a height of 20 ft., with a 10-ft. spread. It has the same cultural and climatic requirements as Lemon Eucalyptus and like that tree is an excellent specimen plant. The bark of Gungurru Eucalyptus is dull white and the leaves are gray-green. In winter the tree produces a profusion of rose-colored flowers.

Eucalyptus ficifolia

Eucalyp´tus ficifo´lia
Scarlet Eucalyptus

Australia

Features: Flowers, habit

Use: Street, screen, specimen

Scarlet Eucalyptus is a compact, low-branching tree with dark red-brown, persistent bark. It differs from the other eucalypti in its wide-spreading, sturdy branches and its generally heavier appearance. This type produces the most attractive flowers. They bloom practically all year round in temperate climates. Varieties include pink, salmon, red, and intermediate shades. Since it is not possible to obtain true colors of Scarlet Eucalyptus by name, it is advisable to buy the tree when it is in bloom. If the roots are forced downward, in youth, by proper feeding and deep watering, the tree grows to a handsome and practical specimen for use in lining streets. It will thrive only in temperate or warm, coastal areas and is entirely intolerant of cold.

Conformation

Height: 15 to 35 ft. (50 ft.). Spread: 10 to 25 ft. (40 ft.).

A dense, low-branching, compact, roundheaded tree with rough, furrowed, dark red-brown bark which peels only slightly. The leaves, alternate, or opposite on young shoots, simple, and entire, with wavy margins, are 3 to 5 in. long and 1 to 2½ in. wide. They are dark green above, distinctly paler beneath; the new growth is a bronzy red.

Flowers

Pink to crimson, fluffy flowers in large, showy panicles all over the tree. They attract bees and are an important source of honey. They bloom intermittently throughout the year, and most heavily from Jan.-Feb. and July-Oct.

Fruit

Brown, urn-shaped capsules, ¾ to 1½ in. long, which persist throughout the year.

Root System: The strong, shallow roots spread laterally and are voracious.

Rate of Growth: Moderate to slow

Natural Requirements

Climate: Tolerates heat; will not stand cold. Thrives only in mild or warm coastal areas.

Soil: Prefers a light, well-drained, fertile soil. Tolerates drought.

Exposure: Sun. Tolerates smoke, dust, fog, and some wind.

Care

Pruning: Head high and stake, when tree is young. Remove suckers and dead and broken branches. Prune lightly each year to shape as a street tree. Time: Spring.

Feeding: Apply manure annually in the fall, especially when tree is young.

Watering: No special attention necessary. Provide plenty of moisture, when tree is young. Good drainage is essential.

Pests and Diseases: Thrips; spray with DDT, lindane, or malathion in spring and fall as a preventive measure and repeat when needed. A bacterial disease sometimes, though rarely, attacks and kills the tree; there is no cure; remove the tree.

Faults: Makes some litter, but not much. Branches are brittle. Stump sprouts.

Eucalyptus globulus

Eucalyp´tus glob´ulus

Tasmanian Blue Eucalyptus;
Blue Gum

Australia

Features: Foliage, habit

Use: Windbreak, screen, erosion control

Blue Gum grows to a huge roundheaded tree with bright green foliage and a bluish-white, peeling bark. The leaves on young shoots are smoky blue and almost round; they are set close against the stems. This tree attains too great a size and has roots too voracious for use in any but the largest gardens; even there, it should be planted only in the outlying areas, to mark boundaries or provide screens and windbreaks. Blue Gum enjoys moist air and thrives in foggy coastal areas, or along river bottoms where humidity is high.

Conformation

Height: 70 to 150 ft. (200 ft.). Spread: 40 to 60 ft. (80 ft.).

An open-growing, roundheaded tree with an erect, straight trunk. The outer bark peels in long strips to reveal an inner bark delicately tinged with blue. The leaves are alternate, or opposite on young shoots, simple, and entire. The leaves on young shoots are almost as wide as long, with the base of the leaf pressed tight against the stem; they are smoky blue and tomentose. Older leaves are lanceolate, somewhat curved or sickle-like, 6 to 13 in. long and 1 to 1¾ in. wide, and equally bright green on both surfaces.

Flowers

Fragrant, large white flowers, 1 to 1½ in. in diameter. They attract bees and are an important source of honey. Jan.-April.

Fruit

Red-brown, angular, rough, valve-shaped capsules, ¾ to 1 in. long. They are gray when young. Summer.

Root System: The strong, shallow roots spread laterally and are very voracious.

Rate of Growth: Rapid

Natural Requirements

Climate: Tolerates heat but not desert atmosphere. Tolerates cold as low as 25° F. Widely adaptable but grows best in coastal areas and river bottoms where there is moisture in the air.

Soil: Tolerates a variety of soils; prefers a good, deep, moist soil. Stands sterile and alkali soils. Tolerates drought.

Exposure: Sun. Tolerates wind and seacoast conditions.

Care

Pruning: Head high and stake, when tree is young. Remove suckers and dead and broken branches. Time: Spring.

Feeding: No special feeding necessary.

Watering: No special attention necessary.

Pests and Diseases: Thrips; spray with DDT, lindane, or malathion in spring and fall as a preventive measure and repeat when needed.

Faults

Makes much litter. Branches are brittle. Stumps sprout. Roots invade sewers, drains, and other installations and upheave sidewalks.

Eucalyptus polyanthemos

Eucalyp´tus polyan´themos

Australian-Beech;
  Redbox Eucalyptus

Australia

Feature: Foliage

Use: Street (desert areas), windbreak, screen

Australian-Beech grows in many irregular patterns, varying greatly in shape and size according to the climate where it is planted. The soft, silver-gray leaves provide an agreeable contrast note in the landscape and are excellent for use in indoor decoration. Australian-Beech is serviceable as a windbreak and screen, and as a street tree in desert areas, where it grows to a medium-sized tree. It is very durable, standing heat, desert atmospheres, and seacoast conditions and even tolerating some degree of cold.

Conformation
Height: 30 to 70 ft. Spread: 10 to 40 ft.

A picturesque tree, much-branched in irregular patterns from a trunk which is often multiple. The bark is gray, persistent, and somewhat furrowed. The leaves are alternate, or opposite on young shoots, simple, and entire, 2 to 4 in. long and 1½ to 3 in. wide. They are a soft and silvery gray.

Flowers
Small white flowers, ¼ in. in diameter, in stalked umbels 3 in. wide; not effective ornamentally. They attract bees and are an important source of honey. Jan.–March.

Fruit
Urn-shaped brown capsules, ¼ in. or less long; not effective ornamentally. May–June.

Root System: The strong, shallow roots spread laterally and are very voracious.

Rate of Growth: Fairly rapid

Natural Requirements
Climate: Tolerates heat and some degree of cold but will not endure prolonged freezing. Tolerates desert atmosphere.
Soil: Prefers a good, light, well-drained soil. Tolerates drought.
Exposure: Sun. Tolerates wind and seacoast conditions.

Care
Pruning: Head high and stake, when tree is young. Remove suckers and dead and broken branches. Time: Spring.
Feeding: No special feeding necessary.
Watering: No special attention necessary.
Pests and Diseases: Thrips; spray with DDT, lindane, or malathion in spring and fall as a preventive measure and repeat when needed.

Faults
Makes some litter, but not much. Branches are brittle. Stump sprouts.

Eucalyp´tus pulverulen´ta, Dollarleaf Eucalyptus, grows to a height of 30 ft., with a 10-ft. spread. It has an open, rounded crown and silver-gray, roundish leaves which look like silver dollars. The tree has the same cultural and climatic requirements as the Australian Beech and is used in landscaping for windbreaks and screens.

Eucalyptus rudis

Eucalyp′tus ru′dis
Desert Gum; Moitch Eucalyptus

Australia

Features: Habit (under difficult conditions), foliage

Use: Shade, street, windbreak, screen

Desert Gum is a dense, compact tree with heavily pendulous branches and a red-brown bark. The foliage is a dark bluish green and provides a pleasing background for the bronzy-red young growth. Although the tree requires moisture at its roots, it is remarkably tolerant of dry atmosphere and maintains an excellent shape under desert conditions. It is also tolerant of moisture in the air, growing well in seacoast areas and even enduring some degree of cold.

Conformation
Height: 25 to 50 ft. (100 ft.). Spread: 30 to 40 ft.

An erect, compact, dense tree with many drooping branches. The bark is red-brown, rough, and spongy but is not deeply furrowed; it is usually persistent. The leaves are alternate, or opposite on young shoots, simple, and entire, 3 to 6 in. long and ¾ to 2¼ in. wide. They are dark bluish green when mature, and bronzy red when they first open.

Flowers
White flowers, ½ in. in diameter, in stalked umbels; not effective ornamentally. They attract bees and are an important source of honey. Sept.–Nov.

Fruit
Top-shaped brown capsules, 1/3 to 1/2 in. wide, in clusters of four to eight. Oct.–Dec.

Root System: The strong, shallow roots spread laterally and are very voracious.

Rate of Growth: Rapid

Natural Requirements
Climate: Tolerates heat and will stand some degree of cold but not prolonged freezing. Tolerates desert atmosphere.
Soil: Prefers a moist, light, well-drained soil.
Exposure: Sun. Tolerates wind and seacoast conditions.

Care
Pruning: Head high and stake, when tree is young. Remove suckers and dead and broken branches. Time: Spring.
Feeding: No special feeding necessary.
Watering: Water deeply once a month.
Pests and Diseases: Thrips; spray with DDT, lindane, or malathion in spring and fall as a preventive measure and repeat when needed.

Faults
Makes some litter, but not a great deal. Branches are brittle. Stump sprouts.

Eucalyptus sideroxylon rosea

Eucalyp´tus siderox´ylon rose´a
(*E. leucoxylon sideroxylon rosea*)
Mulga Island Eucalyptus; Mulga Island Ironbark; Red Ironbark

Australia

Feature: Flowers
Use: Street, specimen

The tall, straight trunk of Mulga Island Eucalyptus remains unbranched for a good part of its height and rises to a slender, light, and open crown of narrow, bright green leaves which have a bluish cast. The showy flowers are a deep, soft rose color and occur in large clusters; they bloom in winter when flowers are very scarce. Mulga Island Eucalyptus is a useful street tree or a specimen plant for average-sized gardens, holding its shape well under adverse conditions. It stands heat, desert atmosphere, and seacoast conditions, and even tolerates some degree of cold.

Conformation
Height: 30 to 50 ft. Spread: 10 to 40 ft.

A slender, open-headed, upright tree, usually unbranched for some distance up the trunk. The bark is red-brown, rough, and persistent. The leaves are alternate, or opposite on young shoots, simple, and entire, 4 to 6 in. long and ½ to 1 in. wide. They are bright green with a bluish cast.

Flowers
Rose-colored flowers, 3/4 to 1 1/8 in. in diameter, in stalked umbels. They bloom profusely and make a handsome winter display. They attract bees and are an important source of honey. Nov.-Feb.

Fruit
Brown capsules, ½ in. long, usually clustered in threes; not effective ornamentally.

Root System
The strong, shallow roots spread laterally and are very voracious but do not usually come to the surface.

Natural Requirements
Climate: Grows best in warm, coastal areas. Stands some degree of cold. Tolerates desert atmosphere.
Soil: Grows best in light, well-drained soil. Tolerates poor, shallow, sterile soils and also alkali soils. Tolerates drought.
Exposure: Sun. Tolerates wind and seacoast conditions. Tolerates smoke and dust.

Care
Pruning: Head high and stake, when tree is young. Remove suckers and dead and broken branches. Time: Spring.
Feeding: No special feeding necessary.
Watering: No special attention necessary.
Pests and Diseases: Thrips; spray with DDT, lindane, or malathion in spring and fall as a preventive measure and repeat when needed.

Faults: Makes some litter, but not much. Branches are brittle. Stump sprouts.

Eucalyp´tus siderox´ylon purpurea has the same use, habit, and cultural and natural requirements as Mulga Island Eucalyptus, but its flowers are bright purple. *Eucalyp´tus siderox´ylon pal´lens* has the same use, habit, and cultural and natural requirements as Mulga Island Eucalyptus but has red flowers and silver-gray leaves.

Eugenia paniculata

Eugénia paniculáta

(*E. hookeri; E. hookeriana*)

Brush-Cherry

Australia

Features: Foliage, flowers, fruit, habit

Use: Hedge, patio, tub, specimen

Brush-Cherry matures from a columnar young tree to a densely rounded pyramid. Neat and distinctive at every stage of its growth, it is effective for use in hedges or in patios and tubs. Unfortunately, it is sensitive to wind, heat, and cold, and thrives only in temperate areas.

Conformation

Height: 10 to 25 ft. (45 ft.). Spread: 8 to 15 ft. (20 ft.).

A columnar tree when young, and a rounded, dense pyramid with slightly pendulous branches when mature. The leaves are simple, opposite, and entire, 2½ to 4¼ in. long and ¾ to 1½ in. wide. They are dark green and glossy; the young growth is tinged with bronzy red.

Flowers

Creamy-white flowers, ½ in. in diameter, with numerous, prominent stamens. They are scattered all over the tree in loose terminal clusters. June–Aug.

Fruit

Edible, rose-purple fruit, ¾ in. long, in clusters 8 to 12 in. long. It makes excellent jelly. Oct.–Nov.

Root System: Shallow

Rate of Growth: Rapid

Natural Requirements

Climate: Prefers temperate areas. Will not tolerate extreme heat or cold.

Soil: Prefers a heavy, well-drained, moist soil.

Exposure: Sun or partial shade. Protect from wind.

Care

Pruning: Stands any amount of shearing. Crotches are weak; lighten branches to prevent breakage. Time: Spring.

Feeding: Apply a small quantity of commercial fertilizer annually in spring. Do not apply manure.

Watering: Provide plenty of moisture. Good drainage is essential.

Pests and Diseases: Thrips; spray with DDT, lindane, or malathion in spring and fall as a preventive measure and repeat when needed.

Faults

Branches tend to break under the load of leaves unless the tree is properly thinned and pruned.

Eugénia paniculáta austrális (*E. myrtifolia*), Australian Brush-Cherry, grows to the same height and width as the species; it has the same cultural and natural requirements and is used for the same landscaping purposes. However, it is more compact and has smaller leaves, which are arranged tightly on the branches and boil up in rounded patterns to a dense, columnar shape. Its fruits, smaller and less attractive than those of the species, ripen intermittently throughout the year.

Acména smithi (*E. smithi*), Lilli-Pilli Tree, grows slowly to a height of 30 ft. It has bronze-tinged foliage, white flowers, and lavender-pink berries in handsome, loose, drooping clusters. It grows best in partial shade.

Feature: Foliage

Use: Shade, specimen

Moreton Bay Fig is a handsome, impressive tree, spreading to an enormous girth and characterized by a large, bulging, buttressed trunk. The leaves are tropical-appearing, large, and leathery, a dark, shiny green above and brownish beneath. Moreton Bay Fig is a useful heavy-shade tree or specimen plant for large gardens, but it should never be used in small gardens or in areas where its large root system is likely to become a nuisance. It thrives only in temperate or warm coastal regions.

Conformation
Height: 40 to 60 ft. Spread: 60 to 100 ft.

A wide-spreading tree with thick, stout branches forming a broad, dense, rounded crown. The trunk is conspicuously swollen at the base and is buttressed. The bark is light gray and —in older specimens—wrinkled, seemingly like an elephant's hide. The leaves are simple, alternate, and entire; 6 to 10 in. long and 3 to 4 in. wide; thick and leathery. They are dark green and glabrous above and brownish beneath.

Flowers
Not effective ornamentally.

Fruit
Inedible, purplish fruit, ¾ to 1 in. in diameter, spotted with white. June–Aug.

Root System
Strong, shallow roots, usually bulging and surfacing around the base of the tree.

Rate of Growth: Moderate

Natural Requirements
Climate: Grows best in subtropical climates. Tolerates heat but will stand only a slight degree of cold.
Soil: Tolerates a variety of soils.
Exposure: Sun or shade. Tolerates wind and seacoast conditions.

Care
Pruning: Prune very little; the tree grows naturally to a good shape. When cut, it bleeds a white, milky substance, which is unsightly but not harmful. Time: Summer.
Feeding: No special feeding necessary.
Watering: No special attention necessary.
Pests and Diseases: Relatively free from both.

Faults
Its roots surface and heave up the ground around it.

Ficus retusa (*F. nitida*), Indian Laurel Fig, grows rapidly to a height of 50 ft. It is densely covered with dark-green, oval leaves, 2 to 4 in. long. It has yellowish-red fruit, about ¼ in. long. In landscaping, it is used for shade, streets, patios, and tubs. The tree thrives in temperate areas.

Ficus macrophylla

Fi´cus macrophyl´la

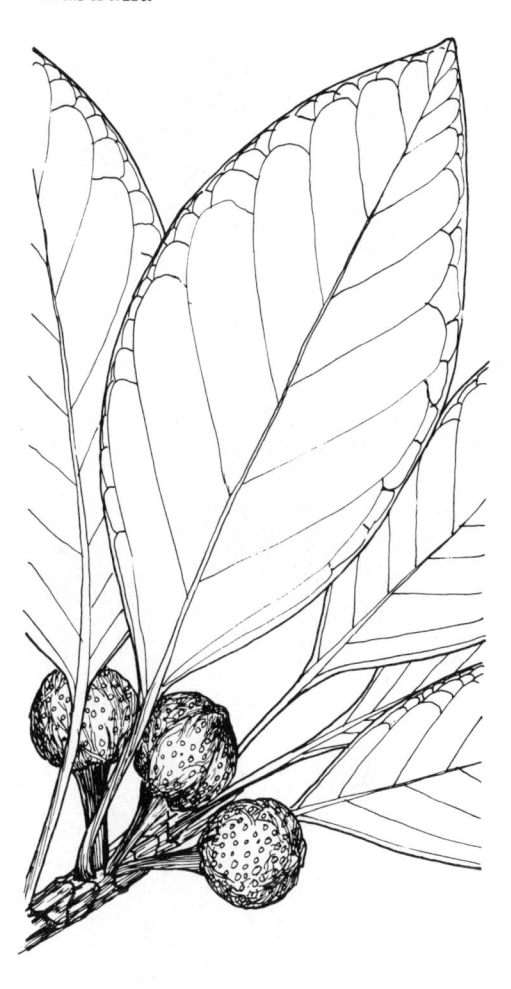

Moreton Bay Fig

Australia

Fremontia californica

Fremont́ia califor′nica
Flannel Bush

California

Feature: Flowers
Use: Hedge, screen, accent, erosion control

Flannel Bush is shrublike in habit and does not assume a good natural shape. The foliage is variable but is usually maple-like and dark green, with whitish or rusty, hairy undersurfaces. The tree is grown exclusively for its large, yellow flowers, which bloom profusely and almost continuously throughout the early summer months. Growing readily in poor, dry soils, Flannel Bush is a cheerful and effective plant for use in difficult areas. It tolerates wind, desert atmosphere, and seacoast conditions but will not stand extreme cold.

Conformation
Height: 10 to 20 ft. Spread: 6 to 18 ft.

An open-growing, shrublike plant with a haphazard branching habit. The leaves are simple, alternate, and variable, usually three- to five-lobed and maple-like, ½ to 3 in. long and ¼ to 2 in. wide. They are dark green and rough above, brownish or felty whitish beneath, and thick.

Flowers
Solitary, lemon-yellow flowers, 1½ to 2½ in. in diameter; very profuse. May–July.

Fruit
Hairy, conical capsules, about 1 in. long, which tend to persist on the tree. Sept.–Oct.

Root System: Shallow

Rate of Growth: Rapid

Natural Requirements
Climate: Tolerates heat and some degree of cold but will not endure extremely cold areas. Tolerates desert atmosphere.
Soil: Prefers a light, dry soil. Tolerates drought.
Exposure: Sun. Tolerates wind and seacoast conditions.

Care
Pruning: Head high to shape as a tree. Prune to maintain a good shape. Time: Spring.
Feeding: No special feeding necessary.
Watering: Little moisture is required. Good drainage is essential. Do not water in summer.
Pests and Diseases: Aphids; spray with nicotine, lindane, or malathion when needed.

Fremont́ia mexica′na has the same cultural and natural requirements as Flannel Bush and is used for the same landscaping purposes. It is perhaps preferable to Flannel Bush as an ornamental because the leaves are more consistently maple-like and larger. The flowers, too, are larger and are a deeper yellow; the undersides of the petals are tinged with orange.

Features: Foliage, flowers

Use: Screen, specimen (for outlying areas), erosion control

Silk-Oak is a narrow tree, growing to many picturesque shapes, with dark-green feathery foliage and slender sprays of showy orange flowers, which bloom in summer. The tree is prized for its decorative features; but it must be used with caution because of its invasive roots and brittle branches. Definitely, it should be relegated to the outlying areas of large gardens where it can be admired safely from a distance. The extensive use of Silk-Oak in tubs is entirely impractical, for its roots can not be confined for very long. The tree tolerates heat and some degree of cold but will not stand prolonged freezing.

Conformation

Height: 30 to 70 ft. (100 ft.) Spread: 10 to 35 ft.

An open-headed, narrow, picturesque tree with many large, upright-spreading branches. The foliage is alternate and twice-compound, 6 to 12 in. long and as wide, and composed of numerous toothed or entire leaflets. These are a deep, dark green above and silky white beneath.

Flowers

Numerous, bright orange flowers in slender sprays 2 to 4 in. long. The flowers are highly decorative. May–June.

Fruit

Brown, woody pods containing one or two flat, winged seeds; not effective ornamentally. Sept.–Oct.

Root System: Shallow. Roots strong and voracious.

Rate of Growth: Rapid

Natural Requirements

Climate: Grows best in mild, dry regions. Tolerates heat and some cold but will not endure prolonged freezing. Tolerates desert atmosphere.

Soil: Grows best in dry, infertile, well-drained, light soils. Tolerates poor, sandy or rich, deep soils and also drought.

Exposure: Sun. Will not tolerate wind.

Care

Pruning: Head back, when tree is young, to eliminate brittle branches. Remove dead or broken branches; otherwise do not prune. Time: Late spring.

Feeding: No special feeding necessary. Withstands neglect.

Watering: No special moisture requirements. Prefers a rather dry soil.

Pests and Diseases: Scale and mealy bug; spray with malathion or an oil emulsion in summer and repeat when needed; spray with oil in winter.

Faults

Makes litter. Has brittle branches and invasive and voracious roots.

Grevillea robusta

Grevil´lea robus´ta

Silk-Oak

Australia

Harpephyllum caffrum

Harpephyl´lum caf´frum
Kafir-Plum

South Africa

Features: Foliage, fruit

Use: Shade, quick effects, specimen

Kafir-Plum grows naturally to a roundheaded tree but can be pruned, when young, to assume many picturesque shapes. The leaves are a glossy dark green when mature, and a clear, bright red when they first open. The dark-red fruit, which ripens in summer, is edible; it has a thin pulp and an acid flavor. The tree is highly useful in providing quick effects in new gardens, growing rapidly to a good size. It thrives only in temperate regions.

Conformation

Height: 30 ft. Spread: 20 ft.

A roundheaded tree with numerous, spreading branches. The leaves are alternate and compound, composed of numerous curved and sickle-shaped leaflets, 2½ in. long. They are a bright red when they first open and are a glossy dark green when mature.

Flowers

Tiny white flowers in axillary panicles; not effective ornamentally.

Fruit

Edible, dark red fruit, the size and shape of a large olive. It has a thin pulp and a very acid taste. June-Aug.

Root System: Average depth

Rate of Growth: Rapid

Natural Requirements

Climate: Grows best in mild or warm, coastal climates. Tolerates heat; will not stand freezing.
Soil: Prefers a light, moist, well-drained soil.
Exposure: Sun or partial shade. Tolerates wind and seacoast conditions.

Care

Pruning: When tree is young, prune to any desired shape. Thin out head occasionally. Time: Spring.
Feeding: Apply a balanced commercial fertilizer annually in spring.
Watering: Water deeply once a month. Good drainage is essential.
Pests and Diseases: Relatively free from both.

Features: Flowers, habit

Use: Street, lawn, patio, tub, specimen

Sweetshade is a slender tree with a symmetrical, upright habit of growth and shiny, neat, dark-green foliage. In late spring and early summer the tree is covered with large, fragrant, honey-colored flowers, which grow in loose clusters at the ends of the branches. Sweetshade makes a good street tree in wind-free areas and is a useful specimen for lawns, patios, or tubs. It will not tolerate extremes of heat and cold and thrives only in temperate or warm, coastal areas.

Conformation

Height: 10 to 40 ft. (50 ft.) Spread: 5 to 20 ft.

An open-headed, symmetrical tree with a slender, neat, pyramidal habit, often characterized by three strong, forked branches arising from a single long, bare trunk. The leaves are simple, alternate, entire or sometimes undulate, 2 to 6 in. long and 1 to 2 in. wide, and pointed sharply at the apex. They are dark green and glabrous and are often crowded at the ends of the branches.

Flowers

Jasmine-fragrant, tubular, honey-colored flowers marked with red at the throat; in loose terminal clusters. The flowers are 1 in. in diameter. They attract bees. May–June.

Fruit

Smooth, flat, lantern-like capsules, 1 in. long and nearly as wide. June–July.

Root System: Average depth

Rate of Growth: Moderate

Natural Requirements

Climate: Grows best in temperate areas. Should be protected from heat and cold.
Soil: Tolerates any moist, well-drained soil.
Exposure: Sun. Tolerates warm coastal conditions. Protect from wind.

Care

Pruning: Prune, when tree is young, to eliminate weak branches at base. Time: Spring
Feeding: No special feeding necessary.
Watering: Water deeply once a month. Good drainage is essential.
Pests and Diseases: Resistant to both.

Faults

Branches are brittle unless pruned to strong crotches when young.

Hymenosporum flavum

Hymenos´porum fla´vum
Sweetshade

Australia

Ilex aquifolium

I ́lex aquifo ́lium
English Holly

Southern Europe; northern Africa; western Asia

Features: Fruit, leaves

Use: Lawn, hedge, patio, tub, specimen

English Holly grows to a narrow, oval-topped tree with numerous, slender branches reaching almost to the ground. The shiny, prickly foliage and bright red berries are well-known features of the winter landscape and are used extensively in indoor decoration. The tree grows best in cool, humid areas and is an effective specimen for lawn, patio, tub, and hedge planting.

Conformation

Height: 20 to 40 ft. Spread: 10 to 20 ft.

A dense, erect, somewhat oval-topped tree with numerous but not wide-spreading branches that reach almost to the ground. The leaves are simple and alternate and have strong, spiny teeth, 1½ to 3 in. long and 1 to 1½ in. wide. They are a shiny dark green. Varieties are available with foliage marked and edged with silver, white, yellow, and gray-green. A variety, Vantol, or Dutch Holly, has larger individual berries than the species and larger leaves, which are somewhat twisted near the apex; the leaves are spineless or are armed with a few spiny teeth.

Flowers

Tiny, fragrant white flowers; not effective ornamentally. Male and female flowers occur on different trees. May–June.

Fruit

Bright red berries, 1/3 in. in diameter, which grow in large clusters on the previous year's growth. Only female trees bear fruit; it is best to buy trees in berry. Pollination is essential to set fruit; therefore, on grounds where there is not room for both male and female trees, female trees that have been grafted with male branches should be planted. Fall and winter.

Root System: Deep

Rate of Growth: Slow

Natural Requirements

Climate: Grows best in cool areas where plenty of moisture is in the air. Tolerates both cold and heat but does not thrive in dry atmosphere.

Soil: Grows best in deep, rich, moist, well-drained, fairly heavy soil. Will not tolerate alkali soils.

Exposure: Partial shade or sun, in cool areas. Tolerates wind and seacoast conditions.

Care

Pruning: Prune, when tree is young, to a single trunk; later, head in when necessary. The tree bears on the previous year's wood and stands severe pruning. It is usually pruned by cutting for berries in the winter, but can be pruned all year round.

Feeding: Apply a small quantity of balanced commercial fertilizer annually in spring; apply manure annually in the fall.

Watering: Provide plenty of moisture. Good drainage is essential.

Pests and Diseases: Relatively free from both When holly-leaf miner is present, spray with lindane, chlordane, or malathion; destroy infested leaves whenever possible.

Features: Foliage, flowers

Use: Street, patio

Sugarplum Tree, when it is full grown, has a dense, pyramidal shape and an unusually symmetrical branching habit. The leaves are two-toned—olive-green above and gray beneath—and the flowers, which open in summer, are like small, rose-colored hibiscus blossoms. The tree is effective in patios or near houses, especially with redwood as a background, and is an excellent specimen for street plantings. Unfortunately, it produces unsightly and persistent pods which cause a skin irritation and itching. It thrives only in temperate areas.

Conformation

Height: 20 to 40 ft. Spread: 10 to 20 ft.

A dense, pyramidal tree with regularly spaced, ascending branches. The leaves are simple, alternate, and entire, 2 to 4 in. long and ¾ to 1½ in. wide. They are thick and leathery, a dark olive green above and gray and scurfy beneath.

Flowers

Soft rose-pink (rarely white), solitary flowers, 2 in. in diameter, which resemble a small hibiscus bloom. They are profuse and quite showy. Summer.

Fruit

Drab, fuzzy pods, which persist on the tree and are unsightly. They cause an itching of the skin. Oct.-Dec.

Root System: Average depth to deep.

Rate of Growth: Moderate

Natural Requirements

Climate: Prefers temperate areas. Will not tolerate cold.
Soil: Grows best in deep, fertile, sandy soil. Develops poorly in shallow, heavy, or sterile soils.
Exposure: Sun. Tolerates wind and seacoast conditions.

Care

Pruning: Thin out branches occasionally. Time: Spring.
Feeding: No special feeding necessary.
Watering: No special attention necessary.
Pests and Diseases: Relative free from both.

Faults

Unsightly and persistent pods cause skin irritation.

Lagunaria patersoni

Laguna´ria paterso´ni

Sugarplum Tree;
   Queensland Pyramid Tree

Australia

Laurus nobilis

Laúrus nóbilis

Sweet Bay; Grecian Laurel; True Bay

Mediterranean region

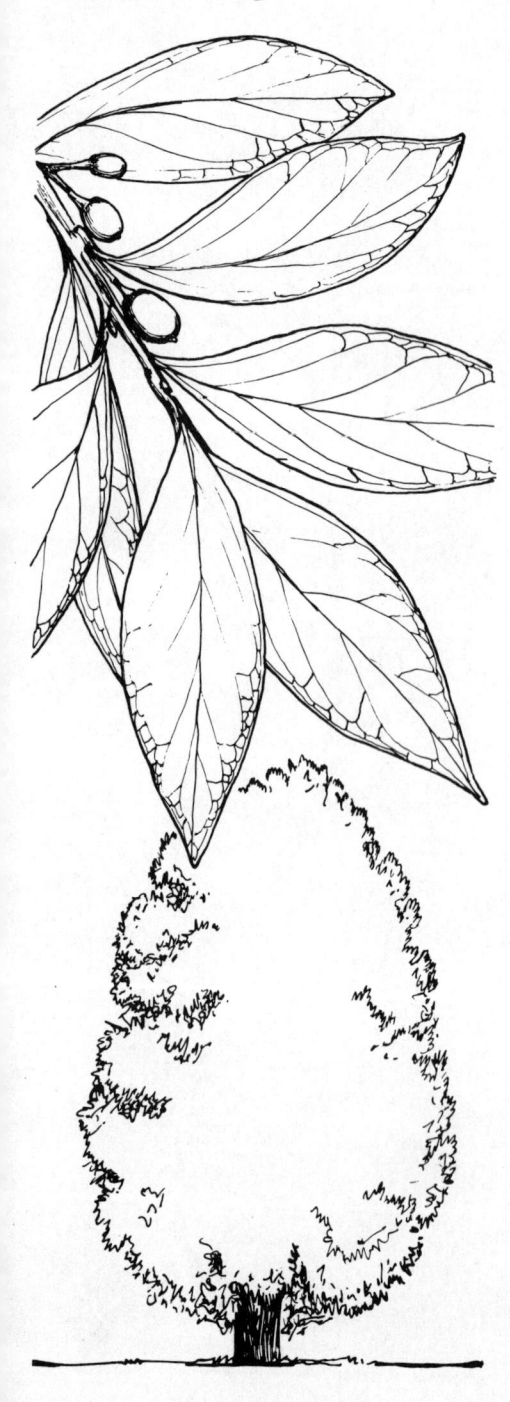

Feature: Foliage

Use: Shade, hedge, tubs

Sweet Bay grows naturally to a multiple-trunked tree with a perfectly round shape and dense foliage which casts heavy shade. However, it is seen in gardens more often as a tubbed specimen, trained either in the shape of a globe, or a pyramid, or an oval, depending upon the type of architecture it is planned to complement. Because of its slow growth and beautiful dark-green foliage, it is well suited to this use. Historically, Sweet Bay is the tree which has symbolized truth and achievement throughout the ages, and it was the favorite tree of poets and scholars in ancient Greece. It will tolerate heat and some degree of cold but grows at its best in mild coastal areas where moist air is prevalent.

Conformation

Height: 20 to 40 ft. (60 ft.) Spread: 20 to 40 ft. (60 ft.)

A dense, bushy, roundheaded, often multiple-trunked tree, with many, wide-spreading, ascending branches. The bark is gray and deeply wrinkled. The leaves are simple, alternate, and entire, 2¼ to 4 in. long and ¾ to 1¾ in. wide. They are a shiny dark green, stiff, and leathery and are densely arranged on the tree. Leaves are used for seasoning foods and flavoring confections.

Flowers

Small greenish or yellowish-white flowers; not effective ornamentally. Spring.

Fruit

Purple-to-black berries, 1/4 to 3/8 in. in diameter; not effective ornamentally. An oil extracted from the berries is used to make perfume. Fall.

Root System: Average to deep

Rate of Growth: Slow

Natural Requirements

Climate: Tolerates heat. Will stand a good deal of frost but will not endure prolonged freezing. Prefers mild, coastal areas where moist air is prevalent.
Soil: Prefers a rich, moist, well-drained, sandy loam.
Exposure: Sun or shade. Tolerates a fair amount of wind and seacoast conditions.

Care

Pruning: Stands severe pruning. Trim to required shape, taking proper precautions not to mutilate the leaves. Time: Spring or summer.
Feeding: Requires annual feeding. Apply liquid manure or a manure mulch in spring or early summer.
Watering: Provide plenty of moisture. Good drainage is essential.
Pests and Diseases: Scale; spray with malathion or an oil emulsion in summer and repeat when needed; spray with oil in winter.

Ligustrum lucidum

Ligus´trum lu´cidum

(L. japonicum macrophyllum; L. spicatum)

Glossy Privet

China; Korea; Japan

Features: Foliage, flowers

Use: Street (narrow parkways), hedge, screen, patio, tub

Glossy Privet is typically a many-stemmed shrub; to make a specimen tree it must be pruned, when young, to a single trunk. When so trained, it forms a tight, round head of closely placed, dark-green, glossy leaves, which are graced in summer by large, erect clusters of white flowers. This tree is easy of culture and maintains a bright, clean look all year round, except in areas where extreme and prolonged winter cold causes some dropping of leaves.

Conformation

Height: 10 to 25 ft. (30 ft.). Spread: 20 to 40 ft.

A tree with many upright branches and a dense, compact, round head. The leaves are simple, opposite, and entire, 2½ to 5 in. long and 1¼ to 2 in. wide, and have a rounded base and pointed apex. They are a very glossy dark green, thick, and leathery; most of them are half-folded or trough-shaped.

Flowers

Tiny fragrant white flowers, closely set in pyramidal clusters 4 to 8 in. long. July-Aug.

Fruit

Black, berry-like fruit, ¼ in. in diameter, which has some ornamental significance. Sept.-Feb.

Root System: Deep

Rate of Growth: Rapid in youth, slowing toward maturity.

Natural Requirements

Climate: Tolerates heat. Stands some degree of cold but tends to lose leaves in colder climates. Adaptable.

Soil: Tolerates a wide variety of soils and also drought.

Exposure: Sun or shade. Tolerates seacoast conditions, and wind to some extent.

Care

Pruning: Stands severe pruning. Train, when tree is young, to a single trunk, and later trim to maintain shape. Avoid all unnecessary pruning, for bearing and blooming qualities suffer from too much cutting. Time: All year round in mild climates; spring in cold areas.

Feeding: Apply a small quantity of balanced commercial fertilizer mixed with bone meal in spring; apply manure in the fall.

Watering: No special attention is necessary. Good drainage is essential.

Pests and Diseases: Relatively free from both.

Lyonothamnus floribundus

Lyonotham´nus floribun´dus

Catalina Ironwood

Islands off the southern California coast

Features: Foliage, bark, flowers
Use: Hedge, specimen

Catalina Ironwood is an unpredictable tree, varying from slender to wide-spreading and often branching from the base with many crooked stems. The reddish-brown bark peels in long, vertical strips, and these weather to a silver gray. The leaves are variable; they are dark green, sometimes simple and bladelike, sometimes compound and fernlike, and they afford a charming texture contrast on the tree. In summer, large flat-topped clusters of tiny white flowers appear at the extreme ends of the branches. The variety *asplenifolius* has a preponderance of compound leaves and is considered more ornamental than the species. The trees thrive only in temperate areas.

Conformation
Height: 25 to 50 ft. (80 ft.). Spread: 15 to 40 ft. (varies).

An unpredictable tree which varies from slender to wide-spreading, assuming many picturesque forms, often with many crooked stems rising from the base. The bark is dark reddish brown and peels in long, vertical strips, which gradually turn a silver gray. The leaves are opposite and of two kinds: a simple, bladelike leaf, 4 to 6 in. long and ½ in. wide, with numerous minute teeth; and a compound, fernlike leaf composed of three to eight deeply cut leaflets. They are dark green above, paler beneath.

Flowers
Tiny white flowers, ¼ in. in diameter, in large, flat-topped, loosely branched, terminal clusters, 4 to 8 in. wide. June–July.

Fruit
Woody capsules, ¼ in. long; not effective ornamentally.

Root System: Average depth

Rate of Growth: Moderate

Natural Requirements
Climate: Will not tolerate extreme heat or cold. Prefers mild, coastal areas.
Soil: Prefers a well-drained soil of some fertility. Tolerates drought.
Exposure: Sun. Tolerates seacoast conditions.

Care
Pruning: Stands severe pruning. If a specimen is desired, prune to a single trunk, when tree is young. Thereafter, prune only to shape. Time: Spring and summer.
Feeding: No special feeding necessary.
Watering: No special attention necessary. Good drainage is essential.
Pests and Diseases: Relatively free from both.

Faults
Stump sprouts.

Features: Fruit, flowers

Use: Patio, tub, specimen

Macadamia ternifolia

Macada´mia ternifo´lia

Queensland Nut

New South Wales

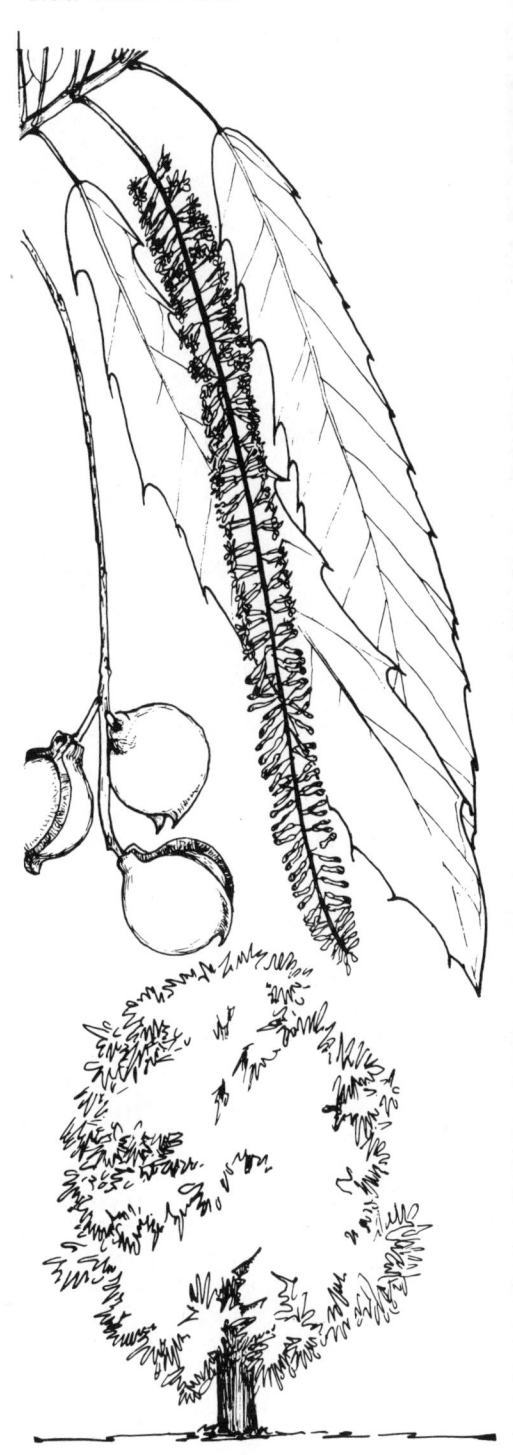

Macadamia is a low-branching, roundheaded tree which is covered each spring with long sprays of delicate white flowers. The fruit is a small, round, edible nut, which tastes like a Brazil nut but has a milder flavor. Macadamia grows very slowly and should be planted in the garden where other trees will supply the necessary landscape features while it is maturing. The tree is quite sensitive to cold and to dry heat and should be considered for use only in mild or subtropical areas.

Conformation

Height: 25 to 30 ft. (50 ft.). Spread: 20 to 30 ft.

An erect, low-branching, roundheaded tree of dense habit, which often has a multiple trunk. The leaves are simple, arranged in whorls of three or four, and entire to irregularly spined, 5 to 12 in. long and 1 to 2 in. wide. They are bright green. Leathery, smooth, and lustrous, they somewhat resemble elongated holly leaves.

Flowers

Small white flowers, in pairs and in racemes nearly 12 in. long. Spring.

Fruit

Round, edible nuts, 1 to 1¼ in. in diameter, enclosed in hard, leathery husks. They have a rich, white meat. Macadamia nuts will fill well only in subtropical climates; they are ripe when they fall from the tree. Fall. The tree will bear when six to eight years old.

Root System: Deep

Rate of Growth: Slow

Natural Requirements

Climate: Likes heat but not dry heat. Will not tolerate cold below 26° F. Prefers mild, subtropical areas and will bear good fruit only in such areas.

Soil: Prefers a deep, rich, moist loam. The tree survives in dry soils, but its rate of growth slows almost to a stop.

Exposure: Sun.

Care

Pruning: Little is required. Time: Spring.

Feeding: Apply a small quantity of balanced commercial fertilizer annually in spring.

Watering: Provide plenty of moisture. Good drainage is essential.

Pests and Diseases: Relatively free from both.

Magnolia grandiflora

Magnólia grandiflóra
Southern Magnolia; Bull-Bay

Southeastern United States

Features: Flowers, foliage, habit

Use: Shade, street, lawn, tubs, specimen, espalier

Southern Magnolia is a wide-spreading, heavy, rounded tree with a very symmetrical shape. The large, glossy dark-green leaves have rusty undersurfaces and are used effectively in indoor decoration. The flowers, although huge and heavily fragrant, have a delicate and fragile appearance — the buds are tightly folded like those of a rose and open into pure-white, cup-shaped blossoms. The tree blooms intermittently throughout the year and most profusely from April to July. Wherever space permits its proper development, Southern Magnolia makes a handsome specimen for use in streets, lawns, and tubs, and provides deep and heavy shade. In smaller gardens, patios, or tubs, or for espalier, the variety *exoniensis* is particularly adaptable. This variety has the same foliage, habit, and flowers as the species but grows only to a height of 25 to 30 ft. and blooms when very young.

Conformation
Height: 40 to 60 ft. (80 ft.). Spread: 50 to 70 ft.

An erect, dense, compact, symmetrically roundheaded or pyramidal tree with wide-spreading branches. The bark is dark brown and rough. The leaves are simple, alternate, and entire, 4 to 10 in. long and 2 to 3½ in. wide. They are a very glossy dark green above, rusty-tomentose beneath, and are stiff and leathery.

Flowers
Pure-white, waxy, cup-shaped flowers, 6 to 10 in. in diameter, usually 6-petaled. They have a heavy, soapy fragrance. The species blooms only when mature, though var. *exoniensis* blooms when young. Intermittently throughout the year; most heavily April–July.

Fruit
Egg-shaped fruit, 3 to 4 in. long and 1 to 1½ in. wide, pink changing to brown, tomentose, and with scarlet seeds on the surface. Late summer.

Root System: Deep

Rate of Growth: Slow in youth; moderate toward maturity

Natural Requirements
Climate: Grows best in hot, humid regions. Tolerates heat and a good deal of cold but not prolonged freezing.
Soil: Grows best in deep, moist, well-drained, heavy, fertile soil; tolerates a slight acidity.
Exposure: Sun. Tolerates a fair amount of wind.

Care
Pruning: When tree is young, thin out to reduce weight and establish framework. Time: Feb.–March. Large branches may be cut for indoor decoration at any time of year without damage to the tree.
Feeding: Apply a manure mulch once every two years.
Watering: Water deeply once a month. Good drainage is essential.
Pests and Diseases: Relatively free from both. Scale sometimes is a nuisance; spray with malathion or an oil emulsion in summer and repeat when needed; spray with oil in winter.

Faults
Difficult to transplant unless roots are properly balled or boxed.

Features: Habit, foliage

Use: Street, lawn, screen, copse, specimen

Chile Mayten is a narrow, graceful, pendulous tree with dense, light-green foliage, which is used effectively in indoor decoration. The tree tends to have a multiple trunk and should be pruned, when young, to shape as a specimen plant. Dainty and delicate in appearance, the Mayten is excellent for small gardens, streets, or lawns; when planted in groups, it makes a lovely grove or screen. It stands some degree of cold but will not tolerate prolonged freezing and grows best in mild, coastal regions.

Conformation

Height: 20 to 30 ft. Spread: 10 to 20 ft.

A narrow, graceful, roundheaded tree with many long pendulous branchlets and a wiry trunk which tends to divide into several main stems. The leaves are simple, alternate, and fine-toothed, 1 to 2 in. long and ¼ to ½ in. wide. They are smooth and thin and are a soft light green. Although the leaves are very densely arranged on the branches, the tree has a dainty and delicate appearance.

Flowers

Minute greenish-white flowers in axillary clusters; not effective ornamentally. May–June.

Fruit

Small, scarlet capsules, about the size of a pea; not highly ornamental. Aug.–Sept.

Root System: Average depth to deep

Rate of Growth

Moderate, as a rule. Rapid for the first few years, then slower.

Natural Requirements

Climate: Tolerates heat and some degree of cold but will not endure prolonged freezing.

Soil: Prefers a rich, moist, well-drained soil.

Exposure: Sun or shade. Tolerates seacoast conditions.

Care

Pruning: When tree is young, prune to a single trunk; later remove suckers and thin top. Stands any amount of shearing.
Time: Spring or fall.

Feeding: Apply a small quantity of balanced commercial fertilizer annually in spring. Apply manure annually in the fall.

Watering: Provide plenty of moisture. Good drainage is essential.

Pests and Diseases: Relatively free from both.

Maytenus boaria

Mayte´nus boa´ria
(M. chilensis)
Chile Mayten Tree

Chile

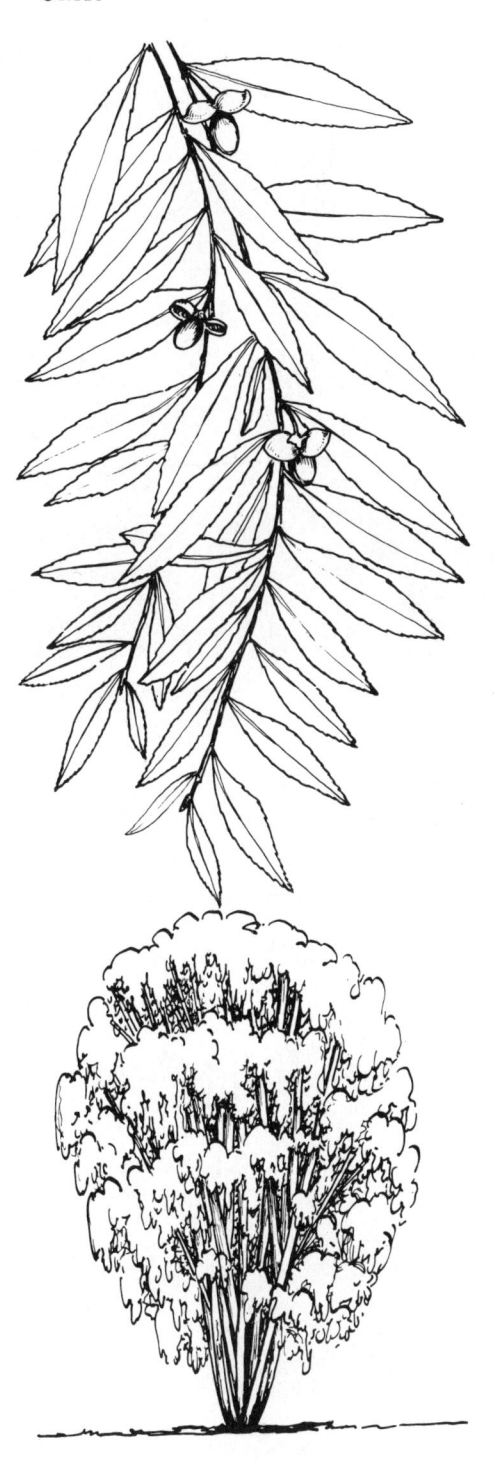

Melaleuca leucadendron

Melaleu'ca leucaden'dron

Cajeput Tree; Swamp Tea Tree; Punk Tree

Australia

Features: Flowers, young foliage

Use: Street, lawn, patio, erosion control

Cajeput Tree is a tall, slender, upright-spreading tree with graceful, pendulous branches. Long clusters of white flowers appear in summer and last for a long while. The young foliage, too, opens like a flower, red and silky-textured. Cajeput Tree is a strong-growing plant which displays an amazing tolerance of adverse conditions. It will grow in dry or swampy areas, even where there is salt in both soil and air. It does well on the seacoast and in the desert, and even tolerates some degree of cold.

Conformation

Height: 40 ft. Spread: 15 ft.

An upright-growing, slender tree with pendulous branches. The bark is gray, thick, and spongy and sheds in many thin layers. The leaves are simple, alternate, and entire, 2 to 4 in. long and 3/8 to 3/4 in. wide. They are pale green and glabrous on both surfaces, and the young growth is red when it opens. From the leaves an oil is extracted which is used in making medicines.

Flowers

Creamy-white flowers, displaying prominent stamens, clustered in spikes 1½ to 4 in. long. July-Oct.

Fruit

Red-brown cup-shaped capsules, 3/16 in. wide, in 1½- to 3-in. cylinders. They are attractive and interesting but not highly ornamental and tend to persist on the tree.

Root System: Average depth

Rate of Growth: Rapid

Natural Requirements

Climate: Tolerates heat and some degree of cold but will not endure prolonged freezing. Tolerates desert atmosphere.

Soil: Tolerates any soil—alkali, salt, or swampy. Tolerates drought.

Exposure: Sun. Tolerates salt air, wind, and other seacoast conditions.

Care

Pruning: When tree is young, head high and prune to promote a bushy crown. Since new growth does not spring from old wood, care must be exercised in trimming. Time: Spring.

Feeding: No special feeding necessary.

Watering: No special moisture requirements.

Pests and Diseases: Resistant and relative free from both.

Faults

Reseeds excessively in moist soils.

Features: Flowers, foliage

Use: Street, hedge, patio, tub

New Zealand Christmas Tree is a much-branched tree somewhat resembling the California Live Oak in appearance. The leaves are medium-sized and dark green, and the undersurfaces are covered with white woolly hairs. In summer, large clusters of dark-red flowers bloom at the ends of the branches and are quite showy in contrast to the green-and-white leaves. Because of its slow growth, New Zealand Christmas Tree remains a reasonable size for a good many years and is therefore useful in small gardens, patios, or tubs. It will thrive only in warm, coastal areas.

Conformation
Height: 20 to 30 ft. (60 ft.) Spread: 35 to 40 ft. (70 ft.)

A wide-spreading tree with many, sturdy branches that start close to the ground. The leaves are simple, opposite, and entire; 1 to 4 in. long and ½ to 1½ in. wide; thick, and leathery. They are dark green above and usually white-tomentose beneath.

Flowers
Showy dark-red flowers, in dense clusters, 4 to 6 in. in diameter, at the ends of the branches. The stamens of each flower are quite prominent. June–July.

Fruit
Brown, cup-shaped, leathery, woody capsules, 3/8 in. long, in clusters, 2 to 3 in. in diameter. July–Aug. Persist on the tree into the following year.

Root System: Average depth

Rate of Growth: Slow, particularly in heavy soils

Natural Requirements
Climate: Grows best in warm, coastal regions. Tolerates heat; will not stand cold.

Soil: Grows best in fairly fertile, moist, well-drained, sandy soil.

Exposure: Sun. Tolerates seacoast conditions.

Care
Pruning: Thin out occasionally to remove dead wood. Time: Spring.

Feeding: Apply a small quantity of balanced commercial fertilizer and bone meal annually in spring.

Watering: Water deeply once a month. Good drainage is essential.

Pests and Diseases: Relatively free from both.

Faults
Capsules are persistent.

Metrosideros tomentosa

Metrosíde′ros tomento′sa

New Zealand Christmas Tree; Iron Tree

New Zealand

Olea europaea

O´lea europae´a
Common Olive

Mediterranean region; western Asia

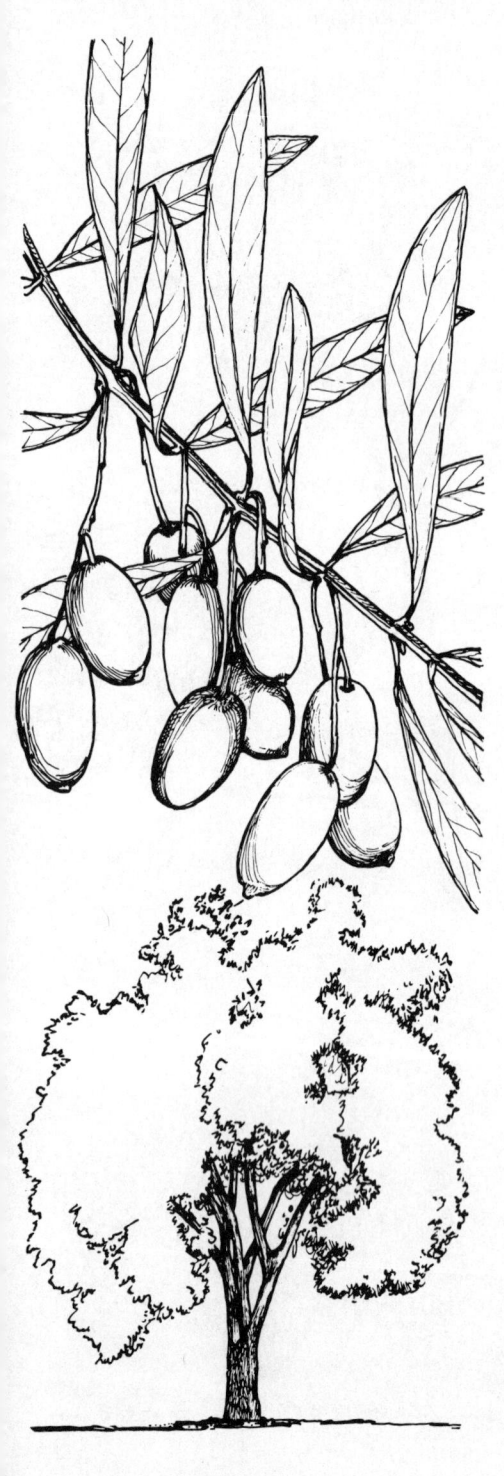

Features: Fruit, foliage

Use: Street, lawn, hedge, orchard, patio, tubs

The habit of the Olive is conditioned by the soil in which it grows; it becomes a dense, rounded tree in poor soils, and an open-growing specimen in good ones. It is a small tree adaptable for use where space is limited; it tolerates heat and some degree of cold.

Conformation
Height: 15 to 30 ft. (50 ft.). Spread: 20 to 40 ft.

A tree of variable habit: densely rounded in poor soils, open and asymmetrical in good ones. At maturity, the trunk becomes gnarled and boils up at the base. The bark is smooth and gray. The leaves are simple, opposite, and entire, 1½ to 2¾ in. long and 3/8 to 5/8 in. wide, leathery in texture, and tapering at the base. They are dull, gray-green above and silvery tomentose beneath.

Flowers
Not effective ornamentally. Olive trees should never be transplanted when in flower. April–May.

Fruit
Shiny, purple-black fruit, ¾ to 1½ in. long, shaped like a tiny football. Crops are heaviest every other year. The fruit is edible, when cured; olive oil is extracted from its flesh and seed. The outstanding varieties are Mission and Manzanillo. Nov.–Dec. The tree bears when three to five years old.

Root System: Deep

Rate of Growth: Moderate to slow

Natural Requirements
Climate: Tolerates extreme heat; needs some winter chill for fruiting but will not stand frost below 10° F. Tolerates desert atmosphere.

Soil: For fruiting, provide a deep, moist, well-drained, fertile soil. Tolerates dry, meager or rich, fertile or alkali soils.

Exposure: Sun or partial shade; shade decreases yield. Tolerates wind.

Care
Pruning: Stands heavy pruning but needs little. Thin out bearing branches. Fruit forms on previous season's growth on outer 2 to 3 ft. of the branches; the tree should not be hedged if fruit is desired. Time: May, early June; Aug.

Feeding: For fruits, apply a small quantity of nitrogen fertilizer annually in spring. For ornamental use, no special feeding necessary.

Watering: For fruits, irrigate monthly, especially in spring and late fall. For ornamental use, no special attention necessary.

Pests and Diseases: Scale (especially in coastal areas); spray with malathion or an oil emulsion in summer and repeat when needed; spray with oil in winter. Thrips; spray with DDT, lindane, or malathion in early spring and fall and repeat when needed. Olive knot causes swelling on trunk, branches, twigs, and leaves; prune out infected areas and spray with Bordeaux. Leaf spot and fruit rot; spray with Bordeaux. Root rot; remove tree and fumigate soil.

Faults
Fruit drops and litters the ground.

Features: Flowers, design of branches

Use: Street, hedge, specimen

Jerusalem Thorn is an open-growing tree with many forked and zigzagging branches spreading widely with an airy grace. The strange, vertebra-like foliage consists of long, flat, leaf blades covered with evenly but sparsely distributed, minute light-green leaflets. Attractive yellow flowers appear on the tree in early summer and, under cultivation, bloom intermittently throughout the year. Jerusalem Thorn is an adaptable tree, standing desert atmosphere, seacoast conditions, heat, and some degree of cold.

Conformation

Height: 15 to 30 ft. Spread: 15 to 30 ft.

An open-growing, wide-spreading tree with slender, spiny, zigzagging, pendulous branches. The bark is smooth and reddish. The leaves are light green. They are twice pinnately compound and alternate, 6 to 12 in. long, and composed of forty to eighty entire leaflets about 1/8 in. long. They tend to drop in cold weather.

Flowers

Bright yellow flowers, ½ to ¾ in. in diameter, lightly flecked with red, in slender, erect spikes 3 to 6 in. long. Early summer and intermittently throughout the year.

Fruit

Narrow brown pods, 2 to 6 in. long, in pendulous spikes and enclosing beanlike seeds. Fall.

Root System: Deep

Rate of Growth

Moderate. Growth rate is more rapid when tree is young.

Natural Requirements

Climate: Tolerates heat and some degree of cold but will not endure prolonged freezing. Tolerates desert atmosphere.
Soil: Thrives in dry, sandy soils. Tolerates alkali and drought.
Exposure: Sun. Tolerates salt spray and other seacoast conditions.

Care

Pruning: Prune to train and shape, only occasionally. Time: Spring.
Feeding: No special feeding necessary.
Watering: No special attention necessary.
Pests and Diseases: Relatively free from both.

Parkinsonia aculeata

Parkinso´nia aculea´ta

Jerusalem Thorn; Palo Verde; Retama

Tropical America

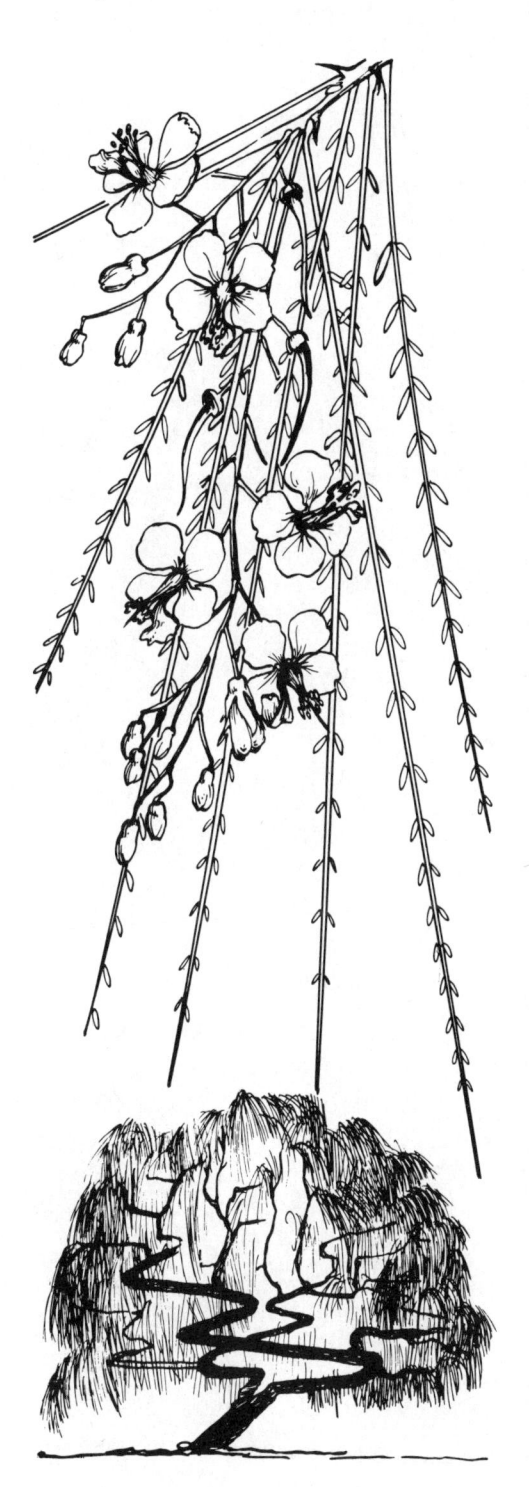

Persea americana

Per´sea america´na

(P. gratissima)

American Avocado; Alligator-Pear

Tropical America

Features: Fruit, habit

Use: Lawn, orchard, patio, tubs

Even in areas where it will not set fruit, the Avocado is planted as a desirable ornamental for its irregular, picturesque habit of growth and its large, dark-green leaves. The tree makes a handsome lawn specimen, and dwarf varieties have been developed which are excellent for use in patios and tubs. Although the Avocado prefers mild or tropical areas, varieties are available which are adaptable to other climates.

Conformation
Height: 20 to 40 ft. Spread: 20 to 60 ft.

A picturesque tree of irregular habit, with a straight trunk and grayish bark. The leaves are simple, alternate, and entire, 4 to 10 in. long and 1½ to 3 in. wide. They are dark green and shiny above, paler beneath, and are thick and leathery in texture.

Flowers
Not effective ornamentally. Winter-Spring.

Fruit
Edible, greenish or purplish, pear-shaped fruit, 3 to 6 in. long, with yellowish, oily flesh. It is a highly nutritive food. It should be picked when green and allowed to ripen for use. Cross-pollination insures the best fruit production, and care must be taken to obtain compatible varieties. Local nurserymen should be consulted about varieties best adapted to the climate. Among the varieties are: Anaheim (coastal areas; large green fruit; June-Nov.), Benedict (colder areas; small black fruit; Sept.-Oct.), Duke (colder areas; small green fruit; Sept.-Nov.), Fuerte (mild areas; large green fruit; Nov.-June, but temperamental), and Haas (mild areas; small black fruit; May-Oct.). Early summer to late spring, depending upon the variety selected. The tree will bear when three years old.

Root System: Shallow. Do not cultivate around the tree.

Rate of Growth: Rapid

Natural Requirements
Climate: Prefers mild or tropical areas. Tolerates heat but will not endure cold below 26° F.

Soil: Prefers a fertile, moist, well-drained soil. Will not thrive in boggy areas.

Exposure: Sun. Protect from wind.

Care
Pruning: Trim out weak branches and head low when tree is young. Prune as little as possible. Time: Spring.

Feeding: Apply a small quantity of balanced commercial fertilizer annually in spring; mulch with manure in the fall.

Watering: Provide plenty of moisture. Good drainage is essential.

Pests and Diseases: Aphids (nicotine, lindane, or malathion); thrips, and white fly (DDT, lindane, or malathion); spray when needed. Scale and mealy bug; spray with malathion or an oil emulsion in summer and repeat when needed; spray with oil in winter. Tip fungus; spray with Bordeaux.

Faults
Does not transplant well.

Feature: Fruit
Use: Hedge, erosion control

Toyon is a shrubby tree of rather haphazard branching habit. Its ornamental significance lies in the profusion of bright red berries, which adorn the tree throughout the winter and are used extensively in indoor decoration. Toyon is best adapted to gardens as a hedge where its indifferent habit can be channelled and controlled. It is also useful for erosion control. The variety *macrocarpa* is recommended for its larger fruit. The trees survive in poor soils and under drought conditions, tolerating heat and some degree of cold.

Conformation
Height: 10 to 20 ft. Spread: 12 to 25 ft.
A roundheaded, shrubby tree, tending to multiple branching from the base. The bark is smooth and dark brown. The leaves are dark green and thick. They are simple and alternate, 2 to 4 in. long and 1 to 1¾ in. wide, and fine-toothed along the edges.

Flowers
Very small white flowers, in clusters 2 to 4 in. long. They are charming but not highly ornamental. May-June.

Fruit
Showy, bright red berries, 1/4 to 1/3 in. long in clusters 5 to 6 in. long. Oct.-Dec. Persist throughout the winter.

Root System: Shallow and spreading
Rate of Growth: Moderate

Natural Requirements
Climate: Tolerates heat and some degree of cold but will not endure prolonged freezing.
Soil: Tolerates a variety of soils and also drought.
Exposure: Sun. Mildews in damp, shady places. Tolerates some wind.

Care
Pruning: If a specimen tree is desired, prune to a single trunk when tree is young. Time: Spring, to shape tree; or winter, for berries.
Feeding: No special feeding necessary.
Watering: Requires very little moisture, especially in summer. Good drainage is essential.
Pests and Diseases: Scale; spray with malathion or an oil emulsion in summer and repeat when needed; spray with oil in winter. Thrips; spray with DDT, lindane, or malathion in spring and fall as a preventive measure and repeat when needed.

Faults: Tends to have an unkempt, gangling appearance.

Photinia serrulata, Chinese Photinia (10 to 30 ft. high and as wide) is a much more handsome tree than the Toyon although its berries are not so dependable nor so spectacular. The leaves are 4 to 7 in. long and 1 to 2¼ in. wide and are usually waved and glossy. They are dark green most of the year but are a beautiful red-bronze when they first open and turn bright crimson in the fall. It is a good practice to prune the branch tips throughout the year, to encourage new growth and so perpetuate the red color on the tree. Chinese Photinia has the same cultural and natural requirements as Toyon.

Photinia arbutifolia

Photin´ia arbutifo´lia
(*P. salicifolia; Heteromeles arbutifolia; H. salicifolia*)
Toyon; Christmas-Berry

California

Pittosporum undulatum

Pittos'porum undula'tum
Victorian-Box; Orange-Berry Pittosporum; Mock-Orange

Australia

Features: Flowers, foliage, fruit

Use: Shade, street, lawn, hedge, patio, tubs

The Victorian Box is naturally shrubby in habit, and if it is to be a specimen tree, it must be pruned when young. After the framework is established, the plant grows to a handsome, dense, rounded shape with a smooth, straight trunk. The wavy-margined, light-green leaves, highly fragrant white flowers, and bright orange berries combine to make the Victorian Box a handsome and interesting specimen at every season of the year. The tree is well adapted for use in small gardens. It grows best in mild or warm coastal regions and will not endure extreme cold.

Conformation

Height: 20 to 40 ft. Spread: 30 to 45 ft.

A dense, compact, roundheaded tree, often with a multiple trunk and low-branching shrubby habit. When the tree is headed high, the trunk is smooth and straight. The bark is smooth and very dark brown. The leaves are simple, alternate, and entire, with wavy margins, which become smooth with age. They are 3 to 5 in. long and 1 to 1¾ in. wide. A beautiful, soft light green when young, they deepen to a shiny dark green with age.

Flowers

Highly fragrant, cream-colored flowers, ½ in. long, in clusters 3 in. in diameter, and quite profuse. The fragrance resembles that of orange blossoms, and the flowers are very attractive to bees. Winter, spring, and summer.

Fruit

Bright orange berries, ½ in. in diameter, in clusters 4 to 6 in. wide. They are fragrant and are excellent for use in indoor decoration. Fall. Persist into winter.

Root System: Deep

Rate of Growth: Rapid

Natural Requirements

Climate: Grows best in mild or warm, coastal areas. Tolerates heat and some degree of cold but will not endure prolonged freezing.

Soil: Tolerates a wide variety of soils and also drought. Good drainage is essential.

Exposure: Sun or partial shade. Tolerates wind and seacoast conditions.

Care

Pruning: Stands severe pruning. If tree shape is desired, prune to a single trunk when tree is young. Time: Spring, or any time of the year in mild climates.

Feeding: Apply manure annually in the fall, a small quantity of balanced commercial fertilizer annually in spring. The tree develops into a better specimen when properly fed.

Watering: Good drainage is essential. Provide plenty of moisture, when tree is young. The tree will stand neglect later but develops into a better specimen when watered deeply once a month.

Pests and Diseases: Relatively free from both. Occasional infestations of aphids and mealy bug. Aphids; spray with nicotine, lindane, or malathion when needed. Mealy bug; spray with malathion or an oil emulsion in summer.

Prunus caroliniana

Prúnus caroliniána
(*Laurocerasus caroliniana*)

Carolina Laurel-Cherry

Southeastern United States

Feature: Foliage

Use: Street, hedge

Carolina Laurel-Cherry must be pruned, when young, to shape as a tree; and it should be pruned annually thereafter if a specimen plant is desired. Although its white flowers are attractive, the tree is grown mostly for its handsome foliage, which is dark green and has a remarkable sheen. Carolina Laurel-Cherry is well adapted for use in small gardens and grows naturally to a neat hedge. It tolerates heat and some degree of cold but will not stand prolonged freezing.

Conformation

Height: 20 to 40 ft. Spread: 15 to 35 ft.

A spreading tree with slender, horizontal branches forming a dense, rounded crown. The leaves are simple, alternate, and entire, 2 to 4 in. long and ¾ to 1¼ in. wide. They are a rich dark green above, paler beneath, and are very lustrous and leathery.

Flowers

Tiny, cream-colored flowers in dense racemes ¾ to 1½ in. long. The flowers are often sacrificed when the plant is heavily pruned. April–June.

Fruit

Shiny black berries, ½ in. long; not effective ornamentally. Fall. Persist until the following spring.

Root System: Average depth to deep

Rate of Growth: Rapid

Natural Requirements

Climate: Grows best in mild regions. Tolerates heat and some degree of cold but will not endure prolonged freezing. Tolerates desert atmosphere.

Soil: Tolerates a wide variety of soils and also drought.

Exposure: Sun or partial shade. Tolerates seacoast conditions.

Care

Pruning: Stands heavy pruning. It must be pruned when young if a tree shape is desired. Prune annually, to shape. Time: Any month.

Feeding: Apply a small quantity of balanced commercial fertilizer annually in spring; apply manure annually in the fall.

Watering: No special attention necessary. Good drainage is essential.

Pests and Diseases: Relatively free from both.

Prúnus lyóni, Catalina Cherry (15 to 35 ft. high; 10 to 45 ft. wide) has the same cultural and natural requirements as Carolina Laurel and is used for the same landscaping purposes. The leaves, fruit, and clusters of flowers are somewhat larger, but the conformation and handsome sheen of the leaves are essentially the same.

Prúnus lusitaníca, Portuguese Laurel, achieves a height of 15 to 35 ft. with a spread of 10 to 20 ft. Shrublike in habit, it branches severally from the base and grows naturally to a fine specimen hedge. White flowers in showy racemes, 5 to 10 in. long, bloom in May and June. Portuguese Laurel has the same cultural and natural requirements as Carolina Laurel-Cherry.

Quercus agrifolia

Quer´cus agrifo´lia

California Live Oak; Coast Live Oak

California

Feature: Habit

Use: Shade, lawn, specimen, erosion control

California Live Oak defies description in the manifold, artistic forms it assumes, whether under cultivation or growing in its wild state along the coastal ranges of the California countryside. Its massive, wide-spreading branches take their configuration from the pressure of the wind, and the trees seem always to blend with and conform to their surroundings. California Live Oak is adaptable for use only in gardens in which there is room for the tree to develop without hindrance.

Conformation

Height: 30 to 75 ft. Spread: 60 to 100 ft.

A highly picturesque tree, assuming many artistic shapes, with wide-spreading heavy, thick branches forming a broad, round crown. The trunk is often divided at ground level, or a few feet above it, and the branches arch downward and sweep the ground at their outer edges. The bark is dark gray and is broken into irregular plates. The leaves are simple and alternate, with margins finely to coarsely spiny-tipped, somewhat like those of the holly. They are a dull dark green, 1 to 3 in. long and 3/4 to 2 in. wide, stiff and leathery.

Flowers: Not effective ornamentally.

Fruit

Brown, rounded acorn, 1 to 1½ in. long, with the broadly top-shaped cup enclosing only the base of the nut. Matures the first year. Aug.–Oct.

Root System: Deep

Rate of Growth

Moderate. Fairly rapid when growing conditions are good.

Natural Requirements

Climate: Prefers a climate similar to that of the coastal ranges. Tolerates heat and some degree of cold but will not endure prolonged freezing.

Soil: Tolerates a variety of soils, from sand and gravel to heavy clay. Prefers a light loam with a gravelly subsoil. Endures drought or wet soils. Rate of growth slows in poor soils.

Exposure: Sun or partial shade. Tolerates seacoast conditions.

Care

Pruning: Stands fairly heavy pruning. Remove suckers and poorly formed branches. Time: Fall.

Feeding: Apply manure annually in the fall.

Watering: Little moisture is required. Do not water in summer.

Pests and Diseases: Caterpillars, mites, thrips (host); spray with DDT, arsenate, lindane, or malathion in spring and fall as a preventive measure and repeat when needed. Scale; spray with malathion or an oil emulsion in summer and repeat when needed; spray with oil in winter. Anthracnose causes a mottling of the leaves and cankers and blight on the twigs; spray with Bordeaux in early spring and repeat two weeks after first spraying.

Quer´cus su´ber, Cork Oak, has the same natural and cultural requirements as *Q. agrifolia* and is used for the same landscaping purposes. It grows to a height of 50 ft. with a 70-ft. spread. Commercial cork is obtained from the bark of the tree.

Features: Foliage, habit

Use: Shade, street, lawn, windbreak, erosion control

Holly Oak grows to a wide-spreading tree with a rounded crown and branches which arch downward at the ends. The leaves are spiny-edged and dark green, somewhat resembling those of the holly except that the undersurfaces are covered with short, yellow or gray, felty hairs. The leaves on the same tree vary widely: they may be small, round, narrow, or curly. Trees in which the deviations have proved consistent have been propagated and offered as separate named varieties. Holly Oak is excellent in large gardens for shade and lawn plantings, and its uniformity of shape makes it well suited for use in streets. Because of its tolerance of wind and poor soils, it is used as a windbreak and for erosion control. The tree is very sensitive to cold but stands full exposure to wind and spray at high-tide line on the seacoast.

Conformation

Height: 20 to 60 ft. Spread: 20 to 50 ft.

A broad, wide-spreading tree with a domelike crown and branches arching downward at the ends. The bark is gray and rather smooth. The leaves are simple and alternate, irregularly and finely toothed or entire, and 1¼ to 2½ in. long and ½ to 1 in. wide, though their size and shape vary. They are a very dark green or black-green above, yellow or gray tomentose beneath, and are glossy, stiff, and holly-like.

Flowers: Not effective ornamentally.

Fruit

Brown acorn, ¾ to 1¼ in. long, ovoid, with a top-shaped cup enclosing about half the nut. The nut is edible. Matures the first year. Summer.

Root System: Deep

Rate of Growth: Moderate

Natural Requirements

Climate: Tolerates heat but not cold. Tolerates dry air.

Soil: Prefers a deep, warm loam. Tolerates a variety of soils, including heavy, well-drained, or light, sandy ones, as well as acid and alkali.

Exposure: Sun. Tolerates wind and stands full exposure to salt spray at high-tide line.

Care

Pruning: Stands fairly heavy pruning. Remove suckers and poorly formed branches. Time: Fall.

Feeding: No special feeding necessary.

Watering: Little moisture is required.

Pests and Diseases: Caterpillars, mites, thrips (host); spray with DDT, arsenate, lindane, or malathion in spring and fall as a preventive measure and repeat when needed. Scale; spray with malathion or an oil emulsion in summer and repeat when needed; spray with oil in winter. Anthracnose causes a mottling of the leaves and cankers and blight on the twigs; spray with Bordeaux in early spring and repeat two weeks after the first spraying.

Quercus ilex

Quer′cus i′lex
Holly Oak; Holm Oak

Southern Europe

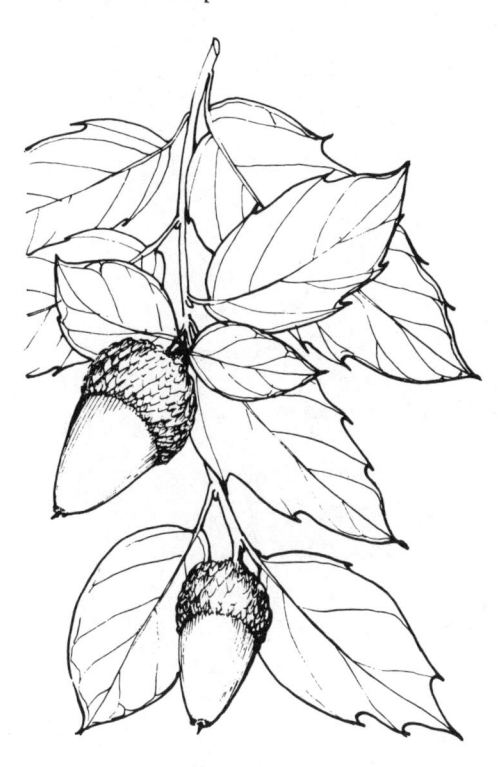

Schinus molle

Schi′nus mol′le

California Pepper Tree;
Peruvian Mastic Tree

Peru

Features: Fruit, habit, foliage

Use: Shade, erosion control, accent

California Pepper has a broadly rounded crown with graceful, pendulous branches and a short, knotty, gnarled trunk. The soft light-green foliage is very fine and feathery. The tree is covered throughout the winter with loose, grapelike clusters of rose-colored berries, which are excellent for use in indoor decoration. Unfortunately, the behavior of the tree in the garden belies its delicate appearance. It has shallow, voracious roots which invade sewers and crack pavements; it distributes an unbelievable amount of litter in twigs, leaves, and fruit; and it is subject to scale and must be sprayed regularly. The tree should be used only in the outlying areas of large gardens as a shade tree or an accent. It tolerates extreme heat and some cold but will not endure bitterly cold areas.

Conformation
Height: 15 to 50 ft. Spread: 15 to 70 ft.

A roundheaded, dense tree with wide-spreading, pendulous branches that often reach to the ground. The trunk is short, gnarled, and knotty; the bark is red-brown. The shiny, light-green leaves are alternate and compound, 6 to 12 in. long, composed of twenty to sixty leaflets 1 to 2 in. long and ¼ in. wide, which are toothed or sometimes entire.

Flowers
Tiny yellowish flowers in much-branched, drooping panicles; male and female flowers on different trees. They attract bees and are not effective ornamentally; their pungent odor is rather offensive. All year round; most heavily in early summer.

Fruit
Light rose-colored berries, ¼ in. wide, in grapelike clusters, 8 to 10 in. long. The fruit forms only on female trees; it is not a true pepper. Fall. Persists throughout the winter.

Root System: Shallow and voracious

Rate of Growth: Rapid

Natural Requirements
Climate: Tolerates heat and some cold but will not endure prolonged freezing. Tolerates desert atmosphere.

Soil: Tolerates a variety of soils, even hard, packed ones. Tolerates drought.

Exposure: Sun or partial shade. Tolerates seacoast conditions.

Care
Pruning: Prune, when tree is young, to establish framework. Later, thin and cut back to encourage new growth. Time: Spring.

Feeding: Apply commercial fertilizer and manure annually to keep the roots from spreading out and stealing fertility from the soil.

Watering: Provide plenty of moisture when tree is young, to force the roots downward. Good drainage is essential.

Pests and Diseases: Scale; spray with malathion or an oil emulsion in summer and repeat when needed; spray with oil in winter.

Faults: Twigs, leaves, and fruit make much litter. Branches are brittle. Invasive and voracious roots invade sewers and crack pavements. Subject to scale.

Schinus terebinthifolia

Schí´nus terebinthifo´lia

Brazilian Pepper Tree;
Christmas-Berry Tree

Brazil

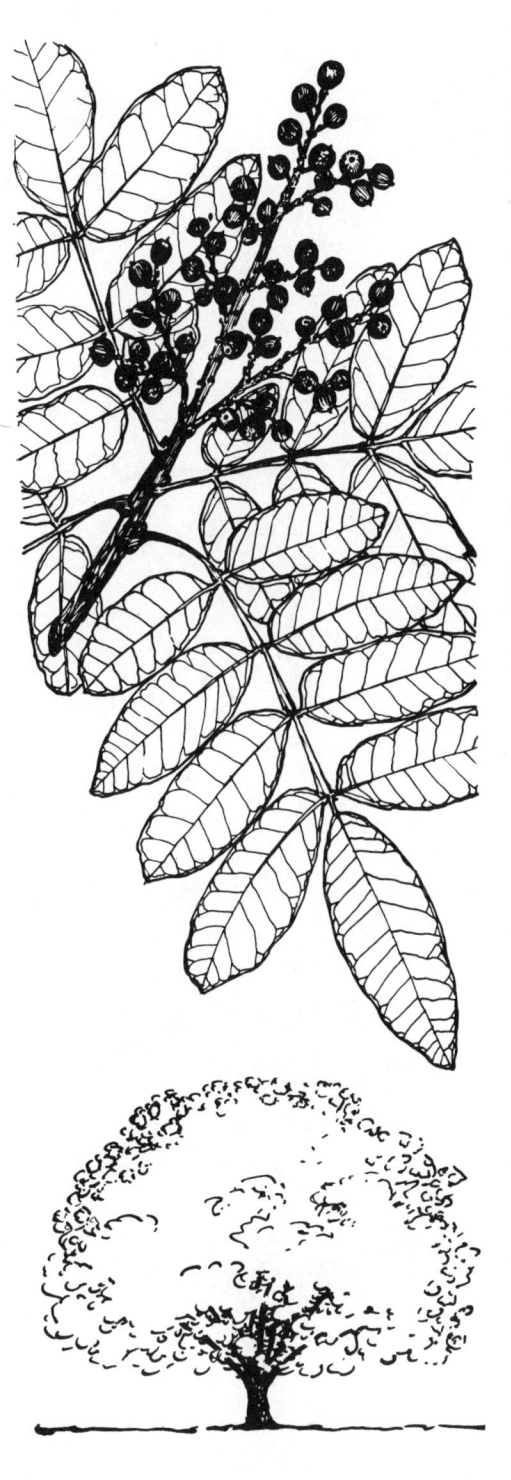

Features: Fruit, habit, foliage

Use: Shade, street, lawn, patio, tubs

Brazilian Pepper Tree has a stiffly upright branching habit and grows to an erect tree with a broad, rounded crown. The foliage is dark green, and the winter berries are an attractive bright red. Brazilian Pepper Tree differs greatly from California Pepper Tree in general appearance and individual performance. It is a clean tree with a well-behaved root system, and it is not subject to attack by scale. Therefore, it succeeds as an ornamental in small gardens, streets, lawns, patios, and tubs, and makes an excellent small shade tree. Brazilian Pepper tolerates seacoast conditions and desert atmosphere but will not stand cold areas.

Conformation
Height: 15 to 30 ft. Spread: 25 to 50 ft.

A roundheaded tree with stiffly erect, wide-spreading branches. The bark is rough and gray-brown. The leaves are 6 to 8 in. long; they are alternate and compound, composed of seven leaflets 1 to 2 in. long and ½ to ¾ in. wide, and toothed or sometimes entire. They are shiny dark green above, paler beneath.

Flowers
Small white flowers in compact clusters; male and female flowers on different trees. Not effective ornamentally. June–July.

Fruit
Bright red berries, 1/8 in. in diameter, in grapelike clusters 2 to 3 in. long; on female trees only. They are quite showy and are excellent for use in indoor decoration. The fruit is not a true pepper. Fall. Persists throughout the winter.

Root System: Average depth

Rate of Growth: Rapid

Natural Requirements
Climate: Tolerates heat and some degree of cold but will not endure prolonged freezing. Tolerates desert atmosphere.
Soil: Tolerates a wide variety of soils and also drought.
Exposure: Sun or partial shade. Tolerates smoke, dust, and seacoast conditions. Needs protection from strong winds.

Care
Pruning: Little pruning is required, since the tree grows naturally in a neat, compact shape. Time: Spring.
Feeding: Apply a small quantity of a balanced commercial fertilizer annually in spring.
Watering: No special attention necessary. Good drainage is essential.
Pests and Diseases: Resistant to and relatively free from both.

Schínus lentiscifolia, Pinkberry Pepper, resembles California Pepper in general appearance but has a more erect and compact habit of growth. The foliage is bright green, the berries deep pink. Since the bad features of California Pepper are not found so extensively in this tree, it is useful in smaller gardens if properly fed and watered. It has the same natural requirements as California Pepper.

Tamarix aphylla

Tam´arix aphyl´la
(T. articulata)
Desert Athel; Athel

Western Asia; northern Africa

Feature: Foliage

Use: Hedge, windbreak, erosion control

Desert Athel grows in a rather haphazard fashion with many upright-spreading branches forming a bushy crown. The twigs are jointed and are covered with minute, scalelike leaves, which persist and give the tree an evergreen appearance. Desert Athel is effective as a windbreak or hedge. It exhibits a remarkable tolerance of poor and dry soils, wind, desert atmosphere, and seacoast conditions but will not stand severe cold.

Conformation

Height: 20 to 35 ft. Spread: 10 to 25 ft.

An irregular tree with numerous branches forming a bushy crown. The branches are very slender. The gray, jointed twigs are covered with minute, scalelike leaves, 1/16 in. long.

Flowers

Tiny pink flowers, in branched, terminal clusters; not highly ornamental. Summer.

Fruit: Not effective ornamentally.

Root System: Average depth

Rate of Growth: Rapid

Natural Requirements

Climate: Tolerates heat and some degree of cold but will not endure prolonged freezing. Tolerates desert atmosphere.
Soil: Tolerates a wide variety of soils. Prefers a light, sandy soil. Tolerates alkali, salt, and drought.
Exposure: Sun. Tolerates wind, salt air, salt spray, and seacoast conditions.

Care

Pruning: Prune annually to shape and to encourage new growth. The current year's growth bears the flowers. Time: Winter.
Watering: No special attention necessary.
Feeding: Apply manure annually in the fall.
Pests and Diseases: Resistant to and relatively free from both.

Faults

The tree sheds branchlets almost constantly.

Tristania conferta

Tristánia conférta
Brisbane-Box

Australia

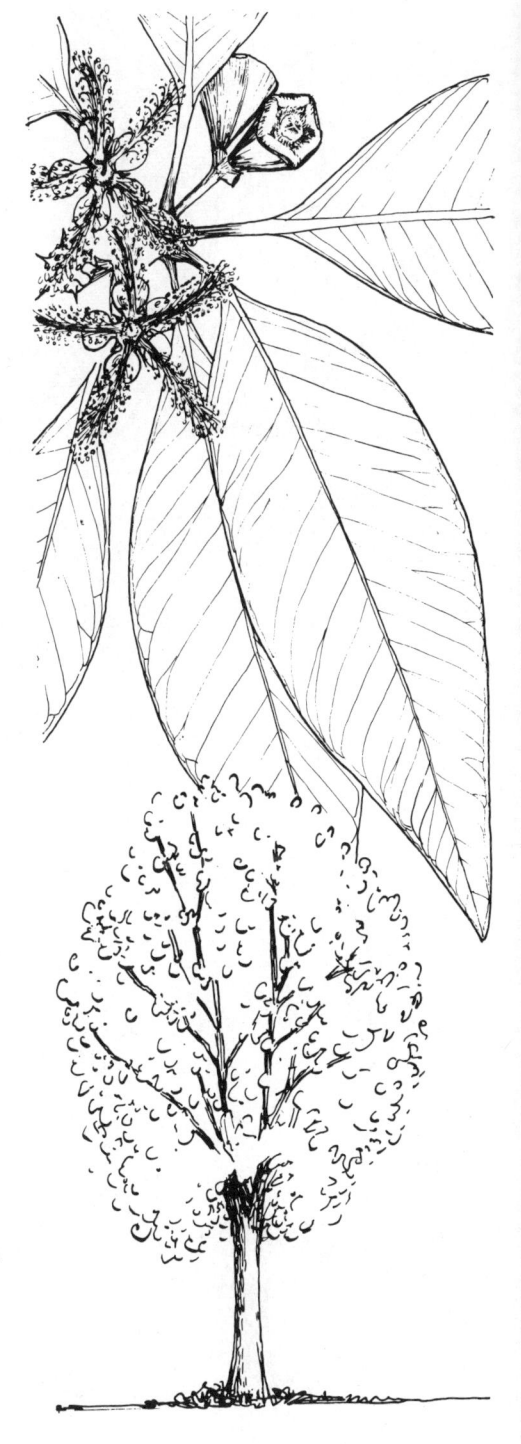

Features: Foliage, habit, bark, flowers

Use: Street, specimen

Brisbane-Box is a slender, oval-topped tree with many, short-spreading, steeply ascending branches and a smooth red-brown bark. The leaves are dark green, thick, and leathery, and carry a high gloss. The white flowers are star-shaped, with numerous protruding stamens which create a fringed appearance; they bloom in small clusters. Brisbane-Box makes a good specimen plant for foliage effect and should be planted where its handsome red bark can be fully displayed. It is well adapted for use in small or large gardens and is effective for lining streets. It thrives only in mild regions.

Conformation

Height: 40 to 75 ft. (100 ft.). Spread: 30 to 50 ft.

An oval-topped tree, somewhat columnar in shape when young, of open growth, with steeply ascending branches. The bark is smooth and a clear reddish brown. The leaves are simple, alternate, and entire, 3 to 6 in. long and 1½ to 2½ in. wide. They are glossy and leathery; dark green above, paler beneath; and arranged in clusters at the ends of the branches. The individual leaves closely resemble those of the Scarlet Eucalyptus; in their juvenile stages it is difficult to tell the two trees apart.

Flowers

Star-shaped white flowers, 1½ in. in diameter, with numerous prominent stamens. They bloom in small clusters in the leaf axils. May–June.

Fruit

Woody capsules ½ in. in diameter; not effective ornamentally. July–Aug.

Root System: Average depth

Rate of Growth: Moderate to rapid

Natural Requirements

Climate: Grows best in mild areas. Tolerates heat but not cold.

Soil: Grows best in fairly rich, sandy loam. When tree is old, it displays some tolerance to drought.

Exposure: Sun.

Care

Pruning: To produce a well-shaped tree, head back when plant is young. Time: Spring.

Feeding: Apply a small quantity of a balanced commercial fertilizer annually in spring.

Watering: Provide plenty of moisture when tree is young; later, water deeply once a month.

Pests and Diseases: Scale; spray with malathion or an oil emulsion in summer and repeat when needed; spray with oil in winter.

Ulmus parvifolia

Ul'mus parvifo'lia
Chinese Elm

China; Japan; Korea

Feature: Habit

Use: Shade, hedge, screen

The branches of the Chinese Elm are pendulous and are best described as arching downward; for the framework of the tree is sturdy and the branches strong, and there is no suggestion of the limp, wispy quality that characterizes many weeping types. The tree is used effectively as a heavy-shade tree, a hedge, and a screen, and is excellent in patios or as a canopy for oriental gardens. Though evergreen in mild climates, it defoliates with even the slightest degree of cold, the leaves turning red and purple before dropping. The variety *sempervirens*, Evergreen Elm, has leaves that are more tenacious in cold climates, and wide-spreading branches which arch and sweep the ground. The Chinese Elm is often confused, in the trade, with the Siberian Elm, a deciduous tree of uncertain habit; its ornamental qualities are distinctly inferior to those of the Chinese Elm.

Conformation

Height: 20 to 60 ft.   Spread: 30 to 70 ft.

A wide-spreading, round-topped tree with heavy, pendulous branches. The bark is dark brown and mottled, often shedding in irregular spots to reveal a lighter-colored inner bark. The leaves are simple, alternate, and fine-toothed, ¾ to 2½ in. long and 3/8 to 7/8 in. wide. They are a glossy dark green above, paler beneath, and turn red or purple before dropping from the tree in cold weather.

Flowers

Not effective ornamentally.

Fruit

Light-brown, winged nuts, 3/8 in. long; not effective ornamentally.

Root System: Shallow

Rate of Growth: Rapid

Natural Requirements

Climate: Tolerates heat and stands a large degree of cold but drops its leaves in cold weather. Tolerates desert atmosphere.
Soil: Tolerates a wide variety of soils; prefers a rich, moist, well-drained loam.
Exposure: Sun or shade. Tolerates seacoast conditions.

Care

Pruning: Thin crown and trim branches as desired, when tree is young, but do not top leader. Little pruning is required after the first three years, for the tree assumes a good natural shape. Time: Spring.
Feeding: Apply a balanced commercial fertilizer annually in spring; apply manure annually in the fall.
Watering: Provide plenty of moisture. Good drainage is essential.
Pests and Diseases: Scale; spray with malathion or an oil emulsion in summer and repeat when needed; spray with oil in winter.

Faults

When old, the tree has a tendency to upheave the ground; proper feeding and deep watering to force the roots downward is the best insurance against this.

Umbellularia californica

Umbellula´ria califor´nica

California Laurel; Oregon-Myrtle; California Bay Tree; Pepperwood

Oregon to California

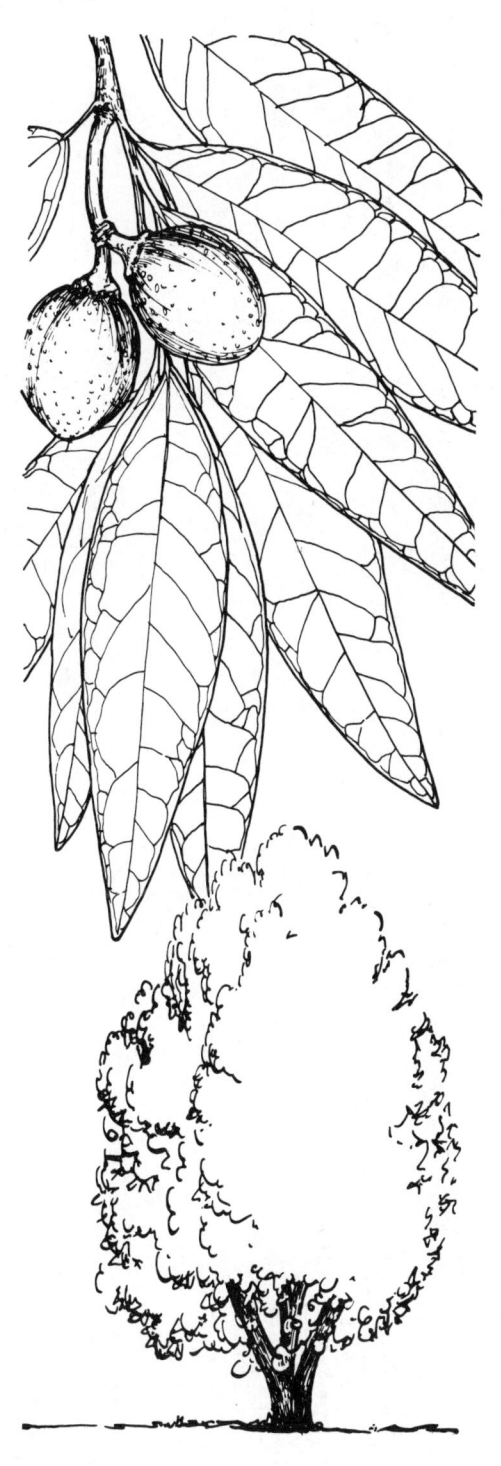

Features: Habit, foliage

Use: Lawn, hedge, water edge, tub, specimen

California Laurel is a heavy, stately tree with stiffly ascending branches forming a rounded crown. In youth, the tree is a dense pyramid of large, shiny, dark-green leaves and is well suited for use as a tubbed specimen. The leaves are highly aromatic, with a clean, spicy, bay fragrance; they are used in cooking to flavor soups and meats. California Laurel needs plenty of food and moisture to attain its best development and becomes shrubby and gangling in dry, infertile soils. It is a fairly hardy tree.

Conformation

Height: 20 to 75 ft. (100 ft.).   Spread: 30 to 50 ft. (100 ft.).

A dense, roundheaded tree with many, stiffly ascending branches. The bark is grayish brown and smooth, in young trees, and becomes dark brown and scaly as the tree grows older. The leaves are simple, alternate, and entire, and are 3 to 5 in. long and ¾ to 1½ in. wide. They are glossy, deep, dark green above, paler beneath, and have a thick, leathery texture and a spicy aroma.

Flowers

Small, pale-yellow flowers, in small, dense clusters; not effective ornamentally. May–June.

Fruit

Fleshy, olive-shaped fruit, 1 in. long. The fruit is at first yellow-green and turns purplish brown at maturity. Aug.–Oct.

Root System: Average depth

Rate of Growth: Rapid (under favorable conditions)

Natural Requirements

Climate: Tolerates heat and a large degree of cold.

Soil: Prefers a fertile, moist, well-drained, light loam.

Exposure: Sun or shade. In hot regions, grows best in shade. Tolerates wind.

Care

Pruning: Stands heavy pruning. Prune, when tree is young, to a single trunk. Thin crown regularly to prevent top-heaviness. Time: Spring or summer.

Feeding: Apply a balanced commercial fertilizer annually in spring; apply manure annually in the fall.

Watering: Provide plenty of moisture. Good drainage is essential.

Pests and Diseases: Scale; spray with malathion or an oil emulsion in summer and repeat when needed. Spray with oil in winter.

Faults

Tree topples if crown is allowed to become too top-heavy.

CHART FOR THE ORNAMENTAL USE AND CLIMATIC TOLERANCE OF BROAD-LEAVED EVERGREEN TREES

Rate of growth: R=rapid; M=moderate; S=slow
Leaf-blade size: L=large, 6 or more in. long; M=medium, 2 to 6 in. long; S=small, less than 2 in. long
Leaf color: gr=green
Fruit: E=edible; O=ornamental

X: areas where the particular tree may be grown easily
(X): areas where the particular tree may be grown, but with some reservations

	ORNAMENTAL USE						CLIMATIC TOLERANCE			
STREET TREES	Rate of Growth	Habit	Leaf-Blade Size	Leaf-Blade Color	Flowers	Fruit	Temperate Coastal	Desert	Cool Coastal	Temperate Inland
Acacia melanoxylon	R	Dense	S	Dark gr	White		X	X	X	X
Brachychiton populneus	S	Dense	M	Light gr	White	O	X	X	X	
Ceratonia siliqua	S	Dense	S	Dark gr	Yellow	E, O	X	X	X	X
Cinnamomum camphora	S	Dense	M	Light gr			X		X	X
Crinodendron dependens	M	Dense	S	Bright gr	White	O	X	X	X	
Eriobotrya japonica	M	Dense	L	Dark gr	White	E, O	X		X	
Eucalyptus ficifolia	M	Dense	M	Dark gr	Red		X		X	
Eucalyptus rudis	R	Dense	M	Dark gr	White		X	X	X	X
Eucalyptus sideroxylon pallens	R	Open	M	Gray	Red		X	X	X	X
Eucalyptus sideroxylon purpurea	R	Open	M	Bright gr	Purple		X	X	X	X
Eucalyptus sideroxylon rosea	R	Open	M	Bright gr	Pink		X	X	X	X
Ficus retusa	R	Dense	M	Dark gr			X			
Hymenosporum flavum	M	Open	M	Dark gr	Yellow		X			
Lagunaria patersoni	M	Dense	M	Gray	Pink		X			
Ligustrum lucidum	R	Dense	M	Dark gr	White		X	X	(X)	X
Magnolia grandiflora	S	Dense	L	Dark gr	White		X		X	X
Maytenus boaria	M	Dense	S	Light gr			X			
Melaleuca leucadendron	R	Open	M	Light gr	White		X	X	X	
Metrosideros tomentosa	S	Dense	M	Dark gr	Red	E, O	X		X	
Olea europaea	M	Varies	M	Gray	Yellow		X	X	X	X
Parkinsonia aculeata	M	Open	S	Light gr	White	O	X	X	X	X
Pittosporum undulatum	R	Dense	M	Dark gr	White	O	X		X	X
Prunus caroliniana	R	Dense	M	Dark gr	White	O	X	X	X	X
Prunus lyoni	R	Dense	M	Dark gr		O	X	X		X
Quercus ilex	M	Dense	S	Dark gr		O	X			
Schinus terebinthifolia	R	Dense	S	Dark gr			X	X	X	
Tristania conferta	M	Open	M	Dark gr	White		X			
SHADE TREES										
Acacia melanoxylon	R	Dense	M	Dark gr	White		X	X	X	X
Agonis flexuosa	S	Dense	M	Bright gr	White		X	X	X	
Brachychiton populneus	S	Dense	M	Light gr	White		X	X	X	
Casimiroa edulis	M	Dense	L	Bright gr		E, O	X			X

ORNAMENTAL USE OF BROAD-LEAVED EVERGREEN TREES

SHADE TREES (continued)	Rate of Growth	Habit	Leaf-Blade Size	Leaf-Blade Color	Flowers	Fruit	Temperate Coastal	Desert	Cool Coastal	Temperate Inland
Ceratonia siliqua	S	Dense	S	Dark gr	Yellow	E,O	X	X	X	
Cinnamomum camphora	S	Dense	M	Light gr			X		X	X
Eriobotrya japonica	M	Dense	L	Dark gr	White	E,O	X	X	X	X
Eucalyptus rudis	R	Dense	M	Dark gr	White		X	X	X	
Ficus macrophylla	M	Dense	L	Dark gr			X			
Ficus retusa	R	Dense	M	Dark gr			X			
Harpephyllum caffrum	R	Dense	S	Dark gr		E,O	X			
Laurus nobilis	S	Dense	M	Dark gr			X	X	X	X
Magnolia grandiflora	S	Dense	L	Dark gr	White		X		(X)	X
Persea americana	R	Dense	L	Dark gr			X			
Pittosporum undulatum	R	Dense	M	Dark gr	White	E,O	X		X	X
Quercus agrifolia	M	Dense	S	Dark gr		O	X		X	X
Quercus ilex	M	Dense	S	Dark gr		O	X		X	
Quercus suber	M	Dense	S	Dark gr		O	X			
Schinus lentiscifolia	R	Dense	S	Bright gr		O	X	X	X	X
Schinus molle	R	Dense	S	Light gr		O	X	X	X	X
Schinus terebinthifolia	R	Dense	S	Dark gr		O	X	X	X	X
Ulmus parvifolia	R	Dense	S	Dark gr		O	X	X	X	X

LAWN TREES										
Brachychiton populneus	S	Dense	M	Light gr	White	O	X	X	X	
Crinodendron dependens	M	Dense	S	Bright gr	White	O	X	X	X	X
Eriobotrya japonica	M	Dense	L	Dark gr	White	E,O	X	X	X	
Hymenosporum flavum	M	Open	M	Dark gr	Yellow	O	X			
Ilex aquifolium	S	Dense	M	Dark gr			X		X	X
Magnolia grandiflora	S	Dense	L	Dark gr	White		X		(X)	X
Maytenus boaria	M	Dense	S	Light gr			X		X	X
Melaleuca leucadendron	R	Open	M	Light gr	White		X	X	X	X
Olea europaea	M	Varies	M	Gray		E,O	X	X	X	X
Persea americana	R	Dense	L	Light gr		E,O	X			
Pittosporum undulatum	R	Dense	M	Dark gr	White	O	X		X	X
Quercus agrifolia	M	Dense	S	Dark gr		O	X		X	X
Quercus ilex	M	Dense	S	Dark gr		O	X		X	
Quercus suber	M	Dense	S	Dark gr		O	X			X
Schinus terebinthifolia	R	Dense	S	Dark gr		O	X	X	X	
Umbellularia californica	R	Dense	M	Dark gr		O	X		X	X

CLIMATIC TOLERANCE

ORNAMENTAL USE OF BROAD-LEAVED EVERGREEN TREES

	Rate of Growth	Habit	Leaf-Blade Size	Leaf-Blade Color	Flowers	Fruit	Temperate Coastal	Desert	Cool Coastal	Temperate Inland
WINDBREAKS										
Acacia melanoxylon	R	Dense	M	Dark gr	White		X	X	X	X
Casuarina equisetifolia	R	Open	S	Light gr	White		X	X	X	X
Eriobotrya japonica	M	Dense	L	Dark gr	White	E,O	X	X	X	
Eucalyptus citriodora	R	Open	M	Bright gr	White		X			X
Eucalyptus globulus	R	Open	L	Bright gr	White		X	X	X	X
Eucalyptus polyanthemos	R	Open	M	Gray	White		X	X	X	
Eucalyptus pulverulenta	R	Open	M	Gray	White		X	X	X	
Eucalyptus rudis	R	Dense	M	Dark gr	White		X	X	X	
Quercus ilex	M	Dense	S	Dark gr		O	X		X	
Tamarix aphylla	R	Open	S	Light gr	Pink		X	X		X
HEDGES										
Acacia longifolia	R	Open	M	Light gr	Yellow		X		X	
Acacia melanoxylon	R	Dense	M	Dark gr	White		X		X	
Acacia riceana	R	Dense	S	Light gr	Yellow		X		X	
Acacia verticillata	R	Dense	S	Dark gr	Yellow		X	X		
Acmena smithi	S	Dense	M	Dark gr	White	O	X			
Casuarina equisetifolia	R	Open	S	Light gr			X	X	X	X
Ceratonia siliqua	S	Dense	S	Dark gr	Yellow	E,O	X	X	X	X
Citrus, Grapefruit	M	Dense	M	Dark gr	White	E,O	X	X	X	
Citrus, Lemon	M	Dense	M	Light gr	White	E,O	X			
Citrus, Lime	M	Dense	M	Light gr	White	E,O	X			
Citrus, Orange	M	Dense	M	Dark gr	White	E,O	X	X		X
Citrus, Tangerine	M	Dense	L	Dark gr	White	E,O	X	X		X
Corynocarpus laevigata	M	Dense	L	Dark gr	White		X	X	X	X
Eriobotrya japonica	M	Dense	M	Dark gr	White	E,O	X		X	
Eugenia species	M	Open	M	Dark gr	Yellow	E,O	X	X	X	X
Fremontia species	R	Dense	M	Dark gr	Yellow		X	X	X	X
Ilex aquifolium	S	Dense	M	Dark gr		O	X			
Laurus nobilis	S	Dense	M	Dark gr	White		X	X	X	X
Ligustrum lucidum	R	Dense	L	Dark gr	White		X	X	X	X
Lyonothamnus floribundus	M	Dense	M	Dark gr	Red		X			X
Metrosideros tomentosa	S	Dense	M	Gray		E,O	X			
Olea europaea	M	Varies	M	Gray	Yellow		X	X	X	X
Parkinsonia aculeata	M	Open	S	Light gr	Yellow		X	X	X	X
Photinia species	M	Dense	M	Dark gr	White	O	X	X	X	X
Pittosporum undulatum	R	Dense	M	Dark gr	White	O	X		X	X
Prunus caroliniana	R	Dense	M	Dark gr	White	O	X	X	X	X

CLIMATIC TOLERANCE

ORNAMENTAL USE OF BROAD-LEAVED EVERGREEN TREES

	Rate of Growth	Habit	Leaf-Blade Size	Leaf-Blade Color	Flowers	Fruit	Temperate Coastal	Desert	Cool Coastal	Temperate Inland
HEDGES (continued)										
Prunus lusitanica	M	Dense	M	Dark gr	White	O	X	X	X	X
Prunus lyoni	R	Dense	M	Dark gr	White	O	X	X	X	X
Tamarix aphylla	R	Open	S	Light gr	Pink		X	X	X	X
Ulmus parvifolia	R	Dense	S	Dark gr			X			X
Umbellularia californica	R	Dense	M	Dark gr			X			
SCREENS										
Acacia longifolia	R	Open	M	Light gr	Yellow		X		X	
Acacia riceana	R	Dense	S	Light gr	Yellow		X		X	
Acacia verticillata	R	Dense	S	Dark gr	Yellow		X		X	
Arbutus menziesi	S	Varies	M	Dark gr	White	O		X		X X
Casuarina equisetifolia	R	Open	S	Light gr			X		X	
Corynocarpus laevigata	M	Dense	L	Dark gr			X		X	
Eucalyptus citriodora	R	Open	M	Bright gr	White		X		X	X X X X X X
Eucalyptus ficifolia	M	Dense	M	Dark gr	Red		X		X	
Eucalyptus globulus	R	Open	L	Bright gr	White		X	X	X	
Eucalyptus polyanthemos	R	Open	M	Gray	White		X	X	X	
Eucalyptus pulverulenta	R	Open	M	Gray	White		X	X	X	
Eucalyptus rudis	R	Dense	M	Dark gr	White		X	X	X	
Fremontia species	R	Open	M	Dark gr	Yellow		X	X	X	
Grevillea robusta	R	Open	S	Dark gr	Orange		X	X		
Ligustrum lucidum	R	Dense	M	Dark gr	White		X	X	X	
Maytenus boaria	M	Dense	S	Light gr			X		X	
Ulmus parvifolia	R	Dense	S	Dark gr			X		X	
ESPALIERS										
Citrus, Grapefruit	M	Dense	M	Dark gr	White	E,O	X	X	X	X
Citrus, Lemon	M	Dense	M	Light gr	White	E,O	X			X
Citrus, Lime	M	Dense	M	Light gr	White	E,O	X			
Citrus, Orange	M	Dense	M	Dark gr	White	E,O	X	X		X
Citrus, Tangerine	M	Dense	M	Dark gr	White	E,O	X	X		X
Eriobotrya japonica	M	Dense	L	Dark gr	White	E,O	X		(X)	X
Magnolia species	S	Dense	L	Dark gr	White		X			
PATIO AND TUB TREES										
Acacia baileyana	R	Open	S	Gray	Yellow		X		X	
Acacia longifolia	R	Open	M	Light gr	Yellow		X		X	

CLIMATIC TOLERANCE

ORNAMENTAL USE OF BROAD-LEAVED EVERGREEN TREES

PATIO AND TUB TREES (cont'd)	Rate of Growth	Habit	Leaf-Blade Size	Leaf-Blade Color	Flowers	Fruit	Temperate Coastal	Desert	Cool Coastal	Temperate Inland
Acacia riceana	R	Dense	S	Light gr	Yellow	O	X		X	
Acmena smithi	S	Dense	M	Dark gr	White	E, O	X			
Casimiroa edulis	M	Dense	L	Bright gr			X	X		X X
Citrus, Grapefruit	M	Dense	M	Dark gr	White	E, O	X			X
Citrus, Lemon	M	Dense	M	Light gr	White	E, O	X			
Citrus, Lime	M	Dense	M	Light gr	White	E, O	X			
Citrus, Orange	M	Dense	M	Dark gr	White	E, O	X	X		X
Citrus, Tangerine	M	Dense	M	Dark gr	White	E, O	X	X		X
Eriobotrya japonica	M	Dense	L	Dark gr	White	E, O	X	X		X
Eucalyptus caesia	R	Open	M	Gray	Pink		X			
Eugenia species	R	Dense	M	Dark gr	White	E, O	X		X	
Ficus retusa	R	Dense	M	Dark gr			X		X	
Hymenosporum flavum	M	Open	M	Dark gr	Yellow	O	X			
Ilex aquifolium	S	Dense	M	Dark gr			X		X	X
Lagunaria patersoni	M	Dense	M	Gray	Pink		X	X	X	X X
Laurus nobilis	S	Dense	M	Dark gr	White		X	X	X	X X
Ligustrum lucidum	R	Dense	M	Dark gr	White	E, O	X			
Macadamia ternifolia	S	Dense	L	Bright gr	White		X		(X)	X X X
Magnolia grandiflora exonensis	S	Dense	L	Dark gr	White		X	X	X	X X
Melaleuca leucadendron	R	Open	M	Light gr		E, O	X	X	X	
Olea europaea	M	Varies	M	Gray		E, O	X			
Persea americana (dwarf)	R	Dense	L	Dark gr	White	O	X			X
Pittosporum undulatum	R	Dense	M	Dark gr		O	X			
Schinus terebinthifolia	R	Dense	S	Dark gr			X	X	X	
Ulmus parvifolia	R	Dense	S	Dark gr			X	X	X	
Umbellularia californica (tubs)	R	Dense	M	Dark gr			X			X

CLIMATIC TOLERANCE

CONIFERS

Conifers may be broadly defined as cone-bearing plants which retain their foliage throughout the year. But there are exceptions, as there are in many other classifications in horticulture: the Yews, Junipers, Podocarpus, and California Nutmeg bear fleshy fruits; and the Larch, Bald Cypress, and Dawn Redwood lose their leaves in winter. Ornamentally, conifers are heavy and ponderous and should be used sparingly in garden design. Large gardens or very formal ones benefit from their use as accents and specimens or as hedges and windbreaks. They are seldom useful as shade trees and, in general, are not to be recommended for streets. Throughout the years, many varieties have been developed from the original species, and these often take dwarf forms; they are useful in small gardens or in patios and tubs. But even in dwarf types, the symmetry of form and general compactness make them heavy accent plants which should be used sparingly and with careful attention to over-all design.

Abies concolor

A´bies con´color
White Fir

Colorado to Mexico

Features: Habit, foliage
Use: Lawn, specimen

The tiered branches of White Fir spread gracefully into a perfect pyramid; because of its popularity as a Christmas tree, it is frequently misplanted in small gardens or close to houses, where subsequent growth is a perpetual embarrassment. It must be remembered that White Fir is a forest tree which grows to immense size and should be used only in areas where plenty of room is available for its development. It grows to its best form in cold areas.

Conformation

Height: 60 to 100 ft. (200 ft.). Spread: 40 to 60 ft.

A formal, perfectly pyramidal tree covered to the ground with branches arranged loosely in tiers, the upper ones more upright, the lower ones somewhat pendulous, and all side-branching in flat sprays. The bark is ashy gray and resinous. The leaves vary in young trees from yellowish green to blue-green, and they turn whitish with age. They are short, stiff, needle-like and bluntly pointed, ¾ to 2½ in. long, and cover the branches densely.

Fruit

Purplish, olive-green or dark yellow-green cylindrical cones, 2 to 5½ in. long, which stand upright on the branches.

Root System: Deep
Rate of Growth: Moderate to slow

Natural Requirements

Climate: Tolerates cold and grows best in cold areas.
Soil: Prefers a deep, rich, moist, light loam. Tolerates coarse, dry soil; will not tolerate heavy clay.
Exposure: Sun.

Care

Pruning: None required.
Feeding: Apply manure annually in the fall.
Watering: Water deeply once a month.
Pests and Diseases: Relatively free from both.

A´bies nordmannia´na, Nordmann Fir, attains a height of 150 ft. but grows very slowly. It has beautiful splayed branches and dark-green, shiny foliage with a silvery undersurface. It is used for the same landscaping purposes as White Fir and has the same cultural and climatic requirements.

A´bies pinsa´po, Spanish Fir, grows to a height of 40 or 60 ft. and has the same general shape as White Fir. The leaves are very rigid and acute and are so arranged as to completely surround the branchlets. A much smaller tree than either White or Nordmann Fir, it is better adapted for use in small gardens. It is the only fir of the group which will grow well in warm climates and seacoast areas.

Araucaria araucana

Arauca´ria arauca´na
(*A. imbricata*)
Monkey-Puzzle

Chile

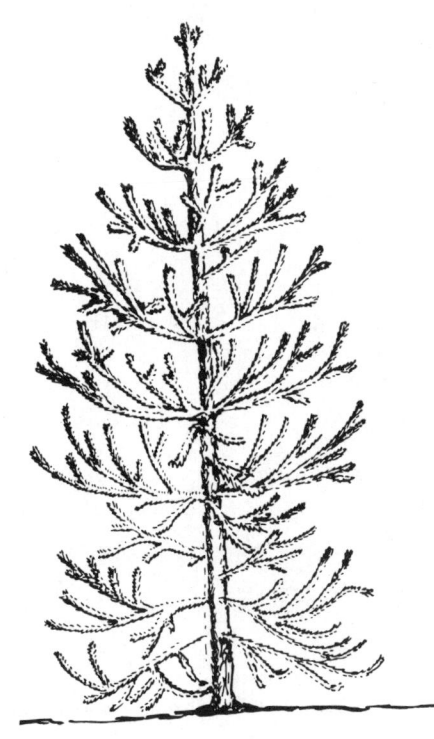

Feature: Habit

Use: Lawn, tub, novelty, specimen

The strange, twisted arrangement of branches, which would presumably baffle a monkey trying to climb the tree, gave rise to the popular name Monkey-Puzzle. The branches dip down, then rise in a gently swinging arc, evolving curious patterns, each branch standing out clearly in its particular contortion, and each clothed tightly with very dark green, sharp-pointed, overlapping leaves. Too great a curio to be used indiscriminately in the garden, the Monkey-Puzzle is best when left to stand almost alone. In its youth, it can be used very effectively in tubs.

Conformation

Height: 15 to 30 ft. (100 ft.). Spread: 8 to 15 ft. (30 ft.).

An erect, pyramidal tree with grotesquely twisted branches dipping downward, then swinging up in a gently curving arc. The bark is rough and brown. The leaves are very dark green, stiff, and sharp-pointed, ¾ to 2 in. long and ¼ to 1 in. wide. They overlap closely on the branches.

Fruit

Huge, globular cones, 5 to 8 in. long. They develop only when the tree is quite old.

Root System: Average depth to deep

Rate of Growth: Moderate

Natural Requirements

Climate: Tolerates heat and cold. Tolerates frost but needs protection from prolonged freezing when young.

Soil: Tolerates a variety of soils; prefers a moist, well-drained loam.

Exposure: Sun. Tolerates wind.

Care

Pruning: None required.

Feeding: No special feeding required.

Watering: Maintain uniform moisture content of soil. Good drainage is essential.

Pests and Diseases: Relatively free from both.

Araucaria bidwilli

Arauca´ria bid´willi
Bunya-Bunya

Queensland

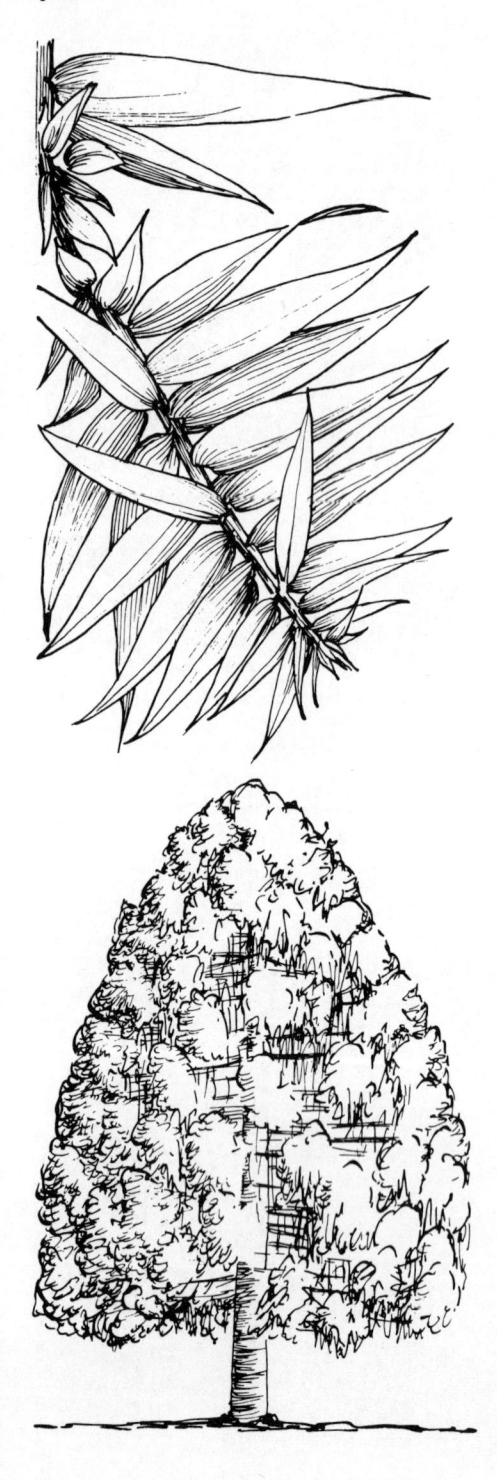

Feature: Habit

Use: Lawn, specimen

Bunya-Bunya when mature is pyramidal and is densely clothed with flat, sharp-pointed, glossy dark-green leaves. The branches dip downward, then rise in a gently swinging arc—the lower branches sweeping the ground, then curving up and away from it at the tips. Bunya-Bunya makes an excellent specimen for large lawns. It stands cold but will not tolerate prolonged freezing.

Conformation

Height: 30 to 80 ft. Spread: 40 to 60 ft.

A large, dense, wide-spreading, pyramidal tree with horizontal branches that dip gradually downward and turn up at the tips. The bark is dark brown and rough. The leaves are a glossy dark green and are 1/2 to 3 in. long and 1/4 to 3/8 in. wide. They are flat, leathery, and needle-like—sharp as thorns to the touch. They persist on the tree for a number of years.

Fruit

Pineapple-shaped cones 7 to 10 in. long and 6 to 8 in. wide. The large seeds are used for food in the tree's native land.

Root System: Average depth to deep

Rate of Growth: Moderate

Natural Requirements

Climate: Tolerates heat and cold but will not stand prolonged freezing.
Soil: Tolerates a variety of soils; prefers a moist, well-drained loam.
Exposure: Sun. Tolerates wind.

Care

Pruning: None required.
Feeding: No special feeding necessary.
Watering: Water deeply once a month.
Pests and Diseases: Scale; spray with malathion or an oil emulsion in summer and repeat when needed; spray with oil in winter.

Feature: Habit

Use: Lawn, tub, specimen

Norfolk-Island-Pine is a very formal, pyramidal tree with beautifully proportioned branches spreading out in horizontal planes and densely covered with small, bright green, needle-like leaves. The branches are arranged around the trunk like the spokes of a wheel, and are spaced far enough apart for light to penetrate through the tree, making each branch distinct. In younger trees, the upper branches usually form a perfect star. The tree makes a striking specimen for lawns and in its juvenile stages is an excellent subject for tub culture. It attains its best growth in temperate regions.

Conformation

Height: 20 to 40 ft. (70 ft.). Spread: 15 to 25 ft.

A formal, pyramidal tree with branches spreading out in horizontal planes, one above the other. The bark is a warm light brown. The leaves are a rich bright green, short and needle-like, 1/2 in. long and 1/8 in. wide. They overlap on the branches and hug them tightly.

Fruit.

Nearly round cones, 4 to 6 in. in diameter, on very old trees only.

Root System: Average depth to deep

Rate of Growth: Moderate

Natural Requirements

Climate: Grows best in warm, temperate areas. Tolerates heat but not cold.

Soil: Tolerates a variety of soils; prefers a moist, well-drained, sandy loam.

Exposure: Sun. Tolerates wind and seacoast conditions.

Care

Pruning: None required.
Feeding: No special feeding necessary.
Watering: Water deeply once a month.
Pests and Diseases: Relatively free from both.

Araucaria excelsa

Arauca´ria excel´sa
Norfolk-Island-Pine; Star-Pine

Norfolk Islands

167

Cedrus atlantica

Cédrus atlántica
Atlas Cedar

Northern Africa

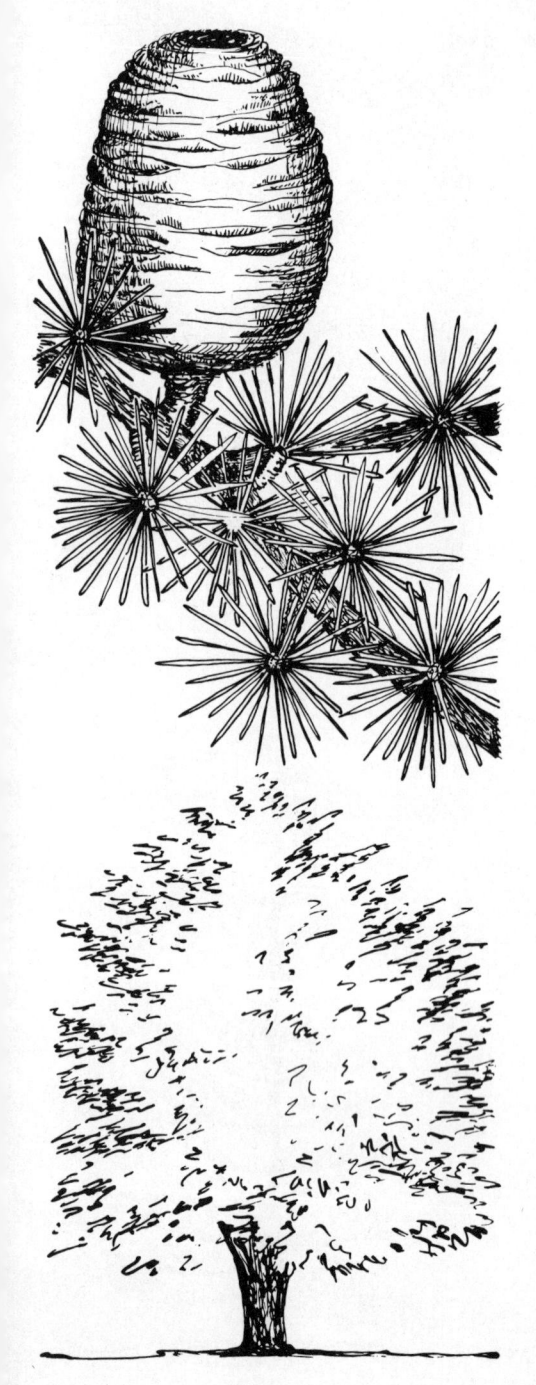

Features: Habit, foliage (var. *glauca*)

Use: Lawn, specimen

Atlas Cedar is a very large, pyramidal tree of open growth habit, with branches that are arranged in formal, precise patterns. Young trees of Atlas Cedar are usually very spindly and have a deceptively fragile appearance. It is probably for this reason that the ultimate size of the tree is underestimated and it is often planted in small gardens where it has no chance to develop properly. *Cédrus atlántica glaúca,* Blue Atlas Cedar, is an outstanding variety, exceptional for its sparkling light-blue foliage. Both trees are very hardy.

Conformation

Height: 30 to 100 ft. Spread: 30 to 60 ft.

A large, wide-spreading, formal, pyramidal tree of open growth habit, with upright, horizontal branches and a crushed leader tip. The bark is rough and dark brown. The leaves are bluish green, short, and needle-like, ¾ to 1 in. long. Var. *glauca* has light-blue foliage.

Fruit

Cones, 2 to 3 in. long and flat or concave at the top. They mature in two years.

Root System: Deep

Rate of Growth: Very slow

Natural Requirements

Climate: Tolerates heat and cold and even endures prolonged freezing.

Soil: Prefers a well-drained loam or clay. Will not tolerate boggy soils.

Exposure: Sun. Tolerates wind.

Care

Pruning: None required.

Feeding: No special feeding necessary.

Watering: Water deeply once a month. Good drainage is essential.

Pests and Diseases: Relatively free from both.

Cédrus líbani, Cedar of Lebanon, resembles Atlas Cedar so closely that it is difficult for the layman to distinguish between them. The two species have the same natural and cultural requirements and are used for the same landscaping purposes. Only when Cedars of Lebanon are hundreds of years old do they form the incomparably picturesque patterns so well known in paintings and line drawings of the tree.

Cedrus deodara

Cedrus deodara
Deodar Cedar

Himalayas

Feature: Habit

Use: Lawn, windbreak, specimen

When young, Deodar Cedar is a pyramidal tree with a dense habit and wide-spreading branches which droop gracefully at the tips. As the tree matures, the branches become more rigid and have a tiered appearance, but irregular open spaces between them alleviate the strict formality. The leaves vary from bright green to yellow-green and are crowded densely on the branches. Like Atlas Cedar, Deodar needs plenty of room in which to develop and is useful only in large gardens. It is not so hardy as Atlas Cedar but it will stand some cold.

Conformation

Height: 50 to 100 ft. Spread: 40 to 60 ft.

A large, compact, formal tree with upright, horizontal branches which are pendulous at the tips, when young, and become more rigid with age. The bark is brown and deeply furrowed on old trees, gray and smooth on young ones. The leaves are bright green, yellow-green, or bluish green; they are 1 to 2 in. long, stiff and needle-like, and arranged densely on the branches.

Fruit

Cones, rounded at the top, 3 to 5 in. long and 2½ in. wide. They take two years to mature.

Root System: Deep

Rate of Growth: Rapid

Natural Requirements

Soil: Prefers a well-drained loam or clay. Will not tolerate boggy soils. Tolerates drought.

Climate: Tolerates heat and some degree of cold but will not endure extreme cold or prolonged freezing.

Exposure: Sun. Tolerates wind.

Care

Pruning: None required.

Feeding: No special feeding necessary.

Watering: Water deeply once a month. Good drainage is essential.

Pests and Diseases: Relatively free from both.

Chamaecyparis lawsoniana

Chamaecyp′aris lawsonia′na

Port-Orford-Cedar; Lawson-Cypress; Lawson-Fir

Southwestern Oregon to northwestern California

Feature: Habit

Use: Lawn, tub (when young), specimen, accent

Port-Orford-Cedar is a large forest tree with durable, aromatic, light-colored wood which is valuable for cabinetmaking, shipbuilding, and innumerable other uses. Its wide-spreading, pendulous branches, covered with sprays of lacy foliage, form a dense, pyramidal tree of infinite grace and charm. Many deviations from the type have been preserved and propagated, and many of these are better known than the species. Port-Orford-Cedar makes an excellent tub subject when young and is an exceptionally beautiful lawn specimen in its more mature stages. The tree should of course have plenty of room in which to develop. It will not stand hot, dry winds or extremely cold climates.

Conformation

Height: 75 to 100 ft. Spread: 30 to 50 ft.

A pyramidal tree with wide-spreading, pendulous branches and a crushed or nodding leader tip. The bark is spongy, ridged, and scaly, and is reddish brown. The leaves are bright green and scalelike, the young growth appearing in flat, upright sprays.

A few of the many varieties under cultivation are: Var. *al′lumi* (Scarab-Cypress), 12 to 30 ft. in height; a fat, pyramidal tree with bright blue, scalelike foliage. Var. *ell′woodi* (Ellwood-Cypress), 12 to 30 ft. in height; a very compact, almost columnar, pyramidal tree with small, soft blue foliage and a very slow rate of growth. Var. *stew′arti,* 15 to 30 ft. in height, an upright, slender, pyramidal tree with gold-tipped, scalelike leaves. Var. *wis′seli,* 15 to 20 ft. in height, a slender, columnar tree with dark bluish-green foliage which is twisted in many interesting arrangements on the branches. This variety is unfortunately somewhat subject to disease and insect infestation.

Flowers

Bright red catkins. They are interesting but not conspicuous enough to be of any great ornamental value.

Fruit

Small, brown, shiny cones, ¼ in. in diameter.

Root System: Deep

Rate of Growth: Moderate

Natural Requirements

Climate: Grows best in cool, humid or coastal areas. Tolerates heat and cold but will not endure extreme cold.

Soil: Grows best in moderately moist, well-drained, sandy loam. Tolerates drought.

Exposure: Sun or partial shade, preferably partial shade. Grows best in cool, coastal areas. Needs protection from hot or dry winds.

Care

Pruning: None required.

Feeding: No special feeding necessary.

Watering: Water deeply once a month.

Pests and Diseases: Relatively free from pests. Var. *wisseli,* however, should be sprayed each spring and fall with an all-purpose insecticide-fungicide as a preventive measure.

Chamaecyparis obtusa

Chamaecyp´aris obtu´sa
Hinoki-Cypress

Japan

Features: Habit, foliage

Use: Patio, tub, specimen

Hinoki-Cypress is a wide-spreading tree with gently pendulous branches which are densely covered with flat sprays of scalelike leaves. It grows slowly and remains a small tree for a good many years. A number of horticultural varieties have been developed, the most important of which are dwarf forms with various foliage deviations. Both the species and the varieties make unusually fine tub and patio plants and are excellent subjects for small gardens. They are interesting, even when quite young, and can be grown in any climate where winters are not very severe.

Conformation

Height: 10 to 30 ft. (90 ft.). Spread: 5 to 20 ft.

A formal, pyramidal tree with horizontal-spreading branches that are pendulous at the tips. The bark is reddish brown and sheds in long, narrow strips. The branches are heavily clothed with flattened, scalelike leaves, bright green above and marked with whitish lines beneath.

A few of the varieties under cultivation are: Var. *gracilis*, a pyramidal form, growing to a height of 20 ft., with dark-green foliage and gently pendulous branches. Var. *nana*, a very compact, dwarf type, usually growing no more than 3 ft. high, with dark-green foliage arranged in flat planes. Var. *nana aurea*, a dwarf type with young foliage a golden yellow.

Fruit

Tiny cones, ¼ in. in diameter; not effective ornamentally.

Root System: Deep

Rate of Growth: Slow

Natural Requirements

Climate: Grows best in cool, coastal areas where moist air is available. Tolerates heat and cold but will not stand extreme cold.

Soil: Prefers a deep, well-drained, sandy loam with some moisture. Tolerates dry soils.

Exposure: Partial shade. Tolerates seacoast conditions. Protect from dry winds.

Care

Pruning: None required.
Feeding: Apply manure annually in the fall.
Watering: Water deeply once a month.
Pests and Diseases: Relatively free from both.

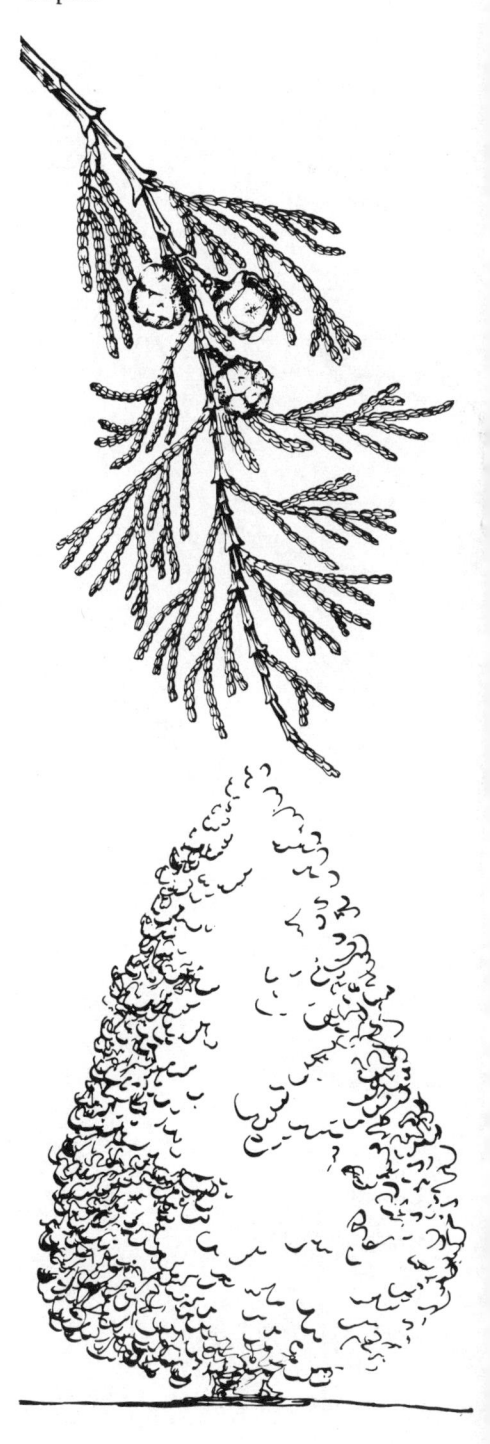

Chamaecyparis pisifera

Chamaecyp´aris pisif´era
Sawara-Cypress

Japan

Features: Habit, foliage

Use: Lawn, specimen

Sawara-Cypress is a large, narrowly pyramidal tree with an open habit of growth and a tendency to lose its lower branches quite early in life. The foliage on the inner branches also frequently dies out and new growth must be spurred by annual pruning. Horticultural varieties are more frequently planted than the species and are noteworthy for their foliage characteristics. Sawara-Cypress stands cold but will not tolerate prolonged freezing. It should have plenty of room in which to develop.

Conformation

Height: 20 to 30 ft. (90 ft.). Spread: 10 to 15 ft. (40 ft.).

A loosely pyramidal tree with wide, horizontal-spreading branches, pendulous at the tips. The bark is reddish brown and peels in long, thin strips. The leaves are bright, glossy green above and marked with whitish lines beneath. They are scale-like and sharp-pointed and are arranged loosely on the branches.

A few of the many varieties are: Var. *filifera* (Thread Sawara-Cypress), which grows to a height of 10 ft. and has weeping branches and dark-green, threadlike leaves; there are also dwarf and golden-foliaged forms of this variety. Var. *plumosa* (Plume Sawara-Cypress), which grows to a height of 20 or 30 ft. and assumes a broad, pyramidal shape. The leaves are very feathery and have a bluish cast when young. Var. *squarrosa* (Moss Sawara-Cypress), which grows to a height of 20 or 30 ft. and has a bushy, irregular habit of growth and soft, feathery, gray-green foliage. An improved form is *squarrosa veitchi*, with light blue-green foliage of very soft texture.

Fruit

Cones, 1/3 in. in diameter; not effective ornamentally.

Root System: Deep

Rate of Growth: Slow

Natural Requirements

Climate: Grows best in cool, coastal areas. Tolerates heat. Stands light frost but will not endure extreme cold or prolonged freezing.

Soil: Prefers a deep, well-drained, sandy loam with plenty of humus and average moisture conditions.

Exposure: Partial shade. Protect from dry winds.

Care

Pruning: Prune branches to keep tree under control and to force new foliage growth on the inside of the branches. Remove dead branches. This should be done annually. Time: Spring or fall.

Feeding: Apply manure annually in the fall.

Watering: Water deeply once a month.

Pests and Diseases: Relatively free from both.

Faults

Inner foliage has a tendency to die out.

Cryptomeria japonica

Cryptomé'ria japon'ica

Cryptomeria

Japan

Features: Habit, foliage, fall color (var. *elegans,* a bronzy red)

Use: Lawn, hedge, specimen

Cryptomeria is a pyramidal tree with a distinguished branching habit and awl-shaped leaves resembling those of the Giant Sequoia. The species is quite old—like the Redwood and Ginkgo it can be traced to a remote geological epoch. It is a forest tree of great economic importance in Japan today. Var. *elegans* is planted more extensively than the species for ornamental use, and grows to a dense pyramid with soft, feathery, bright green foliage which turns a bronzy red in winter. When used in the garden, sufficient space should be allowed these trees for their appropriate development and display. They will not tolerate excessive heat or excessive cold.

Conformation

Height: 25 to 35 ft. (100 ft.). Spread: 15 to 25 ft. (50 ft.).

An open-growing, pyramidal tree with spreading branches which ascend at the tips. The trunk is straight and slender and is covered with cinnamon-colored, peeling bark. The leaves are bright green, soft, and needle-like, curving upward at the tips in an awl shape. They are $\frac{1}{4}$ to 1 in. long.

Var. *elegans* grows to a dense, compact pyramid with soft, feathery, bright green leaves which turn bronzy red in winter.

A useful form for tub and patio culture is the very small and compact variety *compacta,* with bright green, needle-like foliage which turns bronzy red in winter.

Fruit

Cones, 1 in. in diameter; June–Aug.

Root System: Deep

Rate of Growth: Slow

Natural Requirements

Climate: Prefers mild climates. Will not tolerate extreme heat or extreme cold.

Soil: Grows best in rich, moist, well-drained loam; will not tolerate hard, dry soils.

Exposure: Sun or partial shade. Protect from wind.

Care

Pruning: None required.

Feeding: Apply manure annually in the fall.

Watering: Provide plenty of moisture. Good drainage is essential.

Pests and Diseases: Relatively free from both.

Cupressus arizonica (Hort.)

Cupres´sus arizo´nica
(Cupressus glabra)

Arizona Cypress; Roughbark Cypress; Redbark Cypress

Southern Arizona

Features: Foliage, bark
Use: Hedge, windbreak, erosion control, specimen

Young specimens of Arizona Cypress are used extensively as Christmas trees in the Pacific Southwest because of their compact, uniform shapes, straight, tapering, red-barked trunks, and handsome blue-green foliage. The mature tree is less attractive, growing in a variety of forms from dense to open-headed and having dull gray-green foliage and dark-brown bark. Arizona Cypress is used for reclamation purposes in desert areas and on rocky slopes; it also makes an excellent hedge or windbreak. It will stand light frost but will not tolerate prolonged freezing.

Conformation

Height: 20 to 60 ft. Spread: 8 to 30 ft.

A narrowly pyramidal tree with a straight, tapering trunk, covered with plated red bark, and horizontal branches; mature trees are dense or open-growing with deeply furrowed dark-brown bark. The leaves are scalelike and glaucous blue-green on young trees and become dull gray-green as they mature.

Fruit

Small cones, about 7/8 to 1 in. long, which are at first green, then turn gray, and finally become dark brown or purplish. Fall.

Root System: Shallow, spreading. Fibrous roots.

Rate of Growth: Rapid

Natural Requirements

Climate: Tolerates heat. Will stand light frost but will not endure extreme cold or prolonged freezing. Tolerates desert atmosphere.
Soil: Tolerates dry, sterile, or sandy soils and drought.
Exposure: Sun. Tolerates wind.

Care

Pruning: Stands heavy shearing, which is necessary when the tree is used as a hedge. Time: Spring or fall.
Feeding: No special feeding necessary.
Watering: Not required after plant is established.
Pests and Diseases: Relatively free from both.

Cupres´sus macrocar´pa, Monterey Cypress, has enjoyed a long period of unmerited popularity and has been vastly overplanted. It is not recommended here for ornamental use. It has voracious, wide-spreading, soil-depleting roots and is the host plant for a number of insects which spread from it to ravage other plants in the garden. Under cultivation it has no outstanding ornamental qualities which would relate it, even remotely, to the wind-configurated specimens growing wild on the Monterey Peninsula. *Cupres´sus forbesi*, or Tecate Cypress, a tree which grows 15 to 30 ft. high, with a spread of 10 to 30 ft., can be used more effectively. In youth, this tree is compact and narrowly conical, with rich green foliage and an amazing resistance to hot, searing winds. It makes an excellent hedge or windbreak. Older trees are wide-spreading, with broad crowns and beautifully mottled red-and-green bark. They are used extensively to provide shade.

Cupressus sempervirens

Cupres´sus sempervi´rens

Italian Cypress

Southern Europe; western Asia

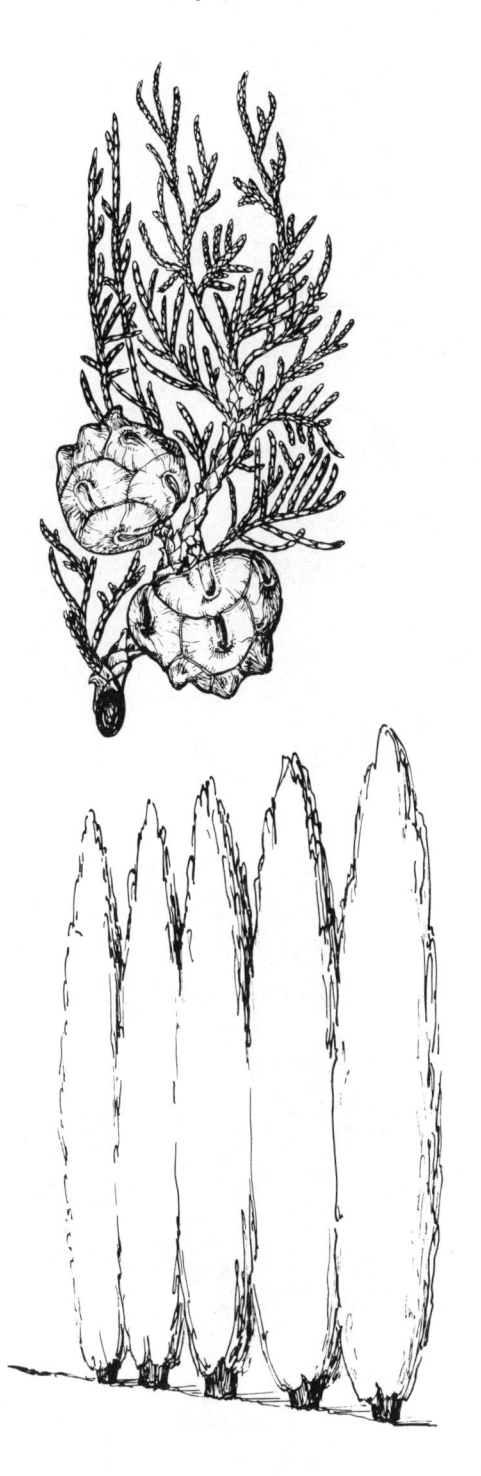

Feature: Habit
Use: Specimen, accent

Italian Cypress is a tapering, conical tree, tall, narrow, and covered to the ground with dense, very dark green foliage. It is used in landscaping to create and emphasize formal effects and to accent the vertical line. On large estates, it can be used to border wide walks which serve as approaches to the house. Italian Cypress should not be allowed too much moisture or too rich a soil, for this stimulates an overgrowth of foliage and causes the branches to bend out and down, destroying the beautiful, compact shape. The tree will not stand severe cold and is not consistently long-lived in cooler, coastal areas of the Pacific Coast.

Conformation

Height: 20 to 60 ft. Spread: 8 to 15 ft.

A narrowly conical tree with thin, grayish-brown bark and a very compact branching habit. The very small leaves are deep, dark green and are arranged very densely on the branches.

Fruit

Cones, to 1½ in. in diameter; not effective ornamentally.

Root System: Deep

Rate of Growth: Slow

Natural Requirements

Climate: Tolerates heat. Stands light frost but will not endure extreme cold or prolonged freezing.

Soil: Prefers a deep, well-drained, not too fertile soil.

Exposure: Sun.

Care

Pruning: None required except to remove dead branches.
Feeding: No special feeding necessary.
Watering: Not required after plant is established.
Pests and Diseases: Relatively free from both.

Ginkgo biloba

Gink'go bilo'ba

Maidenhair Tree; Silverfruit; Sacred Tree of China

Eastern China

Features: Foliage, habit, fall color (golden yellow)

Use: Street, lawn, tubs

Ginkgo is a slender-branched, lacy tree which assumes a conical shape, with age. The foliage is entirely unusual in that each leaf is a perfect replica of a miniature fan, deeply notched at the center apex and spreading out from the leafstalk in the form of a semicircle. The leaves are a delicate light green and turn golden yellow before dropping. Female Ginkgo plants have fruit which exudes a highly offensive odor; it is therefore most important to obtain only male plants for use in the garden. The tree is effective in street or lawn plantings and is well adapted to tub culture. It is very hardy, withstanding extremes of heat and cold.

Conformation

Height: 75 to 120 ft. Spread: 50 to 80 ft.

A deciduous, open-growing, conical tree with slender, ascending branches. The trunk is straight and tapering and the bark is tan and deeply furrowed. The leaves are simple, alternate, and entire, distinctly fan-shaped and notched in the center, and 2 to 3½ in. wide. They are light green, turning golden yellow in the fall and lasting on the tree far into December.

Flowers

Not effective ornamentally. Trees do not bloom until they are at least twenty years old.

Fruit

Small, silver, plumlike fruit, 1 in. in diameter, fleshy outside and hard inside; on female plants only. In some countries it is used for food, though it has an obnoxious odor and taste. Aug.-Oct.

Root System: Deep

Rate of Growth: Moderate

Natural Requirements

Climate: Tolerates extremes of heat and cold. Adaptable.

Soil: Prefers a deep, well-drained loam. Tolerates a wide variety of soils. Good drainage is essential.

Exposure: Sun or shade. Tolerates smog, wind, and seacoast conditions.

Care

Pruning: Little pruning is required or advised. Time: Early spring.

Feeding: No special feeding necessary.

Watering: Water deeply once a month. Never allow water to stand at the base of the plant.

Pests and Diseases: Relatively free from both.

Faults

Obnoxious odor of flowers and fruit on female trees.

Juniperus chinensis

Juníp´erus chinen´sis
Chinese Juniper

Features: Habit, foliage
Use: Hedge, windbreak, erosion control, specimen (var. *torulosa* in patios or tubs)

Chinese Juniper is a medium-sized tree which grows to a compact, pyramidal shape, with blue-green foliage tightly clothing the branches. Varieties are available with different growth habits and foliage colors; the most desirable is *torulosa*, the Twisted or Hollywood Juniper. Except for this one, Chinese Juniper and its varieties are best restricted to use in the outlying areas of the garden as windbreaks or hedges and for erosion control since they tend to become scraggly with age. Hollywood Juniper, however, may be used as a specimen or accent plant in the garden or in patios and tubs. It is an erect tree with a main trunk which ascends in an undulating line, and from which spring many uneven, artistically twisted side branches. The foliage is bright green to dark green and covers the branches densely. Chinese Juniper and its varieties have a wide climatic tolerance, standing heat, cold, drought, and seacoast conditions.

China; Japan

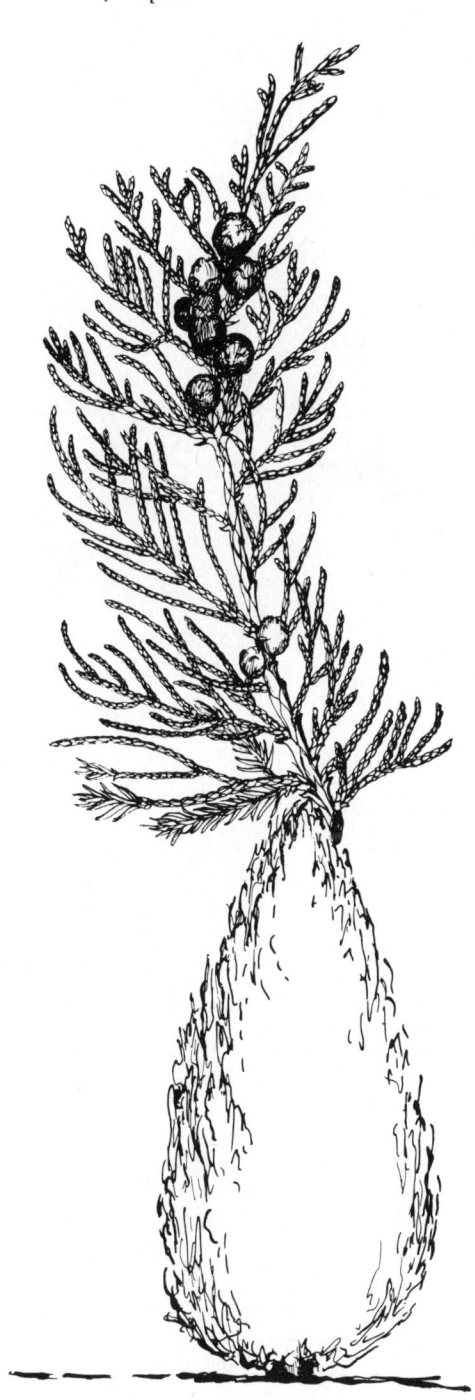

Conformation
Height: 10 to 30 ft. Spread: 6 to 12 ft.

A low-branching, pyramidal tree with an upright habit of growth and many slender, ascending branches. The bark is grayish brown. The leaves are blue-green and densely cover the branches. They are of two kinds: short, prickly, and needle-like; and scalelike.

Among the varieties worthy of consideration are: Var. *columnaris*, which grows in a narrow pyramid to a height of 20 ft. and has silvery blue-green foliage; and var. *torulosa* (Hollywood Juniper), which grows to a height of 25 ft. and has an undulating trunk and twisted branches that form a bright to dark-green pyramid.

Fruit
Decorative, blue to purple berries, 1/4 to 3/8 in. in diameter. These mature the second year; the fruit appears on female plants only, and if berries are desired, the plants must be selected when they are in fruit. Fall and winter.

Root System: Average, spreading

Rate of Growth: Slow. Rate is faster in mild regions.

Natural Requirements
Climate: Tolerates heat and cold. Adaptable.
Soil: Tolerates light, sandy, rocky, or gravelly soils. Tolerates alkali and drought but grows best if it has some moisture.
Exposure: Sun. Tolerates wind and seacoast conditions.

Care
Pruning: Prune to shape. Stands any amount of shearing. Time: Spring or fall.
Feeding: No special feeding necessary.
Watering: Water deeply once a month. Good drainage is essential.
Pests and Diseases: Red spider; spray with malathion at first sign of infestation and repeat when needed. Juniper rust; spray with "fermate" in spring and repeat when needed.

Juniperus communis

Juníp´erus commú´nis
Common Juniper

Eastern United States; Europe; Asia

Features: Habit, foliage

Use: Hedge, windbreak, erosion control, accent

The varieties of Common Juniper are more frequently used for ornamental purposes than is the species itself. The two most important varieties are *hibernica*, Irish Juniper, with bluish foliage, and *suecica*, Swedish Juniper, with yellowish-green foliage; both are narrow, columnar or pyramidal trees. The Swedish Juniper is the hardier of the two; the Irish tends to frost burn in cold regions. However, they both have a wide climatic tolerance. They are used to accent vertical lines or for hedges, windbreaks, and erosion control.

Conformation

Height: 20 to 40 ft. Spread: 10 to 20 ft.

A slender, pyramidal tree with upright-spreading branches and reddish-brown bark which sheds in papery scales. The foliage covers the branches densely and is composed of short, prickly, needle-like leaves, 1/3 to 3/4 in. long. The species has blue-green foliage; var. *aurea* has leaves tipped with golden yellow; var. *hibernica* has blue leaves with whitish undersurfaces; and var. *suecica* has light yellowish-green leaves.

Fruit

Decorative, bluish-purple berries, ¼ in. in diameter, which mature the second year and on female plants only. If berries are desired, the plants must be selected when they are in fruit. Fall and winter.

Root System: Average depth, spreading

Rate of Growth: Slow. More rapid in milder regions.

Natural Requirements

Climate: Tolerates heat and cold. Var. *hibernica* is subject to foliage burn in bitterly cold areas.
Soil: Tolerates light, sandy, rocky, or gravelly soils and alkali and drought, but grows best if it has some moisture.
Exposure: Sun. Tolerates wind and seacoast conditions.

Care

Pruning: Prune to shape, when necessary. Stands any amount of shearing. Time: Spring or fall.
Feeding: No special feeding necessary.
Watering: Water deeply once a month. Good drainage is essential.
Pests and Diseases: Red spider; spray with malathion at first sign of infestation and repeat when needed. Juniper rust; spray with "fermate" in spring and repeat when needed.

Juníp´erus virginiá´na, Eastern Red-Cedar, is a rapid-growing, pyramidal tree which has the same natural and cultural requirements as Common Juniper and is used for the same landscaping purposes. It varies in height and spread, being from 10 to 30 ft. high and from 5 to 10 ft. broad, depending upon the climate in which the tree is grown. The foliage is bright green in spring, deepens gradually to darker green throughout the summer, and becomes pinkish or reddish in winter. There are many varieties of Eastern Red-Cedar under cultivation, differing in foliage color from dark green to blue, silver, and gold.

Juniperus pachyphloea

Juníp´erus pachyphloe´a
Alligator Juniper

Southwest United States and Mexico

Features: Habit, foliage, bark
Use: Shade, specimen, accent, erosion control

Alligator Juniper grows from a young tree of twisted, columnar shape with bluish-white foliage to an irregularly spreading, pyramidal tree with a short, thick trunk and blue-green foliage. The shape varies greatly in individual plants, but it is always picturesque. The most outstanding characteristic of the tree is its red-brown, checkered bark; broken by checks and furrows into numberless, flattened plates, it has a remarkable resemblance to an alligator's hide. Alligator Juniper is a handsome specimen tree, excellent for use in hot, dry areas. It will not tolerate extreme cold.

Conformation

Height: 30 to 40 ft. (60 ft.). Spread: 15 to 60 ft.

A twisted, columnar tree with bluish-white foliage when young, which becomes a picturesque, irregularly spreading specimen when mature. The trunk is short and thick and is covered with a red-brown bark, divided into many scaly plates. When mature, the leaves are blue-green and scalelike and are about 1/16 in. long.

Fruit

Reddish-brown berries, 1/8 in. in diameter, which are covered with a whitish bloom when young. They mature the second year; fruit appears on female plants only, and if berries are desired, the plants must be selected when they are in fruit.

Root System: Average depth, spreading

Rate of Growth: Slow

Natural Requirements

Climate: Tolerates heat. Stands light frost but will not endure extreme cold. Tolerates dry atmosphere.
Soil: Tolerates light, sandy, rocky, gravelly, or alkali soils and drought.
Exposure: Sun. Tolerates wind and seacoast conditions.

Care

Pruning: Tree stands pruning, but is best when left to take its natural shape.
Feeding: No special feeding necessary.
Watering: No special moisture requirements. Good drainage is essential.
Pests and Diseases: Red spider; spray with malathion at first sign of infestation and repeat when needed. Juniper rust; spray with "fermate" in spring and repeat when needed.

Libocedrus decurrens

Liboce'drus decur'rens
Incense-Cedar

Oregon; northern California

Features: Habit, foliage, fruit

Use: Hedge, windbreak, specimen, accent

Incense-Cedar is a narrowly columnar tree with pendulous branchlets and flat sprays of lustrous, bright green to yellowish-green leaves, which yield a spicy fragrance when crushed. The urn-shaped cones are red-brown and look somewhat like carved flowers. The wood of the tree is light and durable and is used, among other things, to make moth-proof chests; an oil extracted from the wood is used in making perfume. In landscaping, Incense-Cedar is used for hedges and windbreaks and as specimens to create formal effects and to accent vertical lines. It is a strong-growing tree, tolerating extremes of heat and cold.

Conformation

Height: 50 to 150 ft. Spread: 12 to 50 ft.

A tall, compact, narrowly columnar tree with a sharply tapering trunk. The branches extend to the ground and have a distinct upward turn; the branchlets are pendulous. The bark is cinnamon brown, thin, and furrowed; it peels in long strips. The leaves are bright green to yellowish green and exude a spicy fragrance when crushed. They are 1/8 to 1/4 in. long and are arranged in the form of flat sprays.

Fruit

Red-brown, urn-shaped cones, ¾ to 1 in. long, pendulous on the branches. They look somewhat like carved flowers.

Root System: Deep

Rate of Growth

Very slow until the tree is established, then moderate to rapid

Natural Requirements

Climate: Tolerates heat and cold.

Soil: Tolerates a variety of soils, including heavy ones. Prefers a deep, well-drained loam.

Exposure: Sun or shade. Resents smog. Tolerates wind and seacoast conditions.

Care

Pruning: None required.

Feeding: No special feeding necessary. For regular feedings use sulphate of ammonia only.

Watering: Water deeply once a month. Avoid frequent light watering.

Pests and Diseases: Relatively free from both.

Picea pungens

Pi´cea pun´gens
Colorado Spruce

Features: Habit, foliage
Use: Lawn, specimen

Colorado Spruce is a sturdy, upright-growing, pyramidal tree with heavy, wide-spreading branches which are densely covered with stiff, bright green to bluish-green leaves. It grows to a large specimen and needs plenty of room in which to develop. Two blue-foliaged varieties, *glauca* and *kosteriana*, are perhaps more widely planted than the species: Colorado Spruce and its varieties will not tolerate extreme heat but will stand cold and cool, humid areas.

Rocky Mountains, Utah to New Mexico

Conformation

Height: 80 to 100 ft. Spread: 40 to 50 ft.

A formal, pyramidal tree, sturdy and upright in growth, with wide-spreading branches extending to the ground. The bark is grayish brown, scaly, and deeply furrowed. The leaves are bright green with a bluish tinge, stiff and needle-like, and ¾ to 1¼ in. long. They are spiny and curved and spread out from the branches in all directions. Var. *glauca* (Colorado Blue Spruce) has bright blue foliage and var. *kosteriana* (Koster Blue Spruce) has bright blue to light-blue foliage. The needles are on short leafstalks, or "pegs."

Fruit

Cones, 2½ to 4 in. long, pendulous on the branches. Aug.–Oct.

Root System: Shallow, with long, slender rootlets.

Rate of Growth: Moderate to slow

Natural Requirements

Climate: Tolerates cold; cannot stand extreme heat. Tolerates mild, humid areas.
Soil: Tolerates a variety of soils. Good drainage is essential.
Exposure: Sun or shade

Care

Pruning: None required.
Feeding: No special feeding necessary.
Watering: Water deeply once a month. Good drainage is essential.
Pests and Diseases: Red spider; spray with malathion at the first sign of infestation and repeat as needed. Parasitic fungi cause wood decay; there is no cure; remove and burn the tree.

Pi´cea a´bies (P. excelsa), Norway Spruce, when young, is a stiffly branching, formal, pyramidal tree with light-green foliage, similar to but shorter than Colorado Spruce. It grows more rapidly and matures earlier than most spruce and fir trees, and in its ragged old age, it is likely to be somewhat of a problem in a garden. It grows to a height of 70 to 125 ft., spreads 30 to 50 ft., and has the same cultural and natural requirements as Colorado Spruce. It is very useful as a hedge or windbreak or specimen in large gardens, but it should not be planted in small ones, because of its ultimate size.

Pinus canariensis

Pi´nus canarien´sis
Canary Pine

Canary Islands

Feature: Foliage

Use: Accent, erosion control

Canary Pine is distinctive for its long, pendant, gray-green needles, which droop gracefully from slender, spreading branches. Characteristically pyramidal when young, it becomes a broad, graceful specimen with a delicacy unusual in pines. Because of its rapid rate of growth and its tolerance of drought, it is useful for fixing soils or for planting on rocky hillsides. It achieves its best growth in temperate regions.

Conformation
Height: 60 to 80 ft.   Spread: 25 to 35 ft.

A pyramidal tree with slender, spreading branches, which becomes roundheaded and graceful when mature. The bark is slightly fissured, thick, scaly, and reddish brown. The needles are gray-green, slender, and pendulous. They are 9 to 12 in. long and are clustered in tufts at the ends of the branches, in bundles of three. They persist on the tree for two years.

Fruit
Oblong cones, 4 to 8 in. long. They ripen in two years.

Root System: Deep

Rate of Growth: Rapid

Natural Requirements
Climate: Prefers temperate regions. Tolerates heat; will not endure extreme cold.
Soil: Grows best in sandy, not too fertile loam. Tolerates poor or gravelly soils.
Exposure: Sun. Tolerates seacoast conditions.

Care
Pruning: None is required.
Feeding: No special feeding necessary. Apply ½ lb. sulphate of ammonia for each inch of trunk diameter at regular two- to three-year feeding periods.
Watering: No special attention necessary.
Pests and Diseases: Relatively free from both.

Faults
Stump sprouting makes it difficult to eliminate the tree from the garden.

Pi´nus pondero´sa, Western Yellow Pine, grows to a height of 60 to 200 ft. and a spread of 30 to 40 ft. It is an important lumber tree but is much too large for use in small gardens. Its chief landscaping value is its climatic adaptability and its tolerance of adverse soil and exposure conditions. It is a narrow tree, with a spirelike crown; richly colored, red-brown bark; and bright yellow-green needles, which stand out stiffly on the branches. The needles are 5 to 10 in. long, clustered in bundles of three. Moderate to slow in growth rate, it has the same natural and cultural requirements as Canary Pine, but is more alkali tolerant. Var. *scopulo´rum*, Rocky Mountain Yellow Pine, is a smaller tree, growing to a maximum height of 75 ft. It has stiff blue-gray needles, 5 to 7 in. long, and under adverse conditions is not so strong-growing as the species.

Pinus halepensis

Pi'nus halepen'sis
Aleppo Pine

Mediterranean regions

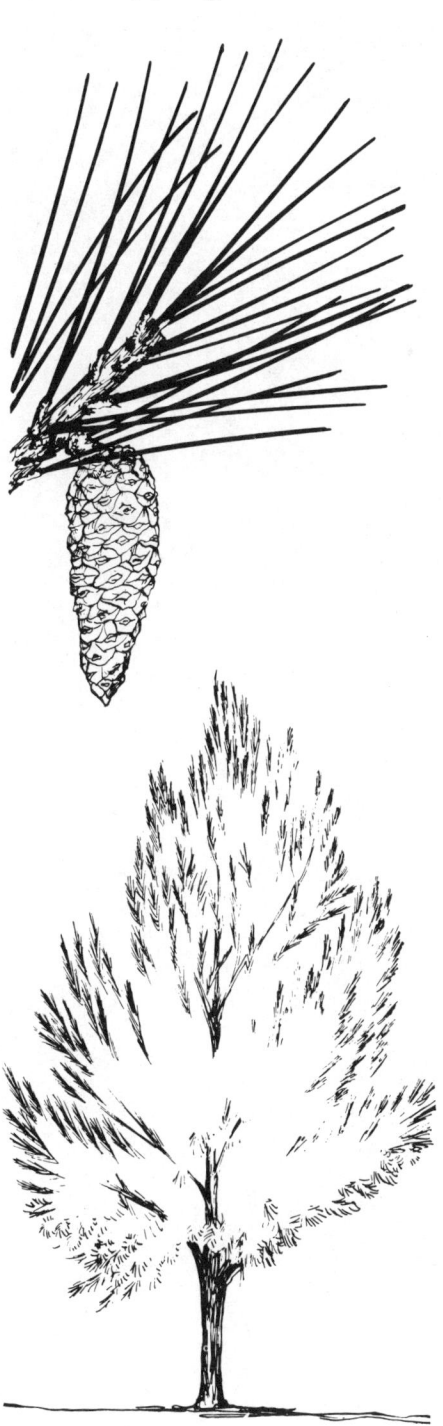

Feature: Foliage

Use: Windbreak, erosion control

Aleppo Pine has an open habit of growth with no particular distinction in pattern or design. Its gray-green needles are attractive but are sparsely distributed. The tree is not of the highest ornamental quality; its importance in landscaping comes from its great tolerance of heat, wind, and arid soils, which makes it a valuable subject for erosion control and windbreaks in dry, hot areas and on the seacoast. It is not, however, tolerant of desert conditions.

Conformation

Height: 30 to 60 ft. Spread: 20 to 30 ft.

An open-growing tree with many short, slender branches often twisting to peculiar and unattractive shapes. The bark is smooth and silvery gray when the tree is young, and becomes brown, scaly, and furrowed as it matures. The gray-green needles are in sparse tufts at the ends of the branches. They are very slender, 2½ to 5½ in. long, and in bundles of two (rarely three). They persist on the tree for two years.

Fruit

Nearly symmetrical, ovoid cones, 2½ to 4 in. long. They ripen in two years.

Root System: Deep

Rate of Growth: Rapid

Natural Requirements

Climate: Grows best in temperate areas. Tolerates heat; will not stand extreme cold.

Exposure: Sun. Tolerates seacoast conditions and also dry, hot winds.

Care

Pruning: None required.
Feeding: No special feeding necessary.
Watering: Not required after plant is established.
Pests and Diseases: Canker is sometimes present on the branches; prune out dead wood and infected areas and treat with Bordeaux.

Faults

Slow, uncertain growth in youth.

Pin'us pinas'ter, Cluster Pine, is an excellent tree for fixing soils in seacoast areas in southern and central California. Its needles are bright green, stiff, and glossy, 4 to 9 in. long, and in bundles of two.

Pinus nigra

Pí′nus ní′gra
Austrian Pine

Central and southern Europe; Asia Minor

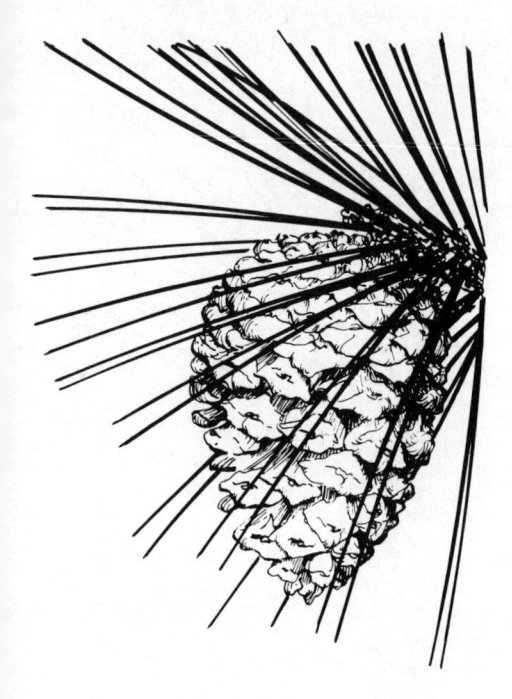

Features: Habit, foliage

Use: Lawn, windbreak, accent, erosion control

Austrian Pine grows to a densely pyramidal, wide-spreading shape with a rounded top and a precise arrangement of branches, which it maintains even when mature. The needles are stiff and cover the branches closely. They are dark green to almost black and have a rich sheen. This tree rivals all the pines in durability under adverse conditions, growing in seacoast, high desert, and mountain areas with equally good form. Wind tolerant, salt tolerant, and surviving in any soil, it is excellent for erosion control and windbreaks. In the garden it is used with lighter-foliaged plants as an effective contrast accent.

Conformation

Height: 35 to 50 ft. Spread: 25 to 40 ft.

A pyramidal tree with stout, wide-spreading branches, rounding at the top with age but maintaining its lower branches. The bark is dark gray and rough. The leaves are shiny dark green to almost black, very stiff, and arranged densely on the branches. They are 3 to 6 in. long, in bundles of two, and persist for four years.

Fruit

Dark-brown ovoid cones, 2 to 3½ in. long. They ripen in two years.

Root System: Deep

Rate of Growth: Rapid

Natural Requirements

Climate: Tolerates heat and cold. Stands high altitudes and high desert conditions.

Soil: Will grow in any soil. Tolerates alkali, salt, and drought.

Exposure: Sun or shade. Tolerates wind, salt spray, and seacoast conditions. Tolerates smoke and dust.

Care

Pruning: None required.

Feeding: No special feeding necessary.

Watering: No special attention necessary.

Pests and Diseases: Austrian Pine is subject to tip blight, which causes the ends of the branches to die back. Should the disease occur, the tips should be cut back to healthy wood in the dry season, and the tree sprayed with Bordeaux. It is very important that the pruned wood be burned immediately to prevent spreading of the disease.

Pí′nus thunbergí, Japanese Black Pine, is a seacoast pine with dense, dark-green foliage and wide-spreading branches which assume many irregular and picturesque forms. It is a slow-growing tree of great beauty, which is used extensively for dwarfing and also makes an excellent patio or tub subject. The needles are 3 to 4½ in. long, and occur in bundles of two.

Pinus pinea

Pi´nus pine´a
Italian Stone Pine

Mediterranean region

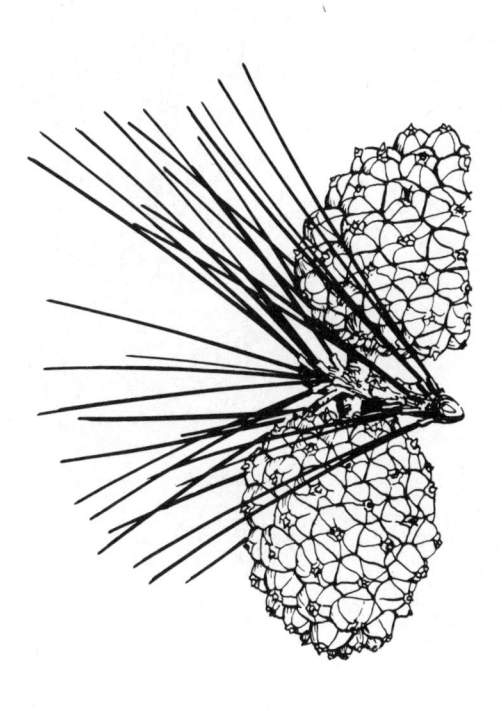

Features: Habit, foliage

Use: Shade, lawn, specimen, accent

The massive, bare branches of the Italian Stone Pine fork close to the ground, spreading steeply upward and extending outward to form a heavy, flat-topped, umbrella-like crown. Long, bright green, shiny needles cover the crown very densely and cast heavy and abundant shade. The appearance of this pine has been compared to a volcano in eruption: the tree grows in a vertical column and then spreads laterally to form a flat mass. Its predictable, uniform shape, makes it an excellent specimen tree for use in medium-sized gardens. It is very strong growing but will not tolerate extreme cold.

Conformation
Height: 30 to 50 ft. (70 ft.). Spread: 40 to 50 ft.

A flatly roundheaded tree with long, massive branches ascending steeply and spreading outward on all sides. The bark is gray-black, thick, and deeply fissured. The shiny, bright green needles are arranged very densely on the branches. They are 3½ to 7 in. long, very stiff, and occur in bundles of two.

Fruit
Reddish-brown, ovoid cones, 3½ to 5 in. long. They ripen in two years and contain seeds which are used for food.

Root System: Deep

Rate of Growth: Moderate

Natural Requirements
Climate: Grows best in temperate areas. Tolerates heat. Stands light frost but will not endure extreme cold.
Soil: Grows best in light, well-drained, sandy loam. Tolerates drought.
Exposure: Sun. Tolerates wind.

Care
Pruning: None required.
Feeding: No special feeding necessary.
Watering: No special attention necessary.
Pests and Diseases: Relatively free from both.

Pi´nus mu´go, the Swiss Mountain Pine, attains a height of 10 to 40 ft. and a spread of 12 to 30 ft. It has dense, stiff, bright green needles, 2 in. long and in bundles of two, and grows from a pyramidal shape, when young, to a wide-spreading picturesque tree, with age. It is resistant to cold and grows well under a variety of adverse conditions. The best-known variety, *mu´ghus*, or Mugo Pine, is a dwarf, shrublike tree extensively used in patios and in tub culture. Var. *mughus* should be pinched back occasionally at the tips and fed a well-balanced commercial fertilizer annually in early spring for the best growth and foliage color.

Pinus radiata

Pi´nus radia´ta

Monterey Pine

California

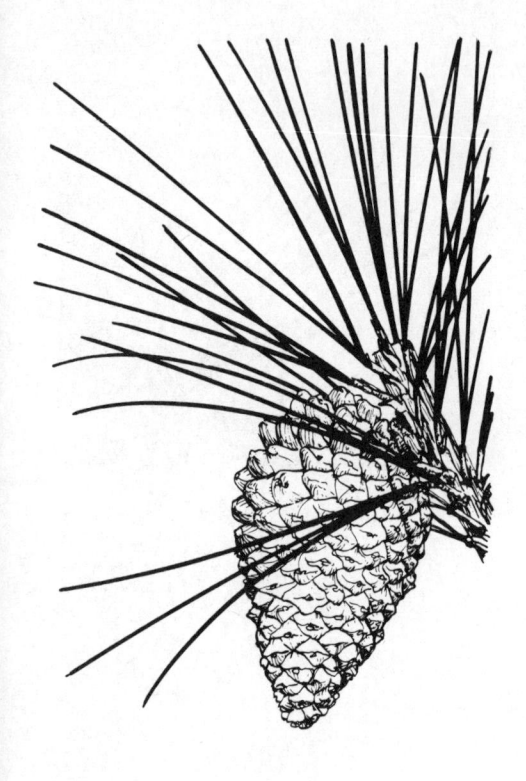

Features: Habit, foliage

Use: Shade, hedge, windbreak, erosion control

Compact and pyramidal in youth, Monterey Pine is a narrow, roundheaded, somewhat variable tree when mature. The foliage covers the branches densely and is a rich, bright green; on older trees it has a handsome, blue-black sheen. This is one of the pines admired for their wind configuration on the Pacific Coast. Under cultivation, it is used extensively for hedges and windbreaks and for erosion control. It has a wide climatic adaptability but grows best in cool, mild, coastal areas.

Conformation

Height: 40 to 80 ft. Spread: 30 to 50 ft.

A narrow, compact, roundheaded tree, pyramidal in youth and assuming a variety of more or less conventional shapes at maturity. The bark is dark brown to almost black and is deeply ridged. The needles are rich, bright green, flexible, and 3½ to 6 in. long; needles of older trees have a blue-black sheen. In bundles of three, they are densely crowded on the branches. They persist on the tree for four years.

Fruit

Broad, uneven, grayish cones, 2 to 5 in. long, in clusters of three to five. They persist on the tree for many years.

Root System: Deep

Rate of Growth: Rapid. Slower in colder areas.

Natural Requirements

Climate: Grows best in cool, coastal areas. Tolerates heat and cold.

Soil: Any kind. Grows best in light, well-drained, sandy soil. Tolerates drought.

Exposure: Sun or partial shade. Tolerates wind, salt spray, and other seacoast conditions.

Care

Pruning: Stands any amount of pruning, but little is required except to shape for use as a hedge. Time: Spring or fall.

Feeding: No special feeding necessary.

Watering: No special attention necessary.

Pests and Diseases: Relatively free from both.

Pi´nus murica´ta, Bishop Pine, has the same climatic and cultural requirements as Monterey Pine and is used for the same landscaping purposes. Perfectly pyramidal in youth, it becomes a handsome, rounded specimen, 40 to 80 ft. high, when mature. The needles are dark green, 4 to 6 in. long, and occur in bundles of two. The cones are oblong-ovoid and are 3½ in. long. *Pinus remora´ta*, Santa Cruz Island Pine, is similar in growth habit to Bishop Pine and, due to its much smaller size, is a useful substitute for it in smaller gardens.

Podocarpus elongatus

Podocar´pus elonga´tus
Fern Podocarpus

South Africa

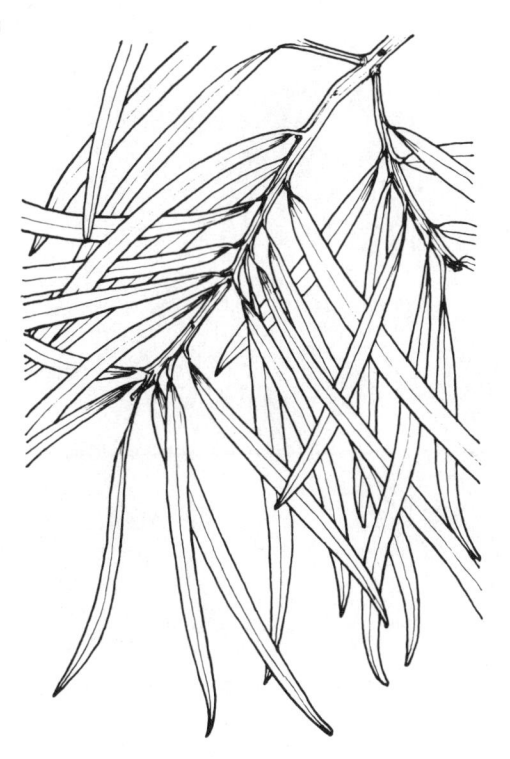

Features: Habit, foliage

Use: Shade (with age), street, screen, espalier, patio, tub, specimen, accent

Fern Podocarpus is a graceful, informally rounded tree with pendulous branches and soft, narrow, bright green, willow-like leaves. The branches are very pliable and can be trained to assume many shapes, including espalier. The tree makes an excellent tub or patio subject and when mature is a good shade or street tree. Podocarpus grows best in temperate areas and is intolerant of any degree of cold.

Conformation

Height: 15 to 60 ft. Spread: 10 to 50 ft.

An informally rounded tree with pendulous branches, which becomes dense with age. The leaves are bright green and are soft, narrow, and flexible. They are 3 in. long and 1/8 in. wide and taper at both ends.

Fruit

Purplish fruit, 1/3 in. in diameter. Fall.

Root System: Average depth

Rate of Growth: Moderate

Natural Requirements

Climate: Prefers temperate areas. Will not tolerate dry heat or cold in any degree.

Soil: Prefers a well-drained loam to which plenty of leaf mold has been added.

Exposure: Partial shade. Protect from wind, when young. Mature trees tolerate full sun and a fair amount of wind.

Care

Pruning: Prune to train as an espalier, or as a specimen tree, by heading high; and prune to maintain form and size desired. Time: Spring or fall.

Feeding: Apply manure annually in the fall.

Watering: Provide plenty of moisture, when tree is young. Mature trees require less watering.

Pests and Diseases: Relatively free from both.

Podocar´pus gracil´ior is often confused with *P. elongatus* and sold under that name. The leaves of *P. gracilior* are longer than those of *P. elongatus*; but otherwise the trees are almost indistinguishable, when young. They have the same cultural and climatic requirements and are used for the same landscaping purposes.

Podocar´pus macrophyl´lus, Yew Podocarpus, grows to a height of 20 to 50 ft., with a spread of 10 to 50 ft. It is very slow growing; it has a columnar shape when young and thus makes a good lighter-foliaged substitute for the Irish Yew. The tree has the same natural and cultural requirements as Fern Podocarpus, but the foliage is much larger and stiffer and is densely arranged in spiral-fashion on the branches. The Yew Podocarpus stands shearing well and can be easily trained for use as a hedge.

Pseudotsuga taxifolia

Pseudotsu´ga taxifo´lia

(*P. douglasi*; *P. mucronata*)

Douglas-Fir; Douglas-Spruce; Red-Spruce; Yellow-Spruce; Oregon-Pine

Rocky Mountains and Pacific Coast

Features: Habit, fruit, foliage

Use: Hedge, windbreak

Douglas-Fir is an important timber tree, growing to enormous size, with a pyramidal shape and drooping branchlets. The foliage is blue-green, fragrant, and very dense; the cones are large and pendulous. It is popularly known as the "old-fashioned Christmas tree," and many people prefer its graceful habit and fragrant leaves to the more formally branched fir and spruce, which are also used for this purpose. Under cultivation, Douglas-Fir should have plenty of room in which to develop; it is definitely not a tree for small gardens. It is useful as a windbreak in places where wind velocity is not likely to become too strong, and it makes an excellent hedge plant. It stands extreme cold and prefers a moist atmosphere.

Conformation

Height: 70 to 250 ft. (300 ft.). Spread: 30 to 60 ft.

A pyramidal tree with horizontal branches uptilted at the ends and with pendulous branchlets. The trunk is clear to one-third of the tree's height, and the bark is reddish brown and plated. The fragrant leaves are bluish green above, soft green beneath, and are in the form of short, flat needles, ½ to 1½ in. long. They are densely arranged on the branches and remain on the tree for from five to eight years.

Fruit

Reddish-brown, ovoid cones, 2 to 3½ in. long, with conspicuous, narrow, three-pointed bracts between the scales. They hang from the branches on long, stout stems. Fall and winter.

Root System: Deep and wide-spreading

Rate of Growth: Rapid

Natural Requirements

Climate: Grows best in a moist atmosphere. Tolerates cold.

Soil: Grows best in deep, well-drained, sandy loam. Tolerates a wide variety of soils. Will not tolerate boggy, water-logged soils.

Exposure: Sun. Tolerates some shade and a moderate amount of wind.

Care

Pruning: Tip prune, when tree is young, to obtain a more compact and symmetrical specimen.

Feeding: No special feeding necessary.

Watering: No special attention necessary. Good drainage is essential.

Pests and Diseases: Borer; spray with DDT in April, May, or June and repeat three weeks after first spraying.

Faults

Young trees have a thin and ragged habit of growth.

Sequoia gigantea

Sequoi´a gigan´tea

(*S. wellingtonia; Sequoiadendron giganteum*)

Big Tree; Giant Sequoia

California

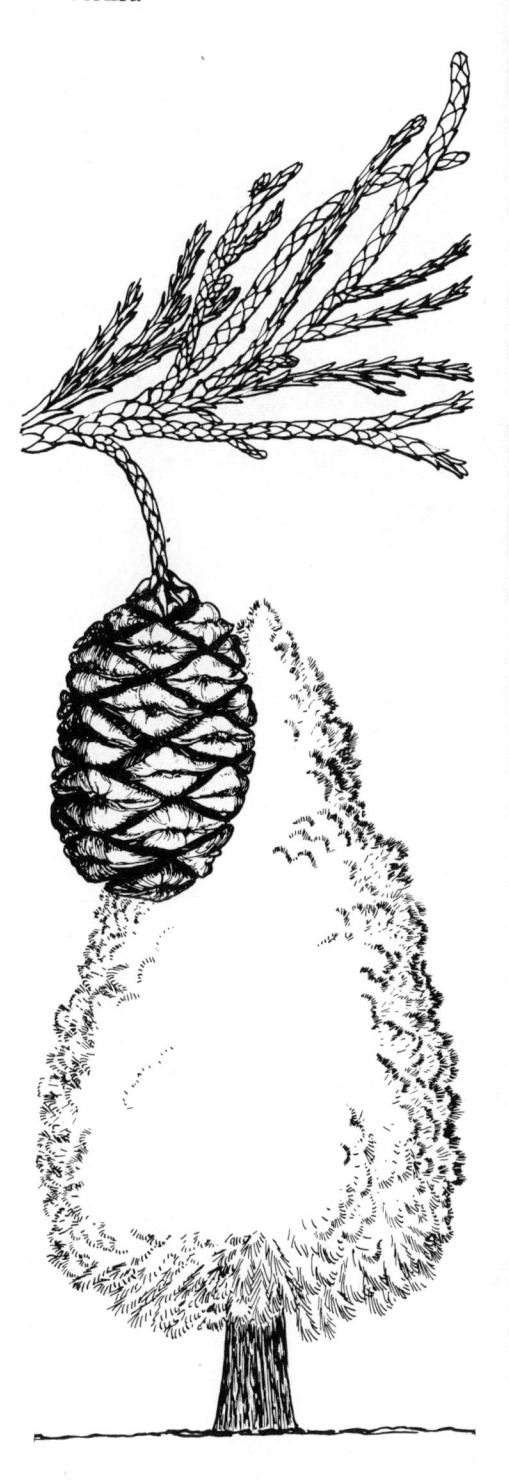

Feature: Habit

Use: Lawn, specimen, accent

Although the Redwood grows somewhat taller, Giant Sequoia is rated the largest tree in the world because of its great height and huge, massive trunk, which in some specimens has reached a diameter of 36 feet. The tree has heavy and thick branches, which grow upward at first and later curve downward to form a compact, pyramidal crown. The foliage is arranged spirally on the branches; it is blue-green when young and turns a clear, bright yellow-green as it matures. Giant Sequoia should never be considered for use in small gardens; but in very large gardens, where space is ample to display its craggy beauty, it makes an excellent lawn specimen. It survives high altitudes and cold and thrives in a moist atmosphere.

Conformation

Height: 150 to 300 ft. Spread: 75 to 100 ft.

A dense, compact tree with stout branches forming a pyramidal crown. The trunk is straight, thick, and massive and is covered with red-brown bark which is deeply furrowed and ridged. The leaves, about 1/8 in. long, hug the branches closely. They overlap in a somewhat scalelike fashion. Blue-green when young, they turn to a bright yellow-green as they become older. They persist on the tree from three to four years.

Fruit

Dark reddish-brown cones, 2 to 3 in. long and 1 to 1½ in. wide. They mature the second year.

Root System: Deep

Rate of Growth: Rapid

Natural Requirements

Climate: Tolerates cold, even in high altitudes. Thrives in a moist atmosphere.

Soil: Prefers a deep, rich, well-drained soil with abundant moisture.

Exposure: Sun.

Care

Pruning: None required.
Feeding: No special feeding necessary.
Watering: Provide plenty of moisture.
Pests and Diseases: Remarkably pest and disease resistant.

Sequoia sempervirens

Sequoi'a sempervi'rens
Redwood

Southern Oregon and California

Feature: Habit

Use: Lawn, hedge (when topped), grove, specimen, accent

Redwood is a narrow, conical tree which grows to a towering height and has dark-green, needle-like leaves arranged in flat sprays. Because of its great height, the tree should never be considered for use in small gardens; in large gardens it can be used as a lawn specimen or can be planted in groups to simulate groves. Successful hedges are made of the trees by topping and trimming them, although it seems a form of desecration to destroy such tall, stately grace. Redwood tolerates cold and some heat and grows best in a moist atmosphere.

Conformation

Height: 100 to 340 ft. Spread: 20 to 40 ft.

A narrowly conical tree with a thick, straight, slightly tapering trunk. The bark is reddish brown, scaly, and ridged. The dark-green, needle-like leaves are ½ to ¾ in. long and are arranged in flat sprays. They persist for three or four years, clinging to the tree one to two years after they have died.

Fruit

Reddish-brown cones, 1/2 to 1 1/8 in. long, in clusters at the ends of the branchlets. They mature the first year.

Root System: Shallow

Rate of Growth: Rapid

Natural Requirements

Climate: Tolerates cold and some heat. Grows best in a moist, humid atmosphere.

Soil: Prefers a deep, rich, well-drained soil with plenty of moisture.

Exposure: Sun. Tolerates seacoast conditions. Cannot stand dry air. Protect from prevailing winds.

Care

Pruning: Prune only to train as a hedge by topping and occasional trimming.

Feeding: No special feeding necessary.

Watering: Provide plenty of moisture.

Pests and Diseases: Remarkably pest and disease resistant.

Faults

Suckers may prove a nuisance in lawn or specimen plantings.

Taxodium distichum

Taxo´dium dis´tichum
Bald-Cypress

Features: Foliage, bark

Use: Water edge, swamps, erosion control, specimen

Bald-Cypress is a large, deciduous tree with a pyramidal shape and feathery foliage which drops each year in the fall. The leaves are a soft, light yellow-green and make an exquisite display against the lightly fissured, cinnamon-brown bark. The tree becomes too large for use in small gardens, but in larger ones it makes an excellent specimen. Due to its marvelous root system it is very adaptable to various moisture conditions in the soil. It tolerates swamps and dry areas equally well, growing to a wide-spreading specimen in wet soils and to a narrow pyramid in dry ones. Bald-Cypress is heat and cold tolerant but needs protection from frost, when young.

Southeastern and south central United States

Conformation

Height: 60 to 125 ft. Spread: 30 to 75 ft.

A pyramidal tree, when young, becoming broad and irregular with pendulous branches, when mature. The bark is cinnamon brown and lightly fissured. The leaves resemble those of the Redwood. They are a soft, light yellow-green and turn brown each year before dropping with the branchlets in the fall. They are flat, ¾ in. long, and are two-ranked on the branches.

Fruit

Brown, globular cones, to 1 in. in diameter. They mature the first year on the previous year's wood.

Root System:

Shallow. In swampy areas, long serpentine roots spread out from the trunk at the base of each buttress. Elongated, spongy cones, or "knees," rise from these roots, a few in a cluster, 5 or 6 ft. above the mud surface. They are covered with bark and are hollow, and they usually die when the water is permanently drained or when the parent tree is cut. They help to anchor the tree and are believed to supply air to the roots.

Rate of Growth: Moderate

Natural Requirements

Climate: Tolerates heat and cold. Young trees need protection from frost.
Soil: Any kind, wet or dry.
Exposure: Any kind. The tree's marvelous root system sustains it against the strongest winds.

Care

Pruning: None required.
Feeding: No special feeding necessary.
Watering: Thrives under any moisture conditions.
Pests and Diseases: Relatively free from both.

La´rix decid´ua, European Larch, is a graceful, pyramidal tree with soft, shimmery, bright green foliage arranged in tufts along pendulous branches. Used chiefly as a specimen and accent tree, it grows to a height of 30 to 70 ft. with a spread of 18 to 35 ft. Its woody cones resembling rosebuds persist for many years. European Larch has a deep root system and does not tolerate boggy soils; it grows best in moist, well-drained soil and in a moist, humid atmosphere.

Taxus baccata

Tax´us bacca´ta
English Yew

Europe; northern Africa; western Asia

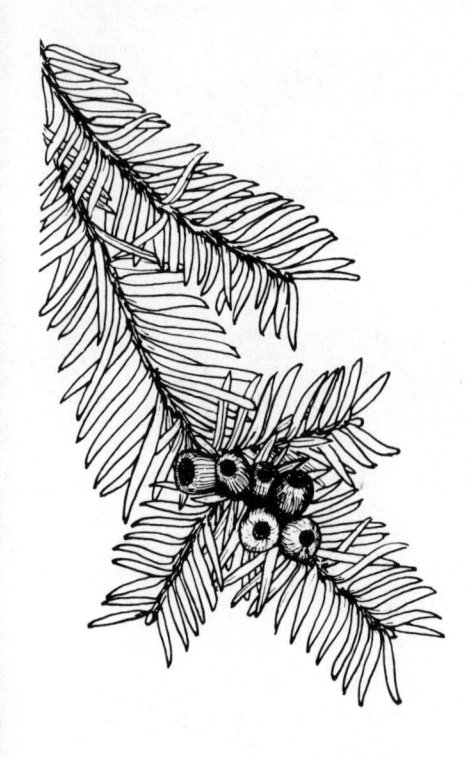

Features: Habit, foliage

Use: Hedge, specimen, accent

English Yew is a wide-spreading tree with a broad, rounded crown and dense, dark-green to almost black foliage. Because of its neat habit and foliage, the tree is excellently adapted for use as a hedge, and the dark color of its leaves makes it effective in accent contrasts. Among the many varieties of English Yew, the one most frequently seen is var. *stricta*, Irish Yew, a narrowly columnar tree which is used extensively to accent vertical lines. English Yew and its varieties tolerate cold to some degree but will not stand prolonged freezing.

Conformation

Height: 10 to 60 ft. Spread: 15 to 80 ft.

A compact, wide-spreading tree with a broad, rounded crown and thin, scaly, reddish-brown bark. The leaves are sharp-pointed and dense, a shiny dark green to almost black above and paler beneath. They are two-ranked, 3/4 to 1 1/4 in. long, and are arranged spirally on the branches.

Among the many varieties are: Var. *aurea*, which has golden-yellow leaves. Var. *stricta*, which has a dense, upright, columnar habit, with branches extending to the ground and dark-green to almost black leaves. Var. *stricta aurea*, which is densely columnar in habit and has golden-yellow foliage.

Fruit

Scarlet berry-like fruits, 1/3 to 1/2 in. in diameter, with the fleshy, red outer growth almost enveloping the seed. Fruit appears on female trees only.

Root System: Average depth

Rate of Growth: Slow

Natural Requirements

Climate: Tolerates heat. Stands cold to some degree but will not endure prolonged freezing.

Soil: Tolerates a variety of soils. Prefers a moderately moist, well-drained, sandy loam.

Exposure: Sun, partial shade, or complete shade. Tolerates seacoast conditions.

Care

Pruning: Stands any amount of shearing. Time: Spring or fall.
Feeding: Apply manure once every two years in fall.
Watering: Water deeply once a month.
Pests and Diseases: Relatively free from both.

Faults

Does not transplant well. Leaves are poisonous.

Thuja orientalis

Thu´ja orienta´lis
Oriental Arborvitae;
  Chinese Arborvitae

Northern China and Korea

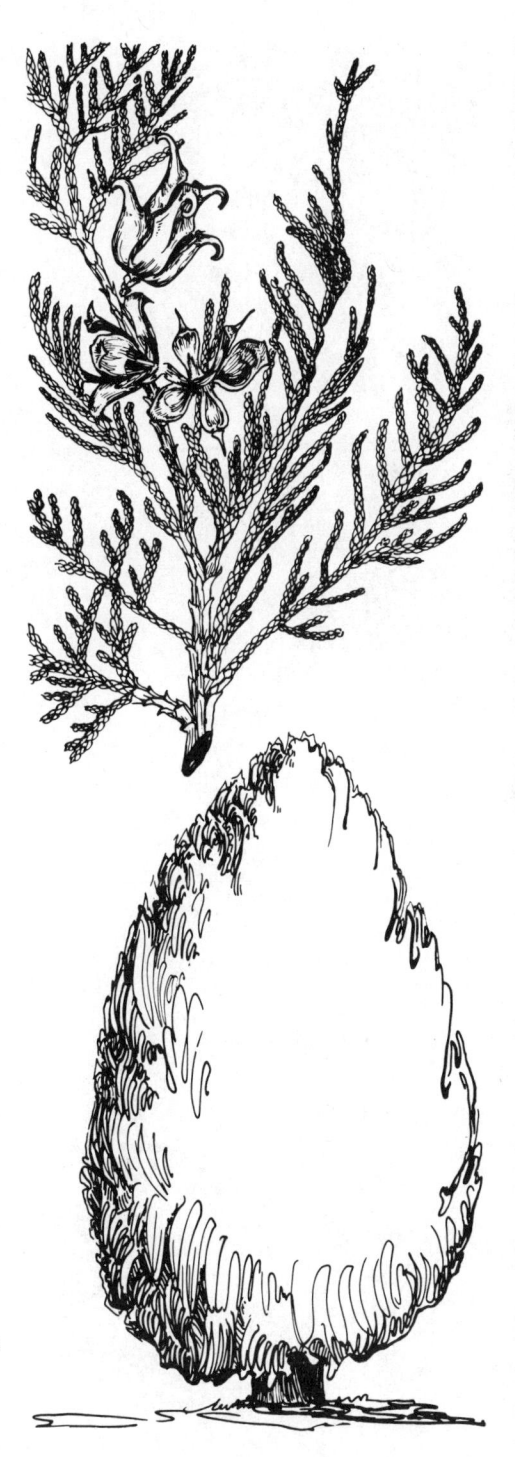

Feature: Habit

Use: Lawn, hedge, water edge, specimen, accent

Oriental Arborvitae is a bushy, compact, pyramidal tree with flattened sprays of bright green foliage carried on the ends of the branches. Many horticultural varieties are available which differ in color of foliage or in habit. Some of these are columnar, some rounded, and some dwarf; all are excellent for accent or specimen plants. Oriental Arborvitae is not so hardy as American Arborvitae but will stand some degree of cold. Like the American species, it thrives best in moist soil and atmosphere.

Conformation

Height: 25 to 40 ft. Spread: 10 to 30 ft.

A small, bushy tree with spreading and ascending branches forming a compact, narrow, pyramidal crown. The bark is thin and reddish brown. The leaves are fernlike and are arranged in flat, vertical sprays. They are bright green above and yellowish green beneath.

Many varieties are available. Var. *beverleyensis* grows to a medium-sized pyramid and has gold-tipped foliage; var. *bonita* grows to a narrow, cone-shaped pyramid and has gold-tipped foliage.

Fruit

Bluish cones, ½ to 1 in. long, which become light brown as they mature. They are ovoid and are tipped with small horns, or hooked. They scatter their seeds and persist on the tree throughout the year. The seeds attract birds.

Root System: Average depth

Rate of Growth: Slow

Natural Requirements

Climate: Grows best in a moist atmosphere. Tolerates heat and stands a good deal of cold.
Soil: Grows best in rich, moist, well-drained soil.
Exposure: Sun. Becomes loose and gangling in shady areas.

Care

Pruning: Stands pruning, but little is required. When pruning, cut from the inside of the tree; do not clip the ends. Time: Spring or fall.
Feeding: Apply manure annually in the fall.
Watering: Provide plenty of moisture.
Pests and Diseases: Scale occurs occasionally in dry atmospheres; spray with malathion or an oil emulsion in summer and repeat when needed. Blight; spray with Bordeaux when necessary.

Thu´ja occidenta´lis, American Arborvitae, resembles *T. orientalis* in general appearance but grows to a larger, wider tree, with a height of 40 to 60 ft. and spread of 30 to 50 ft. It has the same cultural requirements as Oriental Arborvitae and is used for the same landscaping purposes; however, it will stand more cold and shade and needs more moisture for good growth. It is not as well suited for use in small gardens as Oriental Arborvitae as its habit is somewhat unpredictable.

Thuja plicata

Thu´ja plica´ta

Giant Arborvitae; Canoe-Cedar; Western Red-Cedar

Alaska to northern California and Montana

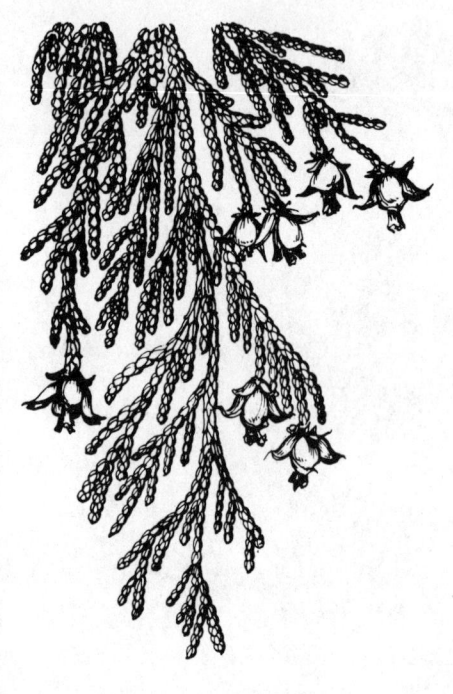

Features: Habit, foliage

Use: Lawn, hedge, water edge, specimen, accent

Growing to a height of 180 ft. in the forest, Canoe-Cedar is a giant pyramid with slender branches covered with bright green, lacy foliage and extending almost to the ground. Historically, the tree has played an intimate part in the life of the American Indian, who used it, among other things, as a base on which to fashion his interesting and ingenious totem-pole art. Canoe-Cedar is contained to a reasonable size by its slow rate of growth and by occasional pruning. It makes an excellent hedge plant or specimen for large lawns. The tree stands extremes of heat and cold and thrives in coastal and humid areas.

Conformation

Height: 50 to 180 ft. Spread: 35 to 60 ft.

A pyramidal tree with a narrow crown and a straight, tapering trunk which is buttressed or fluted at the base. Even on older specimens, the branches clothe the tree nearly to the ground; they are short and horizontal-spreading, the upper ones ascending, the lower ones gently pendulous. The bark is grayish brown and is seamed into narrow strips which extend the length of the trunk, connected at intervals by diagonal ridges. The leaves are scalelike and are arranged in flat, lacy sprays. They are bright green above and often have whitish spots beneath. They are highly aromatic and persist on the tree for three years.

Among the varieties are *atrovirens*, which has very dark green foliage; *aurea*, which has gold-tipped foliage; and *fastigiata*, which is columnar in habit.

Fruit

Cinnamon-brown cones, 3/8 in. long, clustered at the ends of the branches. They persist on the tree until the following summer.

Root System: Shallow

Rate of Growth: Slow

Natural Requirements

Climate: Grows best in humid or coastal areas. Tolerates heat and cold.

Soil: Tolerates a wide variety of soils. Grows best in rich, moist, well-drained loam.

Exposure: Sun or shade.

Care

Pruning: Stands any amount of pruning. Time: Spring or fall.

Feeding: Apply sulphate of ammonia once every two or three years. Does not respond to manure applications.

Watering: Provide plenty of moisture.

Pests and Diseases: Relatively free from both.

Features: Habit, foliage

Use: Shade, lawn, specimen, accent

California-Nutmeg is a yewlike tree, conical when young and becoming rounded and domelike with age. The leaves are stiff and pointed and carry a high gloss as though varnished. They are arranged in one plane all along the branches. California-Nutmeg makes an excellent shade and lawn tree for large gardens; it is also useful in smaller gardens if planted well away from paths or walks. It will stand some degree of cold but will not tolerate prolonged freezing.

Conformation
Height: 15 to 60 ft. Spread: 20 to 40 ft.

A pyramidal young tree, becoming roundheaded when mature, with wide-spreading, whorled branches. The bark is grayish brown tinged with orange and is thin and smooth. The leaves are 1 to 2½ in. long and are arranged in one plane along the branches; they are flat, rigid, spiny-pointed, and very prickly to the touch. They are a shiny dark yellow-green above, with two whitish bands beneath.

Fruit
Green or purplish fruit, 1 to 1¾ in. long, somewhat resembling a small plum. Only female plants bear fruit.

Root System: Deep

Rate of Growth: Slow

Natural Requirements
Climate: Grows best in a cool, moist atmosphere. Tolerates heat. Stands cold to some degree but will not endure extreme cold.

Soil: Prefers a moist, well-drained loam.

Exposure: Shade or partial shade. Protect from strong winds.

Care
Pruning: None required.

Feeding: No special feeding necessary.

Watering: Provide plenty of moisture. Good drainage is essential.

Pests and Diseases: Relatively free from both.

Faults
When the tree is cut down, it exudes a fetid odor. Leaves are prickly.

Torreya californica

Tor´reya califor´nica

California-Nutmeg

California

Tsuga canadensis

Tsu´ga canaden´sis

Canadian Hemlock; Eastern Hemlock; Hemlock-Spruce

Northeastern North America

Features: Habit, foliage

Use: Lawn, hedge, specimen, accent

Canadian Hemlock is a graceful, pyramidal tree with long, slender, horizontal to gently pendulous branches. The leaves are needle-like, very dense, and a dark yellow-green. There are many named varieties of this tree, which differ in size, color, and type of leaf, and in general shape. Whether trimmed or untrimmed, Canadian Hemlock and its varieties make fine hedges and are frequently used for this purpose. They are very hardy.

Conformation

Height: 60 to 80 ft. Spread: 30 to 40 ft.

A pyramidal tree with a broad top and a gracefully drooping leader tip. The tree spreads to its full width in its early years, then grows straight upward. The long, slender branches, yellowish when young and a smooth reddish brown when mature, spread outward on a horizontal plane or slope very gently downward. The bark is brown, scaly, and deeply furrowed. The leaves are needle-like, 1/3 to 3/4 in. long and 1/16 to 1/8 in. wide, and two-ranked, forming flat sprays. Yellow-green above, they are marked with two narrow white bands beneath. They persist on the tree for three or more years.

Fruit

Reddish brown cones, ½ to 1 in. long, usually pendulous on the tree, which mature in the first year. They are profuse and persist for more than a year after dropping their seeds. Fall.

Root System: Shallow. Tree transplants easily.

Rate of Growth: Slow

Natural Requirements

Climate: Tolerates heat and cold.
Soil: Prefers a fertile, moist, well-drained loam.
Exposure: Shade. Will not tolerate full exposure in hot, dry areas. Grows best in a moist, cool atmosphere. Protect from wind.

Care

Pruning: Stands any amount of shearing; but prune only to train as hedge. Time: Spring or fall.
Feeding: No special feeding necessary.
Watering: Provide plenty of moisture. Good drainage is essential.
Pests and Diseases: Hemlock borer; spray with DDT in April, May, or June, and repeat three weeks after first spraying.

Faults

Topples in wind.

Tsu´ga mertensia´na, Mountain Hemlock, is a graceful, delicate tree which grows to approximately the same size as Canadian Hemlock. The shiny, blue-green needles are arranged spirally around the branches in starlike patterns; they hold their color throughout the winter. The branches are long and slender and, like the leader tip, are gently pendulous. Mountain Hemlock has the same cultural requirements and landscaping use as the Canadian Hemlock and grows best in a cool, moist area.

CLIMATIC TOLERANCE CHART FOR CONIFERS

X: areas where the particular tree may be grown easily

(X): areas where the particular tree may be grown, but with some reservations

	Temperate Coastal	Desert	Cool Coastal	Temperate Inland	Cold Winters
SHADE TREES					
Cupressus forbesi	X	X	X	X	X
Juniperus pachyphloea	X	X	X	X	X
Pinus pinea	X	X	X	X	
Pinus radiata	X	X	X	X	
Podocarpus elongatus	X		X		
Torreya californica	X	X	X	X	X
LAWN TREES					
Abies concolor			X	X	X
Abies nordmanniana			X	X	X
Abies pinsapo	X		X	X	X
Araucaria araucana	X	X	X	X	
Araucaria bidwilli	X				
Araucaria excelsa	X				
Cedrus atlantica and var.	X	X	X	X	
Cedrus deodara	X	X	X	X	
Cedrus libani	X	X	X	X	X
Chamaecyparis lawsoniana	X		X	X	
Chamaecyparis pisifera	X	X	X	X	
Cryptomeria japonica	X		X	X	
Ginkgo biloba	X	X	X	X	X
Picea pungens and vars.	X	X	X	X	X
Pinus nigra	X	X	X	X	X
Pinus pinea	X	X	X	X	
Thuja species	X	X	X	X	X
Torreya californica	X	X	X	X	X
Tsuga species			X		X
WINDBREAKS					
Cedrus atlantica and var.	X	X	X	X	
Cedrus deodara	X	X	X	X	
Cedrus libani	X	X	X	X	X
Cupressus species	X	X	X	X	X
Juniperus species	X	X	X	X	X
Libocedrus decurrens	X	X	X	X	X
Pinus halepensis	X	X	X	X	

CLIMATIC TOLERANCE CHART FOR CONIFERS

	Temperate Coastal	Desert	Cool Coastal	Temperate Inland	Cold Winters
WINDBREAKS (Continued)					
Pinus muricata	X	X	X	X	
Pinus nigra	X	X	X	X	X
Pinus ponderosa	X		X	(X)	X
Pinus radiata	X	X	X	X	
Pseudotsuga taxifolia			X	X	X
HEDGES					
Cupressus species	X	X	X	X	X
Cryptomeria japonica	X		X	X	
Cryptomeria japonica elegans	X		X	X	
Juniperus chinensis	X	X	X	X	X
Juniperus communis	X	X	X	X	X
Juniperus virginiana	X	X	X	X	X
Libocedrus decurrens	X	X	X	X	X
Picea abies	X	X	X	X	X
Pinus mugo	X	X	X	X	X
Pinus muricata	X	X	X	X	
Pinus radiata	X	X	X	X	
Podocarpus macrophyllus	X		X		
Pseudotsuga taxifolia			X	X	X
Sequoia sempervirens	(X)		X	(X)	X
Taxus baccata	X		X	X	
Thuja species	X	X	X	X	X
Tsuga species			X		X
PATIO AND TUB TREES					
Araucaria araucana (tubs)	X	X	X	X	
Araucaria excelsa (tubs)	X				
Chamaecyparis lawsoniana vars.	X		X	X	
Chamaecyparis obtusa vars.	X	X	X	X	(X)
Cryptomeria japonica compacta	X		X	X	
Ginkgo biloba	X	X	X	X	X
Juniperus chinensis torulosa	X	X	X	X	X
Pinus mugo mughus	X	X	X	X	X
Pinus thunbergi	X	X	X	X	X
Podocarpus species	X		X		

PALMS AND OTHER TROPICALS

The palms have stout, columnar, unbranched stems on which no true bark is developed, but only a sort of woody rind. These trunks rise to crowns of large, often strangely dissected leaf blades which are evergreen in nature. Palms, bananas, tree ferns, and other plants in this division are used ornamentally to create dramatic, tropical, and sometimes oriental effects. Their bold lines and striking characteristics add charm and interest to the landscape, whether used in groups, patios, tubs, or lawns. Some of them are excellent for bordering streets or lining long approaches to large estates. However used, they become very much the center of any design motif. The climatic range of this group is quite limited, and close attention should be paid to regional preferences before a plant is selected for garden use.

Arecastrum romanzoffianum

Arecas´trum romanzoffia´num
(*Cocos plumosa*)
Queen Palm

Central Brazil

Features: Trunk, leaves

Use: Street, group, patio, tubs, specimen, accent

The clean, ringed, slightly tapering trunk of the Queen Palm rises to a dense head of feathery, blue-green leaves, which ascend steeply and arch gradually outward to form a graceful vase-shaped crown. This tree presents no maintenance problem, but it will not survive in areas in which winter temperatures drop below 20° F. It makes an excellent street, patio, or tubbed specimen.

Conformation

Height: 15 to 40 ft. Spread: 10 to 25 ft.

A tall feather palm with a dense crown of long, stiffly ascending leaves which arch gradually outward and are somewhat recurved. The slender trunk, 8 to 12 in. thick, is smooth, ringed with leaf scars, and thatchless except for a few leaves hanging near the summit. The leaves are bright bluish green and are 9 to 12 ft. long. They are pinnately divided and are composed of numerous soft, flexible, usually entire segments, 14 to 18 in. long and not more than 1 in. wide.

Flowers

Creamy-white, bell-like flowers in clusters, 2 to 3 ft. long, blooming among the leaves, from a hard, woody, boat-shaped sheath nestled among the leaves and partly obscured by them.

Fruit

Orange fruit, about 1 in. long, in large, pendulous clusters among the leaves. It resembles a date in appearance but is not edible. Fall.

Root System: Shallow, spreading

Rate of Growth: Rapid

Natural Requirements

Climate: Tolerates heat. Will not stand cold below 20° F.
Soil: Grows best in light, sandy loam. Tolerates any well-drained soil and drought.
Exposure: Sun. Protect from strong winds.

Care

Pruning: Remove old leaves when necessary.
Feeding: Apply manure once every two years in winter.
Watering: Water deeply once a month. Provide plenty of moisture when plant is young.
Pests and Diseases: Relatively free from both.

Faults

Topples in heavy winds.

Cordyline australis

Cordyli´ne austra´lis
(Dracaena australis)

Giant Dracena; Green Dracena; Cabbage Tree

New Zealand

Feature: Habit

Use: Street, palm groups, patio, tub, specimen, accent

Giant Dracena is a palmlike tree with an erect trunk which rises to a compact, branched head of tufted, bladelike leaves. The steeply ascending branches extend their patterns each year after the flowering period. Because of its well-defined, meticulous habit, Giant Dracena makes an effective specimen for use in patios and tubs, creating an interesting and unusual tropical effect. The tree stands considerable cold.

Conformation

Height: 15 to 40 ft.   Spread: 10 to 15 ft.

A tall, palmlike plant with a single stem or trunk and steeply ascending branches growing in irregular patterns. The numerous branches rise to rosette-like crowns of tufted, bladelike leaves, 18 to 36 in. long and 1 to 2½ in. wide, which stand erect or spread out from the branches. They are dull to bright green.

Flowers

Decorative, waxy-white, cup-shaped, fragrant flowers, 1 in. in diameter, in erect or drooping, much-branched clusters, 12 to 14 in. long. Summer.

Fruit

White or bluish-white fruit, ¼ in. in diameter, in branched, terminal clusters. Fall to winter.

Root System: Shallow, spreading

Rate of Growth: Rapid

Natural Requirements

Climate: Tolerates heat. Stands some degree of cold but will not endure prolonged freezing.
Soil: Tolerates a wide variety of soils. Prefers a well-drained, moist, sandy loam. Tolerates drought but prefers moisture.
Exposure: Sun. Tolerates wind and seacoast conditions.

Care

Pruning: None required except to shape when tree is very old.
Feeding: Apply manure annually in winter.
Watering: Water deeply once a month. Provide plenty of moisture when plant is young.
Pests and Diseases: Relatively free from both.

Cordylí ne indivi´sa, Blue Dracena, has the same cultural requirements and serves the same landscaping purposes as Green Dracena; but its climatic tolerance is limited, and it grows well only in temperate regions. It is smaller than Green Dracena, being only 25 ft. high with a 15 ft. spread when mature; but its leaves are blue-green and are twice as long and twice as wide as those of the other plant.

Dracae´na dra´co, Dragon Tree, is a grotesque, wide-spreading, flat-headed tree, 25 to 60 ft. high and 30 to 60 ft. wide. Heavy branches spring from a short, stout trunk and are completely bare to the outermost tufts of dark-green, bladelike leaves. The tree is so precise as to seem almost unnatural; its landscape use should be as novelty accent only. It has a moderate rate of growth and will survive only in temperate regions.

Dicksonia antarctica

Dicksonia antarctica

Hardy Tree Fern;
 Tasmanian Dicksoni

Australia

Features: Fronds, habit

Use: Fern groups, shaded dell, patio

The dark-brown trunk of Hardy Tree Fern rises to a large crown of feathery, arching fronds. The fronds are dark green and are minutely and delicately dissected to a fine, lacy texture. Although tree ferns are frequently planted in tubs, they do not show to the best advantage under these conditions, since tubs large enough to provide adequate space for the proper development of the plant usually appear out of proportion to it. The plants are excellent patio subjects, used singly or combined in group plantings with lower-growing ferns. They stand some degree of cold but will not tolerate prolonged freezing.

Conformation

Height: 30 to 35 ft. Spread: 12 to 15 ft.

A large, spreading tree fern with a sturdy dark-brown trunk covered with remnants of the old leaf stems and matted with aerial rootlets. The trunk rises to a dense crown of arching dark-green fronds, 5 to 6 ft. long. The fronds are thrice compound, the ultimate segments lance-shaped, toothed, and about 2 in. long. A good trunk produces thirty or forty fronds a year and retains them until the next set is mature.

Flowers and Fruit: None

Root System: Shallow, spreading

Rate of Growth: Rapid

Natural Requirements

Climate: Grows best in mild, coastal areas and moist atmosphere with protection from wind. Tolerates light frost but will not stand prolonged freezing.

Soil: Grows best in light, moist soil of high leaf-mold content.

Exposure: Partial shade or complete shade. Protect from wind.

Care

Pruning: Remove old fronds as they die.

Feeding: Apply leaf mold annually at any time of year.

Watering: Provide constant moisture—the plant may die if not watered every day. During the growing season, it should be watered twice a day; the watering should then be gradually tapered off until the winter months, when the plant must be kept uniformly moist but does not need quite so much attention.

Pests and Diseases: Relatively free from both.

Alsophila australis, Australian Tree Fern, has the same cultural requirements as Hardy Tree Fern and is used for the same landscaping purposes; but it is a lower-growing tree, with an ultimate height and spread of 20 ft. The fronds are light green above and bluish green beneath and are 10 ft. long. Australian Tree Fern is a remarkably handsome and striking plant, but it can be used only in temperate areas. It will not stand any cold and tolerates very little heat, growing best in full shade in temperatures ranging around 60° F.

Musa ensete

Mu´sa ense´te
Abyssinian Banana

Abyssinia

Feature: Leaves

Use: Patio, tub, accent

The trunk of the Abyssinian Banana rises to a crown of large, bright green, gracefully arching leaves, which are sharp-pointed at the base and at the apex. The Abyssinian Banana needs constant attention to feeding and watering and will survive only in temperate or tropical regions. It is used in tubs and patios as an accent plant to create tropical effects.

Conformation

Height: 20 to 40 ft. Spread: 15 to 25 ft.

A treelike, herbaceous plant with a large, central stem swollen at the base and composed of the sheathing bases of the old leaf stems. The crown is composed of numerous, spirally arranged, bright green leaves, 10 to 20 ft. long and 2 to 3 ft. wide, which arch slightly downward and are sharp-pointed at both apex and base. The midribs of the leaves are red, and the leaf stems are very short.

Flowers

Erect flower spikes composed of twenty or more flowers, 1½ to 2 in. long, which are surrounded by reddish-brown bracts, 9 to 12 in. long. The tree dies soon after flowering but it is two to three years before flowers appear, depending upon care and growing conditions.

Fruit

Dry, inedible fruit, 2 to 3 in. long, in bunches and bearing a few black seeds.

Root System: Shallow

Rate of Growth: Rapid

Natural Requirements

Climate: Will survive only in temperate or tropical areas. Will not tolerate cold.
Soil: Prefers a rich, light, moist loam.
Exposure: Sun. Protect from wind.

Care

Pruning: None required.
Feeding: Apply liquid manure once a month in the growing season.
Watering: Provide plenty of moisture; overhead watering is beneficial.
Pests and Diseases: Relatively free from both.

Mu´sa paradisi´aca, Plantain Banana, is a smaller tree without the red midrib in the leaves and with long leafstalks. The fruit is edible, when cooked. The plant that bears the fresh, edible banana is *M. p. sapientum*, a variety which is not so effective ornamentally as *Musa ensete*.

Phoenix canariensis

Phoénix canariensis
Canary Date Palm

Canary Islands

Features: Habit, leaves

Use: Street (wide), lawn, specimen, accent

Erect, massive, and wide-spreading, Canary Date Palm is graceful and majestic, with long, arching, feather-like leaves which ascend steeply at the top of the tree, spread horizontally near the center, and droop heavily at the base of the crown. The trunk is thick and stout and covered—at least near the summit—with woody remnants of the old leaf stems. The tree thrives in temperate zones and is widely adaptable—enduring heat, wind, cool coastal conditions, and even cold areas where there is no prolonged frost. It is admirably suited for use as a lawn specimen or to line wide avenues where adequate parkway space is available.

Conformation

Height (of trunk to crown): 10 to 50 ft. Spread: 20 to 40 ft.

A large, wide-spreading feather palm, with a dense crown of strongly arching leaves which stand at different angles from the main leafstalk. The trunk is stout, 2 to 5 ft. thick, and is covered—at least near the summit—with woody remnants of the old leaf stems. The leaves are pinnately divided, 15 to 20 ft. long, and composed of numerous segments 12 to 16 in. long and 1 to 2 in. wide. They are light green and are folded upward and lengthwise. The leaf stems are short and are armed with stiff spines.

Flowers

Small yellowish flowers, on long, drooping, branched stalks, the male and female flowers on different trees. Spring.

Fruit

Orange-yellow fruit, ½ to ¾ in. long, produced in clusters at the base of the lower leaves and by female plants only. The fruit resembles a date but is not edible. Fall.

Root System: Deep. Transplanting is most successful if done in the fall or early spring.

Rate of Growth: Rapid

Natural Requirements

Climate: Tolerates heat. Will stand some degree of cold but will not endure prolonged freezing.

Soil: Prefers a light, moist, well-drained, sandy loam to which humus has been added. Tolerates drought but grows best with moisture.

Exposure: Sun. Tolerates wind and seacoast conditions.

Care

Pruning: Remove old leaves.
Feeding: Apply manure annually in winter.
Watering: Provide plenty of moisture.
Pests and Diseases: Relatively free from both.

Features: Fruit, leaves, habit (at maturity)

Use: Street (male trees), lawn, novelty, orchard, accent

Date Palm is not a good ornamental tree when young, but as it matures it becomes highly decorative, with long, feathery, bluish-green leaves half arching to form a dense, vase-shaped crown. Although it will produce fruit only in areas where there are long periods of hot, dry summer heat, it will thrive as an ornamental in cool, coastal regions and in colder sections where temperatures do not fall much below 17° F. Since the dropping of fruit is a nuisance, male trees should be selected for use on streets.

Conformation

Height: 25 to 75 ft. (100 ft.). Spread: 15 to 30 ft.

A large feather palm with a slender trunk that tends to lean at a slight angle from the ground and is covered with woody remnants of the old leaf stems. The bluish-green leaves, 15 to 20 ft. long, half arch to form a vaselike crown. They are pinnately divided and are composed of numerous very narrow segments, 12 to 18 in. long, folded upward and lengthwise.

Flowers

Male and female flowers on separate trees: the male flowers waxy and cream-colored and crowded on the flower stalks; female flowers white and arranged in groups. Spring to summer.

Fruit

Brown fruit, 1 to 3 in. long, on strands of the female flower stalks. It has a sweet pulp and is edible whether fresh or dried. One male tree will pollinate fifty female trees. One of the best varieties available is Deglet Noor, a semidry, late-ripening type. The fruits ripen individually, becoming soft and brown when mature. Fall to winter.

Root System: Deep

Rate of Growth: Rapid

Natural Requirements

Climate: Prefers hot, dry desert areas and will produce fruit only in such places. Will not stand cold much below 17° F.

Soil: Prefers a light, moist, sandy loam to which plenty of humus has been added.

Exposure: Sun. Will grow in cool, seacoast areas but will not produce fruit there.

Care

Pruning: Thin fruit by removing individual strands from inflorescence or by cutting back inflorescence by one-third. Time: Immediately after fruit has taken form.

Feeding: Apply manure annually in winter.

Watering: Provide plenty of moisture; do not allow the plant to dry out.

Pests and Diseases: Scale is sometimes, though not often, a nuisance; spray with malathion or an oil emulsion in summer and repeat when needed; spray with oil in winter. Do not spray with poisonous materials near fruit-ripening time.

Faults: Suckers. Young trees are not good ornamentals.

Phoenix dactylifera

Phoénix dactylifera
Date Palm

Uncertain (Western Asia or northern Africa)

Phoenix reclinata

Phoénix reclina´ta
Senegal Date Palm; Cape Palm

Africa

Feature: Habit

Use: Lawn, groups, patio, specimen, accent

The trunk of Senegal Date Palm is slender and delicate and rises to a loose, feathery crown of dark-green leaves, which spread in a well-defined arc to form an open oval or rounded shape. Senegal Date Palm suckers frequently; sometimes four or five trunks will rise from a single base and head to a beautiful, large mass of several crowns. This clumping is perhaps the most attractive form the tree assumes, and it should be encouraged in specimens used for patios or lawns. Senegal Date Palm is much less hardy than others of the Phoenix group and should be planted only in temperate areas.

Conformation

Height (of trunk to crown): 10 to 25 ft. Spread: Determined by number of stems allowed to develop.

A narrow, open-growing feather palm with a loose crown of half-arching leaves which stand at different angles from the main leafstalk; the upper ones growing stiffly erect, the center ones spreading horizontally, and the lower ones pendulous. The slender trunk, 8 to 18 in. thick, is ringed with leaf scars, and covered—at least near the summit—with woody remnants of the old leaf stems. The dark-green leaves are pinnately divided, 5 to 7 ft. long, composed of numerous rigid, spiny segments 12 in. long and 1 in. wide, and recurved downward at the ends. All fold upward and lengthwise.

Flowers

Small yellowish flowers on long, drooping, branched stalks, the male and female flowers on different trees. Spring.

Fruit

Brown or reddish fruit, ½ to ¾ in. long, produced in clusters at the base of the lower leaves and by female plants only. The fruit resembles a date but is not edible. Fall.

Root System: Average depth, spreading

Rate of Growth: Rapid

Natural Requirements

Climate: Prefers temperate regions. Tolerates heat. Withstands some degree of cold but is much less hardy than others of the Phoenix group.

Soil: Prefers a light, moist, well-drained, sandy loam to which humus has been added.

Exposure: Sun.

Care

Pruning: Remove old leaves.

Feeding: Apply manure annually in winter.

Watering: Provide plenty of moisture. Do not allow plant to dry out.

Pests and Diseases: Relatively free from both.

Features: Leaves, trunk

Use: Street, patio, tub, specimen, accent

It would be difficult to find a more oriental-appearing tree than Windmill Palm. The slender trunk, covered with stringy black hairs, starts from a very narrow base and thickens gradually as it rises to a compact crown of lacy, fan-shaped leaves. The leaves are a rich dark-green, tipped with yellow at the margins, and are deeply divided, almost to the base, into many ribbon-like segments. Windmill Palm is a quaint and delicate specimen plant particularly adaptable for use in patios and in tubs. It tolerates some degree of cold but will not stand prolonged freezing.

Conformation

Height (of trunk to crown): 10 to 30 ft. Spread (of crown): 10 to 15 ft.

A small, slender fan palm with handsome leaves forming a compact crown. The trunk is slender and thickens gradually as it rises from a narrow base. It is densely covered with hairy black fibers and the woody remnants of the old leaf stems. The leaves are nearly round, 2 to 5 ft. in diameter, and are deeply slashed to the middle or almost to the base. The segments are ribbon-like, stiff, and firm, and the leaf blades are carried on slender leafstalks 2 to 3 ft. long and ½ to 1 in. wide. They are a rich dark green and are tipped with yellow on the margins.

Flowers

Small orange flowers in clusters on short, branched flower stalks among the leaves. Spring.

Fruit

Small, oblong, purplish fruit in clusters on the flower stalks. The fruit is about the size of a pea and is three-lobed. Summer.

Root System: Shallow. Roots are fibrous.

Rate of Growth: Moderate

Natural Requirements

Climate: Tolerates heat. Will stand some degree of cold but will not endure prolonged freezing.
Soil: Prefers a light, moist, well-drained, sandy loam. Tolerates drought but prefers moisture.
Exposure: Sun. Tolerates wind.

Care

Pruning: None required.
Feeding: Apply manure annually in winter.
Watering: Keep moist. Water deeply at least once a month.
Pests and Diseases: Relatively free from both.

Trachycarpus fortunei

Trachycarpus fortúnei
(T. excelsus; Chamaerops excelsa)
Windmill Palm; Fortune's Windmill Palm

Burma; Indo-China; Japan

Washingtonia filifera

Washingtónia filif´era
(*Brahea filamentosa; B. filifera;
Pritchardia filamentosa;
P. filifera*)
California Washington Palm

California

Feature: Leaves

Use: Street, lawns, groups, specimen, accent

The tall, thick, shag-covered trunk of California Washington Palm rises to an open crown of large, fan-shaped leaves, which at first stand erect, then droop gradually, and finally die and rest like a brown thatch skirt round the trunk. The shag should be left on the trunk, for otherwise the tree is out of proportion and has a naked, artificial appearance. This palm, because of its large size and heavy, burdened trunk, should be used only in large gardens or to line wide streets or avenues. It tolerates some degree of cold but will not stand prolonged freezing.

Conformation

Height (of trunk to crown): 20 to 75 ft. Spread (of crown): 8 to 20 ft.

An open-growing fan palm with leaves that are erect when young, droop gradually as they mature, and rest finally against the trunk, where they remain almost indefinitely. The trunk is stout and columnar, averaging 3 ft. thick, and conspicuously swollen at the base and only slightly narrower above. The clear bright green leaves are 3 to 6 ft. long and a little less broad; they are extended on spiny leafstalks, which usually are longer than the blades. The center part of the leaf is intact; the outer edges are deeply dissected into forty to seventy narrow, ribbon-like, somewhat pendulous divisions, which are margined by threadlike filaments.

Flowers

Hundreds of fragrant, tiny, creamy-white, vase-shaped flowers in tight clusters all along the branches of 12-foot-long flower stalks. They somewhat resemble corn tassels spreading out in the midst of the crown. After the fruit has formed and gone, they die and become part of the shag around the trunk. Spring.

Fruit

Ovoid black fruits hanging in large clusters from the stalk. They have a thin skin and a sugary, edible flesh and were used by the Indians for food. Summer.

Root System: Shallow. Roots are fibrous.

Rate of Growth: Rapid to moderate

Natural Requirements

Climate: Tolerates heat. Stands some degree of cold but will not endure prolonged freezing. Thrives in dry atmospheres.
Soil: Grows best in light, moist, well-drained, sandy loam to which plenty of humus has been added.
Exposure: Sun. Subject to crown rot in coastal areas.

Care

Pruning: Not necessary. Shag may be removed without harming the health of the tree, but the tree has a better appearance if the shag is left.
Feeding: Apply manure annually in winter.
Watering: Provide plenty of moisture.
Pests and Diseases: Relatively free from both. Subject to crown rot in coastal areas.

Faults: Subject to crown rot in coastal areas.

Washingtonia robusta

Washingtónia robús'ta
(W. gracilis; W. sonorae)

Mexican Washington Palm

Probably Lower California

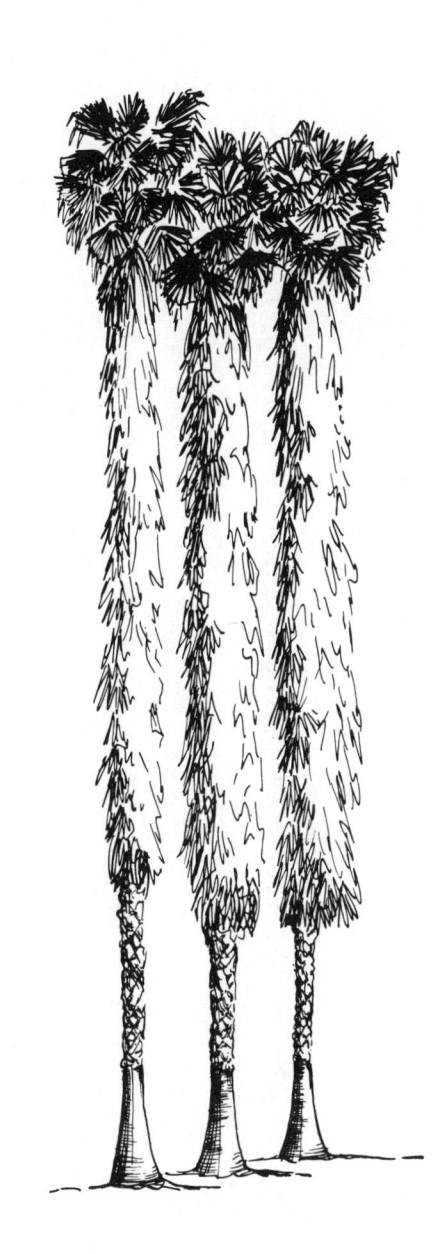

Features: Leaves, trunk

Use: Street, lawn, groups, specimen, accent

Mexican Washington Palm has a slender trunk which rises to a dense crown of deeply slashed, fan-shaped leaves that are arranged in a perfect oval. The trunk is covered with the thatch-like residue of the old leaves; the best form of the tree is maintained when this shag is left to hang naturally from the trunk. Mexican Washington Palm is used successfully in parkway plantings on either narrow or wide streets and as a single specimen to accent tall, straight lines. It is cold tolerant to some degree but will not stand prolonged freezing.

Conformation

Height (of trunk to crown): 40 to 100 ft. Spread (of crown): 5 to 10 ft.

A tall, slender fan palm with large leaves forming a dense, oval crown. The trunk is slender and tapers gradually from a slightly swollen base. It is 1 to 2 ft. in diameter and is covered with shag, which persists for a long time. The bright green leaves are 2½ to 5 ft. long and about 3 ft. wide; they are suspended on reddish-brown petioles 2 to 3 ft. long. The center part of the leaf is intact; the outer edges are deeply slashed into seventy or eighty narrow, ribbon-like, somewhat pendulous divisions.

Flowers

Slightly fragrant, tiny, creamy-white, vase-shaped flowers, in clusters all along the branches of long flower stalks, which spread horizontally from the crown of leaves. The hanging sprays somewhat resemble corn tassels. After the fruit has formed and gone, they die and become part of the shag around the trunk. Spring.

Fruit

Small black, nearly round fruit which hangs in large clusters from the branched stalks. It has a thin skin and sugary, edible flesh and was used by the Indians for food. Summer.

Root System: Shallow. Roots are fibrous.

Rate of Growth: Rapid

Natural Requirements

Climate: Tolerates heat and desert atmosphere. Stands some degree of cold but will not endure prolonged freezing.

Soil: Grows best in light, moist, well-drained, sandy loam to which plenty of humus has been added.

Exposure: Sun. Tolerates seacoast conditions.

Care

Pruning: Not necessary. Shag may be removed without harming the health of the tree, but the tree has a better appearance if the shag is left until it falls.

Feeding: Apply manure annually in winter.

Watering: Provide plenty of moisture.

Pests and Diseases: Relatively free from both.

CHART FOR THE ORNAMENTAL USE AND CLIMATIC TOLERANCE OF PALMS, TREE FERNS, AND OTHER TROPICAL-APPEARING PLANTS

Rate of growth: R = rapid; M = moderate; S = slow

Fruit: E = edible; O = ornamental

X: areas where the particular tree may be grown easily

(X): areas where the particular tree may be grown, but with some reservations

ORNAMENTAL USE						CLIMATIC TOLERANCE			
	Rate of Growth	Habit	Leaf Color	Flowers	Fruit	Temperate Coastal	Desert	Cool Coastal	Temperate Inland
STREET TREES									
Arecastrum romanzoffianum	R	Dense	Dark green	White	O	X			
Cordyline australis	R	Dense	Bright green	White		X	X	X	X
Cordyline indivisa	R	Dense	Novelty			X			
Phoenix canariensis	R	Dense	Light green	Yellowish		X	X	X	X
Phoenix dactylifera (male trees)	R	Dense	Dark green	White		X	X	X	
Trachycarpus fortunei	M	Dense	Dark green	Orange		X	X	X	X
Washingtonia filifera	R	Open	Bright green	White	E, O	X	X		X
Washingtonia robusta	R	Dense	Bright green	White	E, O	X	X	X	X
LAWN TREES									
Arecastrum romanzoffianum	R	Dense	Dark green	White	O	X	X	X	
Phoenix canariensis	R	Dense	Light green	Yellowish		X	X	X	X
Phoenix dactylifera	R	Dense	Dark green	White	E, O	X	X	X	
Phoenix reclinata	R	Open	Dark green			X	X	X	
Trachycarpus fortunei	M	Dense	Dark green	Orange	E, O	X	X	X	X
Washingtonia filifera	R	Open	Bright green	White	E, O	X	X	X	X
Washingtonia robusta	R	Dense	Bright green	White	E, O	X	X	X	X
PATIO AND TUB TREES									
Alsophila australis	R	Dense	Light green			X			
Arecastrum romanzoffianum	R	Dense	Dark green	White	O	X			
Cordyline australis	R	Dense	Bright green	White		X	X	X	X
Cordyline indivisa	R	Dense	Novelty			X			
Dicksonia antarctica	R	Dense	Dark green			X		X	X
Musa ensete	R	Dense	Bright green	White		X			
Musa paradisiaca	R	Dense	Bright green	White	E, O	X			
Musa paradisiaca sapientum	R	Dense	Bright green	White	E, O	X			
Phoenix reclinata	R	Open	Dark green			X	X	X	
Trachycarpus fortunei	M	Dense	Dark green	Orange		X	X	X	X

Glossary

Acorn. A nutlike fruit consisting of a nut proper and a fibrous or woody capsule, or saucer, or cup.

Alternate. Growing singly at the nodes or axils; not opposite and not whorled.

Axillary. Situated in or originating from the axil, or point at which a stalk or branch diverges from the stem.

Bark. The outer woody or corky layer of the stems functioning as a protector of the tissues within. The bark is composed of two layers, the outer and the inner, both distinct in structure, color, texture, and function.

Berry. A fleshy fruit with more than one seed but no true stone.

Bract. A modified or undeveloped leaf extending under a flower, fruit, or stalk.

Branchlet. The ultimate division of a branch.

Bur. A prickly covering, or fruit husk.

Buttressed. Projecting or swollen at the base.

Capsule. A dry fruit of more than one cell, usually splitting lengthwise along two or more seams. The fruits of the poplar, willow, and horse-chestnut are capsules.

Catkin. A slender, compact flower cluster in which unisexual flowers are developed upon an elongated axis and are subtended or more or less concealed by conspicuous bracts. The willow, birch, alder, walnut, and oak have catkins.

Checkered. Marked by horizontal cracks or grooves.

Compound. A single organ usually composed of two or more similar parts. A once-compound leaf has leaflets arranged on a single, unbranched axis; in a twice-compound leaf the axis is branched.

Cone. A series of overlapping scales arranged round an axis; the seeds form at the base of the scales.

Conifers. Cone-bearing plants.

Crown. In a tree, the head or canopy of foliage.

Deciduous. Having leaves, fruits, or flowers which fall periodically; generally applied to plants which shed their leaves annually at the end of the growing period.

Entire. With smooth, untoothed margins.

Evergreen. Never without foliage. All evergreens eventually lose their leaves, but not all at once, and not before new growth has replaced them.

Filler. A rapid-growing plant used for temporary planting.

Fissured. Cleft.

Frond. Used to designate a spray of foliage.

Glabrous. Completely smooth; without hairs or any sort of roughness.

Glaucous. Covered with an extremely fine whitish or grayish powder, which rubs off easily. Leaves that are glaucous are usually blue-green or gray-green.

Habit. The form or shape of a plant.

Habitat. The site where a wild plant grows.

Hardpan. A layer of compact clay or silt, too tight to allow the penetration of roots.

Head. Any tight flower cluster; in a whole tree, the crown.

Head back. See illustration, pages 6 and 7.

Hybrid. The offspring of a cross-fertilization between two different but related species. Hybrids may or may not breed true.

Indigenous. Growing or living naturally in a country or climate; native.

Internode. The part of a leaf or branch between two successive nodes which serves to space them apart.

Lateral. On or at the sides; not terminal.

Leader. Central growing shoot.

Leaflet. A single division of a compound leaf.

Lobe. A part or division of an organ, especially of a petal or a leaf.

Midrib. The principal vein of a leaf.

Needle. A long, narrow leaf.

Node. The place at which a leaf, bud, flower, or branch appears on the stem to which it is attached.

Nut. A hard, usually large, one-celled fruit that does not split open.

Nutlet. A small, hard, one-celled fruit that does not split open.

Opposite. Appearing in pairs at the same node or axil but on opposite sides of the stem; not alternate.

Palmate. With the leaflets of a compound leaf, or the lobes of a simple leaf radiating from one point like the fingers of a hand.

Palmately compound. With the leaflets radiating from the summit of the leafstalk.

Panicle. A compound, loosely branched flower cluster.

Phyllodes. Expanded leafstalks which resemble leaves, as in some species of *Acacia*.

Pinna. One of the ultimate divisions of a compound leaf.

Pod. A dry fruit which splits open at maturity.

Pollination. The transfer of pollen from the anther to the stigma; union of male and female elements for purposes of fertilization.

Pubescent. Covered with soft or downy hairs.

Raceme. An elongated flower cluster with many individual flower stalks springing from a single main stalk.

Rate of growth. Rapid: an annual growth of 3 or more feet each year. Moderate: an annual growth of 1 foot, or slightly more, each year. Slow: an annual growth of less than 1 foot.

Recurved. Bent, turned, or folded back.

Ringed. Said of palm trunks, when the scars of the old leaf bases form distinct rings around them.

Scale. A much-reduced leaf or bract.

Sheath. Any tubular structure, often leaflike, surrounding an organ or part. Some bracts are sheathing, as in the palms. In bananas, sheathing leaf bases make up the stems. In pines, the sheaths are papery tubes enclosing the base of the bundles.

Simple. Said of a leaf having only one blade, in which the midrib is unbranched and is united continuously with the blade; not compound.

Species. A group of individual plants resembling each other more than they differ from each other, and breeding true to reproduce their own kind.

Specimen. A tree which has some outstanding characteristic (or characteristics) which serves to center interest.

Spike. A flower cluster with the individual flowers stalkless, or nearly so, and set along a central axis.

Sucker. A shoot arising near the base of a plant, from the roots or from the lower part of the stem or trunk.

Taproot. The main central root of a plant, usually extending straight down into the ground on a line with the main stem.

Terminal. At the end of a branch.

Tomentose. Covered with short, flat, matted, dense hairs.

Trifoliate. Having three leaves or, loosely, three leaflets.

Twig. The ultimate division of a branch; a branchlet.

Umbel. A flower cluster in which all flower stalks arise from the same point. The cluster can be flat-topped or round, depending upon the length of the individual flower stalks.

Undulate. Wavy, or wavy-margined.

Variety. A group of individuals within a species set aside from others by their slight deviation from the typical form.

Whorled. Having three or more leaves, branches, twigs, or other organs arising in a circle from one point, or node.

Wing. A thin, flat expansion of an organ.

Bibliography

Abjornson, Eberhard. Ornamental Dwarf Fruit Trees. New York, De La Mare, 1929.

American Joint Committee on Horticultural Nomenclature. Standardized Plant Names. Harrisburg, Pa., J. H. McFarland, 1942.

Bailey, L. H. The Standard Cyclopedia of Horticulture. 3 vols. New York, Macmillan, 1925.

Bailey, L. H., and Ethel Zoe Bailey, Hortus Second; a Concise Dictionary of Gardening...in North America. New York, Macmillan, 1941.

Bomhard, Miriam L. Palm Trees in the United States. U. S. Dept. of Agriculture, Agriculture Information Bulletin 22. Washington, D.C., U. S. Dept. of Agriculture, Forest Service, 1950.

Brooks, Reid M., and Claron O. Hesse. Western Fruit Gardening. Berkeley and Los Angeles, University of California Press, 1953.

Chandler, W. H. Evergreen Orchards. Philadelphia, Lea & Febiger, 1950.

Chandler, W. H., and Ralph D. Cornell. Pruning Ornamental Trees, Shrubs, and Vines. California Agricultural Extension Service Circular 183. Berkeley, College of Agriculture, University of California, 1952.

Collingwood, G. H., and Warren D. Brush. Knowing Your Trees. Washington, D.C., American Forestry Assn., 1947.

Dallimore, W., and A. Bruce Jackson. A Handbook of *Coniferae* Including *Ginkoaceae*. London, E. Arnold & Co., 1923.

Dodge, Bernard O., and Harold W. Rickett. Diseases and Pests of Ornamental Plants. New York, Ronald Press, 1948.

Hanson, Roy L. Sunset Pruning Handbook. Menlo Park, Calif., Lane Publishing Co., 1952.

Hinds, Norman E. A. Evolution of the California Landscape. California Department of Natural Resources, Division of Mines, Bulletin 158, 1952.

Hottes, Alfred Carl. The Book of Trees. New York, De La Mare, 1932.

Hoyt, Roland Stewart. Check Lists for the Ornamental Plants of Subtropical Regions. Los Angeles, Livingston Press, 1938.

Jepson, W. L. A Manual of the Flowering Plants of California. Berkeley and Los Angeles, University of California Press, 1951.

Kuck, Loraine E., and Richard C. Tongg. The Tropical Garden. New York, Macmillan, 1936.

Lyon, T. Lyttleton, and Harry O. Buckman. The Nature and Properties of Soils. New York, Macmillan, 1922.

Macmillan, H. F. Tropical Planting and Gardening with Special Reference to Ceylon. 5th ed. London, Macmillan, 1943.

McMinn, Howard E., and Evelyn Maino. An Illustrated Manual of Pacific Coast Trees. Berkeley and Los Angeles, University of California Press, 1951.

Martin, R. Sanford. How to Prune Fruit Trees. Hollywood, Calif., Murray & Gee, 1944.

Neal, Marie C. In Gardens of Hawaii. Bernice P. Bishop Museum, Special Publication 40, Honolulu, 1948.

Pirone, P. P. Maintenance of Shade and Ornamental Trees. 2d ed. New York, Oxford University Press, 1948.

Pirone, P. P. Modern Gardening; a Complete Guide to the Agricultural Uses of Modern Chemistry's Miracle Drugs. New York, Simon and Shuster, 1952.

Taylor, Norman, The Garden Dictionary. Boston and New York, Houghton Mifflin, 1936.

Tufts, Warren P. Pruning Deciduous Fruit Trees. California Agricultural Extension Service Circular 112. Berkeley, College of Agriculture, University of California, 1939.

Wescott, Cynthia. The Gardener's Bug Book: 1,000 Insect Pests and Their Control. New York, Doubleday, 1946.

Wyman, Donald. Trees for American Gardens. New York, Macmillan, 1951.

Index

Abies concolor, 164
   nordmanniana, 164
   pinsapo, 164
Acacia, Bailey, 102
   baileyana, 102
   baileyana purpurea, 102
   Blackwood, 105
   Broadleaf, 104
   Constantinople-, 21
   dealbata, 103
   decurrens dealbata, 103
   False-, 83
   julibrissin, 21
   latifolia, 104
   longifolia, 104
   longifolia floribunda, 104
   lophantha, 107
   melanoxylon, 105
   nemu, 21
   pycnantha, 105
   Rice, 104
   riceana, 104
   Star, 104
   Sidney Golden, 104
   verticillata, 104
Acer circinatum, 12
   dasycarpum, 17
   eriocarpum, 17
   japonicum, 14
   negundo, 13
   negundo californicum, 13
   palmatum, 14
   platanoides, 15
   platanoides schwedleri, 15
   polymorphum palmatum, 14
   rubrum, 16
   saccharinum, 17
   saccharum, 17
Acmena smithi, 128
Aesculus californica, 18
   carnea, 19
   carnea brioti, 19
   hippocastanum baumanni, 19
Agonis flexuosa, 106
Ailanthus altissima, 20
   glandulosa, 20
Albizzia julibrissin, 21
   julibrissin rosea, 21
   lophantha, 107
   Plume, 107
Alder, Red, 22
   White, 22
Algaroba, 112

Alligator Wood, 50
Almond, 66
Alnus oregana, 22
   rhombifolia, 22
   rubra, 22
Alsophila australis, 202
Andromeda arborea, 60
Annona cherimola, 23
Apple, 54–55
   Custard-, 23
   Mexican-, 110
Apricot, 67–68
   Flowering, 68
Araucaria araucana, 165
   bidwilli, 166
   excelsa, 167
   imbricata, 165
Arborvitae, American, 193
   Chinese, 193
   Giant, 194
   Oriental, 193
Arbutus menziesi, 108
   procera, 108
Arecastrum romanzoffianum, 200
Ash, Arizona, 42
   Leatherleaf, 42
   Modesto, 42
   Velvet, 42
   Mountain, 86
Aspen, Quaking, 65
Athel, Desert, 154
Avocado, American, 146

Banana, Abyssinian, 203
   Plantain, 203
Basswood, American, 89
Bay, Bull-, 140
   California, 157
   Sweet, 136
   True, 136
Beech, American, 39
   Australian-, 125
   European, 39
   Purple, 39
Beefwood, 111
   Horsetail, 111
Betula alba, 24
   papyrifera, 24
   pendula, 24
   pendula dalecarlica, 24
   pendula youngi, 24
   verrucosa, 24
Big Tree, 189

Birch, Canoe, 24
   Cutleaf Weeping, 24
   European, 24
   Paper, 24
   White, 24
Bottle Tree, Kurrajong, 109
Box, Brisbane-, 155
   -Elder, 13
   -Elder, California, 13
   Victorian-, 148
Brachychiton populneus, 109
Brahea filamentosa, 208
   filifera, 208
Broussonetia, 85
Buckeye, California, 18
Bunya-Bunya, 166
Buttonwood, 63

Cabbage Tree, 201
Cajeput Tree, 142
Camphor Tree, 113
Camphora officinarum, 113
Canoe Wood, 51
Carob, 112
Caroub, 112
Carpinus betulus, 25
Carya illinoensis, 26
   pecan, 26
Casimiroa edulis, 110
Castanea americana, 27
   dentata, 27
   mollissima, 27
Casuarina equisetifolia, 111
   stricta, 111
Catalpa bignonioides, 28
   Common, 28
   Southern, 28
   speciosa, 28
   syringaefolia, 28
   Western, 28
Cedar, Atlas, 168
   Blue Atlas, 168
   Canoe-, 194
   Deodar, 169
   Eastern Red-, 178
   Incense-, 180
   of Lebanon, 168
   Port-Orford-, 170
   Western Red-, 194
Cedrela, Chinese, 90
   sinensis, 90
Cedrus atlantica, 168
   atlantica glauca, 168
   deodara, 169

Cedrus - *Continued*
    libani, 168
Celtis australis, 29
Ceratonia siliqua, 112
Chamaecyparis lawsoniana, 170
    lawsoniana allumi, 170
    lawsoniana ellwoodi, 170
    lawsoniana stewarti, 170
    lawsoniana wisseli, 170
    obtusa, 171
    obtusa gracilis, 171
    obtusa nana, 171
    obtusa nana aurea, 171
    pisifera, 172
    pisifera filifera, 172
    pisifera plumosa, 172
    pisifera squarrosa, 172
    pisifera squarrosa
        veitchi, 172
Chamaerops excelsa, 207
Cherimoya, 23
Cherry, Australian Brush-, 128
    Brush-, 128
    Carolina Laurel-, 149
    Catalina, 149
    Duke, 70
    Flowering, 71
    Pie, 70
    Sour, 70
    Sweet, 69-70
Chestnut, American, 27
    Chinese, 27
China Tree, 47
Christmas-Berry, 147
Christmas-Berry Tree, 153
Christmas Tree,
    New Zealand, 143
Cigar Tree, 28
Cinnamomum camphora, 113
Citrus aurantifolia, 114-115
    limetta, 114
    limon, 116
    limonia, 116
    paradisi, 117
    sinensis, 118
Cladrastis lutea, 30
Cocos plumosa, 200
Cordyline australis, 201
    indivisa, 201
Cornus florida, 31
    florida rubra, 31
    nuttalli, 31
Corylus maxima, 32

Corynocarpus laevigata, 119
Cotinus coggygria, 33
    coggygria purpurea, 33
Crabapple, 55
    Flowering, 56
Crataegus acerifolia, 36
    carrierei, 34
    cordata, 36
    lavallei, 34
    oxyacantha, 35
    oxyacanthoides, 35
    phaenopyrum, 36
    populifolia, 36
Crinodendron dependens, 120
Cryptomeria japonica, 173
    japonica compacta, 173
    japonica elegans, 173
Cupressus arizonica, 174
    forbesi, 174
    glabra, 174
    macrocarpa, 174
    sempervirens, 175
Cynoxylon floridum, 31
Cypress, Arizona, 174
    Bald-, 191
    Ellwood-, 170
    Hinoki-, 171
    Italian, 175
    Lawson-, 170
    Monterey, 174
    Moss-Sawara-, 172
    Plume Sawara-, 172
    Redbark, 174
    Roughbark, 174
    Sawara-, 172
    Scarab-, 170
    Tecate, 174
    Thread Sawara-, 172

Date, 205
    Chinese-, 94
Davidia involucrata, 37
Dicksonia antarctaria, 202
    Tasmanian, 202
Diospyros kaki, 38
    virginiana, 38
Dogwood, Flowering, 31
    Pacific, 31
Dove Tree, 37
Dracaena australis, 201
    draco, 201
Dracena, Blue, 201
    Giant, 201
    Green, 201

Dragon Tree, 201

Ebony, Green-, 45
Elm, American, 91
    Asiatic, 92
    Chinese, 156
    English, 91
    Evergreen, 156
    Siberian, 92
Empress Tree, 61
Eriobotrya japonica, 121
Eucalyptus caesia, 122
    citriodora, 122
    Dollarleaf, 125
    ficifolia, 123
    globulus, 124
    Gungurru, 122
    Lemon, 122
    leucoxylon sideroxylon
        rosea, 127
    maculata citriodora, 122
    Moitch, 126
    Mulga Island, 127
    polyanthemos, 125
    pulverulenta, 125
    Redbox, 125
    rudis, 126
    Scarlet, 123
    sideroxylon pallens, 127
    sideroxylon purpurea, 127
    sideroxylon rosea, 127
    Tasmanian Blue, 124
Eugenia hookeri, 128
    hookeriana, 128
    myrtifolia, 128
    paniculata, 128
    paniculata australis, 128
    smithi, 128

Fagus americana, 39
    grandifolia, 39
    sylvatica, 39
    sylvatica atropunicea, 39
Fern, Australian Tree, 202
    Hardy Tree, 202
Ficus carica, 40
    macrophylla, 129
    nitida, 129
    retusa, 129
Fig, Common, 40
    Domestic, 40
    Moreton Bay, 129
    Indian Laurel, 129

Filbert, Giant, 32
Fir, Douglas-, 188
   Lawson-, 170
   Nordmann, 164
   Spanish, 164
   White, 164
Firmiana simplex, 41
Flame Tree, Chinese, 47
Flannel Bush, 130
Fraxinus standleyi, 42
   velutina, 42
   velutina coriacea, 42
   velutina glabra, 42
Fremontia californica, 130
   mexicana, 130

Ginkgo biloba, 176
Gleditsia
   triacanthos inermis, 43
Goldenchain Tree, 48
Goldenrain Tree, 47
Grapefruit, 117
Grevillea robusta, 131
Gum, Black-, 59
   Blue, 124
   Desert, 126
   Lemon-scented, 122
   Red-, 50
   Sour-, 59
   Sweet-, 50

Hackberry, European, 29
Halesia carolina, 44
   tetraptera, 44
Harpephyllum caffrum, 132
Hawthorn, English, 35
Heaven-Wood, 20
Hemlock, Canadian, 196
   Eastern, 196
   Mountain, 196
Heteromeles arbutifolia, 147
   salicifolia, 147
Hicoria pecan, 26
Holly, Dutch Vantol, 134
   English, 134
Hornbeam, European, 25
Horse-Chestnut, Baumann, 19
   Red, 19
Hymenosporum flavum, 133

Ice-Cream Tree, 23
Ilex aquifolium, 134
Indian-Bean, 28

Ironbark, Mulga Island, 127
   Red, 127
Iron Tree, 143
Ironwood, Catalina, 138

Jacaranda acutifolia, 45
   mimosaefolia, 45
   ovalifolia, 45
   Sharpleaf, 45
Juglans hindsi, 46
   nigra, 46
   regia, 46
Jujube, 94
Juniper, Alligator, 179
   Chinese, 177
   Common, 178
   Hollywood, 177
   Irish, 178
   Swedish, 178
   Twisted, 177
Juniperus chinensis, 177
   chinensis columnaris, 177
   chinensis torulosa, 177
   communis, 178
   communis aurea, 178
   communis hibernica, 178
   communis suecica, 178
   pachyphloea, 179
   virginiana, 178

Karakanut, New Zealand, 119
Koelreuteria paniculata, 47
   formosana, 47

Laburnum parksi, 48
   vossi, 48
   watereri, 48
Lagerstroemia indica, 49
Lagunaria patersoni, 135
Larch, European, 191
Larix decidua, 191
Laurel, California, 157
   Grecian, 136
   Portuguese, 149
Laurocerasus caroliniana, 149
Laurus camphora, 113
   nobilis, 136
Lemon, 116
Libocedrus decurrens, 180
Ligustrum
   japonicum macrophyllum, 137
   lucidum, 137
   spicatum, 137

Lilac, Japanese Tree, 87
Lilli-Pilli Tree, 128
Lily-of-the-Valley Tree, 120
Lily Tree, White, 120
Lime, 114-115
Limequat, 115
Linden, American, 89
   Littleleaf, 89
Liquidambar styraciflua, 50
Liriodendron tulipifera, 51
Locust, Black, 83
   Common, 83
   Moraine, 43
   New Mexican, 83
   Pink Flowering, 83
   Thornless Honey, 43
   Thornless Sweet, 43
   Yellow, 83
Loquat, 121
Lyonothamnus floribundus, 138
   floribundus
      asplenifolius, 138

Macadamia ternifolia, 139
Maclura aurantiaca, 52
   pomifera, 52
Macrocatalpa, 28
Madrone, Pacific, 108
Magnolia grandiflora, 140
   grandiflora exoniensis, 140
   Japanese, 53
   Saucer, 53
   soulangeana, 53
   Southern, 140
Maidenhair Tree, 176
Malus, 56
   baccata, 55
   ioensis, 55
   pumila, 54
Maple, Ashleaf, 13
   Crimson King, 15
   Japanese, 14
   Mountain, 12
   Norway, 15
   Red, 16
   River, 17
   Scarlet, 16
   Silver, 17
   Soft, 17
   Sugar, 17
   Swamp, 16

Maple - *Continued*
    Vine, 12
    White, 17
Mastic Tree, Peruvian, 152
Mayten Tree, Chile, 141
Matenus boaria, 141
    chilensis, 141
Melaleuca leucadendron, 142
Melia azedarach
    umbraculiformis, 57
Metrosideros tomentosa, 143
Micromeles, 86
Mimosa, 21
Monkey-Puzzle, 165
Morus alba, 58
    nigra, 58
    rubra, 58
Mulberry, Black, 58
    Kingan, 58
    Persian, 58
    Red, 58
    White, 58
Musa ensete, 203
    paradisiaca, 203
    paradisiaca
        sapientum, 203
Myrtle,
    Australian Willow-, 106
    Crape-, 49
    Oregon-, 157

Nectarine, 73
Negundo aceroides, 13
    fraxinifolium, 13
Nettle Tree, 29
Nutmeg, California-, 195
Nyssa sylvatica, 59

Oak, California Black, 81
    California Blue, 81
    California Live, 150
    Coast Live, 150
    Cork, 150
    Holly, 151
    Holm, 151
    Pin, 82
    Red, 80
    Scarlet, 80
    She-, 111
    Silk-, 131
Olea europaea, 144
Olive, Common, 144
Orange, Mock-, 148
    Osage-, 52

Sweet, 118
Oxydendron arboreum, 60

Pagoda Tree, Japanese, 85
Palm, California
        Washington, 208
    Canary Date, 204
    Cape, 206
    Date, 205
    Fortune's Windmill, 207
    Mexican Washington, 209
    Queen, 200
    Senegal Date, 206
    Windmill, 207
Palo Verde, 145
Paradise Tree, 20
Parasol Tree, Chinese, 41
Parkinsonia aculeata, 145
Paulownia imperialis, 61
    Royal, 61
    tomentosa, 61
Peach, 72-73
    Flowering, 74
Pear, 79
    Alligator-, 146
Pecan, 26
Pepper, Brazilian, 153
    California, 152
    Pinkberry, 153
Pepperidge, 59
Peppermint Tree, 106
Pepperwood, 157
Persea americana, 146
    gratissima, 146
Persimmon, Common, 38
    Kaki, 38
Phoenix canariensis, 204
    dactylifera, 205
    reclinata, 206
    Tree, 41
Photinia arbutifolia, 147
    arbutifolia macrocarpa, 147
    Chinese, 147
    salicifolia, 147
    serrulata, 147
Picea abies, 181
    excelsa, 181
    pungens, 181
    pungens glauca, 181
    pungens kosteriana, 181
Pine, Aleppo, 183
    Austrian, 184
    Bishop, 186
    Canary, 182

Cluster, 183
Italian Stone, 185
Japanese Black, 184
Monterey, 186
Mugo, 185
Norfolk-Island-, 167
Oregon-, 188
Rocky Mountain
    Yellow, 182
Santa Cruz Island, 186
Star-, 167
Swiss Mountain, 185
Western Yellow, 182
Pinus canariensis, 182
    halepensis, 183
    mugo, 185
    mugo mughus, 185
    muricata, 186
    nigra, 184
    pinaster, 183
    pinea, 185
    ponderosa, 182
    ponderosa
        scopulorum, 182
    radiata, 186
    remorata, 186
    thunbergi, 184
Pistache, Chinese, 62
    Common, 62
Pistacia chinensis, 62
    sinensis, 62
    vera, 62
Pittosporum,
    Orange-Berry, 148
    undulatum, 148
Plane Tree, California, 63
    London, 63
Planera japonica, 93
Platanus acerifolia, 63
    californica, 63
    orientalis, 63
    racemosa, 63
Plum, 75-76
    Damson, 75-76
    European, 75-76
    Flowering, 77
    Japanese, 75
    Kafir-, 132
Podocarpus elongatus, 187
    Fern, 187
    gracilior, 187
    macrophyllus, 187
    Yew, 187
Pomelo, 117
Poplar, Blue-, 51

Poplar - *Continued*
   Bolleana, 64
   Carolina, 64
   Lombardy, 65
   White, 64
   Yellow-, 51
Populus alba, 64
   alba pyramidalis, 64
   canadensis eugenei, 64
   nigra italica, 65
   tremuloides, 65
Pride-of-India, 47
Pritchardia filamentosa 208
   filifera, 208
Privet, Glossy, 137
Prune, 76
Prunus, 71, 75-76, 77
   amygdalus, 66
   armeniaca, 67
   avium, 69-70
   caroliniana, 149
   cerasus, 70
   lusitanica, 149
   lyoni, 149
   mume, 68
   persica, 72-73
   persica, Flowering, 74
   persica nectarina, 73
Pseudotsuga douglasi, 188
   mucronata, 188
   taxifolia, 188
Pterocarya stenoptera, 78
Punk Tree, 142
Pyrus aucuparia, 86
   communis, 79

Queensland Nut, 139
Queensland Pyramid
   Tree, 135
Quercus agrifolia, 150
   borealis, 80
   coccinea, 80
   douglasi, 81
   ilex, 151
   kelloggi, 81
   palustris, 82
   suber, 150

Redwood, 190
Retama, 145
Rhus cotinus, 33
Robinia neomexicana, 83
   pseudoacacia, 83
   pseudoacacia decaisneana, 83

Rowan Tree, 86
Rulac negundo, 13

Sacred Tree of China, 176
Saddle Tree, 51
St. John's Bread, 112
Salix alba vitellina, 84
   babylonica, 84
Sapote, White, 110
Schinus lentiscifolia, 153
   molle, 152
   terebinthifolia, 153
Scholar Tree, Chinese, 85
Sequoia, Giant, 189
   gigantea, 189
   sempervirens, 190
   wellingtonia, 190
Sequoiadendron
   giganteum, 189
Silk Tree, 21
Silverbell, 44
Silverfruit, 176
Smoke Tree, 33
Snowdrop Tree, 44
Sophora japonica, 85
Sorbus aucuparia, 86
Sorrel Tree, 60
Sourwood, 60
Spruce, Colorado, 181
   Colorado Blue, 181
   Douglas-, 188
   Hemlock-, 196
   Koster Blue, 181
   Norway, 181
   Red-, 188
   Yellow-, 188
Sterculia diversifolia, 109
   platanifolia, 41
Sugarplum Tree, 135
Sumac, Chinese, 20
Sweetshade, 133
Sycamore, California, 63
Syringa
   amurensis japonica, 87
   japonica, 87
Tamarix algerica, 88
   aphylla, 154
   articulata, 154
   parviflora, 88
   Smallflower, 88
Taxodium distichum, 191
Taxus baccata, 192
   baccata aurea, 192

   baccata stricta, 192
   baccata stricta
      aurea, 192
Tea Tree, Swamp, 142
Thorn, Carriere, 34
   Jerusalem, 145
   Lavalle, 34
   Pauls Scarlet, 35
   Washington, 36
Thuja occidentalis, 193
   orientalis, 193
   orientalis bonita, 193
   orientalis beverley-
      ensis, 193
   plicata, 194
   plicata atrovirens, 194
   plicata aurea, 194
   plicata fastigiata, 194
Tilia americana, 89
   cordata, 89
   glabra, 89
   nigra, 89
Toon, Chinese, 90
Toona sinensis, 90
Torreya californica, 195
Toxylon pomiferum, 52
Toyon, 147
Trachycarpus excelsus, 207
   fortunei, 207
Tree-of-Heaven, 20
Tricuspidaria dependens, 120
Tristania conferta, 155
Tsuga canadensis, 196
   mertensiana, 196
Tulip Tree, 51
Tupelo, Black, 59

Ulmus americana, 91
   parvifolia, 156
   parvifolia semper-
      virens, 156
   procera, 91
   pumila, 92
Umbellularia californica, 157
Umbrella Tree, Texas, 57

Varnish Tree, 47
   Japanese, 41

Walnut, Black, 46
   English, 46
   Hinds Black, 46
   Persian, 46

Washingtonia filifera, 208
   gracilis, 209
   robusta, 209
   sonorae, 209
Wattle, Cootamundra, 102
   Golden, 105
   Gossamer, 104
   Silver, 103
   Silver-Green, 103
   Sydney Golden, 104

Whitewood, 51
Willow, Babylon Weeping, 84
   Weeping, 84
   Yellow-stemmed Weeping, 84
Wingnut, Chinese, 78

Yellow-Wood, American, 30
Yew, English, 192
   Irish, 192

Zelkova acuminata, 93
   cuspidata, 93
   Japanese, 93
   keaki, 93
   Sawleaf, 93
   serrata, 93
Zizyphus jujuba, 94
   sativa, 94
   vulgaris, 94